DOWN TO THE SEA IN SUBMARINES

DOWN TO THE SEA IN SUBMARINES

A COLD WAR ODYSSEY

DAN CONLEY

Foreword by Admiral Sir Mark Stanhope GCB, OBE, DL

Seaforth
PUBLISHING

Dedication

This book is dedicated to the officers and men who so bravely crewed the submarines of the Royal Navy during the two World Wars. It also commemorates the outstanding service and commitment of the current generation of British submariners who continue to 'Go Down to the Sea in Submarines'.

Copyright © Dan Conley 2024

First published in Great Britain in 2024 by
Seaforth Publishing,
An imprint of Pen & Sword Books Ltd,
George House, Beevor Street, Barnsley S71 1HN

www.seaforthpublishing.com

British Library Cataloguing in Publication Data
A catalogue record for this book is available from the British Library

ISBN 978 1 0361 1368 1 (HARDBACK)
ISBN 978 1 0361 1370 4 (EPUB)
ISBN 978 1 0361 1371 1 (KINDLE)

Pen & Sword Books Limited incorporates the imprints of Atlas, Archaeology, Aviation, Discovery, Family History, Fiction, History, Maritime, Military, Military Classics, Politics, Select, Transport, True Crime, Air World, Frontline Publishing, Leo Cooper, Remember When, Seaforth Publishing, The Praetorian Press, Wharncliffe Local History, Wharncliffe Transport, Wharncliffe True Crime and White Owl

Typeset in 10.75/13.5 Sabon by Mac Style
Printed and bound in Great Britain by CPI Group (UK) Ltd,
Croydon, CR0 4YY

Contents

List of Plates

Foreword

It is a pleasure to have been asked to write the foreword to *Down to the Sea in Submarines* which concisely and informatively narrates the history of the Royal Navy Submarine Service post WW2. Whilst I personally had a varied career in both submarines and surface ships, I define myself as a submariner. I can therefore, with some insight, commend this vivid account of the author's career and the story of the evolution of the 'Silent Service' during his time in the Royal Navy.

Prior to the commissioning in 1963 of the nuclear submarine *Dreadnought*, the Royal Navy's Submarine Service consisted exclusively of diesel submarines, many of which were of WW2 vintage. Within the short space of five years from *Dreadnought* entering service, the first British ballistic missile-armed submarine (SSBN), the Polaris-armed *Resolution*, deployed on patrol. In 1969 Continuous at Sea Deterrence (CASD) was established which means at least one SSBN is always on patrol delivering Britain's independent nuclear deterrent. At the same time, a force of highly capable anti-submarine nuclear attack submarines (SSNs) was being built. These were remarkable national achievements. Meanwhile, the diesel boat submariner, typically of somewhat raffish, jaunty and independent spirit, successfully rose to the challenges of mastering the professionalism and different skill sets necessary to operate nuclear submarines.

Dan Conley joined the Navy in the year *Dreadnought* was commissioned and volunteered for submarines in which he was to serve for the next three decades. Accordingly, he witnessed and was very much a participant in the above remarkable transition. His first years of service were in diesel submarines and he does not demur from the difficulties he experienced as he got to grips with submarine life. I can personally attest that, in diesel boats, this was a rough-and-ready existence, living in extremely close proximity to others, and in winter seas enduring perpetually wet and damp conditions. On the other hand, typical of serving in submarines, responsibility was thrust upon him right from the start and he clearly achieved great satisfaction in overcoming many difficulties. Although he experienced several highly alarming events, there were many instances of levity and fun. He describes many of the latter, very much capturing the ethos, spirit and camaraderie of the British submariner. I found, on reading his humorous anecdotes, much to remember and smile about.

In 1973 the author joined his first nuclear submarine, the SSN *Swiftsure*. Deeper diving and faster than her predecessors, she pushed the bounds of technology in a highly complex platform which incorporated many innovations. As the limits of her capability were explored, there occurred many highly challenging situations, particularly the unexpectedly extreme angles the boat underwent during her manoeuvring trials. As a first-of-class submarine, inevitably there occurred several serious technical problems which were only overcome due to the expertise, innovation and competence of her engineering teams. And he experienced several worrying events. Most notably, when surfaced watchkeeping officer on the bridge, during a violent storm the boat momentarily submerged under an exceptionally large wave. He and his lookout were left reeling and choking seawater after the wave had passed. Only their safety harnesses had saved them from being washed overboard and drowned. A few years later in the same submarine, incidentally my first appointment as a submariner, I experienced a similar, if slightly more troubling, event.

The author uniquely describes life onboard nuclear submarines, both SSNs and SSBNs, and particularly in the case of the latter, how crew members can endure months under the sea, completely out of touch with their families. Fortunate to undertake exchange service in the USN and experiencing time at sea in several of its SSNs, he relates how he found life and perspectives different in American submarines. However, whilst he observed contrasting operating procedures and routines, both submarine services had one key achievement in common; they successfully confronted the massive Soviet submarine fleet of the Cold War. After commanding a diesel submarine, the author went onto command two SSNs, *Courageous* and *Valiant*. He provides dramatic first-hand accounts of his interactions with numerous Soviet submarines, vividly describing the suspense and tension of being in their close proximity, undetected. Having commanded an SSN myself, I personally can certainly relate to his experiences.

Importantly, this book charts the history of the West's submarine operations in the highly demanding environment of operating under the Arctic Ice and also how the Royal Navy developed world-leading expertise in the realms of submarine escape and rescue. The book also sets out the long and difficult introduction into service of the UK's submarine torpedo systems and the frustrations he personally experienced in dealing with a hierarchy which could seen to be at fault in playing down performance and reliability problems.

In the mid-1990s, the UK's nuclear deterrent was modernised by the much more capable and effective Trident weapon system, which is still in service and will be for at least the next four decades. Dan Conley took the lead in the acceptance into service of *Vanguard*, the first-of-class of British submarines which carry this missile system, and he describes many of the teething problems of bringing the UK's Trident submarines into service. *Vanguard* and her three sister submarines are still in service and will be until they start being replaced in the early 2030s by the *Dreadnought* class, currently under construction. The *Vanguard*s have now well exceeded their 25-year design life and accordingly are proving very challenging and expensive to maintain. Owing to stretched hull availability, at times CASD hangs by a thread and on occasions patrol durations have been measured in a considerable number of months. The resulting stress on crew members and their families is clearly a major issue for the Navy Board and indeed the Government to address.

The Cold War era is now long past. However, it is evident that as the West now confronts an aggressive, recidivist Russia and a more aggressive China, Britain's submarine force once again will be key to its ultimate security. This fine memoir is an absorbing read which vividly captures the key events during the Cold War undersea confrontation with the Soviet Navy and, in doing so, will open the reader's eyes to the significance and importance today of the Royal Navy Submarine Service. This book also highlights how it takes a very unique and dedicated person to serve in Britain's submarines.

Admiral Sir Mark Stanhope GCB, OBE, DL

Preface

Cold War Command, co-authored by Captain Richard Woodman and myself, describes my experiences serving in the Royal Navy Submarine Service during the three decades from 1967. During this period, I participated in the intense and highly secretive Cold War undersea confrontation with the massive Soviet submarine force which only in the early 1990s began to decrease in numbers. *Down to the Sea in Submarines* recounts these experiences and other events from a more personal perspective and in greater detail. Importantly, it uniquely captures life at sea in a British submarine during the height of the Cold War.

Down to the Sea in Submarines charts the British submariner's remarkable transformation from the somewhat buccaneering free spirit serving on a rather clapped-out WW2 boat during the sunset of the British Empire, to the highly professional individual who spends prolonged periods under the sea in a platform which matches the complexity of a spacecraft. In particular, the ballistic missile submarine (SSBN) crew has the awesome responsibility for the safe and effective management of nuclear-tipped missiles located only a bulkhead apart from the nuclear reactor.

It takes a unique type of person to serve in submarines and this book describes the British submariner and his way of life in the post-WW2 era. In telling this story, I aim to bring alive the superb camaraderie which most of my peers and I enjoyed. I also describe some of the 'Silent Service's' remarkable achievements and its highly beneficial relationship with the United States Navy Submarine Force. Additionally, I offer a glimpse to the reader of the many humorous situations my colleagues and I participated in, or encountered. While it is too easy to look back with the proverbial 'rose-tinted' spectacles, life in the post-war diesel boat on the whole was fun, with responsibility heaped upon crew members at a very young age. My experiences of serving in a nuclear submarine were much more serious and sometimes alarming. However, despite being under the sea in a powerful, highly complex and sophisticated fighting machine, there were also situations and events of levity and humour.

As I write, at a time of very much heightened tension with an aggressive and threatening Russia, in the deep ocean there is a Royal Navy Trident SSBN crew delivering the United Kingdom's continuous at sea nuclear deterrent. At the same time there are men and women manning the nation's nuclear attack submarines which, at short notice, could be deployed to any ocean in the world. All of these young people are continuing to uphold the fine heritage of the brave and committed men who manned our Submarine Service in the 60 years prior to the commissioning in 1963 of the UK's first nuclear submarine, *Dreadnought*. *Down to the Sea in Submarines* sets out and underlines the remarkable dedication and professionalism of our Submarine Service crews.

Acknowledgements

In writing this book, I am deeply grateful for the immense support of my dear wife, Sue, and close friend Captain Alan Wright. They exuded both great patience and attention to detail in removing the many eccentricities in my initial text and most significantly contributed to making the content both an enjoyable and informative read.

Dan Conley,
January 2024

Glossary and Abbreviations

'Akula' class	Highly capable third-generation Soviet nuclear attack submarine
'Alfa' class	Deep-diving, high-speed Soviet nuclear attack submarine
APLIS	Applied Physics Laboratory Ice Station
ASW	Anti-Submarine Warfare
AUTEC	Atlantic Underwater Test and Evaluation Centre
B2-TC	Batch II *Trafalgar* class – renamed *Astute* class
BUTEC	British Underwater Test and Evaluation Centre
Captain (SM)	Captain of a submarine squadron
CASD	Continuous At Sea Deterrence
CEP	Contact Evaluation Plot
'Charlie' class	Soviet SSGN
CNSA	Commodore Naval Ship Acceptance
CSST	Captain Submarine Sea Training
'Delta' class	Third-generation Soviet SSBN
DSEA	Davis Submarine Escape Apparatus
DSRV	Deep Submergence Rescue Vehicle
'Echo' class	First-generation anti-ship nuclear missile submarines
FAA	Fleet Air Arm
FOSM	Flag Officer Submarines
'Foxtrot' class	Soviet diesel submarines produced in large numbers in the 1960s
'Hotel' class	First-generation Soviet SSBN
HTP	High Test Peroxide
'Juliett' class	Soviet missile-firing diesel submarine
MIZ	Marginal Ice Zone
MoD	Ministry of Defence
MPA	Maritime Patrol Aircraft

'November' class	First-generation Soviet nuclear attack submarine
OOD	Officer-of-the-Day
OOW	Officer-of-the-Watch
PE	Procurement Executive
PWR	Pressurised Water Reactor
SCOSER	Standing Committee On Submarine Escape and Rescue
SINS	Ships Inertial Navigation System
SM3	Captain of Third Submarine Squadron
SOSUS	Long-range underwater sound surveillance system
SSBN	Ballistic missile nuclear submarine.
SSG	Diesel submarine equipped with ballistic or anti-ship missiles
SSGN	Nuclear attack submarine equipped with anti-ship/land-attack cruise missiles
SSK	Diesel or conventionally-powered submarine
SSN	Nuclear attack submarine
STWG	Submarine Tactics and Weapons Group
'Typhoon' class	26,000-ton third-generation Soviet SSBN
VC	Victoria Cross
'Victor' class	Russian second-generation nuclear attack submarine
'Whiskey' class	Soviet diesel submarine produced in large numbers in the 1950s
WRNS	Women's Royal Naval Service
X-Craft	Small 30-ton submarine, designed for harbour penetration, armed with mines
XO	Executive Officer – Second-in-Command
'Yankee' class	Second-generation Soviet SSBN

Chapter 1

The Royal Navy Submarine
Service Heritage

During the nineteenth century there had been several attempts to develop man-powered submarines as fighting vessels but often these involved fatalities. In 1865 a Confederate submarine, the *Hunley*, powered by eight men, succeeded in sinking the Union warship *Housatonic* at the entrance to Charleston harbour. This was the first successful submarine attack but in achieving this the entire crew perished, most probably because their craft was too close to its explosive device when it was detonated. It was not until the introduction of the internal combustion engine in the late nineteenth century that the submarine evolved as an effective weapon system. The first British submarine, the US-designed *Holland I*, embarked on sea trials in 1902. Remarkably, little over half a century later, in 1955 the US commissioned the world's first nuclear-powered submarine, USS *Nautilus*. This event heralded the submarine's fearsome ability of being able to deliver a massive nuclear weapons strike which could potentially destroy the key infrastructure and economy of even the largest of nations.

The early British submarines, and their contemporaries in other navies, were very fragile vessels of only about 100 tons in displacement and powered by highly dangerous petrol engines. These emitted extremely hazardous fumes which could intoxicate the crews and risked lethal explosion. When dived, the boats shifted to battery power and propulsion by a primitive electric motor which gave them a speed of only a few knots. They were limited to a safe depth of about 100ft and, being not very seaworthy, were in the early days limited to coastal defence roles. When on the surface, their open access hatch had dangerously little clearance above the level of the sea. Furthermore, barely visible amongst the waves, they were vulnerable to collision.

Inevitably these boats experienced many accidents. Taking a lesson from the coal-mining community, caged canaries were kept onboard to provide a warning of toxic gasses or fumes. However, these little creatures did not provide a foolproof warning system and, prior to WW1, there were numerous cases of fatal explosions. One such tragedy was the explosion onboard *A4* in 1909 when alongside the Haulbowline naval base near Cork. Six crew members were killed and were buried in Old Church Cemetery in Cobh, where, incidentally, many of the dead resulting from the U-boat sinking of the liner *Lusitania* in 1915 were later interred.

Tragically many of the early boats were involved in fatal collisions, where once the pressure hull was ruptured, they rapidly flooded and plunged to the seabed, all the crew perishing. Notably, the first British designed submarine, the *A1*, was lost with all hands near Spithead in 1904 after being accidentally rammed by a surface vessel. More than half of the thirteen vessels of this class were involved in serious accidents, often with a high number of fatalities. Therefore, it took a very special type of person to volunteer for submarines, especially in an era when the First Sea Lord (1910–11), Admiral Sir Arthur Wilson VC, declared 'Submarines are underhand, unfair, and damned un-English'.

At the outbreak of WW1, larger ocean-going boats were coming out in numbers from Britain's shipyards. These boats were constrained, when dived on the battery, to a maximum speed of about 10 knots in short bursts, but much safer diesel engines were replacing the highly dangerous petrol versions. Diesel fumes are much less flammable and not toxic, albeit they emit a strong, pungent odour which permeates clothes, bedding and any absorbent material onboard. This heralded generations of submariners who, when in uniform, were distinguishable by a distinctive diesel smell. Besides smelling unpleasant, living conditions onboard these early boats were extremely primitive, with inadequate fresh water for regular washing and toilet facilities initially of the 'bucket and chuck-it' type.

During the war, British submarines operated in the North Sea where they contributed to the blockade of German ports and acted as a forward scouting force for the Fleet. But their first great successes came further afield, in the Sea of Marmara, where having penetrated the Turkish-controlled Dardanelles Straits, they acted in support of the ill-fated Gallipoli campaign, destroying significant numbers of Turkish warships, troopships and supply vessels. These submarine crews, in transiting minefields, avoiding submarine nets and negotiating strong currents, displayed remarkable gallantry and boldness. Their attacks were extended to gun actions against shore targets and the landing of demolition parties to destroy railway lines. Such daring engagements, bolstered the submariner's swashbuckling devil-may-care image and the courage of Captains such as Holbrook, Boyle, and Nasmith became legendary. Less well-known were the Submarine Service's operations in the Baltic where they successfully attacked German warships and merchant shipping. In the closing stages of the war our submarines supported White Russian forces opposing the Bolsheviks, a campaign which, of course, was to end in failure. Altogether five Victoria Crosses (VCs) were awarded to submarine Captains during the course of the war, a high number for such a small and evolving fighting arm.

Meanwhile, the German submarine service firmly made its mark soon after the outbreak of war with the sinking, within a few hours, of three British cruisers patrolling off Heligoland by one small submarine, U9, in which 1,459 British crew died, and, on account of this new, extremely potent threat, the Grand Fleet was forced to closet itself in safe anchorages such as Scapa Flow. During the latter stages of the war the U-boat campaign against merchant shipping crossing the Atlantic from America, almost crippled Britain's ability to continue the war effort and to feed its people. The introduction of a convoy system to protect shipping in late 1917 proved the nation's salvation.

During the course of WW1, the Admiralty had wrestled with determining the optimum role for the submarine. At a time when naval aviation was also in its infancy and the use of aircraft for reconnaissance was still evolving, the concept of deploying submarines ahead of the Fleet to scout for and report back the enemy gained favour. The theory was that when these so-called 'Fleet submarines' sighted an enemy warship formation and reported its location and movements to the Fleet, they would then submerge to avoid detection and potentially have the opportunity to attack the enemy. To be successful in this role, submarines would require to sustain a surfaced speed of well over 20 knots to keep up with the Fleet. However, this speed was beyond the capability of the diesel engines of the era. Consequently, a submarine propelled by steam turbines was designed and built. This was the birth of the notorious 'K' class, the first of which first came into service in May 1917.

Seventeen 'K' class were completed to a revolutionary design. Over 300ft long and at 1,800 tons, they were three times the displacement of other contemporary submarines. However, they were dogged by too many hazardous hull openings, including two for retractable funnels, dangerously poor stability and cumbersome manoeuvrability when dived. In the pre-radar era, their low profile when on the surface in the vicinity of the Fleet was a further significant hazard. They were involved in a total of sixteen major accidents incurring an appalling loss of life: one sank on sea trials; three were lost after collisions; a fifth disappeared and another sank in harbour. None were successful in combat. Four decades later with the commissioning of USS *Nautilus*, steam returned as a means of submarine propulsion. This time it proved both highly successful and safe, marking the advent of the first true submarine capable of virtually unlimited endurance under the sea.

There continued a series of British submarine losses in the inter-war years: in 1921 *K5* foundered owing to unknown causes; in the two years 1924 and 1925, *H42*, *L24* and *M1* sank as a result of collisions; *H47* sank in 1929 after a collision with *L12*; *Poseidon* foundered in 1931 after collision with a merchant vessel; *M2* – a seaplane carrier – sank in 1932, probably because of failure of the water-tightness of the hangar; in 1939 *Thetis* sank during Contractor's Sea Trials because of torpedo tube problems. In most cases the entire crew perished with fatalities totalling 441 from a relatively small fighting arm – an absolutely dreadful peacetime figure.

Meanwhile, against a background of the 1922 Washington Naval Treaty constraints and very limited financial resources, the Royal Navy continued to pursue the concept of the Fleet Submarine: a 12in gun was fitted on one boat, *M1*, and a seaplane hangar on another, *M2*. As stated above, both these vessels and their crews were to be lost in accidents. More successful were the three diesel-powered 'River' class boats built in the early 1930s, which at 2,200 tons in displacement, achieved unrivalled surfaced speeds of over 22 knots. However, with the building of battleships capable of over 25 knots, the concept of submarines providing Fleet support was clearly unsustainable. As a concept it was not to re-emerge in the Royal Navy until the 1960s when the high speed and superb manoeuvrability of the nuclear submarine made it viable.

At the outbreak of WW2 Great Britain had about fifty-five operational submarines. Many of these were obsolete (the 'H' and 'L' classes) or, in the event, too big and of limited dived manoeuvrability to be successful in combat, most notably the 1930s 'O' class. Only sixteen were of the more modern 'U', 'S' and 'T' classes, which were to prove highly successful during the course of the war. In addition, four of the of six large *Porpoise* class minelaying submarines were operational. Only one of this class was to survive the war. While surface speeds of 15 knots or more were typical for the British WW2 submarine, dived speeds were at best 10 knots. Underwater endurance was a maximum of about 24 hours before expiration of battery life and a build-up of CO_2 in the atmosphere determined the need to surface.

Whilst the Submarine Service was to have very notable successes in the Norwegian Sea against the German Navy and in the Far East against Japanese forces, it was in the Mediterranean that the Royal Navy submarine was to have a decisive effect. Operating from bases in Gibraltar, Alexandria and Malta, it succeeded in depriving the Italian Navy of sea control of the central Mediterranean. Most importantly by sinking fifty supply ships within three months, our submarines played a key role in choking off vital supplies to Rommel which were required for his North African campaign in the latter half of 1941. Suffering such catastrophic losses, the German drive towards the Suez Canal was repulsed and Rommel eventually defeated. Akin to the Battle of Britain, rarely in the history of warfare have so few men had such a decisive impact upon a campaign of utmost strategic importance.

Conditions endured by the Tenth Submarine Flotilla operating from Malta were particularly challenging and the crews were to share many of the privations endured by the brave Maltese. Often there was no respite for crews when in harbour because of intense bombing. Submarines often had to resort to submerging in the harbour during daylight hours to avoid being hit. Above-ground base facilities and workshops having been destroyed, alternative support functions were set up underground in caves and tunnels, including messing and sleeping quarters. Added to this there was a shortage of reliable torpedoes, and older, less effective variants had to be resorted to.

At sea, Tenth Flotilla submarines harried convoys of supply shipping and troop transports. They also attacked railway lines, landed commandos, conducted reconnaissance and, on one occasion at least, sent out a boarding party to blow up a disabled enemy ship. The larger classes of submarine were also used to bring in vital supplies to Malta when stocks of key materials, such as aviation spirit, were desperately low. However, it was at great cost and a very high proportion of the Tenth Flotilla submarines were lost, particularly to mines. Furthermore, the Italians demonstrated much greater anti-submarine effectiveness than their German allies and, in convoy protection, took a toll of several boats.

Five VCs were awarded to submariners during the Mediterranean campaign. These included three to the Captains of *Upholder*, *Torbay* and *Turbulent*, Lieutenant Commander Wanklyn and Commanders Miers and Linton respectively. The remaining two medals were awarded to Lieutenant Roberts and Petty Officer Gould who very bravely removed an unexploded bomb from underneath the casing of *Thrasher*. But these awards represented merely the pinnacle of the great courage of the crews of operating their boats in the vicinity of minefields and where an attack upon enemy shipping inevitably brought about a severe and terrifying depth-charge pounding.

During the course of the war, Britain developed a number of midget submarines, termed X-Craft. Of only 30 tons displacement and manned by a crew of four, these craft were towed by larger submarines as close to their target as practicable and, after release of the tow, they continued underway with their own propulsion. They were armed with side explosive charges to be released under the designated target vessel. If necessary, a diver could leave and re-enter the boat through a lock-out chamber in order to cut a gap in anti-submarine netting. However, X-Craft operations were extremely hazardous: the hulls of the boats were fragile with a maximum safe depth of 200ft, they had a top dived speed of only 5 knots and their underwater handling had its problems. It therefore took very special and brave people to man them.

X-Craft were used in two highly successful operations. The first of these was carried out in September 1943 against the German battleship *Tirpitz* moored in Altafjord, Norway. Of the six submarines deployed, none returned but two, *X6* and *X7*, successfully placed charges underneath the battleship, causing serious damage and putting her out of action for many months. In the second of these operations, *XE3* sank the Japanese heavy cruiser *Takao* at anchor in the Johore Straits north of Singapore Island. Both attacks involved navigating heavily guarded, enemy-held narrows and very deservedly resulted in the award of four VCs.

During WW2 Britain lost seventy-four submarines and eight X-Craft, most with their entire crews. Consequently, its Submarine Service suffered the highest fatality rate of any of the Royal Navy's fighting arms. For most, being depth-charged was a highly traumatic experience and a submarine attack could be extremely tense and stressful for prolonged periods. Therefore, it is perhaps no surprise that, post war, many submariners who had experienced combat found it difficult to settle into peacetime routines and tempo.

After the war most of Britain's approximately 140 submarines in commission were scrapped or sold overseas. Of those boats which remained operational, the majority were fitted with a snorkel mast (a Dutch invention dating back to the late 1930s) which enabled them to run their engines whilst submerged, avoiding the need to surface to re-charge the batteries and refresh the air. However, snorkelling, more commonly referred to as snorting, has its risks. In April 1951 the *Affray* sank in the English Channel with the loss of seventy-five lives, with strong evidence that the cause was snort-system related.

The loss of the *Affray* was preceded by the sinking of the *Truculent* in January 1950 in the Thames Estuary, after collision with a Swedish oil tanker. The majority of her crew were killed. In 1955 a trials torpedo exploded onboard the submarine *Sidon* in Portland harbour. The boat sank alongside and, again, many of the crew were killed. Therefore, in the decade after WW2 there occurred three submarine losses, somewhat replicating the grim experience post-WW1. Also in the early 1970s, owing to material failures, there occurred serious battery explosions in the 'A' class submarines *Auriga* and *Alliance*. These caused several life-threatening injuries and one fatality.

In the 1950s the Submarine Service was seen as a bit of a career backwater, with its main peacetime role the rather mundane training of surface and airborne anti-submarine forces. Those boats which were retained were streamlined to improve their stealth when dived and a handful were fitted with improved batteries which gave them burst speeds of around 15 knots. As it became evident that the Soviet Union was building a very large submarine force, the Royal Navy submarine's primary role became anti-submarine warfare. In reality, effectiveness in this role would have been constrained by the lack of a capable anti-submarine weapon and limited underwater speed.

While submarines may have been regarded as career constraining and a dangerous occupation, morale was generally high and, indeed, the Service attracted a number of very talented officers who would attain high rank. Admiral of the Fleet the Lord Fieldhouse and Admiral Sir 'Sandy' Woodward, both of Falklands War fame, were but two. No doubt the mystique and excitement of serving in submarines, together with the receipt of submarine pay, were a lure for many. The strong sense of camaraderie and individual responsibility placed upon each member of a submarine's crew, were further key factors in high levels of job satisfaction. Added to these, with submarines based in Canada, Australia, Malta and Singapore, there was plenty of opportunity for the enjoyment of attractive overseas postings and frequent foreign port visits.

Of greater operational significance, a small number of specially-equipped submarines (initially wartime 'T' class) started being deployed to the Barents Sea on highly classified joint US/UK intelligence-gathering missions targeting the Soviet Navy and its shore installations. These missions were extremely demanding and shrouded in great secrecy. The crews which undertook them were regarded by their peers with great respect and a degree of awe and reinforced the mysterious aura of the 'Silent Service'.

On the downside many of the Captains of this era, perhaps as a result of their war experiences, proved difficult to serve under and a small, but notable, minority had a serious drink problem. Until the early 1970s, a drinking culture permeated through all ranks fostered by the wardroom's access to cheap duty-free spirits and the daily rum issue to senior and junior ratings. While crews were, in general abstemious when at sea, it was normal for much alcohol to be consumed onboard their boats when in harbour or when accommodated aboard depot ships.

In 1958 the Royal Navy commissioned its first post-war class of submarine. HMS *Porpoise* was the first of twenty-one vessels of the similar 'P' and 'O' class which were to form the core of its conventional submarine force until the early 1990s. These boats, designated 'SSKs', were 1,850 tons in surface displacement and were much superior to the wartime construction they were replacing. Among their many improvements were deeper diving capability, higher burst speeds of 17 knots, better crew living quarters, greater weapon loads and much longer range. An additional fourteen boats of the 'O' class were sold to Commonwealth and foreign nations.

In the same year, the US-UK Mutual Defence Agreement included the American commitment to provide the Royal Navy with a nuclear attack submarine design together with delivering the associated propulsion plant and its technology. Some five years later, in April 1963, the Royal Navy's first nuclear submarine, HMS *Dreadnought*, was commissioned. An attack submarine, she was designated as an 'SSN'. A few months earlier, in December 1962, at Nassau in the Bahamas, President Kennedy had agreed with Prime Minister MacMillan to supply the UK with the Polaris nuclear ballistic missile weapon system. The Submarine Service in the future would deliver the UK's nuclear deterrent.

I joined the Royal Navy in 1963 and served in the Submarine Flotilla in the three decades from 1967, incidentally the year in which Britain's first ballistic-missile submarine (SSBN) *Resolution*, was commissioned. I was there for the introduction of this class of submarine and participated in its succession by the Trident weapon system in the *Vanguard* class in the 1990s. I also was much involved in the entry into service of the *Upholder* class of diesel submarines. The four vessels of this class all decommissioned in 1994, ending the era of conventionally-powered submarines in the Royal Navy.

Chapter 2

Joining the Submarine Service

From an early age I was fascinated by submarines. I was brought up in Campbeltown, a fishing port at the end of the Kintyre Peninsula in the Firth of Clyde, where my father was skipper of one of two fishing boats owned by our family. The port was regularly visited by submarines, calling in to undertake repairs or to allow the crew a short break ashore. I soon developed a fascination for these underwater craft and, if I spotted one approaching the quayside, I would be there to watch it berthing. Painted black, and silently coming alongside using their main electric motors, to my young self they exuded a sinister aura of mystique and adventure. Their crews came across as confident and cheerful, conducting their berthing manoeuvres with few orders and little fuss, and giving the impression of being thoroughly professional and competent. To be a submariner one day became my ambition from a young age.

Submarine visits to Campbeltown did not always go to plan. One dark and stormy evening in the 1950s the 'T' class boat *Trenchant* got its navigation wrong and ended up aground on the northern side of the loch entrance. For many years a local pub displayed a picture of the stranded boat with a postman in wellington boots, accompanied by his dog, delivering its mail.

In the late 1950s two trial submarines propelled by turbines fuelled by High Test Peroxide (HTP) were commissioned. These were named *Excalibur* and *Explorer* and, together with their tender and specialist fuelling vessel, often used Campbeltown as a forward operating base. HTP technology had been acquired from the Germans at the end of WW2 and enabled these trials submarines to achieve record dived speeds of 26 knots. However, this type of fuel was extremely unstable and the two boats suffered frequent minor fires and explosions, resulting in *Explorer* being nicknamed 'Exploder'! Whether this type of technology could ever have been developed as a safe, reliable form of submarine propulsion is debatable and, in the event, it was soon eclipsed by the advent of the nuclear-powered submarine. Of note, in 2000, an HTP-powered torpedo exploded onboard the Russian nuclear submarine *Kursk* in the Barents Sea, causing it to sink with loss of the entire crew.

In 1955 my father contracted tuberculosis, which ended his fishing career, and the one remaining family boat was sold. Consequently, we moved to Glasgow but I continued to visit Campbeltown on holiday where a highlight was being able to watch the arrival of a submarine. In early 1961, at the age of 14 and determined to join the 'Silent Service', I applied for a Naval Scholarship. Having successfully passed the hurdle of a first interview at the Reserve Headquarters in Leith, I travelled to Gosport that summer to attend the Admiralty Interview Board. There were about half a dozen other candidates in attendance.

On the second evening of the three-day interview process, all candidates were transported to the nearby submarine base, HMS *Dolphin*, for a tour of one of the boats alongside, the recently commissioned *Finwhale*. Two years earlier I had toured the WW2 boat *Tireless* at Rosyth Navy Days and it immediately struck me that *Finwhale*, with a much larger battery and a thicker pressure hull than the former, was considerably more congested in terms of internal space and was much more complex. When we entered the control room, I was absolutely overawed by its mass of pipes, valves, switches and cabinets of electrical equipment and wondered how I would ever get to grips with such complexity. By coincidence I was to undertake the majority of my Submarine Commanding Officer's Qualifying Course in *Finwhale* 14 years later. However, by then I was very much at home and totally familiar with such a living and working environment.

In due course, I learned that I had been successful at the interview and was to be awarded a Naval Scholarship and a reserved place at Britannia Royal Navy College, Dartmouth, as a General List seaman officer. The scholarship was not so significant as I was attending a grammar school where there were no fees to pay, but a maintenance grant was payable which no doubt helped with the family budget. Two years later, in September 1963, I joined the college to start my officer training as a cadet, a rank paid at £16 per month.

At this time the Fleet Air Arm (FAA) was the dominant fighting arm of the Royal Navy and, when I joined, five fixed-wing aircraft carriers were in service. A high proportion of the Service's hierarchy were aviators, and plans were in place to build a new, large 60,000-ton vessel to replace the older, less capable carriers. Despite a very high peacetime fatality rate amongst aircrew, the FAA continued to attract many volunteers to train as fast jet pilots. On the other hand, the specialisation of aircrew observer (navigator) was not popular, not least because it suffered an even higher fatality rate than that of pilot, and many individuals had been pressed into this career path. Thankfully, by our third year of training, when specialisation preferences were called for, there were sufficient applications to become pilots and observers that none of us was forced into the FAA as non-volunteers.

However, the Navy was about to change very profoundly in its structure and allocation of its resources. The 1962 Nassau Agreement set the Royal Navy the aim of training crews to man and maintain a force of five SSBNs and delivering Continuous At Sea Deterrence (CASD) from 1969. At the same time a programme was ongoing to construct a force of SSNs which could be tasked to confront the growing threat from the Soviet Union's huge submarine force and, importantly, could provide support to the SSBN on deterrent patrol.

In 1966, on grounds of cost, the Labour Government made the decision to cancel the new aircraft carrier project and to run down the existing carrier force. This indeed was a great blow to the FAA. Therefore, for many of my peers the Submarine Service was a natural career choice, as it was to become the Navy's most important fighting arm and offered much greater professional opportunities. I was, therefore, pleased and relieved that my choice to specialise in submarines was accepted and I was designated to start submarine training in September 1967, having completed four years of General List professional instruction, courses and sea experience. The latter included three months at sea as a cadet on a frigate in the Dartmouth Training Squadron, as well as a year at sea as a midshipman in a destroyer where I was disappointed at the amount of time spent in these vessels on 'spit and polish' as opposed to achieving fighting effectiveness. These experiences confirmed my strong preference for a career in submarines.

During this period of training, I had had several opportunities to spend short trips at sea in submarines. These further reinforced my enthusiasm to serve in 'boats'. All the crews I went to sea with were clearly highly professional and evidently took pride and enjoyment in explaining the workings of their submarines. When a cadet in the Dartmouth Training Squadron in the summer of 1964, my ship, *Wizard*, together with the other frigates of the squadron, were the targets for one of the weeks of the Submarine Commanding Officers

Qualifying Course, known as the 'Perisher'. The exercises took place in the Clyde Estuary, returning each night to a buoy in Rothesay Bay. Keen to volunteer for submarines, I requested to spend a day in *Narwhal*, the course training boat. Having transferred to the submarine, I joined Lieutenant Gavin Menzies who was Officer-Of-the-Watch (OOW) on the bridge for the surface passage down to the exercise areas. Most unusually for the era, as a seaman officer he was wearing glasses. I spotted that he had a clutch of tissue paper to wipe away the frequent spray which hit the top of the fin. He subsequently passed Perisher and commanded *Rorqual* before an unwise prohibition was placed upon those submarine seamen officers who needed to wear spectacles. Incidentally, after having left the Navy, he went onto write the controversial bestseller *'1421' – the Year China Discovered the World*.

I particularly enjoyed a day at sea in the English Channel on the WW2 boat *Totem*, one of the eight 'T' class all-welded boats which had received an extensive conversion to give them much better underwater performance. As we headed back to harbour, I was invited to the stokers' mess right aft, where I was taught the rudiments of 'Uckers', a board-game similar to but a bit more complicated and aggressive than Ludo, and a favourite of the submarine sailor.

In early September 1967, my training class of twenty-two officers reported to HMS *Dolphin* for 12 weeks of basic submarine training. All volunteers in our early 20s, we were of very diverse social backgrounds: public and grammar schools; two admiral's sons; two individuals promoted from the lower deck and a couple of Australians. Curiously one course member, besides becoming a successful submarine Captain, in later life inherited an earldom and at the time of writing sits in the House of Lords. Of the eighteen RN seamen officers taking part, only four would eventually go onto achieve submarine command. On reflection, a high proportion of my peers left submarines early on in their careers, for a variety of reasons, but too often simply because of personality clashes with their Captains.

The Submarine School was then in HMS *Dolphin*, a shore establishment housed in Fort Blockhouse which formed the western side of the entrance to Portsmouth Harbour. *Dolphin* was established in 1905 as the first Royal Navy Submarine Base and was very much the 'Alma Mater' of the Submarine Service. Generations of submariners had received their basic training there and had an emotional attachment to the place with its informal and friendly, but professional, atmosphere.

The waterfront of the Fort comprised nineteenth-century fortifications and accommodation blocks. The Submarine Flotilla headquarters, Flag Officer Submarines (FOSM) and his staff, were located in a number of buildings overlooking the piers. It was from here that submarines on patrol were communicated with and their command and control exercised.

Dolphin was also the base for the First Submarine Squadron which then consisted of about fifteen operational submarines, mainly of the 'A' class of immediate post-WW2 construction. With support workshops and other technical facilities dotted around the establishment it was, therefore, a busy set-up and evenings in the wardroom were convivial and lively. Memorably the wardroom hall-porters, all retired senior rate submariners, were a great source of information and provided friendly advice to junior officers new to submarines.

The course officer was a senior Lieutenant, Chris Meyer, who was supported by a real character of a Chief Petty Officer, Bill Hoy. Soon after joining, we were ushered in groups to be introduced to Flag Officer Submarines, Rear Admiral Ian McGeoch, DSO, DSC, in his headquarters office. A WW2 submarine hero, he commanded *Splendid* in the Mediterranean, where in late 1942 he sank a record amount of enemy merchant shipping, in addition to several warships. However, after attacking a convoy in April 1943, his boat was depth-charged and badly damaged by a German destroyer. He managed to surface the submarine and scuttle it under the destroyer's withering gunfire. He luckily survived, albeit losing the sight of one eye from a shell splinter. Taken as a prisoner-of-war by the destroyer's crew and incarcerated in Italy, after several attempts he succeeded in escaping and walked 400 miles to neutral Switzerland where he managed to return to Britain under a prisoner-of-war exchange scheme – truly *Boy's Own Paper* stuff. A false eye gave him a somewhat daunting appearance, but he warmly welcomed us into the Submarine Service and we felt very privileged to be serving under him and a cadre of legendary senior officers who had significant submarine war experience.

An early task on arrival at *Dolphin* was to collect an issue of submarine clothing, mainly cold-weather attire (including long johns, never in the event to be worn by myself) and two white submarine sweaters, the iconic sea-going uniform of the British Submariner. Unfortunately these garments did not wash well and soon lost their shape, in particular sagging around the neck. Off-white in colour and usually marked with a few oil stains, the typical submarine sweater was a far cry from the neat, suave attire sported by submarine movie stars such as John Mills.

Early in the course, training was undertaken in the 100ft escape tower. This was built in the 1950s to train crews how to escape from a stricken submarine. Prior to undergoing this training, we all had a thorough medical examination to ensure we could withstand the decompression rigours of ascending from the bottom of the tower where the pressure was three times atmospheric. However, there were no psychological tests to ascertain whether we could withstand being confined to a steel tube under the sea for months on end.

The tower and its staff were run by Lieutenant Commander Matthew Todd, a redoubtable character, who had undertaken several war patrols, including serving under the controversial and difficult Captain of *Thule*, Lieutenant Commander Alastair Mars, DSO, DSC. Todd had himself commanded several submarines, including an X-Craft which, even in peacetime, was dangerous in which to serve. An expert in submarine escape, he had pioneered what was known as the free ascent, whereby an escaper on leaving a stricken submarine would use the capacity of his own lungs to reach the surface. He was supported by a staff of about a dozen senior rates known as 'Swim Boys' who would ensure the students had safe ascents to the surface, but whose equipment merely consisted of goggles and a nose clip. A doctor was also stationed at the top of the tank, available to immediately start treatment on the occasional individual who had suffered medical problems during the ascent.

After a session of classroom training, which included watching a realistic and sobering film depicting escape from a submarine, the first ascent was undertaken individually from a lockout positioned at a depth of 30ft. It was stressed by the trainers that it was absolutely vital to breathe out all the way to the surface to avoid a risk of burst lungs or a fatal embolism. To ensure that this happened, on leaving the lockout, a Swim Boy would check the correct breathing-out posture before allowing the ascent to commence. His colleagues, positioned at stages on the way up, were there to check all continued to be well. For those not breathing out adequately, a Swim Boy's thump in the stomach was normally enough to achieve the right rate of expiration.

All of us successfully completed the ascent from the 100ft lockout at the foot of the tank and most enjoyed the rather thrilling experience of free ascent from this depth. However, we fully realised that the tank conditions of clear, well-lit water at a body temperature of 38°C, would be very different from actually escaping from a stricken submarine. Gut-wrenching fear, darkness and bitterly cold water would characterise the real thing, emphasising the need for thorough training if the escape process was to prove successful in the event of a serious accident.

Against a background of three submarine losses since 1950, the majority of the course instruction was geared towards enabling its students to safely serve as a dived OOW in a 'P' or 'O' class submarine. The individual's responsibility for submarine safety was hammered home throughout as was the consideration that a mistake by even a junior crew member could imperil the whole boat. Therefore, all officers were expected to have a detailed knowledge of each of the submarine's operating systems and procedures and the course content was very much structured to achieve this. Significant time was also allocated to teaching the sonar and weapon systems of the modern diesel submarine.

When a submarine is snorting at periscope depth, running its diesel engines to re-charge its batteries and refresh its air, it incurs additional safety risks. Air is sucked down an induction (snort) mast into the boat through an 18in diameter hull valve. If this mast dips under the sea, other than just for a few seconds, there is a risk of a hazardous quantity of seawater entering the boat, unless the hull valve is quickly shut. Additionally, unless the engines are shut down quickly when the mast dips or when the induction hull valve is shut, they will suck the air out of the submarine, potentially lowering the air pressure to dangerous levels. The engine exhaust is piped out through a separate mast and there is the further hazard, if procedures are not carried out correctly, of lethal carbon monoxide levels building up inside the boat. Finally, when a submarine battery is being fully charged, it will emit hydrogen. If not properly ventilated this can cause an explosion. Therefore, the snort system and its procedures were thoroughly taught and rigorously rehearsed during the course. Of note, owing to material failures, serious battery explosions occurred in the early 1970s in the ageing 'A' class boats, *Auriga* and *Alliance*. Sadly, these incurred one fatality and several significant injuries amongst the two crews.

In the latter stages of the course, a week of training was spent at the attack training simulator at Rothesay on the Isle of Bute. This facility was a left-over from the era when the Third Submarine Squadron depot ship was semi-permanently moored in Rothesay Bay. At its core was a sphere, the inside of which replicated a submarine control room. It rotated in response to ordered course changes, and training attacks were carried out on a surface ship simulated by a light image projected onto a screen. Basic in concept, it worked well in teaching the arts of a submarine attack. On the final attack session of the week, the training staff relished dropping ear-splitting scare charges around the sphere, simulating a depth-charging.

The attack training over, we headed by ferry and train to Glasgow Central Station to embark on the overnight sleeper to Euston Station. Having decanted our luggage into our sleeping compartments, naturally we headed to the bar. There we found Anton Diffring, the German film actor best known for his roles as a fanatical Nazi military officer, enjoying a quiet drink. If he was seeking peaceful solace, he was to be disappointed as we were soon joined by a lively group of Territorial paratroopers. As the train headed out of the station the gathering in the bar became more raucous and, in recognition of the presence of the film star, a number of German drinking songs were attempted. The Sergeant in charge of the paratroopers got really into the mood of the singing. Standing on a table conducting the ensemble, at the words 'Einz Vie Drie' of a particular song, much to the barman's despair, the Sergeant crunched up and ate his whisky tumbler. Mischievously, Chief Petty Officer Hoy then passed him up a British Rail water decanter, which, proving too much for the Sergeant's teeth and gums, punctured his cheek. This resulted in blood everywhere, to the great concern of the barman who recovered the remains of his decanter and hastily produced a first aid kit.

Shortly afterwards a course member, fired up by significant quantities of Scotch, decided to do an impromptu striptease on top of one of the tables. Encouraged by a supporting chorus, he was just getting to the finale as the train pulled into Carlisle station. It was all high-spirited stuff but, needless to say, there were many sore heads as the train arrived in London early in the morning. Diffring must have reflected afterwards that it was somewhat surprising that Britain had won the War.

In the final weeks of the training each of us spent one night at sea in a submarine. This experience consolidated elements of the classroom instruction, as well as offering the individual the opportunity to withdraw from training, even at this late stage, if they viewed life under the sea was not for them. No student took up this option.

About the same time we were invited to submit our submarine squadron preference. There were two British based options on offer, the First Squadron at Gosport, or the Third Squadron at the Clyde Submarine Base, Faslane. There was also one overseas basing opportunity at the Seventh Squadron in Singapore. Although two boats were based in Sydney, Australia, they were due shortly to be withdrawn back to the UK. Therefore, this desirable posting was not on the table. The SSBN Tenth Submarine Squadron was forming at Faslane but at this stage in our careers, we were all destined for diesel boats.

At the closing stages of WW2, a new class of submarine, designed for war in the Pacific was ordered – the 'A' class. In the event sixteen of these boats were completed immediately after the war and fourteen remained operational in 1967. They had a relatively high surfaced speed of 18 knots on a good day, but they were constrained to a maximum dived speed of only 8 knots. Furthermore, their hard-mounted, as opposed to noise-insulated, diesel engines meant they were noisy when snorting. Consequently, these factors determined that they had limited utility in high level operations and would have not been very effective in anti-submarine tasking. Much as the crews which served in them exuded enthusiasm for their 'A'-boat, I considered it not for me, not least because the training course had been totally 'O/P' class systems focused.

Therefore, to avoid appointment to an 'A'-boat, my choice was the Third Submarine Squadron which in addition to three SSNs, consisted exclusively of 'O/P' class diesel boats. I was delighted to learn that I was to be posted to the northern based boat *Odin*, under training and as torpedo officer. After about four months of practical experience in an operational boat I and my peers would undergo a final practical and written examination to qualify as submariners. As an aside, this qualification would then entitle us to Submarine Pay, a significant enhancement in income for both officers and ratings.

The course completed, in early December 1967 I drove north to the Clyde Submarine Base to join *Odin*. I had not received any joining instructions but on arrival at the base wardroom, a telephone call to the boat confirmed they were expecting me and that they looked forward to me arriving onboard the following morning. I was about to start a career in submarines which was to span the next 30 years and take me to sea in more than forty submarines.

Chapter 3

The *Oberon* Class Submarine

Odin, completed at Cammell Laird Shipyard at Birkenhead in 1962, was one of thirteen *Oberon* – 'O' – class submarines built for the Royal Navy. These followed on from the eight boats of the *Porpoise* – 'P' – class built between 1958 and 1961. At the time, three other UK yards were involved in submarine construction: Chatham Royal Dockyard, Vickers Armstrong at Barrow-in-Furness, and Scotts at Greenock on the Clyde.

The boat's pressure hull was a steel cylinder 18ft in diameter and about 250ft in length into which was squeezed machinery, main batteries, torpedo armament and crew accommodation for seventy souls. The 'O' class were very similar to the 'P' class, but they were constructed of superior quality steel and consequently had a deeper safe diving depth of 600ft compared with the 500ft of the 'Ps'. At 1,850 tons in surface displacement, they were considerably larger than the earlier 'T' and 'A' classes. Much of the additional space was required to hold a larger battery which delivered the maximum dived speed of 17 knots, albeit for only about 30 minutes.

Two 'Admiralty' design diesel generators provided power to electric main motors which achieved a maximum speed of about 14 knots on the surface. When dived, the propulsion was shifted to battery drive. Each of the two main battery sections consisted of 224 lead acid cells, similar in fundamental features to a standard car battery but, of course, much larger in size. Once under the water, the diesels would periodically be run, using the snort induction system, to re-charge the batteries and refresh the boat's air.

The 'O/P' classes embodied significant advances in reduction of their acoustic signature when dived and propelling on main motors. This stealth was demonstrated in the case of one boat travelling at slow speed above a number of noise-range listening hydrophones on the seabed and only the patter of rain on the surface of the sea was detected. These boats also enjoyed an excellent range of 15,000 miles and were capable of patrol durations of up to 60 days in length. When running on the surface, they handled well and were absolutely seaworthy in the roughest of sea conditions. The most significant shortcoming of their design was a rather ponderous turning rate when dived and proceeding at slow speed.

With eight torpedo tubes, the 'O/Ps' carried an impressive outfit of up to twenty-six torpedoes. However, until the early 1980s, their main anti-surface ship weapon was the Mark 8 torpedo which had been in service since 1927. Of limited range, and with no target homing capability, this weapon was well overdue for replacement. The two types of anti-submarine warfare (ASW) torpedoes embarked were the useless straight-running Mark 20, and the equally ineffective wire-guided Mark 23, electric torpedoes. Both were unreliable, too slow and had inadequate homing systems. They were replaced in the late 1970s, by the much more capable Tigerfish torpedo. That said, the latter weapon suffered a long gestation and it was not to become fully effective until the mid-1980s.

As completed in build, the 'O' class had sensors and torpedo-control equipment which had advanced little since 1945. While these submarines had to be capable of sinking surface shipping, their primary combat role of hunting and destroying other submarines required effective sonar equipment, together with a capable ASW weapon. The sonars, which nearly always operated in the passive mode (not transmitting) to avoid counter-detection, had only a single narrow trainable beam. Furthermore, the long-range sonar, which had its hydrophones fitted in the ballast tanks, required the submarine to circle slowly to conduct an all-round search. The control room attack equipment relied upon a number of rudimentary paper or Perspex plots which, although effective were manpower intensive and required a considerable degree of skill to determine target parameters and develop torpedo firing solutions.

Two periscopes were fitted: a powerful binocular search periscope where the operator sat on a power-operated chair; and a smaller monocular attack version, the uppermost 3ft of which, to minimise the risk of detection, was only about three inches in diameter. Navigational aids included radar and an echo-sounder and, in coastal waters, the Decca navigator provided an accurate radio aid to fixing the vessel's position. In the deep ocean, the Loran long-range radio wave system could provide an accurate position but it could be fickle to operate successfully. The search periscope was fitted with an artificial horizon sextant for use in astro-navigation but, in practice, it was difficult to operate and to my knowledge few individuals had any success in achieving an acceptable fix from it.

The primary system for receiving signal traffic was via the Very Low Frequency (VLF) long-range, radio wave transmission system delivered by several huge aerial networks which had been established around the UK and Allied countries. These enabled radio signals to be received when the submarine was under the sea at periscope depth. At deeper depths, reception was through a floating wire trailed behind the boat or a retractable buoy system. Less reliable, High Frequency (H/F) signal traffic could also be received or transmitted when on the surface or at periscope depth through one of two aerials. Shorter-range communication to ships or aircraft was achieved by Ultra High Frequency (UHF) aerial systems.

A submarine dives by opening vents to release the pressurised air out of its main ballast tanks, allowing seawater in from below. On diving, an immediate crew action is to achieve neutral buoyancy through adjusting the contents of a number of seawater-filled internal compensating tanks, and to trim the boat fore and aft to ensure that it is balanced out. Prior to leaving harbour, the officer responsible for calculating the optimum state of these tanks, known as the trimming officer, and normally the First Lieutenant, would supervise this process. If he got his calculations wrong and the boat was too light or too heavy on diving, this would not be well received by the Captain. At worst, if drastically over-heavy in trim such that it was proving difficult to maintain periscope depth using the power of the electric motors, surfacing might be necessary, causing much embarrassment and invariably the Captain's wrath.

Once underwater, the submarine changes depth by applying a bow up or bow down angle through the use of hydroplanes, one set fitted forward in the bows, the second set aft and close to the rudder. In older boats of the class, both hydroplane sets and the rudder were controlled by separate individuals who had to work together to achieve good control. During subsequent refits, all of the class were fitted with a one-man control system which uses a single column to control all three surfaces, an arrangement not dissimilar to an aircraft's joystick, and which has the benefit of being much less manpower intensive.

As a submarine goes deeper her hull compresses quite significantly, decreasing its displacement and making it vital that ballast water be pumped out to compensate for the increased negative buoyancy. To surface, high-pressure air retained in immensely strong compressed air cylinders is blown into the ballast tanks where it ejects the water, restoring positive buoyancy and allowing the boat to rise.

The 'O' boat's complement comprised seven officers, approximately 20 senior ratings and 40 or more junior rates. The Captain was normally in his early 30s and the average age of the officers was about 25. The second-in-command, the First Lieutenant (also known as the Executive Officer – XO), would normally be a senior lieutenant, as would the Electrical and Marine Engineer officers. It would be exceptional for anyone serving onboard to be over the age of 45.

Most of the 'O' class crew accommodation was forward, above the main battery compartments. Unlike earlier classes of submarine, no hammocks were slung, and each man had his own bunk although some of the engine room staff lived on portable bunks set up between the two torpedo tubes fitted at the stern. Each crew member was provided with a personal sleeping bag, made from nylon fabric. After a few weeks of use, these emanated a distinct, somewhat unpleasant odour. Temporary bunks were also set up in the torpedo room for trainees or visiting personnel. However, space was extremely tight and even the wardroom, with its seven bunks set up round a central table, was very cramped. The Captain slept separately in a cubby-hole of a cabin but apart from breakfast, traditionally ate in the wardroom where the First Lieutenant presided.

At times of darkness the wardroom lighting, like the control room, was switched to red illumination. This ensured rapid adaption of the eyes when looking through a periscope at night time. During the winter months in northern latitudes, living in virtually perpetual red lighting placed quite a strain on the officers. However, the practice of the control room being in red lighting when the boat was deep, I always thought of dubious value: it was not conducive to the watchkeepers remaining alert, and the prompt detection of leaks, or a system failure.

In a small galley, approximately 9ft square, two chefs sweated and toiled to serve up over 200 meals a day. The quality and variety of the food normally was of a high standard despite the chefs often having to contend with the boat's sometimes violent movements, together with dramatic variations of atmospheric pressure, making baking bread quite a challenge. Many powdered mixes were hygroscopic in nature and, unless perfectly sealed, inevitably attracted the diesel vapour which was always present in the atmosphere. Chocolate pudding mix was particularly susceptible to this problem and, although it looked appealing when served, could disappointingly taste rather acrid. Many of the dishes produced had their own particular nickname, most of which would nowadays be cited as politically incorrect: mentionable examples included tinned individual steak and kidney puddings known as 'Babies' Heads', and sautéed kidneys on fried bread called 'Shit on a Raft'.

Besides providing a cooked breakfast, the galley staff delivered a two-course lunch and dinner in the evening. At tea-time the crew could help themselves to toast and jam, or the occasional chocolate biscuit. 'Wagon Wheels' were always a firm favourite, in an era when this make of biscuit was much larger than today's version. The boat's Coxswain, in addition to being the Senior Rate responsible for maintaining crew discipline, ran the victualling system. He would order all food, supervise its careful storing and the daily issue to the galley. He had a daily allowance per crew member with which to work and, while generous enough to permit highly satisfactory meals in terms of quality and quantity, had to be carefully managed. After two or three weeks at sea, fresh provisions would run out and frozen or tinned food would have to be resorted to, but the menus were in general well-balanced and varied. The Coxswain was also responsible for supervising the daily issue of rum to the crew which normally took place at lunchtime. The rum supplied was 95.5 per cent proof and was the equivalent of three gins and tonic! The rum issue was abolished in 1970.

For medical purposes, a first-aid kit and a small quantity of medicines were carried. The latter included a rather pathetic quantity of six ampules of morphine held by the Captain in his personal safe. This quantity of morphine would almost certainly have proved inadequate in event of a serious accident. The medical kit also included a full tooth extraction set but, in reality, its utility in extracting a tooth from a crew member in severe pain would have proved challenging.

Fresh water was always at a premium, as onboard distillation facilities were limited and the stored water capacity, whilst normally adequate for daily washing, could only cope with the crew occasionally showering, if at all. Sewage and waste water were stored in holding tanks. These were emptied on approximately a daily basis by blowing the contents out of the hull by use of high-pressure air. When dived, garbage was disposed of via a somewhat crude ejection system where bagged rubbish was flushed out using pressurised seawater. There were no laundry facilities other than hand washing clothes in a sink.

Until the 1970s, when at sea, diesel boat submarine crews wore what was known as 'pirate rig' as a matter of practicality. Particularly in the case of the officers, the standard uniform of navy worsted trousers and white shirt with stiff-starched collar was totally unsuitable for wear at sea. Provided it was decent, any type of attire was acceptable. On coming ashore after a few weeks at sea with clothes smelling strongly of diesel oil, typically crew members' wives would insist on all sea-going wear being quarantined until washed separately.

Living in close proximity for weeks on end in the close confines of a diesel submarine, it was essential that the crew got on well together. Inevitably at times there could be tensions between individuals, sometimes arising from trivialities in behaviour or actions. However, in general the British diesel submariner was of relaxed, easy-going personality willing to put up with any eccentric habits of his fellow crew members.

'O/P' boats did not have a separate air induction system for feeding air to the engines when on the surface, as was the case in submarines of other nations. No doubt this was to reduce the number of major hull openings. However, this meant that, to run the diesels on the surface, air was sucked down the conning tower hatch and through the control room to the engine room. Wet and salt laden, this rapidly moving air-stream did little good to the increasing amount of electronic gear being fitted into the control room. In very rough weather where lots of spray and the occasional lump of solid water could be expected down the conning tower, a plastic fabric trunking was mounted below the control room hatch. This in turn was lashed into a three-foot high canvas receptacle with a hose connected to a pump to remove any overflowing seawater, a somewhat Heath Robinson set-up known as the 'bird-bath and elephant's trunk'.

In rough weather at night, with the control room in near-darkness, going on bridge watch dressed in foul weather gear and safety harness involved negotiating a wet, moving and slippery deck, climbing into the 'bird-bath', avoiding falling into any water it contained before battling up the 'elephant's trunk' through a very noisy and violent 100mph rush of indrawn air. Emerging onto the bridge, even the conditions of a Force Eight gale, would seem serene after the experience of the vertical ladder climb against such odds. The later major modernisation of the 'O' class, which incorporated improved lock-out arrangements where the submarine ran on the surface with all conning tower hatches shut and the snort system open, thankfully consigned the 'bird-bath' to history.

Once the boat was dived, the crew would settle into a three-watch system of four hours on watch and eight hours off. Maintenance, cleaning, routine evolutions and regular damage control exercises would always consume quite a bit of the crew's off-watch time. For recreation, besides the playing of cards or board games, each crew mess could enjoy feature films several times a week. The films, often new releases, were supplied by the Royal Naval Film Corporation under the arrangement of a generous concession from the British Film Industry. However, there were severe consequences if a film was lost overboard or when transferred to another vessel: it was said that losing a film involved more paperwork than the emergency disposal of a damaged multi-million-pound aircraft off the flight deck of an aircraft carrier. Films were shown on a 16mm Bell and Howell film projector and the ultimate demonstrated operator skill was the ability to undertake a running reel change without interruption to the screening. The wardroom traditionally used a navigational chart as a screen much to the consternation of the navigator if it became required for actual use. The occasional serving of an ice-cream during a screening was a much-enjoyed treat, as was the showing of a cartoon prior to the main feature.

If the submarine was dived for over 12 hours without snorting, the atmosphere would start to become stale as oxygen levels decreased and carbon dioxide built up. Rudimentary atmosphere control could be effected by burning oxygen candles and running carbon-dioxide removal equipment. However, a poor atmosphere, with its consequences of headaches and lethargy, was something crews put up with when deep for prolonged periods. In an era where smoking was still prevalent amongst the crew, and generally allowed when dived, this habit further worsened air quality.

In stormy sea conditions, the submarine could roll and pitch heavily at periscope depth. Keeping a level trim to avoid the boat broaching the surface could be very demanding on the control room team. Snorting in high sea states could be a further challenge of skill, requiring constant pumping out of seawater draining from the induction system and keeping the boat's angle and depth within the engine running tolerances. If depth increased, causing the snort mast head to be immersed, the engines would start to suck air out of the boat. Watch officers would apprehensively observe the atmosphere pressure gauge nudging towards the red sector, inevitably resulting in a crash stop snorting if the correct depth was not quickly regained. If this occurred, there followed the full drill of recovering the boat's trim and initiating the lengthy procedures required to restart the engines. This could incur the ire of the Captain if he considered that the control room team had not been up to the mark. At night, stress on the control room watch-officers would be intensified as the compartment would be in near total darkness to enable an effective periscope watch, a highly important factor if in an area of shipping or fishing vessel activity. In stormy weather keeping an effective watch for such vessels was made even more difficult by waves washing over the top of the periscope.

Shutting down the engines and going deep beyond a depth of about 150ft, to a stable environment and much more serene conditions, was always a welcome relief to the whole crew. Also the consequent switching to bright red lighting in the control room much relieved the strain upon its watchkeepers.

If a submarine goes below its safe depth through flooding, total loss of power or a high-speed uncontrolled dive, the boat risks being crushed by the immense pressure of the sea causing the loss of all onboard. This point-of-no-return is known as her 'crush-depth' and for the 'O' class submarine it was just over 1,000ft. If, through mechanical failure, the hydroplanes fail to a full-rise or dive position, steep boat angles in excess of 30 degrees can rapidly occur, even at moderate speeds. If the planes happen to fail in the full dive position, the crew must react very quickly indeed to avoid the boat exceeding her crush-depth. Therefore, crews were thoroughly trained and drilled to contend with plane failures.

My personal challenge as I joined *Odin* was to get to grips with the complexity of the systems and procedures, as described above, as rapidly as possible. In particular, as a control room watchkeeper I would need to quickly gain competence in being able to take the right actions in event of an emergency. Of equal importance would be my adapting to submarine life, melding into the wardroom team and gaining the Ship's Company's trust and respect. The latter was by no means a given and would have to be hard won.

Chapter 4

My First Submarine

On a wet Sunday evening in December 1967, I joined *Odin* which was alongside at Faslane situated at the head of the Gareloch. In the absence of joining instructions, I checked into the brand new shore base wardroom and, although I was not expected, a comfortable cabin was allocated. The base, HMS *Neptune*, was in the final stages of completion. Its facilities included new submarine jetties, the Polaris school, workshops, shore accommodation and a newly commissioned floating dock, Admiralty Floating Dock (AFD) 60. The depot ship *Maidstone* and the WW2 landing ship *Lofoten* were alongside providing workshop and accommodation facilities to the Third Submarine Squadron but, as the base facilities came fully on stream, these vessels would soon depart.

The first Royal Navy SSBN, *Resolution*, was also berthed alongside. She had been commissioned two months earlier, remarkably only five years since the US agreed to supply the Polaris weapon system and technology.

The base was a hive of activity, with a positive air of enthusiasm and energy evident. This was an era when the man-in-the-street was much aware of Britain's new seaborne nuclear deterrent and, in general, was strongly supportive of this awesome new capability. Furthermore, there had been lots of upbeat publicity surrounding the build and commissioning of the Polaris force. Consequently, the first crews enjoyed a certain mystique and aura and were considered somewhat special.

In line with the United States' model, the base boasted comprehensive recreational and retail facilities, including a petrol station and cinema, but these were to quickly prove commercially unviable. When off-duty, the British submariner – unlike his US counterpart – spent as little time as possible in the base, preferring the limited entertainment offerings of the nearby town of Helensburgh or venturing further afield to Glasgow, some 40 miles away.

Base security was still in its infancy and there were none of the rigours of today in gaining access to submarines alongside. Officers could conveniently park their cars on the jetties and there was no problem in getting civilian guests onboard the boats for the many parties or other social gatherings which were then the norm. However, there were already ominous signs that the base Ministry of Defence (MoD) Police, whose prime role was ensuring the physical security of the site, would concentrate more upon imposing restrictions on its naval community. In later years there were occasions when occupants of a nearby 'peace camp' succeeded in penetrating the base security barriers and managed to get into the most secure areas. Needless to say, these high profile and very embarrassing intrusions reflected badly upon the competence and effectiveness of the MoD police.

The officers' married quarters had been completed in the nearby village of Rhu and a large estate of ratings' quarters had been established behind Helensburgh. The ratings' houses, however, were not well built and, in due course, the estate became a bleak, soulless place for families, where the father could be away at sea, out of contact, for several months. Although the officers' quarters had won an architectural prize, the exterior of most of the houses looked like giant chicken-coops and were ill-designed to cope with winter weather in the west of Scotland. The estate's nick-name of 'Moon City' was appropriate.

On reporting onboard on the morning after my arrival, I was greeted by the First Lieutenant, Geoffrey Biggs ('GB' – later Vice Admiral Sir Geoffrey Biggs), and introduced to the officers, two of whom, the Engineer Officer and the Navigator, were Australian. Indeed, a number of the crew were also Australian, including the Coxswain, cutting their teeth in *Odin* before being assigned to their own submarines, which were being built at Scotts Shipyard at Greenock. Later when the Captain, Lieutenant Commander David Wardle, arrived onboard, I was introduced to him. He immediately struck me as a quiet, unassuming officer, but now on his second submarine command, confident and knowledgeable. I soon learned he was highly popular with the crew. I also had the opportunity to meet my torpedo division of one Petty Officer and five junior rates.

Clearly *Odin* was in first-rate condition, having completed a successful refit at Rosyth Dockyard a year earlier. She had been designated to join the Seventh Submarine Squadron based in Singapore but, as part of ongoing defence cuts, this was being reduced in size. Instead, she was allocated to the Third Submarine Squadron and a disappointed crew who, instead of enjoying the many attractions of service in the Far East, resigned themselves to much more strenuous operational activities together with the West of Scotland climate.

Soon after joining I experienced disappointment. The submarine was about to undergo her annual Squadron inspection and the crew were focused on bringing the boat up to the highest levels of condition and cleanliness prior to the harbour inspection phase the following week. She was then off to sea for two days of demanding exercises and evolutions where the crew would be put through a wide range of testing scenarios. To my frustration, I was informed that I was to remain ashore for the sea inspection phase. Therefore, initially, I felt a bit of a nuisance and was very much left to my own devices.

Although *Odin's* accommodation was more than adequate when at sea, it was the practice of all submarines in port to accommodate the crew ashore in barrack accommodation, leaving only a duty watch onboard overnight to deal with the routine running and security of the vessel, or to meet any emergencies. As I was one of few submariners at that time living in the base wardroom, this added to my sense of isolation. Furthermore I resented being detailed to help with the painting and cleaning of the torpedo compartment, much to the embarrassment of the senior rating in charge. Prior to the boat proceeding to sea, as I crawled through the knee-chafing nooks and crannies of the outer casing and the conning tower, searching for any loose connection or foreign body which could cause a noise defect, I began to wonder if I had made the right specialisation choice.

Before undertaking harbour Officer-of-the-Day (OOD) duties on my own, I undertook two duties as an understudy. The first of these was with the First Lieutenant who, after we returned from supper together in the depot ship, provided me with a pile of different biro pens of assorted colours. I was then instructed to insert a variety of signatures in the many voids in an array of official documents such as the important-key issue and control room logs. This documentation would be presented as part of the inspection process, but no doubt the Squadron staff would not have been oblivious of such dubious practices. The two understudy duties completed, I was then on my own in charge of the submarine overnight with a duty watch of about fifteen senior and junior rates.

The harbour inspection was successfully completed, but as I stood on the jetty bidding farewell to *Odin* as she slipped astern of her berth and proceeded to sea, I remained aggrieved that I was not with her. The following day, a Friday, I headed to Glasgow to take a girlfriend out to dinner. On arrival back in the base late in the evening, I was informed that *Odin* was back alongside unexpectedly 12 hours early, as the inspection had gone so well. The following morning, on arriving onboard, it was made clear that the Captain was annoyed that I was not on the jetty to meet the boat on her return. Things were not getting off to a good start in my submarine career.

A few days later, I was decanted from the shore wardroom accommodation to the 1938-vintage depot ship *Maidstone*. Moored alongside, this venerable old ship had great character and there was a tremendous sense of camaraderie and spirit amongst the accommodated submarine crews. Dinner in the wardroom was always a convivial occasion, a fair amount of drinking being buoyed by the ebullient presence of a number of Canadian and Australian officers on exchange appointments to British submarines. Also present were the officers of the Israeli submarine *Dakar*, until recently HMS *Totem*, who conducting work-up prior to departure for Israel, added a friendly international dimension to the gatherings. Very sadly, a few weeks later, *Dakar* was lost with all hands in the Mediterranean en route to her new home. The wreck, in deep water, was not located until 1999, but the cause of her sinking has never been established. Too much top weight might have been a contributory factor while on the surface in stormy weather. The boat had been fitted with a swimmer lock-out chamber in the fin during her refit prior to handover and even when alongside, she appeared low in buoyancy. I had got to know some of *Dakar*'s junior officers and this tragedy was a poignant reminder that submarining could be a dangerous profession.

Meanwhile, in addition to my torpedo officer responsibilities, I spent much of my harbour time thoroughly learning the submarine's systems and the layout of its equipment. This involved instruction from specialist senior rates and, clad in overalls, crawling into the tightest of spaces, tracing pipework and identifying the location of key operating valves. If I was to be an effective duty officer in harbour and OOW at sea, a firm grasp of the working of the submarine's many complex systems was vital.

As the most junior officer and a bachelor, I was the natural choice to be on duty on Christmas Day. Before lunch, the Captain arrived onboard with his wife and family and toured the messes, exchanging greetings and very much enjoying a chat with the duty watch. Lunch was not exactly a success as the turkeys arrived from the shore galley wrapped in tin-foil and had been placed in ovens for cooking. It was not appreciated that they already had been partially cooked and the outcome was, when as by tradition served by the Duty Officer, they were much over-cooked. Fuelled by the daily rum ration and beer supplied by the Senior Rates, this did not spoil the occasion and exceedingly dark brown turkey was consumed with relish. In the evening I was invited to join the stokers in their mess right aft, to watch a film. Sadly, it became evident to me that many of those were there for no other reason than they had no families to spend Christmas with: their crewmates essentially were their family.

After a few days leave, I returned onboard on New Year's Day to drop off my personal belongings as we were off to sea the following day. I was greeted by the sight of a somewhat inebriated group of junior ratings, arms linked, doing a 'Can-Can' routine up and down the casing, under the bemused watch of the Duty Officer and Duty Chief Petty Officer. It was bitterly cold with ice evident on the edge of the loch. Despite a couple of individuals at the end of the 'Can-Can' line falling into the extremely cold sea, this did not appear to dampen the gathering's enthusiasm. *Odin*'s Ship's Company were clearly a high-spirited lot.

On 2 January *Odin* slipped and proceeded to sea for a few days independent shake-down exercises in the Clyde Estuary followed by anti-submarine exercises in the deep Atlantic to the west of Ireland. Glad that I was finally at sea in a submarine, I soon settled into *Odin*'s dived routine as a trainee officer. I stood watches in the control room with the First Lieutenant who proved to be an excellent mentor and rapidly delegated tasks to me.

During the week several divings and surfacings were exercised. The former could be urgently executed by a double blast on the klaxon whereupon the crew rushed to close up at their diving stations, the boat speed was increased, main ballast tank vents opened and the bridge evacuated. The upper hatch of the 'O' class conning tower (located inside the fin structure) would be underwater within about 90 seconds, much longer than the 30 seconds typical of WW2 submarines. The alternate, more orderly, diving procedure was to close up at Diving Stations and only order the ballast tank vents open when the engines were stopped and the bridge team brought below.

The conning tower consisted of a steel pressure-tight cylinder about 10ft in height and 4ft in diameter. The upper hatch had two lever-operated stirrup-type clips and would be shut by the surface OOW, taking care that his foul-weather braces did not get entangled in the clips. If that occurred, there was the good-humoured situation of a rescuer being sent up the tower to extricate an embarrassed OOW suspended from the clips.

After blowing high-pressure air into the ballast tanks to surface, this was followed by inserting low pressure air using a blower to gain full buoyancy. If the boat's internal air pressure was less than that of the atmospheric pressure, even by a small degree, the surfacing OOW, on being ordered by the Captain to open up, would require to unclip the stirrup clips and exert his full body leverage to crack open the hatch to allow the pressure to equalise. A large pressure differential would require prior equalisation using the snort induction system. If the boat's internal pressure was greater than that of the atmosphere, the OOW would have to exert great care in using the clips to gradually open the hatch and avoid it flying open under pressure, causing injury to himself.

I soon experienced a particularly demanding and complex workload, snorting at night dived in the Clyde Estuary, one officer keeping watch on the periscope for periods of about 20 minutes, while the other controlled the boat's trim and the snorting procedure, at the same time monitoring the sonar reports. The latter officer plotted the boat's position from visual navigational data provided from the periscope watchkeeper or coordinates provided by the Decca radio navigation system. In poor visibility, radar could be used for both navigation and the avoidance of shipping. At that time there was still a high level of fishing activity in the Clyde and, if unfortunate enough to end up in the proximity of the fishing fleet, with its highly confusing lights at night, it took quite a degree of skill for the periscope watchkeeper to manoeuvre the boat into clear water. Naturally this was all a steep learning curve for myself but I thoroughly enjoyed the challenges.

The second week at sea found Odin in the deep Atlantic providing training as a target for a RAF squadron of Shackleton Maritime Patrol Aircraft (MPA) based at Ballykelly in Northern Ireland. As was usual for January, the weather was stormy which made keeping trim of the boat and snorting at periscope depth difficult. These challenges were compounded by a bout of influenza sweeping through the crew, laying many of them low. The control room watchkeeping routine had to switch from a three-watch to a two-watch system which put extra stress on those who remained well. I soon realised that the First Lieutenant must have had a degree of faith in my abilities, as during more than one night watch, when the boat was deep and well below periscope depth, he arrived in the control room clutching his sleeping bag and a book. The handover completed, he disappeared into the radar office at the rear of the control room with the only instruction to call him if the Captain should wake. However, I was under no illusion regarding the level of the First Lieutenant's confidence in me. He knew that I was surrounded by a highly experienced control room team and if any emergency arose he would have been out of the radar office in an instant.

I was soon to experience the hard way that diesel submarines spend a lot of time on the surface and that open bridge watchkeeping in the winter off the British coast could be an extremely cold, wet experience. The bridge contained only basic equipment, which included a compass repeat and communications connections to the control room, including a voice-pipe. It offered little protection from the elements and in stormy conditions heavy spray or solid seas lashed its occupants. I was to learn that sleeping in damp clothes to dry them off prior to the next bridge watch was the norm. Thankfully, I did not experience the mariner's curse of seasickness. Needless to say, the confines of a rolling, pitching submarine and the strong, pungent smell of diesel vapour challenged even those with the strongest of stomachs.

The exercises with the RAF complete, *Odin* headed north towards Cape Wrath, on route to Newcastle-upon-Tyne for a five-day visit. On the passage, a war-shot Mark 8 torpedo firing was scheduled using the small island of Garvie, situated off the Cape, as target. It is used as a live firing target by all three Services. I was looking forward as torpedo officer to the rare opportunity of firing a war-shot torpedo, albeit at a lump of rock. However, the proving firing for some reason was cancelled, perhaps because the local farmer could not get his flock of sheep off the nearby mainland area in time and the animals would have been at risk if the torpedo went awry.

In very much deteriorating weather, *Odin* ploughed her way on the surface round the north of Scotland heading eastwards towards the Pentland Firth, between the Scottish mainland and the Orkney Islands. Violent seas were soon encountered, with the rising westerly wind, approaching storm force, blowing against the westerly setting tidal stream of over 8 knots. The seas this generated were phenomenal for their steepness and, for a while, little progress was made through the infamous turbulent area – rather oddly named the 'Merry Men of Mey' – as one of the two main propulsion motors had failed due to a defective lubrication oil pump. This reduced the boat's maximum speed to 10 knots, barely enough to make headway. The situation was saved by a jury-rigged Black and Decker heavy duty drill ingeniously being set-up by the engineers to drive the pump, enabling the motor to be restarted. Amazingly, the drill ran continuously for the next 36 hours.

Clear of the Firth, *Odin* swung south into the North Sea on the night of the Glasgow so-called 'hurricane' of 15 January 1968, during which twenty people were killed in Central Scotland. I assumed the bridge watch at 0230 as the storm was at its height, with the wind speed gusting at over 100mph, visibility down to a few hundred yards and the sea a mass of white spume. On *Odin*'s bridge, the seas were breaking over myself and the lookout, making a nonsense of any attempt to keep a proper visual watch. Having gone into the radar office before heading to the bridge, I also knew radar performance was poor owing to intense 'sea-clutter'. As a result, any other vessel would only have been detected at very short range, but fortunately there was little, if any, shipping around.

To prevent the control room flooding, access to the bridge was through the conning tower being used as an airlock, air for the engines being supplied by the snort induction system. When it came to my turn to be relieved at 0430, I experienced real trouble locking back into the submarine. On climbing down to the airlock I found it half flooded by the breaking seas. Two attempts to pump it out proved fruitless, as each time I opened the upper hatch to climb into the lock, the sea poured in after me. I therefore decided to stay in the chamber while it was pumped empty. Crouching at the top of the airlock ladder, my knees in water, suffused in the added surrealism of red lighting and with the pump drawing a vacuum, causing the seawater around me to start vaporising, I was highly relieved when the chamber was emptied and a member of the control room team swung the lower hatch open.

As the officer-under-training, I had been allocated the most uncomfortable of the seven wardroom bunks. Jammed into the curve of the pressure hull and sharing space with the chrome brackets which supported the weight of the bunk above, it was impossible to sleep in it in rough weather. As lying on my bunk was untenable, I decided to sleep under the wardroom table where books, a typewriter and miscellaneous odds-and-ends fell on top of me whenever *Odin* hit a particularly big wave.

The following day, once alongside in Newcastle, as the junior officer, then naturally I found myself OOD at the evening drinks reception for local dignitaries. Towards the end of the gathering I was instructed by the First Lieutenant to somehow manoeuvre a drunken lady mayor out of the submarine by way of the access hatch and up a steep gangplank to her awaiting limousine. This was only achieved with a great degree of difficulty and the help of several members of the duty watch. On reporting to 'GB' 'task accomplished', he responded that I was now needed to eject a drunken alderman who, in upper attire of only a string vest and gold chain of office, was chasing female guests through the boat.

On the day following my onerous duty of discharging the inebriated recipients of the boat's hospitality, I checked into the comfort of the local hotel where the wardroom was accommodated. However, as the cost of the hotel exceeded the daily subsistence allowance, 'GB' quickly decided that the officers, together with their accompanying wives, would move into the far cheaper local Mission to Seamen. The latter charged £1 per night B&B (£17 at today's prices). It proved clean, friendly and hospitable, leaving the balance of our subsistence allowance now available to be spent on other pleasures. However, I was unsure what the wives thought of staying in a Seamen's Mission instead of a well-appointed hotel.

The people of Newcastle had the reputation of being notably hospitable to the crews of visiting warships and their generosity and kindness to Odin's Ship's Company met all expectations. The wardroom bachelors were particularly feted by a group of racehorse owners who, apart from treating us to an excellent dinner at a greyhound racing stadium, offered us an assured tip for a novice horse they were racing for the first time. At long odds, it won by ten lengths at Catterick racecourse the following Saturday. Unfortunately, I did not place a bet.

Our departure was on a Sunday and a large gathering of well-wishers watched from the quay. However, the two tugs required to swing the boat round to heading down-river did not appear at the scheduled departure time. Those gathered were treated to the rather amusing sight of the Captain and the First Lieutenant rummaging through quayside dustbins in search of a local telephone directory to call the tug company. Happily, the tugs appeared soon afterwards negating the need to make a call. When entering the Tyne Estuary, there was the more sobering experience of passing the spot where a few months earlier a colleague had drowned. On heading out to sea in the submarine Truncheon, he had been checking the casing secured when a wave washed him into the sea. Sadly, his life jacket failed to function and before he could be recovered, he drowned.

Odin's next task was to return by way of Cape Wrath to deep ocean areas off the north-west of Ireland to take part in ASW exercises, in the role of the loyal opposition to a group of frigates and destroyers acting as convoy escorts, supported by MPA. Notably, towards the end of the exercises the escort force encountered a Soviet 'Whiskey' class diesel submarine which, after several hours of prosecution by sonar, surfaced and requested by radio a weather forecast. The response was 'You won't need a weather forecast when you are in Siberia'. This incident reminded us that the UK's naval forces and coast were subject to continuous surveillance by Soviet Navy units, both surface and sub-surface. Indeed, for several decades, a Soviet intelligence-gathering ship (known as an AGI) was to be permanently stationed just outside territorial waters to the north of Ireland. Its aim was to monitor the SSBN transit routes to and from their Atlantic patrol areas.

With the exercises completed, *Odin* headed for Lough Foyle and a visit to Londonderry, berthing alongside the WW2 landing ship *Stalker*, which performed limited depot ship support. The Joint Anti-Submarine Warfare Training School, which had run the exercise, was situated in HMS *Sea Eagle*, a shore establishment near the city. Inevitably, submarines arrived last into port and delivered their exercise records after the other participants. With inter-Service rivalry rampant, the trick for a submarine officer reporting into the staff who had been monitoring the exercise was first to closely examine the large floor plot in *Sea Eagle*. Here the exercise had been tracked and set out, so a subtle shift of one's own submarine's position away from the locations of reported submarine detections, especially those by aircraft, afforded a mischievous satisfaction.

Many of the officers of the visiting warships congregated in the evenings in a local hostelry, the *Maiden City* bar, which usually reverberated to loud Irish Republican music, rousing in tempo and melody, if dubious in sentiment for officers of Her Majesty's Navy. 'The Troubles' were yet some months away and although fault lines fractured Ulster society, the lubricating effects of alcohol and Celtic music won the day. Nevertheless, late one evening, while wardroom colleagues and myself were enjoying this convivial and noisy hospitality after official closing-time, the pub was raided by the police. The Royal Ulster Constabulary made rather futile attempts to take the names of the large number of customers present, which included a rather confused group of officers from an American destroyer.

Another favourite haunt was the village hall dance in Muff just across the border in the Irish Republic, where Irish dance bands provided outstandingly good music and the local girls were enthusiastic to dance. Many of the latter worked in a local shirt factory and where the trick was to team up with a dance partner who worked at the end of the production line, thus offering the opportunity of receiving a free shirt. Only tea was served in the hall but, of course, bottles of spirits were smuggled in and no doubt the consequent inebriation provoked fights which had the curious quality of proceeding at the pace of the music being played.

My wardroom colleagues and I were struck by the friendly welcome received from the people of Londonderry who, at that time, never bothered to lock their house doors. However, the city was evidently a poor and deprived place. The armed police patrolling the streets gave hints of the tensions which would tear apart a citizenry divided by two religious factions and plunge Northern Ireland into a dark and bloody era of widespread violence. Despite the disenfranchisement of the Roman Catholic population by the requirement of being a property freeholder to vote in local elections, I found the genuine friendliness of the local population to the Royal Navy was remarkable.

By this time I had truly settled into submarine life and, notwithstanding my earlier reservations, *Odin* proved a happy and efficient submarine, well led and motivated by the strong team of David Wardle and Geoffrey Biggs. Aboard *Odin*, pirate rig was taken to exotic levels. For example, the ratings manning the sonar system dressed as French onion sellers, engine room artificers in Arab garb and the control room watchkeepers were attired as Victorians. I stuck to the more practical garb of a fisherman's sweater and slacks. This non-conforming dress would be prohibited in the early 1970s as, with its increasing number of nuclear submarines, the Royal Navy's Submarine Service underwent the major cultural shift discussed elsewhere. Moreover, the cleaner conditions aboard nuclear submarines and the availability of laundry facilities were more conducive to the wearing of formal uniform.

Off-watch recreational time in the wardroom after dinner in the evening, was frequently spent playing a fast-paced card game known as 'Skats'. A complex and sophisticated version of 'Snap' and of Germanic origins, an unspoken rule was that the Captain's decision was final and it was diplomatic to let him win more often than not. A movie would be run once or twice a week, normally of high quality and recent general release. This was eagerly anticipated, especially at weekends. Many of the officers and crew smoked, availing themselves of the ridiculously cheap duty-free cigarettes sold onboard. As a nonsmoker, I had to get used the unpleasant fug of cigarette smoke which often permeated the wardroom atmosphere, even at breakfast.

Odin was next tasked at short notice to undertake the Submarine Commanding Officer's Qualifying Course. It was known as the 'Perisher' because for those who failed, their submarine career was abruptly over. There were no second chances. For the few days of *Odin*'s participation, the training took place in the Clyde Estuary, returning each evening to a buoy in Rothesay. The course was under the instruction of a submarine Captain of commander's rank, traditionally known as the 'Teacher'.

On the first night in harbour, 'GB' had led the wardroom ashore, visiting several of the Rothesay hostelries, as indeed had the majority of the crew. The following morning, at the scheduled time for calling the hands, the fin door had blown shut and the main access hatch had also been pulled-to to stop the ingress of heavy rain. Therefore, the upper-deck sentry had no way of getting below to start shaking a crew, most of whom would be in a very deep slumber, in an era where there was no control room watchkeeper to call up.

The result was the entire crew below was still turned in as the boat transferring the Perisher course came alongside. The thud of the boat and its propeller noise suddenly woke someone and then all hell broke loose as the crew were urgently shaken and the boat went to Harbour Stations and the engines were started at the rush. The Perisher team, under the ward of a somewhat short-tempered Teacher, was received onboard with a degree of embarrassment but I do not recall what terse words were exchanged.

Having finished the Perisher week, the Ship's Company resolved to take their highly popular Captain on a farewell shore gathering in Campbeltown, as he was shortly due to be relieved. Needless to say, it was an occasion of great revelry, which finished with a noisy parade down the jetty with a chaired David Wardle wearing a Viking helmet, carrying a replica Norse sword as a baton, conducting a rendition of the submarine's song which had the repetitive chorus 'Odin send the wind and waves to make it safe for snorting'. The next day *Odin* proceeded to sea, dived and then sat on the seabed for the morning, allowing the crew to recover from the excesses of the previous evening. Such was life in a typical diesel submarine of the Royal Navy during the 1960s.

Odin next headed on surface passage via the Irish Sea and English Channel to Chatham Dockyard for repairs to her two diesel engines. This was necessary because the greater-than-normal high revolution running of her type of engines had worn the crankshafts which now required replacement. The Clyde Base did not have the capacity to undertake the work but Chatham Dockyard, at that time completing building of the last of three *Oberon*s for the Canadian Navy, *Okanagan*, had the skills and capability. However, for the Ship's Company it meant at least four weeks away from their base port.

I found myself watchkeeping alone on the bridge during the middle night watch as the submarine headed through the Dover Straits. At a time when there were no shipping traffic separation lanes in place, I experienced the somewhat discomforting situation of a high density of merchant vessels coming from all directions. Only too aware that a submarine's unique configuration of navigation lights could be confusing to other vessels, I would have welcomed the Captain's presence on the bridge. However, despite passing frequent reports to him of other vessels passing close, he did not appear on the bridge till the worst was past. On his arrival he gave the impression that he thought I could have handled the situation myself. On reflection, he was rather over-confident of my abilities as I had experienced few night watches on my own and had not yet qualified for a bridge watchkeeping certificate.

The next morning found me again on watch on the bridge, on my own, as the submarine headed up the Thames Estuary towards the Medway River. A Petty Officer in the control room was plotting my visual fixes on a chart but I was heavily relying upon a crude sketch I had made of the courses and navigational marks along the planned track. I was due to be relieved at 1230 which would give me time for lunch prior to the pilot boarding at 1400 at the Medway entrance. However, the handover time came and passed with no sign of my relief. I was not aware that, in the wardroom, a convivial lunch of steak and chips, accompanied by champagne, was in full swing to mark David Wardle's last day at sea in command. Consequently, no one was in a hurry to relieve the junior officer on the bridge. For my part, although both hungry and cold, it gave me a great degree of satisfaction that I had been trusted to navigate the boat more than 30 miles up the Thames Estuary to the Medway. That said, it was a crisp, clear day and as there were copious buoys and navigational marks indicating the channel, it was not difficult. Lunch for me was a quick sandwich before heading onto the casing to embark the pilot.

Soon after arrival in Chatham, at the end of February 1968, I put up my second stripe on promotion to the rank of lieutenant. The officers were initially accommodated ashore in the comfort of Chatham base wardroom. However, because the engine repairs extended beyond the planned four weeks, putting strain on the wardroom accommodation, I and my colleagues were moved to a local NAAFI centre. I was beginning to experience a wide range of shore living quarters.

My period as a trainee was coming to an end and the final hurdle was the successful passing of an oral and written examination, the Submarine Qualification. I took the written part of the qualification in an office ashore in the dockyard under the invigilation of a Coxswain loaned from another submarine refitting alongside. Half-way through my written paper, this helpful Chief Petty Officer left and shortly afterwards returned with two steaming cups of coffee. Sitting down beside me, he obligingly ran through any of the questions I could not answer, contacting his mates by telephone where he could not answer a specific question. Thankfully, when the results were published, I was spared the embarrassment of coming top of my training class in the examinations.

Repairs completed, *Odin* headed back to the Clyde Base. *Maidstone* had departed and, as there was no accommodation available in the shore wardroom, I was temporarily accommodated in *Lofoten*. While its cabin accommodation was perfectly adequate, it was notorious for the rust colour of its fresh water supply and the 'instant sun-tan effect' of having a bath. More importantly, I had unexpectedly received instructions to join *Sealion* as its Navigation Officer, replacing an officer who had been landed ashore injured. Whilst this was an elevation and opened new prospects for me, it was not good news and I would have much preferred to remain in *Odin* where I was well integrated into the wardroom and, importantly, had gained the respect of the Ship's Company. On reflection, despite a bit of a shaky start, responsibilities had been heaped upon me at a very early stage, but this would not have been unusual for the era. Nevertheless, this did engender a great deal of job satisfaction and feeling of worth.

I was now to join a boat with a poor reputation: *Sealion*'s Captain was known to be an aggressive, heavy drinker in harbour and a bully at sea and her crew morale was not good. It was, therefore, with a heavy heart, that in early April I stood on the Clyde Base jetty, waving off *Odin* as she departed off to sea without me.

Chapter 5

Challenging Times

L ike my first boat, *Sealion* belonged to the Third Submarine Squadron. Completed at Cammell Laird's Birkenhead yard in 1961, she was the penultimate example of the 'P' class submarine. With larger internal frames than the 'O' class, she was a bit tighter for internal space but, other than that, she was very similar in layout to *Odin*. However, she had yet to be fitted with the One-Man-Control (OMC) system and required separate operators for the fore and after hydroplanes and the rudder. Therefore, on watch there was a total of three operators instead of the one required to man the OMC.

Sealion had a poor reputation within the Submarine Flotilla and my worst fears were confirmed when, in April 1968, I joined her in a floating-dock, situated in a remote corner of Portsmouth Dockyard. She was undergoing repairs to both of her propeller shafts and was filthy dirty, with crew morale evidently at rock bottom. The stench of her wing bilges, which contained remnants of packed food from past patrols mixed with oily water, added to the usual pungent aroma of diesel-oil. There was long-standing dirt and grime everywhere and much of the deck and bulkhead paintwork and finish had been damaged and not made good. She should have had the same internal appearance as *Odin*, which was only a year younger, so the overall effect upon me was deeply depressing.

There were some mitigating factors. *Sealion* was the last conventional British submarine to conduct Barents Sea intelligence-gathering patrols as part of the highly classified US-led naval surveillance programme. These operations were primarily aimed at gathering intelligence on the characteristics of Soviet ships and submarines and observing their missile firings. There were, however, other intelligence-gathering activities and during a first commission patrol, using a specialist mast, *Sealion* gathered radiation and other data from Soviet nuclear bomb tests on Nova Zemlya. On another occasion, whilst near a stationary barge which was acting as a target for a surface-to-surface missile firing, her periscopes and other masts were detected by a helicopter. She was then harassed for many hours by a group of Soviet destroyers. Despite the interaction occurring in international waters, during the prosecution the destroyers, in an attempt to force her to surface, dropped numerous warning charges close around her. These caused no damage other than shattering the odd light bulb, but they were unnerving to the crew. Nevertheless *Sealion*, after slowly heading west for over 20 hours, made it safely into Norwegian territorial waters. On surfacing, there was the very welcome presence overhead of several NATO aircraft but, cheekily, the closest Soviet destroyer passed by signal light the message 'Good Morning *Sealion*!'.

These northern patrols involved long periods of snorting to and from the patrol areas with consequent increased wear and tear upon both machinery and crew. Indeed, her Engineer Officer, Lieutenant Peter Glendinning, received a national award (MBE – Member of the Order of the British Empire) for keeping her engines running under exceptional conditions. *Sealion* had finished these patrols about a year before but was mechanically worn out and many of her men were also in an exhausted frame of mind. In particular, those responsible for maintaining her weapon systems were a poor lot. If their equipment became defective, they often did not have the ability to repair it: the best men were being drawn away and transferred to support the high-priority Polaris programme. Consequently, clapped-out boats like *Sealion* had to struggle with sub-standard technicians. This unhappy situation was worsened by a highly defective character being in command.

The Captain was in his late 30s and *Sealion* was his third submarine command. Dark-featured and stocky in build, despite a well-groomed moustache and beard, overindulgence in drink and cigarettes was beginning to prematurely age his facial appearance. Doubtless he was only too conscious that, after completing his time in command of *Sealion*, his future appointing options would be very limited, and he was highly unlikely to be promoted to the rank of Commander. But this was no excuse for the shocking state of the boat and this spoke volumes about his laissez-faire attitude to standards of cleanliness and material availability. It was also reflective of his poor relationship with the First Lieutenant, the second-in-command. On the other hand, he had the reputation of being an astute tactician, highly capable in use of the periscope during attack approaches and was an accomplished navigator.

As Navigation Officer, I inherited equipment which was adequate for coastal work, but was not up to the mark for operating in the deep ocean. The long-range Loran-C radio-navigation system was defective, and the echo-sounder was incapable of taking the deep-sea soundings for positioning using seabed contour charts. In an era when satellite navigation was not yet available, this left me with the periscope sextant. This was a complex piece of optical equipment and whilst I was to achieve successful sun observations through it, I never mastered using it to take star sights. The only other available option was the use of dead reckoning with all its inaccuracies caused by the unknowns of deep ocean currents. In extremis an 'action surface', where the boat was surfaced for a minimum period, would enable me to climb to the bridge to take star sights at dawn or evening twilight using a conventional sextant. This evolution strongly risked angering the Captain if my astronomical measurements did not result in an acceptably accurate navigational fix. Thankfully, on the few occasions I was required to undertake this procedure, the outcome was satisfactory.

In due course, with two new stern shafts fitted, *Sealion* proceeded down harbour and secured in Haslar Creek, alongside at HMS *Dolphin*. Here she loaded torpedoes and stores prior to going to sea and, for the first time, I observed my new Captain at close quarters. As Officer-of-the-Day on the final evening alongside, after having dinner in *Dolphin*'s wardroom, the sentry on the casing reported to me that the Captain was coming aboard with some friends, one of whom had brought his dog. I then had to carry a heavy Labrador into the submarine through the accommodation hatch and down a vertical ladder. At the end of an evening where significant quantities of spirits were consumed, I had to reverse the process. Due to the weight and nervousness of the Labrador, this proved more difficult than extricating the Lady Mayor from *Odin*.

To my despair, having said goodbye to his chums, the Captain returned onboard, and sat in the wardroom where I was obliged to keep him company, as he drank whisky and chain-smoked cigarettes, until just before 0600. He then staggered ashore and off to bed in his shore quarters. As the off-duty crew came aboard at 0800, I received them with bleary eyes and was issued an unwelcome reprimand from the First Lieutenant for not clearing away the glasses from the night's drinking session. I was soon to learn he was a weak character, unable to take a stand against the Captain's excesses. The latter returned onboard just before noon and resumed drinking at a reception set up in the control room for the First Submarine Squadron officers to thank them for their support and assistance during *Sealion*'s sojourn in Portsmouth. The guests departed at about 1400, and shortly afterwards the Ship's Company went to Harbour Stations for leaving. As the Captain arrived on the bridge it was evident he was suffering from the effects of the vast quantity of alcohol he had consumed from the previous evening and topped up during lunchtime. *Sealion* slipped her berth at 1500 and I anticipated that the departure would not go smoothly.

On backing out of Haslar Creek, the Captain had to reverse the propellers to avoid a sand dredger heading out to sea which he should have spotted before getting underway. The result was that the almost stationary *Sealion* got caught up in the strong ebb tide sweeping through the narrow entrance to Portsmouth Harbour. On its western side lay the wardroom of HMS *Dolphin* which had a large patio adjoining the sea-wall. Here a group of the Squadron officers were gathered to bid her farewell. They were treated to the sight of *Sealion* heading out to sea, beam-on, athwart the line of the channel and with her bows pointing towards – and passing a few yards away from – them. With a modest shudder accompanied by a muddy disturbance and rising bubbles, the boat's bows grounded at the *Dolphin* saluting-point, while her stern was swung by the fierce tide to point down channel towards Southsea Castle. My immediate thoughts were that I had only been navigating for a few minutes and already we were in a grounding situation.

Fortunately, *Sealion* was quickly drawn off the bottom by the application of full-astern power, thereafter continuing down the buoyed channel stern-first until there was a suitable position to turn her round. Meanwhile for RN publicity purposes, the departure was being filmed onboard a small boat which I had observed nearby. However, I don't think the footage would ever have been used, even for instructional purposes. The Captain's only remark once heading down channel in the right direction was 'I need a cigarette'. This was an inauspicious start to my time as navigator.

Having arrived in the Clyde, *Sealion* undertook several weeks of work-up with the assistance of the Squadron shore-staff. I soon learned that, when things went wrong the Captain was like a raging bull in the control room, yelling at everyone he deemed to have contributed to the cock-up. This included myself and I had frequently to endure the sharp end of his tongue. This was particularly the case when departing from or arriving at the Clyde Base. He had made passage up the Clyde on many occasions and was thoroughly familiar with the route's navigational marks, together with the required headings and course alterations. Consequently, he did not really need my services as navigator. Nevertheless, I would risk a verbal tongue-lashing if I made the smallest error in setting a new course, the more so on leaving harbour when he was likely to be suffering from a hangover.

A number of practice torpedo firings took place during this work-up phase, using the torpedo recovery craft as target. This was standard procedure for such practice firings if a naval vessel was unavailable but, no matter the target, it was a prerequisite to set the depth of the torpedo to pass underneath the target vessel. This was particularly so in the case of the venerable Mark 8 torpedo, where almost two tons of weapon travelling at over 50mph would likely penetrate the thin plating of most modern warships if its depth in error was set at less than the draught of the target. Albeit rare, on occasions exactly this happened. However, Sealion's Mark 8 firings all of those went smoothly, unlike the case of the useless Mark 23 anti-submarine torpedo. Here for the first time I witnessed the ineffectiveness of this weapon, as despite the best efforts of the fire-control team, not one of these weapons which were fired performed correctly.

Work-up complete, there then followed in the deep ocean the successful acceptance trials of a new long-range sonar, Type 2007. This equipment had the distinct advantage of state-of-the art beam-forming technology which provided simultaneous detection capability in all directions. This notable advance, negated the need for the submarine to circle to enable detection on the single beam available on earlier sonars. The Captain demonstrated his strengths in tactical prowess by skilfully interpreting this new sonar's contact information on a recently introduced type of paper plot, known as the Contact Evaluation Plot (CEP). This innovation facilitated the evaluation of each contact's range and its characteristics. Gradually the UK's diesel submarine force was benefiting from new sonar technology.

Meanwhile the First Lieutenant confirmed my initial view that he was demonstrably ineffective and, in particular, was unwilling to support his fellow officers when lambasted by the Captain. Furthermore, it was evident he did not have a grip on maintaining the boat at a basic state of cleanliness, one of his prime responsibilities. As an example, prior to meals being served, the wardroom steward laid out his crockery and cutlery on the filthy mattress of his bunk. Indeed, even for the officers, the quality of life and hygiene onboard *Sealion* verged upon living in squalor.

While *Sealion* passed the work-up phase to the overall satisfaction of the Squadron staff, her commander did not. His excessive drinking in harbour and his aggressive behaviour at sea had been noted and arrangements were put in place to relieve him early. During that time I cut a somewhat lonely figure when in harbour, as I had little empathy with my fellow officers other than Peter Glendinning. Observing the strain I was under, he kindly invited me home for one weekend and, on the Sunday, I had the novelty of being taken to a stock-car racing event at Cowdenbeath. It was certainly a most welcome break away from base life where inevitably of an evening I would encounter the Captain holding forth in the wardroom bar. However, I gradually noticed a change in his attitude to myself: after a few weeks at sea serving with him, he had stopped checking my work and was far less aggressive when I made an error. Indeed paradoxically, I overheard him recount to one of his peers that he reckoned that one day I would make a successful submarine Captain.

Both he and the First Lieutenant were soon to disappear, but not before *Sealion* undertook trials of a prototype Polaris submarine communication buoy. This involved fitting special rails to the after part of the casing to house and recover the buoy which measured approximately 8ft by 6ft. It was attached to the submarine by about 1,000ft of wire. Fitting of the rails was taken in hand by Scotts Shipyard at Greenock which had a distinguished shipbuilding history, and where two *Oberon* class submarines were being completed for the Australian Navy.

At the same time, the opportunity was taken to replace much of *Sealion*'s tired fabric and furnishings, all of this work being concealed in the cost of the rails. However, although the workforce evidently possessed a much better work ethic than I had experienced in the Royal Dockyards, the senior directors were uninspiring and the yard's infrastructure was run-down and under-capitalised. The boat required dry-docking for a few days but the Scott's dock needed the continuous running of pumps to keep the wooden dock floor reasonably free of water. Other evidence of decrepitude was the use of ancient telegraph poles as side-shores, to keep the submarine in position on the blocks. Unsurprisingly, like most other British shipyards which were living on a historical reputation for excellence, Scotts would go out of business a few years later.

The buoy trials took place in the Mediterranean, in waters to the east of Gibraltar. Rough weather encountered crossing the Bay of Biscay on the surface proved the rail design was not robust, and heavy seas tore the newly welded rails from the casing. This required a new set to be manufactured and fitted by Gibraltar Dockyard. Once this had been accomplished, *Sealion* embarked on her trials which involved running eastwards daily from Gibraltar, testing different buoy types, configurations and towing wires at dived speeds up to 16 knots.

Besides having onboard a number of trial scientists and technicians, opportunity was taken to host local guests at sea for the day, including army personnel, the medical staff from the Gibraltar naval hospital and local dignitaries. Accommodated in the wardroom, most commented on the bemusing array of tin cans strung out below the deckhead to catch water from leaking cable seals on the above pressure hull. On one occasion, *Sealion* departed from the dockyard with an army band playing on the forward casing, though some difficulty was experienced getting the drums below through the accommodation hatch when out of the harbour.

When dived in the waters to the east of Gibraltar, the submarine would often be surrounded by schools of dolphins. On encountering the boat, they would break out in a cacophony of chatter which could be heard on the loudspeaker of the underwater telephone system in the control room. To impress our visitors, a favourite trick was to cry 'Shut up' into its microphone. This caused instant silence amongst the dolphins whilst they considered what this strange underwater creature had uttered. After a minute or so there then followed a massive amount of noise, as these intelligent creatures deliberated what they had just encountered.

The buoy trials proved successful in demonstrating the hydrodynamics at a range of speeds but, on the final day, the trial scientists produced a tow wire covered in ostrich feathers which had been fitted with the aim of avoiding wire 'strum'. This was a harmonic oscillation of the wire that occurred as it was drawn through the water and which, by being a potential 'acoustic counter-detection hazard', would possibly betray the position of any submarine deploying the equipment in an acute operational situation. An expedient relying upon ostrich feathers to reduce strum was predictably regarded with cynicism by the crew. On working up to full speed, the wire parted due to the increased resistance of the feathers and the buoy was lost – never to be recovered. On that note, the trials were completed.

Meanwhile there had been a change of officers. Peter Glendinning had departed but was replaced by an equally capable Engineer Officer, Lieutenant David Wright. About the same time the First Lieutenant left to undertake Perisher which he successfully completed. He was relieved by an individual of much stronger character. Unfortunately, he soon turned out to be something of a bully, with an abrasive temperament and badly lacking people management skills. In consequence, the other members of the wardroom, which now included some highly capable individuals, drew together like a 'Band of Brothers', supporting each other and developing into a very effective team. In this atmosphere lifetime friendships were formed.

The Sonar Officer, an Australian, had been relieved by a fellow countryman, Lieutenant Derrick Webster who, although initially under training, was to prove a highly spirited and confident individual who would truck no nonsense from the new First Lieutenant. In terms of command seniority, with only a few months of submarine sea experience, I found myself as Third Hand of the boat beneath the Captain and First Lieutenant. This unexpected elevation was solely a consequence of a shortage of submarine qualified officers as the manpower-intensive two-crewed Polaris boats started commissioning.

The lax atmosphere that prevailed aboard *Sealion* guaranteed that a final departure time from Gibraltar two hours before midnight would result in a significant portion of the Ship's Company returning from shore leave one hour before sailing in a less-than-sober state. This proved to be the case and, shortly afterwards, true to form the Captain arrived by car a few minutes before departure and also staggered across the brow in an inebriated state to take the submarine to sea for his final time. Certain irregular preparations had been made by members of the crew before leaving the berth while the Captain worked up his own departure plan. Ignoring all harbour speed restrictions, and determined to make his last departure a memorable one, he reversed *Sealion* from her berth at maximum speed and created a significant wash on the alongside guard ship, the frigate *Zulu*.

This 'Tribal' class frigate had fitted to either side of her bridge large decorative Zulu shields which had been presented to her. These had now miraculously appeared secured to *Sealion*'s fin and were unsubtly illuminated by lamps. Their sighting by the frigate's watchkeepers caused a flurry of activity and a high-speed rigid raider craft was dispatched to recover the booty. By the time this reached *Sealion*, she was already outside the harbour mole. As the fast boat roared alongside, a Royal Marine Officer, immaculately dressed in his mess kit, stood up in the stern and pleaded for the return of the shields. However, the outgoing Captain was in no mood to surrender the trophies his warriors had gleaned and started bombarding the boat with potatoes from a bag he had had sent up from the galley. The *Zulu* detachment repelled and the shields stowed securely away, he disappeared below to his cabin. There he remained ensconced for most of the next three days as *Sealion* ran north, up the Portuguese coast and headed across the Bay of Biscay.

Something of his state of mind is revealed by the fact that the Captain made no protest when as a tease, I kept the navigational charts under lock and key during the surface passage north off the coast of Portugal and Spain. Apparently indifferent to *Sealion*'s progress until the diving area was reached in the Bay of Biscay, this somewhat sad character departed without ceremony after speedily handing over to his relief when the boat berthed at Faslane. Meanwhile the Zulu shields were somehow returned to the frigate.

With her old Captain gone, *Sealion* rapidly improved. The boat was now much cleaner and her crew, having undergone many changes of personnel, was more competent and efficient. The new Captain, although initially lacking confidence, was a big improvement on his predecessor. Perhaps most enlivening was the arrival of a new wardroom attendant, Leading Steward Elks. He had previously served in the Royal Yacht, but we did not enquire too deeply why his service there had been abruptly terminated. Notably, he displayed unsurpassable ingenuity and pluck in procuring extras for the wardroom. Many a Supply Officer of a warship berthed near *Sealion* must have wondered where the wardroom langoustines, fillet steaks or fresh strawberries had disappeared to, while the recipients of this cunning turned a Nelsonic blind eye.

However, the new Captain proved somewhat accident-prone; early in his command *Sealion* struck the jetty when berthing in Portland harbour, causing it some damage. The berth allocated was a difficult one to come alongside on and as we altered for the final approach it was clear we were going too fast. 'Slow Astern', 'Half Astern' and 'Full Astern!' orders followed in quick succession. Meanwhile the Casing Officer quickly cleared the berthing party from the bow area, yelling with particular urgency and volume at the lone sailor standing right forward of the sonar dome, holding an inadequate fender, to rapidly retreat aft.

As the bow crashed into the wooden piles of the jetty and buried itself under the structure, at first the damage did not seem too bad. However, as stern power began to take effect and the boat was extracted from underneath the jetty, shattered timbers crashed down and I observed a large hole appear on the jetty road. Furthermore, a substantial chunk of road surface tarmac had come to rest incongruously on top of the sonar dome.

The sonar dome itself had been damaged and required emergency repairs in Devonport Dockyard before *Sealion* embarked on Exercise Silver Tower. This was the largest NATO exercise for over a decade and involved the chartering of a dozen or so merchant ships to act as an east-bound convoy crossing the Atlantic. *Sealion*'s role was to play the part of a Soviet submarine with orders to lay a minefield in the approaches to Falmouth and then attack the convoy as it made its way up the English Channel. Having successfully laid six practice moored mines at a selected position, to conserve its battery and avoid detection from searching aircraft, the submarine lay on the bottom of the sea off Start Point.

As the convoy approached in darkness, to minimise the risk of detection the Captain decided to penetrate the surrounding screen of escorts whilst deep. This was successfully achieved without being detected by any of the escorts. He then manoeuvred *Sealion* to a position right in the midst of the convoy and commenced carrying out simulated attacks from deep rather than periscope depth. This ploy worked out perfectly and, in a real situation, the merchant ships would have been sitting ducks. The night sky over the convoy was illuminated several times by green flares fired by *Sealion*, each indicating a simulated attack. After this great success *Sealion*'s crew were cock-a-hoop and the Captain's self-confidence greatly buoyed.

Exercise Silver Tower over, *Sealion* headed north for several weeks of ASW target services in sea areas to the north-west of Ireland with the opposition NATO ships and MPA. The opportunity was taken for an exchange of personnel with the MPA community and we embarked a Dutch Atlantique pilot for a few days experience of operating under the sea. He soon appreciated that the submarine pace of life was relentless with no sojourn to the bar and a pleasant dinner following a day's flying sortie. At the same time Derrick Webster, as the other half of the exchange, enjoyed the thrill of low-level flying in an Atlantique over stormy seas in search of *Sealion*. About the same time another new officer had joined, Sub Lieutenant Alan Wright. Of the Supply specialisation, he was amongst the early officers of that branch to be appointed to submarines and was cutting his teeth in *Sealion* as Torpedo Officer before, in due course, being posted to a nuclear submarine.

After further exercises in the English Channel, *Sealion* headed to Bristol for a pre-Christmas visit. In an era when quite large vessels could still navigate all the way to the centre of the city, there was the challenge of negotiating over five miles of narrow and twisting sections of the River Avon before locking into the berthing basin. On reaching the sharpest turn, known as the Horseshoe Bend, we did not alter course hard enough and the bow buried itself in the soft mud of the northern bank. Fortunately, there was a tug in the lead which quickly pulled us off the bank. With the Portland pier collision not long past, this incident did nothing to improve the Captain's ship-handling confidence. However, soon afterwards there was the cheering and morale-building sight of a class of primary school children lining the river bank robustly singing 'We all live in a Yellow Submarine'.

At the traditional first night cocktail party in the cramped space of the control room, the guests were the usual great and good of Bristol but, amongst them, was one rather colourful character – an outrageously camp and loud personality. It was soon established that he was the proprietor of several Bristol nightclubs and was generously allowing all of *Sealion*'s crew free entry into them. He was, nevertheless, overheard to exclaim to another guest, 'This is a dream come true for me – Tinned Sailors!'. Subsequently some of us went to his most prestigious nightclub accompanying him as personal guests. The star act was a female jazz singer, blonde and buxom and extremely amply proportioned. Her performance really impressed and, as we left the club, she and the proprietor were invited to visit the boat the next morning.

When they arrived at the berth, the boat's engines were running to charge the batteries but, as it was raining, only the accommodation space hatch was open. In consequence a gale of wind rushed down it, feeding air to the diesels. That was fine for the average person but, following her boss down the access ladder, the singer's bulk and clothing filled most of the hatchway and the super-charged engines started creating a vacuum in the submarine. Quick reaction was required to shut down the diesels and equalise the boat's air pressure with the outside atmosphere by opening the conning tower hatch. Meanwhile we were treated to the sight of the proprietor clinging onto his singer's legs in a vain attempt to pull her down through the opening. Thankfully, as the pressure equalised, she managed to scramble down the ladder without further assistance. She took the whole episode in excellent humour and after a restorative large sherry, she treated us to several resounding opera arias in the confines of the wardroom. Thankfully her exit from the boat was achieved without any drama.

Another highlight of the visit was the Harvey's Sherries cellar tour and lunch to which all of the wardroom, with the exception of the Duty Officer, were invited. The company's hospitality was absolutely outstanding and their fine wines flowed generously throughout the meal. Afterwards in the late afternoon as we spilt out onto the streets of Bristol, some of us ill-advisedly did some Christmas shopping, inevitably selecting the most inappropriate of presents.

The departure from Bristol and the passage down the River Avon occurred without incident. The entire Ship's Company had been royally feted by its citizens in an era where each day, somewhere a submarine would be visiting a UK port. These visits besides generating a great deal of goodwill and generous hospitality on the part of the local community raised the profile of the Royal Navy and specifically the Submarine Service. Sadly, today such home-port visits rarely occur, as there are few available operational submarines and, all being nuclear, they attract substantial costs in visiting harbours other than naval ports.

As we made surfaced passage back to Faslane up through the Bristol Channel, arriving on the bridge on the evening of departure to take over the midnight watch, I encountered an incredible sight. The bridge personnel were eerily glowing green all over and the rotating radar aerial was like an illuminated Christmas decoration. It was snowing and, very unusually, an ongoing thunderstorm had caused the snow particles to be charged and briefly emit a green glow. I have met few who have ever experienced this strange phenomenon at sea, but it added to that happy feeling heading for Christmas leave.

Christmas leave over, *Sealion* started 1969 by conducting a few days independent shake-down exercises in the Clyde Estuary to 'shake away the cobwebs'. The morale of the crew had been buoyed by the news that, in the spring, *Sealion* was programmed to accompany the Commander-in-Chief Western Fleet's flagship on official visits to Oslo, Copenhagen and Stockholm. This was in addition to a port call to Lisbon in March on completion of a major NATO exercise.

During one night of the independent exercises, while dived north of Arran, the sound room team made several sporadic contact reports of a vessel of eerily quiet characteristics. Proving almost impossible for the sonar operators to determine its characteristics, it was somewhat of a mystery. Only afterwards on return to base was it determined that we had been sharing the same area as a USN SSBN operating from the Holy Loch. Except under conditions of controlled exercises or operations, submarines never operate dived in the same area to avoid the risk of underwater collision. Clearly there had been an error in the weekly allocation of the Clyde exercise areas to individual submarines.

The independent exercises over, we headed to deep water to the north-west of Ireland to take part in a major submarine versus submarine exercise which involved the participation of seven diesel submarines and the SSN *Warspite*. The weather was appalling for all of the two weeks of exercising, perhaps unsurprisingly as it was January. Few submarines gained contact on each other and consequently little training value was achieved. In our case, the only contact with another boat was sighting *Porpoise* on the surface at about one mile's distance, at the end of the exercise. She was not supposed to be there and, evidently, one of the two boats' navigation had gone awry. When landfall and a good navigation fix was made a few hours later as we headed on the surface for Londonderry, I traced back *Sealion's* track to the plotted end of exercise position. I then demonstrated to the Captain that we had been in the right area and that *Porpoise* had been at fault. However, I am certain her navigator had undertaken the same procedure, assigning the blame to *Sealion*.

With all seven diesel boats alongside, a two-day visit to Londonderry was bound to be a memorable one and the crews thoroughly enjoyed the generous hospitality and friendliness of the locals. On the Sunday evening departure, timed to catch a favourable tide, the police ran out of vans to bring back numerous inebriated sailors and the use of ambulances had to be resorted to. One of our sailors was delivered back by a taxi driver who had found him in the gutter and who refused all offers of payment for his fare. The Londonderry folks' sympathetic accommodation of 'Jolly Jack's' inclination to get drunk ashore, starkly contrasted with events during the not-far-off 'Troubles', with violent rioting breaking out in the city a few months later.

On *Sealion's* return to base in Faslane, repairs were undertaken to equipment damaged during a later-described depth excursion and the crew prepared for an upcoming Squadron sea inspection. The good news for myself, was that another new officer, the Electrical Officer Lieutenant Henry Buchanan, had succeeded in fixing the long-defective Loran-C ocean-going navigation system. The fault was a simple one, the ends of input signal cable in a junction box were not connected, but at long last I could confidently navigate accurately in the deep ocean.

Shortly afterwards, the sea inspection was conducted in the Clyde Estuary with the presence onboard of the Squadron Captain (SM3) and several of his staff. It did not go well for me. After *Sealion* avoided ASW vessels operating to the north of Arran and penetrated an exercise minefield which had been laid some time previously off the coast near the village of Lochranza, my challenge was to safely navigate the boat overnight down the Kilbrannan Sound. This runs between the Kintyre Peninsula and Arran. This was going to be difficult as it was a dark, cloudy night with no moon and few identifiable navigational marks and, for the purposes of the inspection, there was a need to proceed as covertly as possible.

To ensure safe navigation it was planned to use radar to fix the boat's position. However, to avoid counter-detection of its transmissions, it would be operated using a minimal number of sweeps and the Captain directed that a narrow, sector scan facility be used. An officer stationed in the radar office was tasked to report to myself on the control room navigation plot, the range of the pier of the fishing village of Carradale. It was situated on the west side of the sound, about half way down it. Unfortunately, using the radar in such a restricted mode resulted in the radar officer misidentifying this feature. The result was, as the boat approached the narrows off Carradale, on one of his periodic periscope looks, the Captain suddenly realised from the unexpectedly close proximity of the pier, that my plotted position was seriously in error. To avoid a grounding on shallows ahead, he surfaced the boat in emergency. Naturally as navigator this was a black mark for me.

An accurate position achieved while on the surface, the boat was dived again and proceeded to undertake a minelaying exercise at the entrance to Campbeltown Loch, followed by a photo-reconnaissance at first light of the island of Ailsa Craig. Having been engaged in close quarters navigation almost continuously for 14 hours, I snatched a quick breakfast before returning to the control room as watch-leader at the start of the inspection's emergency evolution phase. I was again in the spotlight and, to test my reaction as watch-leader, during a crash stop snorting procedure, a high-pressure air blow was deliberately applied to the aftermost ballast tanks. Amongst all this ongoing noise, I was unaware of this which resulted in the boat taking a steep bow-down angle with the stern sticking out above the surface. I should have simply opened the ballast tank vents to let the air out of them, but to a background of much tutting from the Squadron staff in the control room, I ordered flooding of an internal compensating tank – the wrong solution. The Captain interceded by ordering the vents opened and this brought *Sealion* back on an even keel.

Later in the morning, I had a contretemps with a Squadron Lieutenant Commander who wanted to test the procedure for preparing all classified material for destruction on abandoning ship. This task fell to me, as one of my supplementary responsibilities was being in charge of all classified books and crypto. I considered emptying the contents of one safe into a canvas bag, weighted with several large tins of Heinz baked beans for dropping into the sea, was adequate to demonstrate the procedure. This did not satisfy the Squadron officer who did not see the humour in the tins of beans and insisted I empty all of my safes which numbered about a dozen. I quite correctly refused his instruction on the grounds that having quantities of classified documents and crypto cards scattered along the passageway of *Sealion* whilst evolutions were ongoing, risked loss or compromise of highly classified material. However, this obstinacy towards a senior officer's instruction was noted and was yet another black mark against me.

Several days later, when the boat was back alongside in the base, I was sent for by the Captain in his shore cabin. He gave me a dressing-down for my performance during the inspection. This I deemed unfair as I had been under continuous close scrutiny whilst navigating the boat in highly confined waters during several phases of the inspection and this had been achieved more than satisfactorily. It was my view that the emergency surfacing had occurred owing to the Captain's directive to use the radar in a restricted mode which had undoubtedly resulted in misidentification of a key navigational feature. As I left his room, I felt again that I had chosen the wrong specialisation, but I vowed to myself to ensure that, in future, my standard of navigation would be beyond reproach.

After further exercises in the English Channel and a brief call into HMS *Dolphin*, a coordinated dived transit was made across the Bay of Biscay in company with the elderly 'A' class submarine *Acheron*. With the luxury of a fully-working Loran navigation system, there was no problem in keeping station with the other boat using the minimum of underwater communications. At the end of the transit, on reaching sea areas off the north-west of the Iberian Peninsula without being detected, both boats conducted a successful dual attack on a NATO-escorted convoy at the start of a major exercise. Although somewhat a cast back to the U-boat campaign in the Atlantic, this was a satisfying outcome to a somewhat challenging operation. However, there were few further interactions because during the following two weeks, the exercise was dogged by bad weather as the opposing surface forces proceeded down the west coast of Portugal towards Lisbon.

There followed a five-day visit to Lisbon which was unremarkable, other than it rained most days. What is memorable was a visit to a restaurant by all the wardroom officers, except the First Lieutenant who was onboard on duty. The five us had become a close-knit group who, besides enjoying each other's company, provided robust mutual support in countering the eccentricities and excesses of the XO. Each of us has a firm recollection of the excessive restaurant bill which included a surcharge for a dismal performance of Fado – gloomy Portuguese folk music and dancing. However, good news had been received. One of the two operational Portuguese submarines had developed a serious defect. Rather than returning to Faslane as planned, *Sealion* had been directed to replace her in a forthcoming exercise with the Standing Naval Force Atlantic (STANAVFORLANT), a group of escorts from several NATO nations. The best part was at the end of the week-long exercise, all vessels would visit Funchal, Madeira.

During the course of the exercise, the First Lieutenant, for some very strange reason, calculated that, if war broke out and all the boat's weapons were discharged, in the increasingly warm sea, a diving trim could not be maintained if further fresh water was consumed. Consequently, despite the extreme improbability of this situation, he succeeded in persuading the Captain that strict water-rationing was necessary – and that meant no washing.

I personally found this stricture annoying from the start as, unlike many of my peers, I attempted to wet shave most days – I found chin stubble to be highly irritating and my efforts to grow a beard never came to fruition. As we headed south, the internal temperature in the boat increased, and clearly the water-rationing became more of a concern and irritation to the entire crew. One evening towards the end of the exercise, I observed Leading Steward Elks pass through the control room, heading in the direction of the junior rates bathroom carrying a large bucket of warm water. After a short interval he returned evidently having shaved and washed his hair. Enviously, I challenged him to the effect that he had broken the water-rationing restrictions and questioned him as to where he had got the water from. He replied 'It was the wardroom supper washing-up water Sir'. I recalled the main course had been braised steak and examining the ever-resourceful steward's hair, spotted remnants of that meal, bits of onion and carrot.

More seriously, the First Lieutenant was again up to his excesses, and had imposed stoppage of leave on the wardroom on arrival at Funchal because a number of administrative audits were overdue. Consequently, when at last common sense prevailed and the water-rationing was lifted, there was joy in the ratings' bathrooms as the Ship's Company had a good washdown, looking forward to the forthcoming visit, while the wardroom was in a state of deep gloom. Thankfully, the strong-willed Engineer Officer, David Wright, confronted the Captain regarding this idiotic situation and demanded the stoppage of wardroom leave be rescinded. This was conceded, but it was another episode which exacerbated the fractious relationship between the wardroom and the Second-in-Command.

The berthing in Funchal was not without incident. In manoeuvring alongside, *Sealion*'s stern swung out and nudged a fishing vessel which was moored close to the jetty. The impact did not seem serious but it was enough to breech the fishing boat's hull, requiring it to beach immediately for repairs. This was yet another incident which did not help build the Captain's ship-handling confidence. The fishing boat belonged to Blandy, a long-established family company which owned many interests in the island including the famous Reid's Hotel and Madeira wines. Early in the visit John Blandy, its chairman, and who was also the Honorary British Consul, paid a visit to *Sealion*. He presented the wardroom with a case of his finest Madeira but also left an invoice for an eye-watering sum to meet the cost of repairs to his fishing boat.

However, there was to be another event in the harbour environs involving *Sealion*. Two days into the visit, there was the requirement to move berth to allow the P&O liner *Canberra* alongside. The submarine simply needed to be moved stern first out into the harbour and then re-berthed in a new pier area once *Canberra* had been secured alongside. However, the First Lieutenant who was in charge of the move (with myself also on the bridge), decided it would be much better if *Sealion* cleared the harbour completely. He had not taken into account the risks of encountering a heavy swell outside the harbour mole, with personnel still securing gear on the casing. Soon after leaving the sheltered harbour waters, a large wave swept over the casing causing a Petty Officer to be washed into the sea. As he went in, his smart new cap drifted away and evidently he was in a dilemma – should he swim after his cap or towards *Sealion*? Despite the slight

levity of this situation, I was deeply concerned. Although he was
wearing a life jacket, unless we got him onboard quickly, the strong
current could take him away from the boat into a life-threatening
situation. Moreover, there was no rescue assistance available nearby.
Fortunately, we quickly rescued the Petty Officer as well as his hat,
neither the worse for wear, but it was yet another incident reflecting
the First Lieutenant's poor judgement.

At that time each Royal Navy vessel carried a number of cheques,
known as 'Navy Bills'. These documents set out in grand, elaborate
copper-plate text that the Admiralty would honour the given amount
of sterling currency set out in the bill against witnessing signatures.
The visit to Funchal had not been on our original programme and,
therefore, there was a large shortfall onboard of Portuguese escudos
with which to pay the crew and meet the hotel bills. Lieutenant
Derrick Webster was the Cash Account Officer who had the task of
solving this problem. Having tried to cash a Navy Bill, met universally
with much mirth and bemusement by the Funchal banks, he took
advantage of his previous service with P&O and negotiated cash from
Canberra's Purser using a Navy Bill. This solved the problem but there
were to be repercussions on return to base for the undertaking of such
an unorthodox arrangement with a P&O liner at what proved to be a
very disadvantageous exchange rate.

The Australian on the day of arrival also had the task of booking
the Ship's Company into three hotels, for the officers, senior rates and
junior ratings respectively. Of a rather extravagant disposition, he
billeted the officers in the newly-built five-star Savoy where most of
the guests appeared to be elderly American widows of the blue-rinse
hair stereotype. These ladies seemed to be particularly susceptible to
the charms of equal numbers of local gigolos. For my part, in the hotel
I met a very attractive British girl and invited her onboard Sealion one
evening for a tour of the boat and a drink in the wardroom, which she
willingly accepted. Her father unfortunately insisted in accompanying
her and, furthermore on arrival at the boat, declared that he was
unwilling to go below. Instead, he remained standing on the casing
beside the gangway sentry. Tour over, my suitably impressed guest
was seated in the wardroom, enjoying a glass of cognac, when there
was a report from the sentry that her father had become seasick.
Therefore, he required her to leave the submarine immediately. That
dashed any romantic aspirations as the next day we left Funchal and
headed back to Faslane for maintenance. The sunshine and warm seas
around Madeira quickly became but a pleasant memory.

The maintenance period complete, we headed down the Irish Sea in late April. On surface passage, unusually for that month, we encountered a severe storm. Therefore, the submarine ran shut down and snorted on the surface and, frequently being covered in driving spray, watchkeeping on the bridge was yet again a terribly cold and wet experience. When there was enough daylight and the wind and sea had moderated sufficiently, a damage assessment was made. The gangplank which had been strapped to the forward casing had gone, a sonar dome had been smashed in and a cover over an emergency indicator buoy on the after casing had disappeared. Arriving in a battered state into HMS *Dolphin* for repairs, the opportunity was also taken to off-load a defective Mark 20 torpedo from the after ends. Work complete, *Sealion* was in good shape to commence the Scandinavian tour.

The Commander-in-Chief (C-in-C) Western Fleet's group for the Scandinavian visits consisted of the guided missile destroyer *Kent* and the last of the *Daring* class destroyers in RN service, *Defender*. The C-in-C was Admiral Sir John Bush, who had a highly distinguished wartime record but was known as the 'Burning Bush' for his fiery temper. The aim of the tour was to 'Show the Flag' and engender goodwill with the people of the nations visited. This involved the ships being open to visits by the public. The participation of two submarines, *Sealion* and *Acheron*, would attract a lot of attention and draw large crowds of visitors. However, as will be seen, the presence of submarines could also present unusual problems.

There had been a long ceremonial entry to Oslo, the first port of call. Perhaps, because of noise and exhaust smoke, both submarines had been forbidden to run their diesels. Therefore, soon after the arrival formalities had been completed, and the crews decanted to their respective hotels, both boats needed to put a battery charge on. *Kent* was berthed by the pier, with *Defender* alongside, with the two submarines secured outboard of her. Alan Wright was *Sealion*'s OOD.

Acheron's OOD had the idea of having a timed race to get the diesels started with the prize a large gin and tonic. 'No cutting corners!' was his last utterance as both officers disappeared below to instruct their duty engineers to start the charge. The result was a dead heat. The outboard engine in each boat burst into life at exactly the same moment, resulting in the emission of two very oily black clouds. These then joined forces as a light wind took them inexorably over *Defender* and onto the flight deck of the flagship *Kent*. This coincided with a bugle sounding the alert on the latter.

While both OODs were arguing over who owed to whom the gin and tonic, a vision appeared above them on *Defender*'s deck. It was the Admiral's Flag Lieutenant, a Royal Marine Captain, resplendent in Sam Browne, gleaming sword, white gloves and a pith helmet, pristine but for specks of soot on it. He enquired – almost languidly – whether he was right in thinking that *Sealion* and *Acheron* might be responsible for the black cloud that had just enveloped *Kent*'s flight deck. After it was agreed that this was possible, he then passed on the C-in-C's compliments and informed both officers that they had just covered the Admiral and the King of Norway in 'Shit'. Consequently, the Admiral would be most grateful if both boats were not alongside by the time the King (Olav V) was due to leave. He was apparently staying for lunch, but that still left little time to arrange a move to a new berth.

As the duty watches prepared for slipping, with *Acheron*'s OOD's words ringing in his ear – 'If you're still tied onto me in 30 minutes, you'll be coming anyway!', Alan sent an urgent message to the officers' hotel seeking a qualified 'driver' for the move. Fortunately, the First Lieutenant arrived just in time to slip and both boats spent some time floating around Oslo harbour whilst a harassed Norwegian Liaison Officer found an alternative berth. Otherwise, the visit to Oslo went off without incident and there was no repeat fracas when Frederik IX, King of Denmark, was invited onboard *Kent* during the visit to Copenhagen. On this occasion the submarines were berthed at some distance from the flagship.

A pilot was mandatory for part of the route down the narrow shipping lanes through the Kattegat to Copenhagen. Similarly, a pilot should have been embarked for the 40-plus miles of long and tortuous passage through the archipelago from the Baltic Sea to Stockholm. However, there was an ongoing strike of pilots and, as a contingency, it was planned that *Acheron* embark the one senior pilot not on strike and *Sealion* follow her in. That plan would have been fine but *Acheron* quickly wound up to her maximum 18 knots and, only capable of doing 13 knots, we quickly lost sight of her among the myriad of islands on the horizon. Nevertheless, having carefully planned this particular passage, for me it was a real professional joy to successfully undertake this difficult navigational challenge through many twisting and narrow channels. In calm conditions and brilliant, early morning sunshine, passing close to the immaculate lawns of cottages where Swedes were enjoying their breakfasts, it was one of those wonderfully memorable occasions when one's salary appeared to be an unnecessary bonus.

On arriving alongside in Stockholm, one hour after our so-called pilotage guide, *Acheron*, we were saddened to hear that our Swedish host submarine had recently suffered a battery explosion involving fatalities. Therefore, its crew would not be partaking in the very full social programme arranged by the Royal Swedish Navy and the citizens of Stockholm for the group. However, a highly enjoyable dinner was hosted by its squadron staff in the depot ship *Patricia* for *Sealion* and *Acheron* officers.

Undoubtedly, of the three capitals visited, Stockholm excelled in the remarkably generous hospitality offered to all levels of each ship's crew. This culminated in a dance organised on the final evening for several hundred crew members in the city hall. Much to Jolly Jack's delight there were throngs of highly attractive Swedish young ladies available as dance partners. For my part, I had met another very attractive girl at the official cocktail party on *Kent* who had accompanied her father, a senior surgeon in the Swedish Navy. There followed a memorable romance during that sunny, hot summer, holidaying with her in Gothenburg, where she had started training as a nurse, and spending a few days with her family in a summer cottage to the north of the city. However, sadly for me, our relationship ended a few months later in a very snowy and bitterly cold Gothenburg, when it became clear the attractions of a Royal Navy submariner had been well and truly eclipsed by the advances of a young doctor.

The Scandinavian visits over, *Sealion* headed back to Faslane to undertake preparations for an impending long refit at Rosyth Dockyard on the Firth of Forth. Buoyed up by the enjoyment of the Scandinavian visits, crew morale was high and the wardroom's quality of life had over the months significantly improved. Most passage time was spent on the surface and allowed much more leisure and relaxation time for the Ship's Company. There were plenty of movie showings and the wardroom indulged most evenings in a racy series of poker variations, albeit for very small stakes.

The competence and quality of the crew had also markedly improved since I joined. One notable character was the Coxswain, 'Manny' Scicluna. Of Maltese nationality, he was a loyal, dependable senior rate, highly respected by the entire crew. As Coxswain he acted as helmsman on entering and leaving harbour. On occasions the two of us experienced language interpretation difficulties when passing and receiving orders down the bridge voice-pipe, my Scots accent strongly clashing with his Maltese lilt.

There was one final visit, on this occasion to Campbeltown, for one night alongside. The First Lieutenant was engaged to be married, with his wedding date only a few weeks later. Therefore, despite his unpopularity, the wardroom officers persuaded him to come ashore with them and celebrate some form of stag-night in a local hotel. However, he was not for socialising and notably, towards the end of the evening, assiduously avoided drinking a pint of beer offered to him which, unbeknown to him, contained copious quantities of vodka. During the evening, we had been joined by the Captain of a visiting Royal Naval Reserve minesweeper which was berthed astern of *Sealion*. As we left the hotel, he spotted the untouched glass of beer, and before we could stop him, picked up the glass and downed most of its contents in one go. We observed the colour drain from his face as he took his last gulp.

There was an early 0600 departure from harbour the following morning and, as the Captain joined me on the bridge a few minutes before slipping, notably the First Lieutenant was not present. Just as the first line was about to be let go, he arrived on the bridge, somewhat shame-faced and, as normal, he reported that the boat was ready for sea. However, the situation was not normal, as when he saluted the Captain it was observed that he had a set of handcuffs attached to the wrist of his right hand and the free end was sporting a small part of a wooden bunk. Derrick Webster had managed to get hold of the Coxswain's set of handcuffs and, with the help of Henry Buchanan, secured the sleeping First Lieutenant to his bunk just before the wardroom were awakened. He then threw the keys over the side.

There were no repercussions to this prank which was viewed as the tail-end of the stag-night. However, as *Sealion* passed the minesweeper, a lonely personage was observed standing on its bows. It was its Captain, whose face matched the colour of the light green nightshirt he was dressed in. He piped the 'Still' on a bosun's call as we came abeam and fired a green flare from a Very pistol: evidently he must have thought that we submariners had deliberately given him the spiked glass of beer.

Sealion departed from Faslane in July 1969, flying her paying-off pennant and heading for refit in Rosyth. Prior to her departure, there had been the usual round onboard of farewell parties and consequently the wardroom bar stocks were very low. It was somewhat to our annoyance that, on the morning following her arrival at the dockyard, the Captain unexpectedly announced that he had invited the Admiral Superintendent, accompanied by several senior managers, onboard for lunchtime drinks. The crew had started de-storing and there was gear everywhere, not least in the wardroom where I had laid out all holdings of classified material for muster and bagging up. Therefore, I was not best pleased at stopping the muster midstream and locking away all the books and crypto material. Derrick Webster was not happy either as, in his role of wardroom wine caterer, he was very short of Scotch, known to be the Admiral's favourite tipple.

Therefore, to make up the shortfall, Derrick took the one remaining bottle of Johnny Walker and poured a quarter of it into another bottle which he topped up with gin and vodka. The bottle containing this novel cocktail was marked by a piece of masking tape to distinguish it from the good bottle. The senior guest, Rear Admiral William Ridley, was a formidable individual of large frame and, sporting a monocle in one eye, was of rather fearsome appearance. However, in reality, this belied a benign character and as the whisky flowed he and his managers settled into friendly discussion about the forthcoming refit. Unfortunately, after the admiral had consumed two large tumblers of the good stuff, in error the Captain poured a large quantity of the contents of the suspect bottle into his glass. The monocle fell out of his eye as the first gulp of the cocktail went down his throat but he made no comment and continued to drink it, albeit slowly. Meanwhile his senior managers, who had not been offered drinks from the sound bottle, were eulogising over the taste of their Scotch – 'Aye this is great stuff – I bet you canna buy this in the shops!'. No, you cannot, I thought.

Soon after arrival in Rosyth, apart from the engineering branches, most of the crew departed for new postings. This was also the case for the wardroom where the tight-knit group of five of us sadly, said goodbye to each other. As for the First Lieutenant, some years later he failed to pass the Perisher Course and consequently his submarine career was abruptly over. It was not without some excitement that I had learned that my next appointment was to the eight-year-old *Oberon*, then completing an extensive modernisation at HM Dockyard, Portsmouth. Destined to be a unit of the Seventh Submarine Division, *Oberon* was under orders to proceed to Singapore and I would, at last, be exchanging the miserable weather of the Western Approaches for the tropical climes of the South China Sea. Coincidentally the individual I had clashed with a few months earlier during the sea inspection was to be my new Captain.

My 15 months in *Sealion* had been a tremendous learning experience and a bit of a roller-coaster ride. I had joined her when she was in a filthy state, crew morale rock-bottom and I had to endure the challenges of serving under a Captain who was an aggressive alcoholic. When I departed for my new appointment, she was a clean, happy vessel with a considerably more competent and capable wardroom and crew, except for the First Lieutenant. Under the greatly improved leadership of a new Captain and department officers, crew morale was upbeat and they had developed into a cohesive and mutually supportive Ship's Company. I had had my bad times when I considered that the Submarine Service might not be my metier, but these experiences were more than offset by periods of great professional satisfaction and enjoyment. There had also been many occasions of memorable hilarity. Most importantly, I had made enduring, strong friendships with my fellow wardroom officers, that tight-knit 'Band of Brothers' who had very much supported each other through good times and bad.

Chapter 6

Unexpected Angles

As explained earlier, submarines change depth by moving the hydroplanes to achieve a bow-down angle to increase depth and the opposite to ascend. Extreme care must be exercised to control the amount of angle on the boat as too much bow-down angle, at even modest speed, risks exceeding the safe operating depth. In the case of *Sealion*, this was 500ft and her theoretical crush depth was about 900ft. As an example, in the situation of the boat being at periscope depth at a speed of 10 knots, if the bow-down angle increased to 30 degrees owing to hydroplane failure, if no action was taken, crush depth would be breached in less than two minutes, killing the entire crew. Therefore, as previously stated, watch officers are rigorously drilled in such situations to urgently reduce speed and put the hydroplanes into an emergency recovery mode. In most cases this mode uses high-pressure air to operate the hydroplanes instead of the more usual hydraulic pressure. If these measures were in themselves insufficient to take a bow-down angle off, then the forward ballast tanks are blown. I was to experience two plane failure scenarios in *Sealion*, both very different and one highly frightening.

The first of these emergencies occurred during the exercise period after Christmas in the Clyde areas. At 200ft and proceeding at about 6 knots, all was quiet and routine in the control room during the forenoon watch. In the wardroom the Electrical Officer, who was also the wine-caterer and due to be relieved on return to harbour, was mustering the wardroom bar stocks. In conducting this task, he had placed a significant array of bottles on the wardroom table. I was watch-leader in the control room when suddenly the after-planes failed in a rise position resulting in a steep bow-up attitude of over 20 degrees, before the angle was corrected by applying the after-planes in their emergency mode and reducing speed.

Meanwhile there had been a loud cry of 'Shit!' from the wardroom, followed by a cacophony of glass breaking and bottles hitting the deck. While we in the control room were clinging onto whatever we could, to keep our balance, and taking measures to get the boat level, an avalanche of intact spirit bottles was observed to clatter through the control room at speed on its way to the engine room. They were followed by the Electrical Officer, in a real panic, doing his best to round up his wards. Needless to say, the odd bottle of Scotch was never retrieved.

The second, much more serious incident occurred only a few weeks later when *Sealion* was snorting in deep water to the north-west of Ireland at 10 knots, her maximum snorting speed. We were acting as a sonar target for the SSBN *Resolution*, then undergoing her 'first-of-class' sonar trials. To avoid any possibility of a collision, the two submarines were allocated separate depth zones, *Resolution* running in the deeper of the two, and in a position then unknown to *Sealion*. At about 0020 I had arrived in control room about to take over the watch from the First Lieutenant, but still in the process of getting myself together after only a brief sleep. The control room was darkened, illuminated only by a few dim red lights.

Suddenly the after planesman reported that his hydroplanes had jammed to 'full rise'. He immediately transferred the control of the planes to the separate emergency system and applied 'full dive' to the hydroplanes which, however, remained indicating 'full rise'. The submarine adopted a severe down angle and increased depth rapidly.

The 'Stop Snorting!' order was rapped out and the control systems watch-keeper urgently went through the tasks of shutting hull valves, lowering masts and – as part of his standard procedure – flooding the snort induction mast with seawater to avoid it being over-pressured. The forward planesman put full rise on his hydroplanes, which limited the down angle to about 20 degrees, but he could not counter the effect of the larger and more powerful after-planes.

Part of the 'Stop Snorting' drill in *Sealion* was to empty two small external compensating tanks using high-pressure air to counter the additional weight of water incurred in flooding the snort mast. By mistake, the control systems watchkeeper did this with the tank emptying valves shut and the effect of the high-pressure air caused the relief valves on both tanks to lift with a very loud and explosive report. The reliefs vented through the pressure hull into the control room wing bilges and the blast of high-pressure air from the port relief forced an alarming jet of bilge water into the control room. In the darkness and cacophony of noise, I thought that an explosion had occurred and that the pressure hull had been breached. The spray from the bilge hit the electrical starter of a pump, causing a second violent blast and a flash, followed by a major electrical short-circuit which caused the loss of most of the control room instrument illumination. These all added to my and others' fears that the situation was rapidly getting out of control.

The runaway *Sealion*, with now a significant bow-down angle, was going deep at speed. Preoccupied by their fight to regain control of the submarine the two planesmen had failed to shut off their large-scale shallow water depth gauges. These were only tested to a maximum of 140ft, which *Sealion* had long since passed, and now their gauge-glasses fractured and yet more seawater sprayed into the control room. Meanwhile, the First Lieutenant had failed to order stern power to quickly reduce speed and lessen the effect of the apparently jammed after-planes.

As *Sealion* left her safe depth and she entered the depth zone of *Resolution* beneath her, I grabbed the acoustic underwater telephone microphone and broadcast the alarming report: 'Going deep! Going deep! Out of control!'. Apart from warning the SSBN of our descent, I was determined that if *Resolution* was within reception range she would be aware that *Sealion* was in trouble. There was, however, no response from the SSBN as *Sealion* headed for the depths out of control and, to my mind, apparently flooding. Unless the dive-angle and speed were reduced, *Sealion* would quickly reach her crush depth. Notwithstanding the terror induced by this prospect, I had the curious thought that it was unfair that this was happening before, and not after, the impending Scandinavian visits.

Amid the shouting and confusion, the Captain had rapidly arrived in the control room and immediately ordered the motors to 'Full Astern'. The drag of the reversed propellers slowed the submarine and gradually she levelled out. Much to everyone's relief, she adopted a bow-up angle and ahead propulsion was ordered. However, the boat continued to make sternway and began to increase her depth again. This was because the motor room watchkeepers were having difficulty responding to the ahead order due to problems on the main motor control. The log speed continued to register zero for some time until eventually headway was achieved. Meanwhile, my torch showed me that one of the small calibre deep depth gauges was registering nearly 600ft and the boat was below its safe depth. However, because of the diminutive scale of the gauge, I could not determine in which direction depth was changing.

In response to the rapidly worsening situation, the Captain ordered 'Standby to Surface!'. I was alarmed to hear the First Lieutenant instinctively ordering the cycling of the main ballast tank vents as part of the normal surfacing procedure. *Sealion* was far from being in a normal situation and I was fearful that, having opened the vents, they would not be able to be promptly shut, which was vital to enable high-pressure air being put into these tanks to gain positive buoyancy and reach the surface. However, my heart beating and anxious about the state of the vents – were they open or shut? – I was relieved to hear the high-pressure air rushing into the main ballast tanks. Eventually, after what seemed like a long moment of suspended animation, the boat began to gain headway towards the surface.

As the surface was approached the Torpedo Officer, Alan Wright, was assigned the duty of surfacing OOW. In the absence of the large-scale shallow-water depth gauges, it was difficult to judge when the boat had reached the surface. In consequence, the conning tower upper hatch was ordered opened by the Captain while it was still underwater. The OOW had to fight to open the hatch against the seawater pressure above, but finally succeeded, being rewarded by a deluge of cold seawater. However, this was swiftly replaced by a massive up-draught as the high atmospheric pressure which had built up inside the submarine vented through the hatch. He was only prevented from being blown out of the conning tower and sustaining serious injury by the lookout on the ladder below him, firmly holding his legs until the pressure equalised.

It was afterwards established that the incident had been caused by the failure of the after-planes 'teleflex' indication system. Remarkably, this was the only after-plane indicator in the control room. A further shortcoming was the limitation of *Sealion*'s deep depth gauges which registered a maximum 750ft, well short of the 900ft plus crush depth. Moreover, the small size of the indicator scale on these gauges made it difficult to determine quickly whether the submarine was increasing or decreasing depth, not a good situation. If, like *Affray*, *Sealion* had been lost, it would have been very difficult to establish the cause, giving rise to numerous improbable conspiracy theories, such as *Sealion* having collided with a Soviet submarine spying on *Resolution*.

In reality, *Resolution* had not been in close proximity and had failed to hear my underwater telephone transmissions. As for *Sealion*, repairs were carried out on the surface and, after a few hours, we dived and the trial continued. There was no subsequent inquiry but the one outcome was that, once back in harbour, two new large-scale depth gauges were fitted which could register depths down to 1,000ft. However, there continued to be the serious deficiency of only one indication of hydroplane angle in the control room.

A few moments after the incident, those officers not immediately occupied assembled in the wardroom and, very shaken, each had a glass of Scotch, a most unusual occurrence at sea. However, there had been no panic and indeed the latest new officer, Henry Buchanan, who was still under training, thought the events had been a normal occurrence. As for myself, as a young bachelor, I was not personally worried by what had happened, considering it 'all part of the deal'. I was also confident that this was the general feeling of all of my fellow officers but this acceptance was due in part to our collective submarine inexperience as a wardroom. I had learned the hard lesson that the cause of a hydroplane failure would not always be readily identifiable, but that such systems failures could rapidly result in dangerous loss of control of the boat. On reflection some time afterwards, I concluded that we had come quite close to losing the submarine and that *Sealion* could easily have been the fifth Western submarine to be lost between 1968 and 1970.

A few months after the *Sealion* incident, USS *Chopper*, a WW2 diesel boat, experienced a much more dramatic depth excursion, undoubtedly breaking records where the crew survived to tell the tale. She was participating in an exercise in the Caribbean with a destroyer, proceeding at about 9 knots at 150ft, when her electrical power totally failed, causing both sets of her hydroplanes to move to the full dive position.

Within seconds her angle increased to 45 degrees bow-down and a motor room watchkeeper was to save the day by, on his own initiative, rapidly applying full stern power on the main motors. However, despite this action and the blowing of the forward main ballast tanks, and other efforts to regain control of the submarine, the down angle continued to increase and, within two minutes of the power failure, *Chopper* was nearly vertical in the water, bow-down. The bow is estimated to have reached a depth of over 1,000ft, well beyond her safe depth of 400ft, before the crew's efforts began to take effect.

Then *Chopper*'s bow started to rise, reached level, and continued to climb. She began to ascend with a rapidly increasing up-angle until she was again nearly vertical in the water, now bow-up, before broaching the surface. As the air escaped from the forward ballast tanks, there then followed a plunge to 200ft before resurfacing and control being regained. All these events happened within a few minutes but, remarkably, no one was seriously injured. Most of the crew were, however, highly shaken and, on arrival back in harbour, some immediately requested a transfer out of submarines. Despite being of wartime construction, clearly *Chopper* had been well built but, unsurprisingly having reached more than twice her safe depth, she was a structural write-off.

The *Chopper* incident served to again highlight how, even at moderate speeds, control of a submarine can rapidly be lost with extremely hazardous consequences. The *Sealion* depth excursion was the most severe case of 'unexpected angles' I personally experienced, but there were to be others in submarines I later served in.

Chapter 7

A Different Kind of Submarining

Having departed from *Sealion*, after a short period of leave I joined *Oberon* in refit at Portsmouth Dockyard in July 1969 as Sonar Officer and Third Hand. Despite the Labour Government's declaration of withdrawal of British forces from the Far East at the end of 1971, when her refit and work-up were completed *Oberon* was to be deployed to this region, based in Singapore. Therefore, I considered myself lucky to receive such a desirable appointment but I was well aware that the brightest and best of my peer-group were being drawn into the Polaris programme, or appointed to one of an increasing number of SSNs.

Commissioned in 1961, *Oberon* was undergoing an extensive two-year modernisation. This included improved crew accommodation facilities and, crucially, a much better system for feeding air to the engines. When running on the surface, the snort induction system would be opened up and the two conning tower hatches used as an airlock system for access to and from the bridge. This avoided the newly fitted electronic equipment in the control room being affected by cold, damp air being drawn down the conning tower. In stormy weather conditions there would be no need for the previously described 'Bird-Bath' and 'Elephant's Trunk' arrangements.

Another enhancement of the modernisation was the installation of a significantly improved air-conditioning system. This would be important when operating in Far East waters: when a submarine is dived in tropical waters, without proper air conditioning, inevitably the crew will suffer uncomfortably high temperatures and levels of humidity which can result in heat exhaustion or skin disorders. She was also fitted with two single-man escape towers, one forward and the other aft. These much improved the ability of the crew to safely escape if the submarine became stricken on the seabed. However, despite the costly modernisation, there had been no updating of the sonar suite which remained essentially early 1950s technology and, indeed, the long-range sonar was much less capable than the prototype fitted in *Sealion*.

Oberon was the Captain's second submarine command. Aged in his middle 30s and of a seniority where promotion was most likely, he was clearly determined that commanding *Oberon* should be a successful step to the rank of Commander. His XO, Lieutenant Nick Beattie, had a distinguished father, Captain Stephen Beattie, who was awarded the VC for his part in the daring raid on the dock system at St Nazaire in northern France in March 1942. The Navigator, Lieutenant Mike Gilbert, and the Torpedo Officer, Lieutenant Roger Hornshaw, were, like myself, in their early 20s and each of us had less than two years' submarine experience.

The refit was suffering delays for a number of reasons and the Captain and engineering officers were constantly engaged in dialogue with the dockyard management to somehow instil a sense of urgency to complete the outstanding work. The more time in dockyard hands, the less time the boat would be based in Singapore. As this would be an accompanied deployment, where the families could join married crew members at government expense, there would be less time for the dependents to live there and enjoy the many benefits and pleasures of this foreign posting. Besides generous overseas pay and allowances, Singapore naval base had the attraction of being very family-friendly and offered excellent recreational facilities. Already the refit completion date had slipped by several months and departure was now no longer scheduled for early 1970.

With *Oberon* not likely to be ready for sea for several months, I looked for some sea-time in another boat. Therefore, I contacted my *Odin* First Lieutenant, Geoffrey Biggs ('GB') who, having passed his Perisher Course, was now Captain of *Otus*, and asked that I join his boat for a few weeks. He responded that, by coincidence, his Third Hand, Lieutenant Edwin 'Arkle' Atkinson, was absent horse-eventing with the British team in Belgium and that he was only too pleased that I should take his place. *Otus* would be undertaking Perisher training in the Clyde Estuary, returning to Rothesay and securing to a buoy at the end of each day. I consequently leapt at his offer and shortly afterwards joined *Otus*.

At the end of one evening, when secured to the buoy, 'GB', fuelled by ample quantities of Scotch and fired up by a racy series of games of Skats, declared that the following morning I should take the boat to sea. He had only one instruction: 'Beat Swales out'. Tim Swales was Captain of *Oracle*, the other boat involved in Perisher training. I assumed that 'GB' would be on the bridge, keeping an eye on me as I manoeuvred his submarine out of Rothesay Bay.

The following morning at Harbour Stations I arrived on the bridge, as instructed, to take the boat to sea. With no sign of the Captain, no doubt the Navigation Officer was rather bemused that a visiting officer, with limited submarine experience, should be entrusted to get *Otus* underway. The Perisher transfer boat duly arrived alongside and its students got onboard. Meanwhile, I had ordered slipping from the buoy and gingerly proceeded out of the bay, reporting progress to a messenger in the control room to relay to the Captain. It was a dark, wet morning and anchored frigates had to be avoided. At the same time I had to make sure that I was well ahead of *Oracle*. All the time I was wondering where was the Captain?

In due course, the First Lieutenant arrived on the bridge to report to the Captain that the boat was 'Opened up for Diving'. He was extremely surprised that 'GB' was not supervising the departure and headed down below to find him. I then received information from the control room to the effect that he could not be found and the crew was searching for him.

About 15 minutes later, 'GB' arrived on the bridge as the allocated dived areas were being entered. He looked round quickly and curtly enquired 'Where is Swales?' When I pointed out *Oracle* a few miles astern, he declared 'Fine' and disappeared below to have his breakfast.

The mystery of the missing Captain had meanwhile been solved. When the Perisher course came onboard, they had dumped all their raincoats on top of his bunk, not realising, in its near darkness, that it was still occupied. The messenger, in relaying messages to the Captain, was effectively talking to a pile of coats. During the search for him, someone had clicked that he might still be turned in. Of course, the officer running the Perisher course, Commander Dick Husk, must have been aware of the search for the Captain when he came onboard.

I assumed afterwards that 'GB' had intended to be on the bridge of *Otus* when she left harbour, but for his sleeping soundly under a stack of overcoats. There again, he would have recalled that I had safely navigated *Odin* up the Thames while the wardroom were hosting a farewell lunch for the departing Captain. Whatever, these two episodes contrasted sharply with some of my less than happy experiences navigating *Sealion*.

Shortly after I joined *Oberon*, the Captain addressed the entire Ship's Company and announced the introduction of the 'Military Salary' which put Armed Forces pay on a comparable basis of remuneration with broadly similar civilian occupations. It meant a substantial pay rise for most. However, for myself and my bachelor peers the best part of the deal was that, in the future, we would be paid the same as married men and the archaic practice of paying marriage allowance would be ended. A few months later, what was called a 'Delicate Text' signal was received announcing the end of the 'tot'– the daily rum ration. So ingrained was this tradition, that each of the nation's Polaris submarines had been designed with a built-in rum tank to hold over 200 gallons of strong spirit. Today it is inconceivable that missile and nuclear propulsion plant technicians would carry out their work after possibly having consumed a large slug of neat alcohol at lunchtime.

Re-commissioned in February 1970 at Portsmouth, *Oberon* headed north to the Clyde for two months of trials and work-up. Unlike *Sealion*, she was immaculate in cleanliness and appearance and, with an experienced and competent 65-strong crew, all looked promising for her forthcoming deployment.

The trials and work-up mostly progressed well, although the two stern tubes, which could only discharge the useless Mark 20 anti-submarine torpedoes, never achieved a successful proving firing. These two tubes were subsequently only used for stowage of beer, and the two embarked stern war-shot torpedoes were carried out to the Far East and back again, effectively performing no role other than ballast. The quietness of the 'O' class was emphatically demonstrated during static noise trials in Loch Fyne, with the boat suspended in a dived condition between four buoys above acoustic sensors on the seabed: the trials had to be put on hold on several occasions because ducks were noisily feeding on weed on the buoy wires. Creating more noise than the submarine, they were chased away only to return an hour or so later.

One work-up serial that did not go so well was that of a search for and simulated attack on an 'A' class submarine transiting a sea area to the north of Ireland. The crew had settled down to the ponderous search technique of slowly circling at a depth of 300ft to give the single-beam long-range sonar an opportunity of gaining detection on the opposing submarine at maximum range. In anticipation of soon making contact, 'Action Stations' and 'Shut-Off for Attack' had been ordered. The latter procedure involved shutting the hull valves of those systems which were not in use. However, due to crew error, the control room depth gauges had also been isolated and we were not aware that the boat was gradually rising until it broke surface, still circling. At this point the sound of waves hitting the fin alerted the control room team that all was not well despite 300ft steadily registering on the depth gauges. With members of the work-up staff onboard, this was a highly embarrassing incident but hard lessons had been learned.

Oberon sailed for the Far East in June 1970 and, because at the time the Suez Canal was shut, headed south for the Cape of Good Hope. To enable the passage to be conducted at a reasonable speed, and to avoid undue strain on the engines, the majority of the 12,000-mile route was completed on the surface. As most of the boat's tracks were well away from the shipping lanes, the bridge watchkeepers spent many a night under brilliant starlit skies without seeing another vessel, with the only sounds the subdued rumble of the diesel engines and the noise of the sea breaking on the bows. In starting to plan the passage, the Captain had initially aired the possibility of conducting the entire passage to the Far East dived, thereby achieving a first for a diesel submarine by breaking several endurance records. Of note, the British nuclear submarine *Valiant* had completed an entirely submerged transit from Singapore to the UK in 1967 in 27 days. However, he was soon dissuaded from such a wild notion as, apart from the potential damage to crew morale by foregoing a number of attractive port visits, the 60-plus days of snorting would put significant stress on the engines and other equipment.

Having called at Gibraltar, followed by Las Palmas in the Canary Islands, the next stop was the lonely and isolated British outpost of the mountainous island of St Helena in the South Atlantic. This remote territory, leftover from the days of the British Empire, had a population of just over 4,000, most residing in its only town, Jamestown. As there was no substantial pier, the submarine anchored off the town for a day. The Captain, by tradition, made a call upon the Governor of the island and returned onboard with him for a tour of the boat.

Later in the evening, the Captain and several members of the wardroom, including myself, went ashore to dinner in the Governor's residence, Longwood House. The latter was where Napoleon's body had originally been interred when he died in exile in 1821. A French historian was one of the dinner guests in addition to a visiting Church of England bishop. We were a somewhat motley group who after dinner, were escorted by the Governor to a garden wall to relieve ourselves before port and coffee were served and the ladies rejoined. I did not need this comfort break but I went through the motions anyway with the bishop standing beside me, cassock raised. The following morning as we departed, I wondered what the inhabitants would have made of the very unusual sight of a submarine anchored off their island and their brief glimpse of an entirely different world.

Oberon docked at Simonstown naval base, situated near Cape Town, in mid-July during a sleet squall – not quite the South African weather the crew had envisaged. However, they were soon immersed in the remarkable hospitality offered by the local population which had a great affinity for the Royal Navy. This affection had been cemented during both World Wars when Simonstown had served as an important Royal Navy base.

Several days after arrival, I and a few of my fellow officers were invited to look round the first South African submarine, the newly commissioned *Maria Van Riebeeck*. Of French *Daphne* class design, we were immediately struck by how less robust she was in comparison to the 'O' class. Comparatively small, with a less safe snort induction system and open main battery tanks, we sensed that the *Maria Van Riebeeck* officers, most of who were not experienced in submarines, were uneasy about operating their boat in the notoriously large and violent seas off the exposed South African coast, which has few sheltered harbours or safe anchorages. No doubt the second loss of a French boat of this class, with its entire crew, a few months earlier was fresh in their minds.

After a few days of maintenance, *Oberon* was off to sea for anti-submarine exercises with the South African Navy. The opposition consisted of two Clyde-built frigates *President Pretorious* and *President Kruger*. Towards the end of the exercises, I was transferred by helicopter for two days' experience onboard the *Pretorious*. I found many ways in which the ambience in the ship was like the Royal Navy two decades earlier. Even the wardroom crockery bore the obsolete Admiralty crest. However, manned by white conscripts doing their national service, these ships did not spend much time at sea, and it was clear to me that these men were nowhere near as professional as their British counterparts. Sadly, this observation proved prescient as several years later the *Kruger* was to sink with heavy loss of life after collision with the replenishment tanker *Tafelberg*.

Leaving Simonstown, *Oberon* headed north towards Mombasa, meeting up with the frigate *Lincoln* on her forlorn and futile station off the port of Beira in Mozambique. The 'Beira Patrol' was a blockade intended to choke off oil supplies to the whites-only regime of Prime Minister Ian Smith in Rhodesia which had repudiated its colonial

status by a unilateral declaration of independence. Sanctioned by the
United Nations, the blockade lasted from 1966 to 1975 and involved
a total of seventy-six Royal Navy ships but it proved ineffectual, as
fuel was trucked through South Africa and other contiguous countries.
The Beira Patrol and the many years Royal Navy ships spent on this
thankless and lonely task have long since been forgotten.

On arrival in Mombasa, the entire crew was accommodated in a
British Services recreational camp sited on a beautiful beach, a few
miles to the south of the city. A delightfully relaxed and informal set-
up, we were billeted in simple thatched huts by the beach which we
soon discovered were also home to variety of insects. As for myself, my
room-mate and I shared our shower cubicle with a tarantula perched
just above the shower-head. My fellow officer had been brought up in
Kenya, and thankfully assured me that it was not aggressive but just
to keep an eye on it.

The final port call before Singapore was Colombo in Sri Lanka.
The crew were all accommodated ashore in a large hotel, the facilities
and rooms of which were decrepit and clearly it had seen better days.
In the evening we were saddened to come across many of the staff
sleeping in the stairwells. Evidently these were the only spaces where
they could enjoy a reasonably peaceful sleep.

Sri Lanka was still adjusting to independence. Many of the buildings
from the colonial era were falling into disrepair and there was garbage
everywhere on the streets. One evening I was called to the submarine
because an Able Seaman in my division had been beaten up in a bar
and needed medical attention. I took a taxi to the dock area where
Oberon was berthed but the driver was not allowed access beyond the
entry gate and, therefore, I had no option but to walk the half mile
or so to the pier. Passing several run-down warehouses where sacks
of wheat were being stored, their markings indicated that they had
been donated by the USA. Peering inside the buildings, I witnessed
the chilling sight of the grain being voraciously devoured by hordes
of huge rats.

Arriving onboard, a quick inspection of my sailor indicated that he
was in urgent need of dental treatment as he had lost some front teeth
and others were loose. This was promptly organised but, after the
treatment had been completed, looking into the sailor's mouth it was
clearly a botched job, requiring rectification on arrival in Singapore.
In due course we received the dentist's bill for two appointments. The
size of the bill was eye-watering but its breakdown revealed quite
a lot of gold had been used and there was a charge for two bottles

of gin. When questioned about the gin, the sailor revealed that the dentist had no anaesthetic and in lieu, prior to each session, he had consumed half a bottle of gin. On being asked about what happened to the remaining gin, the response was that the dentist drank it before he started work on his teeth.

Before departing from Colombo, the local Mission to Seafarers chaplain visited the wardroom with a bag of jewellery. He explained that he was selling the jewellery of a friend at very modest prices, some of which I bought. His friend was a Tamil who had fled the country to Australia because, as a vocal opponent of the governing regime, his life was at risk. Of course, we were not to be aware that such personal tragedies augured the outbreak of civil war in Sri Lanka some 13 years later.

Oberon arrived in Singapore in September, as part of the Seventh Submarine Division and secured alongside the ageing depot ship *Forth*, sister ship of the *Maidstone*. *Orpheus* and *Finwhale* were the two other boats in the division. As in a few months the *Forth* would be returning to the UK, I decided, while in harbour, to live in the wardroom of the shore base, HMS *Terror*, a comfortable, airy, colonial-style building, cooled by overhead fans as opposed to air conditioning. Living in a building with no air conditioning had the benefits of rapid acclimatisation to the heat and humidity of Singapore where it rained most days, with a tropical downpour generally in the afternoon.

The Singapore Naval Base of 1970 was very different in character to my previous experience in 1965, when serving as a midshipman in a destroyer during the height of the Indonesian Confrontation. Then, the Royal Navy had three strike aircraft carriers on station supported by dozens of escorts and smaller warships. The Confrontation had ended later that same year when President Sukarno's power base collapsed and the Indonesian threat faded. Fewer warships were now supported by the dockyard which had been taken over by a civilian entity, Sembawang Shipyard. This company had quickly turned it into a highly efficient and successful commercial ship repair and maintenance facility. Everywhere else it was evident that the Royal Navy was winding its presence down and was in the process of shipping equipment and stores back to the UK.

Being populated predominantly by immigrants from China, Singapore had withdrawn from the Malaysian Federation in 1965 owing to an increasingly 'Malaysia for the Malays' policy which favoured those of Malay origin. This policy had sparked riots in several of Malaysia's major cities in 1969, leaving hundreds dead, most from the minority Chinese communities. However, in late 1970, the region was enjoying peace and prosperity despite the Vietnam War raging with increasing intensity a few hundred miles to the north.

Life in Singapore for the crew of *Oberon* was a far cry from that experienced at home. What was known as 'Tropical' routine was worked in harbour, the crew arriving for work at 0700 in the morning and those not on duty securing at 1230. As there was a shortage of naval married quarters, accompanied Ship's Company members were found rented housing locally. For reasons of economy most of the ratings' families were housed in the Malaysian district of Johor Bahru across the causeway which linked Singapore Island to the mainland. Although living in comfortable houses and sometimes with domestic help, many of the young ratings' wives found their existence in Johor when their husbands were at sea very lonely and boring, with no TV and a lack of family or friends. For this reason, although *Oberon* experienced few disciplinary incidents during her time in Singapore, a large number of family welfare problems occurred, many exacerbated by the tropical climate and refuge being sought in alcohol to counter homesickness.

For myself and my fellow officers, apart from the many attractions of the cosmopolitan city of Singapore only a few miles away, there was an excellent officers' club on the base with swimming pool, golf course and other sports facilities. The wardroom's bachelor officers bought a second-hand ski-boat and I spent many afternoons water-skiing on the flat calm waters which separated Singapore from mainland Malaysia, taking picnics onto the smaller islands or many beautiful beaches. During weekends, when in harbour, there were often trips into the Malaysian jungle to an idyllic, secluded spot with a river pool suitable for swimming fed by a picturesque waterfall. For both officers and ratings it was a very different existence to that of the Clyde Submarine Base, Faslane, with its cool, wet climate and much more onerous demands upon crews, with longer periods spent at sea and fewer port visits. However, this life was rather surreal and, in effect, marked the end of an era. It would be a considerable shock to our systems when we returned to Scotland, where *Oberon* was destined to be based on leaving the Far East.

As there was no naval threat or Soviet presence in the region, the three submarines of the Division were primarily tasked to provide anti-submarine training for the still-substantial number of Royal Navy warships in the area. *Oberon*, acting as a Soviet submarine, was to take part in several major exercises involving large numbers of American and allied warships. There was also a series of 'Showing the Flag' visits to countries surrounding the China Sea. Most of these involved a very crowded cocktail party in the crammed confines of the wardroom and control room, where conversation with people having a limited grasp of English was difficult. On one occasion the Captain hosted a black-tie, candlelit dinner party for a dozen dignitaries in the torpedo compartment, a table being set out between the weapon racks in close proximity to thousands of pounds of high explosive.

While on long surface passages, in calm seas, the opportunity was taken to hold barbeques on the casing or to stop and broadcast 'hands to bathe', keeping a sharp lookout for sharks. In the often calm conditions of the Malacca Straits, if on the surface, the Ship's Company could enjoy watching a film on the casing of an evening. The turned-in fore-planes provided an excellent support for a film screen, enabling movies to be shown under the stars. During one such session, where a John Wayne Western was being shown, arrangements had been made to rendezvous with the cruiser *Blake* to receive a boat-transfer of mail and fresh provisions. This evolution was seen as no reason to interrupt the screening but afterwards one of *Blake*'s officers described how the cruiser's bridge watchkeepers had been puzzled as they approached the rendezvous position, to hear horses' hooves and gunfire echoing across the Straits until they identified the source as *Oberon*.

Two months after arrival in Singapore, I was informed by the Captain that I was to be elevated to the position of First Lieutenant, Second-in-Command. There had been an evident personality clash between him and Nick Beattie who was to be moved to a shore job in the base. With only three years' experience in submarines, I knew I would not have been the Captain's first choice as his 'Number One', but presumed there was no alternative at short notice. Difficult months were to follow as I settled into my new responsibilities and now headed up a wardroom consisting of close friends. However, learning from my *Sealion* experience, I was not afraid of privately challenging the Captain whose judgement on occasions could be eccentric and contentious, particularly with respect to its impact upon his officers. Too often he was guilty of currying favour with the senior rates by openly challenging decisions made in good faith by his officers.

One of the duties of being First Lieutenant of a diesel submarine was the ability to safely move berth in harbour. Having demonstrated that I was capable of doing so, the Captain approved that I undertake future harbour moves. However, he cautioned me to the effect that, if I damaged *Oberon*, it would not only be detrimental to his career but also the well-being of his wife and children. Thereafter, when conducting moves of the boat, I could not help but have the image of the Captain's wife and children wandering the streets destitute. That said, perhaps it had the desired effect as in the many changes of berth I subsequently undertook, I never caused any damage to the submarine.

The Captain was determined that *Oberon* should gain the reputation of having the highest standards of cleanliness and appearance. Among his eccentricities in pursuing this, he insisted that the internal passageways of the boat be scrubbed twice daily and, where there were areas of tiling, such as in the control room, that these be wax polished by machine. Needless to say, this type of cleaning, most unusual in a submarine, did not go down too well with the Ship's Company who viewed it as unnecessary and, indeed, potentially hazardous 'bull'. In event of the submarine adopting a steep angle, clearly a polished deck would be a menace. This, and other unnecessary demands upon the officers and crew, soon brought me into confrontation with my superior and I quickly realised that I had to establish firm boundaries of responsibility and delegation. Despite my comparative lack of experience, I knew that I was on firm ground as Nick Beattie was the second First Lieutenant that the Captain had fired and he would be reluctant to make me a third. That said, we eventually developed a strong and highly beneficial working relationship.

Meanwhile, life had been made easier for me by the appointment of a new Engineer Officer who replaced a stubborn and not very cooperative individual, many years my senior in age. His replacement was an Australian, Lieutenant Nick Hornsby, who besides being a first-class engineer, was excellent company in the wardroom and ashore.

Early in March 1971 while *Oberon* was on surface passage in poor weather conditions in the East China Sea, we recued a racing pigeon, off the south-west coast of Japan. I was on watch on the bridge and spotted the pigeon attempting to land on the top of the fin but in the strong gusty wind conditions, it was finding it difficult. After one aborted attempt, the exhausted bird disappeared behind a large breaking wave and I thought it was a 'goner'. As the submarine went to 'Diving Stations' in preparation for several days of exercises with Japanese ASW escorts, I was relieved on the bridge and took up station in the control room, ready to undertake the diving process.

As the diving klaxon sounded, reports were made that the upper lid was shut and clipped. When the bridge OOW came below I noticed a pigeon's head sticking out from the neck of his wet foul-weather jacket. As he clambered down into the submarine, he had found it resting in an exhausted state just above the upper conning tower hatch. Somehow it had made its way to the inside of the fin. With the sea racing up towards the hatch, it had made no resistance to being picked up and stuffed down the foul-weather jacket. The bird was taken forward to the torpedo compartment and, having been dried off and given some food and water, made a rapid recovery from its ordeal. Within a few hours it had made itself completely at home, flying round the compartment and using the top of one of the torpedoes as a roost.

On the final day of the exercises, the submarine surfaced briefly to embark a party of Japanese admirals and, after a coffee and briefing in the wardroom, I escorted them on a tour round the submarine. On reaching the torpedo compartment the visitors, who had little grasp in English, pointed excitedly to the pigeon and clearly thought it was an emergency communications system. When I reverted to the use of sign language to signify it was a racing bird, their excitement gradually subdued on grasping that the Royal Navy Submarine Service did not embark messenger pigeons.

A day later *Oberon* arrived in the port of Shimonoseki and the pigeon was released, quickly heading off on its interrupted journey home. No doubt a Japanese pigeon racing enthusiast received his bird safely back, albeit the best part of a week late and, of course, with no idea that it had spent several days under the sea in a British submarine.

There had not been a visit to Shimonoseki by a Royal Navy vessel since WW2, and both its civic dignitaries and the local naval community proved outstandingly hospitable and welcoming to the crew. Indeed, the wardroom of only eight officers, together with the crew, were almost overwhelmed by the requirement to provide representation at several high-profile events and participation in a number of sports matches. Perhaps the most memorable occasion was a large reception in the City Hall, attended by several hundred citizens. During its closing phases there was a performance of traditional Japanese singing and dancing. On its completion, the convivial hosts, who had enjoyed generous quantities of sake, demanded that their British guests reciprocate. A number of verses of 'Old MacDonald had a Farm', enthusiastically sung and acted by six *Oberon* officers, had the Japanese audience reeling in fits of laughter.

As *Oberon* departed the port, we were treated to a fly-past of aircraft from the nearby naval air station. The Harvard trainers, with 'rising sun' markings, silhouetted against the morning sunshine, looked suspiciously like WW2 Mitsubishi Zeros. It was a fitting finale to an outstandingly successful visit where our small crew had acted as excellent ambassadors for their country.

Sometimes the exercises *Oberon* took part in involved the clandestine night landing of special forces. One of the most common techniques of doing so was to embark four Royal Marines with two canoes. Surfacing well to seaward of the designated landing spot, the craft and their occupants would be placed on the casing, and the submarine would be submerged underneath them. A raised periscope would then pick up a rope rigged between the two craft and the submarine would tow them towards the shore to a suitable release point, where they were let go by simply lowering the periscope. The recovery process was achieved at a pre-determined rendezvous point in darkness by each of the canoes lowering a simple but distinctive acoustic device which the submarine would home onto using its sonar. Steering between the bearings of the two devices enabled the rope between the canoes to be snagged by the raised periscope and the tow out to sea effected. Communication between canoes and submarine was achieved by using a basic code passed both ways by red torchlight through the periscope lens.

I had to admire the Marines as they headed towards tricky landing spots such as mangrove swamps, which harboured a variety of unpleasant and venomous creatures. In later years some of the 'O' class were fitted with diver lockout chambers in the fin which enabled Marines to be exit the submarine without the need for the submarine to surface. This could be a dangerous operation and one trial involving *Orpheus* resulted in the death of two Marines. The exercise, held in Loch Long, went wrong when the submarine, entering less dense water, suddenly lost her trim and went deep. Her Captain increased speed to regain control and the two Marines, having left their chamber and loaded down with kit, were swept off the casing and drowned, unable to reach the surface.

During one major multinational exercise, *Oberon* embarked eight Marines, who were to be covertly landed at night in the Lingayen Gulf in the north of the Philippines. Their objective was to conduct a beach survey to assess suitability for landing craft operations and thereafter mark the optimum stretch of beach for landing. As *Oberon* approached the entrance to the gulf it was soon evident that it was being heavily patrolled by aircraft and warships. This would make it difficult to penetrate undetected. Therefore, the decision was made that, during the afternoon the batteries would be charged by snorting very near to a beach, making radar or visual detection by aircraft highly unlikely. When dark, we would surface and pass close to the shore of the island of Santiago at the Gulf's north-western extremity, before diving again and running in towards the landing area.

The plan worked perfectly. Snorting only about half mile off the beach we evaded detection by the aircraft, and only drew the attention of a sole fishermen who came out in his dugout canoe to investigate the strange smoking object in the sea. He followed us for some distance paddling a few yards behind the snort induction mast and, indeed, made a strange sight through the periscope. When darkness fell, we surfaced and transited round into the Gulf with a few nerve-racking close passes to fishing huts on stilts, watching in the distance several escorts conducting a futile search on sonar. This type of search would be totally ineffective in detecting a surfaced submarine close inshore. The rest of the operation went to plan. Having eluded the patrolling escorts, we dived and ran into the designated beach area in the south-east of the Gulf. When close inshore, we surfaced and the Marines landed in four canoes. As they paddled towards the shore, they commenced their beach survey, taking soundings using hand lead-lines.

Unfortunately, their survey failed to detect a sandbar some distance from the shoreline. As a result, when the assault force of more than a dozen major ships arrived during the following day, several of the landing craft firmly grounded too far off the shoreline to be able to safely disembark their vehicles and troops. Meanwhile, *Oberon* had changed roles and was now tasked to carry out simulated attacks on the landing force. This we did with absolute ease before departing the Gulf still undetected. It was, therefore, an elated, cock-a-hoop 'Limey' submarine crew which arrived in the vast US Naval Base of Subic Bay for the post-exercise wash-up and analysis.

With the Vietnam War at full intensity, on our arrival in the base it was a sobering sight to witness a US aircraft carrier, fresh from bombing operations, coming alongside for repairs and crew recreation. This was in stark contrast to Singapore Naval Base with its leisurely run-down in preparation for the Royal Navy's imminent withdrawal.

The town of Olongapo adjoined the Naval Base and it was where the US sailor headed for relaxation, drink and female company. It was a notorious town, with raised sidewalks and muddy streets resembling something out of the Wild West, an image reinforced by the heavily armed guards at the entrance to most bars and nightclubs. There were numerous erotic shows and large numbers of prostitutes plying their trade to drunken sailors. Sadly, many of the prostitutes were young girls. All servicemen had to be back in the base by 2300 when its gates shut and after visiting a few bars, a ride in a Jeep-type taxi took the Captain and myself back to the base. He had come to grief slipping off a sidewalk into the filthy mud of the street and badly needed a clean-up. As we approached the bridge spanning a drainage channel in front of the main gate, we saw numbers of young girls in boats underneath the bridge, catching coins tossed to them by returning sailors. We had to admire their skill in netting even the most wildly tossed coin before it reached the water but Olongapo was remembered as a terribly sordid and squalid place, with displays of absolute human depravity.

Meanwhile, on 1 July that same year, the 'A' class submarine *Artemis* had sunk while lying alongside a jetty at HMS *Dolphin*. No one was killed in the incident and the three ratings trapped onboard overnight escaped successfully from the forward torpedo compartment. The sinking was not due to material failure but to the incompetence and slack practices of key personnel who failed to monitor the trim of the submarine during fuelling. This allowed flooding to occur through an open hatch near the waterline. Indeed this incident, where there had been a litany of professional failures on the part of the crew from the Captain downwards, was a severe jolt to the Submarine Service which prided itself in its professionalism. It was a wake-up call at a time when there had been a severe dilution of expertise in diesel boats.

Nevertheless, I did think 'There but for the Grace of God'. I recalled, for instance, that, had *Odin* come to grief when I was alone on the bridge transiting the Dover Straits at night, it would have been revealed that I did not possess a bridge watchkeeping qualification and that the Captain, or at least a qualified OOW, should have been with me. *Artemis* had been in refit at Portsmouth Dockyard at the same time as *Oberon* and, therefore, its officers were well known to the *Oberon* wardroom who on hearing about the event the following day, were highly relieved to hear that no one had been killed.

All too soon the deployment was over and, in September 1971, *Oberon* left Singapore heading west across the Indian Ocean to join the Third Submarine Squadron in Faslane, visiting three South African ports en route, before heading north in the Atlantic. Meanwhile, the remains of the Far East Fleet soon afterwards sailed from Singapore for the last time, so ending a 90-year connection with Sembawang. Most of the remaining barracks and shore buildings were transferred to the Australian Army under a five-power agreement (Australia, New

Zealand, the United Kingdom, Singapore and Malaysia) but with no permanent Royal Navy units in the region.

While on surface passage in the middle of the Indian Ocean, in lively weather conditions with quite a heavy swell running, the Chief Petty Officer responsible for maintenance of the sonar reported his concern about the integrity of the pressure-tight seal on the sonar chamber hatch. The sonar chamber was a separate watertight compartment under the bows, only accessible from the external area of the casing aft of the bows, and there was concern that it might flood. Therefore, the decision was made to dive the submarine to check-out the seal.

The Ship's Company was ordered to 'Diving Stations' in preparation to take the boat under the sea. I was in the control room making final adjustments to the submarine's diving trim. Running on the surface for a prolonged period, the fuel consumed in the external tanks was replaced by much heavier salt water and unless compensation was made to the ballasting of the boat, it would sink like a stone on going under the water.

Therefore, I was concentrating hard on the final ballast adjustments when the Petty Officer in charge of the sonar team came up to me and expressed deep concern for the half a dozen teddy-bears for his children he had stowed in the chamber. I responded that because the poor weather conditions prevented safe access along the external casing to the chamber, sadly the bears would have to take their chances if it flooded. Unfortunately, the Captain overheard this conversation and, very much in character, took a more sympathetic view towards the Petty Officer's children's presents and decided that we ought to make an attempt to rescue them from the chamber.

Therefore, the boat's course was reversed to running down sea, which reduced the risk of waves washing over the casing. Having fallen out from 'Diving Stations', three members of the crew and the Petty Officer, kitted out with life jackets and safety harnesses, gingerly made their way forward to the sonar dome. They then proceeded to remove the access plates to get under the casing into the chamber. Shortly afterwards they emerged triumphantly clutching the teddy-bears, buttoned up the casing plates and made their way precariously back to the fin door. I often wonder, if *Oberon* was being tracked and observed by a Russian submarine, what they would have made of the goings-on. Closing back up at 'Diving Stations', the subsequent short dive proved uneventful and, inevitably, the sonar hatch seal proved fine.

Visits were made to the ports of Durban and East London, in addition to periods alongside for maintenance in Simonstown. However, for the majority of the Ship's Company who wanted to return to the UK as soon as possible to re-unite with their family and loved ones, dallying in South Africa for no sound operational reason, was not a good thing. Consequently, morale deteriorated, resulting in a marked increase in disciplinary cases.

Before *Oberon* departed Durban for Simonstown, I requested permission from the Captain to drive across country and join her on arrival in port. This would give me the opportunity en route to visit relatives who lived in Port Elizabeth. During the drive, I stopped for breakfast in Umtata (Mthatha), the capital of the Transkei, one of the so-called homelands established by the regime of the staunch Afrikaner Prime Minister, Henrik Verwoerd. South Africa at the time was in the grip of a draconian policy of apartheid and the aim of the homelands policy was to provide separate development and settlement for the majority black population. Whilst in Umtata I noticed a news bulletin indicating that scores of individuals had been killed in villages just outside the capital, victims of internecine feuding between rival tribes.

Continuing my journey, not far from Umtata and on a lonely stretch of road, I observed a village on fire about a mile from the road. Stopping the car and getting out to get a closer look and to take photographs, I spotted that there were troops and army trucks adjacent to the settlement. Returning to the car, to my great alarm I encountered about twenty semi-naked women, covered in green mud. They had been hiding in a ditch opposite, and ran towards me yelling. I jumped into the car and, while in a real panic fumbling for my ignition key, they started rocking it and banging the doors. Then suddenly they were gone, running off on the other side of the road. To my great relief the car started immediately and as I sped off, noticing in my rear mirror an army truck approaching. Afterwards someone explained that the women had fled the carnage in their villages and in a terrified state were hiding in the ditch, daubing themselves in mud as camouflage. They had probably wanted to hijack my car to get as far away from the scene as possible. Later in the morning I offered a lift to two hitchhikers – female students – who were also heading to Port Elizabeth and proved pleasant, convivial company – what a contrast!

Meeting *Oberon* when she berthed in Simonstown, I soon learned that the four-day passage from Durban had been blighted by exceptionally stormy weather and I quickly sensed that crew morale was low. While, at other times, a forthcoming passage eastwards back up the coast to visit the city of East London would have very much been welcomed by the crew, on this occasion they saw it as a delaying factor to our return to UK. East London, at the time very much an Afrikaner city, proved highly enjoyable for the officers who were well looked after by the local civic dignitaries. When open to visitors, the submarine attracted unprecedently large crowds but it was a bit of a damp squib for the crew who found it rather dull and boring. Soon it was back to Simonstown naval base for repairs to the main generators and maintenance before heading to Las Palmas and Gibraltar on route to UK. In Simonstown, the officers enjoyed staying in a pleasant family hotel in the seaside town of St James a few miles to the north of the base. The crew were, however, billeted in newly-constructed barrack accommodation rather than the hotels they had become used to. This was yet another unwelcome factor in the deterioration of morale.

In the middle of November, after repairs were completed, including work on the main generators, we finally left Simonstown behind and headed north to Las Palmas. But not for long. Three days out, as the air temperature and humidity increased, the insulation in the main generators started deteriorating and the Captain decided to return to Simonstown for further repairs. This was not a good decision as the insulation deterioration was far from being critical and, within a few days after crossing the Equator, humidity and temperature levels would have steadily improved, with a consequent improvement upon the insulation readings. Clearly the Captain did not fully appreciate the adverse impact of his decision upon the morale of the crew who were faced now with a further two weeks in Simonstown, which had few attractions for them, and the cancellation of visits to the much more attractive ports of Las Palmas and Gibraltar.

Fortunately, a wealthy British expatriate, on learning of *Oberon*'s unexpected return and the severe disappointment of the crew, extremely generously invited all of the crew to his house situated in the beautiful Cape wine-growing area. His offer of hospitality was very willingly accepted and, for several days, he accommodated groups of the crew who enjoyed pool activities, barbeques every evening and unlimited wine and beer. Having never been near a horse before, some of the crew underwent horse-riding instruction before being taken around the stunning surrounding countryside on horseback. It was, therefore, happy and contented groups of sailors who returned to the submarine after their memorable few days in the wine-lands. The outstandingly generous hospitality, provided by an individual who had a great affinity for the Royal Navy, had saved the day.

The 6,000-mile surfaced passage back to the UK passed without further incident. So ended the final deployment of a Royal Navy submarine to the Far East. A year later *Odin* deployed to Australia to be attached to the Australian submarine squadron based in Sydney. *Odin's* three-year deployment, included visits to many ports in the Pacific and China Sea. However, as the Australian Navy built up its own squadron of 'O' class submarines, there was no need for the presence of a British submarine and when the deployment ended, it was not to be repeated. The era of overseas basing of our submarines was over. For my part, I was extremely fortunate to experience visiting many countries, witnessing diverse cultures and enjoying a highly different and more relaxed type of submarining.

Chapter 8

Animals in Submarines

The racing pigeon rescue described in the previous chapter, was my only personal experience of a bird or animal onboard a submarine. In the past Royal Navy submarines had occasionally embarked animals including mice in the early petrol-driven submarines. These served to act as a warning of the presence of noxious gasses. However, perhaps the most well-known case of an animal being at sea in a British submarine, was the reindeer onboard the WW2 'T' class submarine *Trident*.

While on operations fighting German forces in the Arctic Circle, in August 1941 the crew of *Trident* was given a gift of a young female reindeer by a Soviet admiral in Murmansk. The Captain of the submarine (Commander Geoffrey Sladen) had mentioned that his wife had trouble pushing her pram through the snow in England – and the Russian Admiral responded 'What you need is a reindeer!' Because it was a gift, the Captain did not want to seem rude by refusing it.

The reindeer, named Pollyanna by the crew, was embarked into the submarine through the torpedo loading hatch and remained onboard while the boat conducted a six-week war patrol. It was hoped she could sleep in the torpedo compartment. However, she apparently had more refined tastes and insisted on sleeping under the Captain's bunk. One can imagine the scene when the submarine surfaced at night to recharge her batteries and refresh the stale air. Pollyanna, to get some fresh air, would barge her way through the narrow passageways to the main hatch in the control room which would be in red lighting, nudging crew out of the way to get a space under the open hatch.

Living with a reindeer underwater in wartime conditions inevitably posed challenges for the crew. A barrel of lichen given by the Russians soon ran out and Pollyanna lived on scraps from the galley. She developed a taste for the wartime favourite, Carnation condensed milk, and she also ate large quantities of cigarettes.

Despite Pollyanna consuming a navigation chart, the crew made it back to the UK to their base in Blyth in Northumberland. However, as the reindeer had over-indulged on the condensed milk, she had to be slimmed down before being winched out of the torpedo loading hatch. As an aside, a few months later, off Norway early in 1942, *Trident* torpedoed and badly damaged the 15,000-ton German heavy cruiser *Prinz Eugen*.

On being landed, Pollyanna was given to London Zoo where she lived out the rest of the war. She died five years later, ironically within a week of her old submarine, *Trident*, which never did get rid of the smell of reindeer, being decommissioned and scrapped in 1947.

There was also the case of the pet chimpanzee known simply as 'Chimp' who was adopted by an 'A' class boat based in Singapore during the 1950s. Chimp lived in the forward end of the boat's engine room but spent a lot of time with the crew of the stokers' mess right aft in the boat. Somehow it had been fixed that he was on the boat's books for victuals and, therefore, drew a daily rum ration and, on special occasions in the stokers' mess he would be offered sips out of his messmates' rum glasses. However, sometimes these sips were more likely to be large gulps and he consequently would be later found in a quiet corner of the boat suffering from a massive hangover.

He almost came to grief one night when the boat was on the surface and he was on the top of the conning tower with the bridge crew. He was tethered to one of the periscope stands and when the submarine unexpectedly crash-dived he was overlooked until someone noticed he was not at his diving station in the engine room. Fortunately, there was time to reverse the dive, blow main ballast, surface and recover a very wet and miserable Chimp who had received a short but total ducking. Brought down below and dried off, he quickly recovered after receiving a large medicinal tot of rum.

However, this story had a sad ending. When his boat visited Malta on route back to the UK he was gifted to a destroyer based there. Otherwise, on arriving in UK, he would have had to face the rigours and costs of six months of quarantine. But he did not settle into destroyer life and he sorely missed the camaraderie of his submarine mess and his daily rum tot. In the more formal life of a surface ship, being a chimpanzee he was not entitled to a rum ration. One day a submarine came into Malta's Grand Harbour where the destroyer happened to be berthed. Chimp spotted it and, on thinking his beloved submarine had returned, he jumped overboard to swim to the boat, but drowned on the way across.

In more recent times, one of our *Resolution* class SSBNs had a goldfish tank installed in a wardroom bulkhead and at least one US SSBN had a heated tropical fish tank but this could simply have been a cover for an illicit still. It was also known that Commander Joe Williams (later Vice Admiral), when Captain of the US SSBN *Robert E. Lee*, embarked a young terrier for the whole duration of the boat's first deterrent patrol in 1961. The dog was a favourite of the crew but he was inclined to crawl round oily pipework and return to his master's cabin in a state of filth. Hence his nickname Mobo, the then US equivalent of Swarfega, which often had to be applied to the dog's coat to remove the oil. Mobo's submarine career was abruptly cut short when, during the post-patrol handover, he bit the relieving Captain on the ankle. The 1995 Hollywood film *Crimson Tide* portrayed the extreme tensions onboard a US SSBN about to be ordered to launch its weapons during a time of international crisis. The SSBN's highly aggressive Captain, played by Gene Hackman, was accompanied throughout by a protective Jack Russel terrier, a feature almost certainly inspired by the story of Mobo.

Chapter 9

Back to Reality

Oberon arrived at the Clyde Submarine Base in mid-December 1971 to join the Third Submarine Squadron. Several Squadron staff officers had embarked for familiarisation of the boat during the passage up the Clyde Estuary and were delighted to be presented with a hearty breakfast of T-bone steaks and fried eggs. The deep-freeze had been full of the finest of steaks, all illicitly acquired in South Africa, and the shortened passage time from South Africa to the UK had resulted in a surfeit of these. Indeed, some of the crew had complained that they had featured too often on the menu. More seriously, on passage we had been informed that after a few days in Faslane to undertake unloading of weapons and non-essential stores, the boat was heading to Vickers Shipyard at Barrow-in-Furness. There she would undergo a two-month docking and maintenance period which had originally been planned to take place in the submarine base. This was not welcome news for those married members of the Ship's Company whose wives, having moved from Singapore to Faslane in August, now faced further separation from their husbands.

The rather grim Cumbrian industrial town of Barrow was a stark contrast to the bright, vibrant, modern Singapore. Although it had the redeeming feature of being very close to the stunning countryside of the Lake District, many of Oberon's crew found it difficult to adjust to the much longer harbour working hours, the routines of submarine life in northern climes and the loss of their generous overseas allowances. A large proportion of the longer-serving officers and ratings, having done their standard two years of time onboard, were being posted elsewhere but their replacements were nowhere near as competent or committed. In particular, three of the new officers had reputations of unreliability and poor standards of overall performance. For my part, despite having been in post for well over two years, disappointingly I was required to remain for another six months for continuity reasons.

The Captain was also posted elsewhere and, soon afterwards, he achieved his goal of promotion to the rank of Commander and was appointed as Perisher Teacher. He and I had developed into a strong team despite the significant gap in age and seniority between us as well as his eccentricities. He had proved to be a patient mentor and delegator and, particularly at sea, had trained me how to conduct visual attacks against aggressive warships. We were both strict disciplinarians who ran a taut and efficient submarine, where the crew knew exactly what was expected in terms of standards of behaviour and performance. Therefore, I was sorry to say farewell to him and was never able to enjoy the same confidence in or rapport with his replacement.

With no barracks accommodation available in Barrow, it was a major challenge to accommodate the crew ashore in the run-up to Christmas, most being set up in lodgings run by kindly and hospitable landladies. I sorted out accommodation for myself in a remote Lake District cottage, where two of the officers standing by the build of the first-of-class SSN *Swiftsure* were already ensconced. The beautiful countryside surrounding the cottage was a welcome contrast to the industrial grime of the shipyard and I was to spend many a happy weekend there, often joined by a long-standing girlfriend, Linda, who later was to become my wife.

Soon after arrival in Barrow, other challenges and complications became evident. Many of the crew had not had the opportunity while in Faslane to acquire new uniforms to replace items of kit which had either worn out or been lost. Therefore, in the early days at the shipyard, the *Oberon* crew had drawn attention to themselves as being a rag-tag bunch. This was resolved when we managed to get a van-load of uniform items brought down from Faslane. There also had been instances of difficulty of access for *Oberon*'s guests in the few days prior to Christmas, when work had not started and the boat still had to be docked. It had to be impressed upon the Vickers security staff that *Oberon* was not a new build which belonged to the company and it was our decision who was allowed onboard, not theirs.

Perhaps the most serious initial problem was the disposal of the 40,000 gallons of diesel fuel which remained in the boat's tanks on arrival at Barrow. Together with the seawater in the tanks, it was pumped out into contractor's trucks for onward disposal. The local HM Customs and Excise officers had learned about the landing of the fuel and presented the Engineer Officer with a large bill for the relevant duty. This took a bit of resolving but what missed the attention of the authorities was an ongoing racket in Faslane and elsewhere of the so-called sludge from submarine fuel tanks not being disposed of in the correct manner. Instead it was being recycled as pure diesel and sold on at a considerable profit.

In 1971 the Vickers shipyard and engineering works was a vast, sprawling complex which employed over 13,000 people, including those who worked in the gun manufacturing facility. Barrow and Vickers were almost synonymous, most of the town's 80,000 population either working for the company or having a close relative involved in it. The shipyard was a hive of activity with two 'O' class boats being built for the Brazilian Navy and, besides *Swiftsure*, two sister nuclear submarines were in various stages of construction. In addition, the first of the Type 42 destroyers, *Sheffield*, was being fitted out and a small commercial liner was on the stocks. However, in marked contrast to Singapore's Sembawang, the yard was far from efficient: trade demarcation remained rife, the layout and geographic spread of its facilities were not in the least conducive to good working practices and planning/project management procedures were weak. That said, the management and workers exuded a great deal of pride in their work and were scornful of many aspects of the standard of work which had been undertaken during the Portsmouth Dockyard refit.

The early 1970s were a dark chapter in British industrial history with high levels of strikes and stoppages and poor management/ worker relations. In January 1972 there occurred the first of a series of strikes by the National Union of Mineworkers (NUM) which severely interrupted fuel supplies to power stations. The government, led by Edward Heath, in February declared a state of emergency which led to factories and offices being restricted to a three-day working week. This delayed *Oberon's* passage through the repair period, which already had been significantly extended by unforeseen defects and the shipbuilder's inclination to complete the work to a costly gleaming, new-build standard.

During the national state of emergency, frequent planned power cuts occurred which made life challenging for those of us living in the cottage. However, our local inn, the fourteenth-century Farmers Arms at Spark Bridge, lit by candles and oil lamps, remained warm and hospitable and somehow managed to provide hot food. Not that food was an issue as lunch was provided for the wardroom in one of three directors/senior managers' dining rooms in the yard, the three being known as the 'gold, silver and bronze troughs' where even the lunchtime repast was consumed strictly accordingly to seniority. The crew could use a canteen close to the floating dock housing *Oberon*. However, in the evening if they wanted a cooked meal, they had to align with night-shift eating times – steak pie and chips at 2330 was not to everyone's taste.

Oberon eventually left Barrow in April 1972 and started work-up and post-repair trials in the West of Scotland. This was a period of great difficulty for those remaining members of the crew who had enjoyed a halcyon existence in the Far East. While satisfactory results were achieved in the work-up, because of a hard core of troublemakers amongst the crew, morale was fragile. There had been several disciplinary cases exasperated by weak leadership on the part of some of the officers. In particular, in disciplinary matters I found it difficult to work with my new superior whom I viewed as having rather a laissez-faire attitude to standards of crew behaviour. The situation was exacerbated by the boat's new Coxswain, the senior rate with responsibility for crew discipline, who proved a mercurial person of questionable loyalty. Consequently, the three of us made a poor team, with strong tensions between us, which in the confines of the submarine, must have been evident to the crew. These management and leadership shortcomings contributed to an atmosphere of poor spirit and weak motivation within the Ship's Company. In 1972, with four SSBNs in commission, each with two crews, and thirty other submarines needing to be manned, the Royal Navy had to truly scrape the bottom of the barrel in crewing *Oberon*.

Events reached a nadir when the submarine was secured to a buoy in Loch Fyne off the picturesque town of Inveraray, while undertaking trials in a nearby noise-range. Several junior ratings when ashore, having consumed large quantities of alcohol, attempted to acquire the Duke of Argyll's flag flying from the top of the highest tower in his loch-side castle. Breaking a window at ground level to gain entry, one individual severely lacerated his leg on the broken glass and through a combination of loss of blood and the effects of too much alcohol, lay unconscious in the Duchess of Argyll's dressing room. He was followed a short time later by his companions who, ignoring his predicament, attempted to access the tower. When this proved impossible, they gave up their attempt to steal the flag, and instead removed four ancient muskets from the walls of the grand hall. Further damage occurred while leaving the castle when they attempted to remove a cannon from the balustrade surrounding the building, and this ended up damaged in a ditch.

The following day, an urgent signal was received from the Captain of our Submarine Squadron requiring a full investigation into events at the Duke of Argyll's castle the previous evening. The Duke was a personal friend of the First Sea Lord, Admiral Sir Michael Pollock (an ex-Flag Officer Submarines), and consequently severe displeasure had been relayed down the command chain. The situation worsened after a search of the submarine revealed the four stolen muskets which had been brought onboard undetected due to the absence on the casing of the Duty Officer when the liberty boat arrived back from Inveraray. The local police handed the case over for the Royal Navy to deal with and disciplinary proceedings swiftly followed against the miscreants. Against a background of squadron pressure, all of them received severe sentences of detention but *Oberon*'s name had been very much sullied at a high level. All this confirmed my strong opinion that it would have been best to change the entire Ship's Company when the submarine returned from the Far East.

As for the Duty Officer's absence on the casing when the boat arrived alongside with the miscreants and muskets, it was quickly established he was asleep at the time. I advised the Captain that this officer's neglect of duty should be severely sanctioned but instead he took a rather benign position and issued a mild reprimand. Later in this officer's career, he was court-martialled and found guilty of serious negligence in the performance of his duties. This perhaps could have been avoided if, from the outset, he had been robustly managed and mentored by his superiors.

Work-up was followed by several weeks during which *Oberon* was designated the training boat for a class of prospective NATO submarine commanding officers, including Norwegian, Danish and German participants. This commitment gave me further insight into the severe stresses and demands of the Perisher course. In the case of the NATO students, these were intensified by their unfamiliarity with the boat's equipment and the necessity of conducting their attacks, issuing rapid orders in their second language, English.

The boat undertook four weeks of periscope attack training in the Clyde Estuary, returning to a buoy at Rothesay each evening, followed by two weeks of operational exercises, both in the deep ocean and coastal waters. The Teacher had a brilliant intellect, but, sadly, a serious alcohol dependency. Consequently, on more than one occasion, the students were subjected by him to all-night drinking sessions in Rothesay. This made for interesting attacks during the course of the following morning.

During the operational exercise phase, the toilets (called heads in the Navy) became blocked and as earlier clearances methods had not proved successful, there was need for recourse to the drastic procedure of high-pressure air being applied to the sewage tank with the hull valve shut in order to blow back the obstruction. The isolation valve on the waste pipe of one toilet pan would be left open and a cover held down by a stoker to keep the tank contents from blowing everywhere.

Unfortunately, in error, the wardroom head's insolation valve had not been shut and the one Dane participating in the course, having not heard the broadcast that the heads and bathrooms were out of action, was in the officers' head when the blow was applied. The result was that as he was finishing his business and was carrying out the flush, he got completely covered in a vast quantity of pressurised excrement which spewed over the top of the head's door and hit the bulkhead opposite. I recall looking down the passageway from the control room aft, at the brown mess everywhere and, in horror, seeing the wardroom head's door handle slowly turn. There appeared a dreadful effigy, only recognised as the Dane by his light blue eyes and very white teeth.

There was nothing for it but to strip him and hose him down with water and lots of disinfectant in the Senior Rates' bathroom. His uniform had to be disposed of down the garbage ejector. He subsequently passed the course.

This period at sea was to be my last in *Oberon* and I was extremely pleased to hand my responsibilities over to Lieutenant Bill Organ. Because of my somewhat fractious relationship with the Captain and my feeling of isolation from several of the new officers, my last six months in the boat had not been happy ones. Furthermore, *Oberon* was no longer the elite, smart, efficient boat it had been in the Far East and was gaining a reputation for poor discipline. After leave and professional courses, I was destined to join my first nuclear submarine, the brand-new *Swiftsure* which I had eyed enviously some months previously when in Barrow.

Chapter 10

The Silent War

During WW2, the Soviet Union's submarine force had some successes, most notably in the Baltic Sea. In January 1945, during the evacuation from East Prussia and the Baltic States of German forces and civilians retreating from the rapidly advancing Red Army, the Russian submarine *S-13* sank the liner *Wilhelm Gustloff* in the southern Baltic. She was heavily overloaded with refugees and more than 9,000 persons perished, the deadliest maritime disaster of all time.

After the war the Soviet Union embarked upon a construction programme geared towards establishing a very large submarine force. This peaked in the 1970s with a force level of more than 350 boats. The majority of these were diesel submarines of the NATO-designated 'Whiskey' class, over 230 of which were built. In comparison, the German U-boat force had only about forty submarines operational at the outbreak of WW2. Therefore, potentially, the Russian submarine fleet had the capability to cripple the sea lines of communication in the Atlantic and Pacific and to win the war at sea without pursuing an all-out war on land.

To meet this threat, the West built up substantial numbers of ASW forces – ships, aircraft, helicopters and submarines. In 1963, when I joined the Royal Navy, the UK possessed a total of ninety escorts, destroyers or frigates, with a further thirty available in reserve. Additionally, the RAF had a large force of over 150 Avro Shackleton MPA. Other NATO and Allied countries also had impressive numbers of ASW assets, and in particular the USN's order-of-battle included over 600 frigates and destroyers. At the same time, most of the West's submarines were reconfigured for the new, primary role of ASW. This was, in part, driven by the consideration that, in the first two decades after the War, the Soviet surface navy was not assessed as a major threat.

To make them suitable for ASW operations, the majority of the West's conventional submarine hulls were streamlined to reduce flow noise and thus enhance the key characteristic of quietness, making them much less likely to be counter-detected. Low radiated noise would also have the benefit of improved sonar performance.

This programme involved removal of all but the most essential fittings or equipment from the external superstructure of the submarine. In the case of the Royal Navy, all of its immediate post-WW2 'A' class boats had their 4in gun removed but their gun-tower and hatch remained in situ forward of the fin. This allowed boats of this class, which patrolled close inshore during the 1960s Indonesian-Malaysian Confrontation, to be backfitted with this type of gun which was required for self-defence while on the surface. One of these boats, *Andrew*, remained in service until December 1974 when it fired its gun for the last time. This marked the end of the era of Royal Navy submarine gunnery.

A number of WW2 submarines were also enlarged to take bigger main batteries and more powerful main motors. This programme in the USN was known as the Greater Underwater Propulsion Programme (GUPPY) which gave the boats a maximum submerged speed of 15 knots instead of the 8 to 10 knots previously. This increase in speed further improved their anti-submarine capability. 'Guppies' were to remain in service in several navies until the 1980s and indeed the Argentine Navy deployed one of this type (ARA *Santa Fe* ex USS *Catfish*) during the Falklands War. However, with hard-mounted as opposed to noise-insulated diesel engines, the 'Guppies' had the significant disadvantage of being relatively noisy when snorting. The Royal Navy converted eight boats of the wartime 'T' class to GUPPY equivalent performance and several of these were still operational when I joined the Submarine Service in 1967.

Quietness, or stealth, provides the submarine with the ability to approach and deliver an attack upon an enemy submarine completely undetected. As submarines are much less vulnerable to attack than ships and aircraft, they also can be deployed close to enemy bases, where there will be a greater concentration of hostile warships and submarines. A technological race started between the Western Powers and the Soviet Union where each had the aim of gaining and retaining superiority in the undersea confrontation. For the Western Alliance, this was a crucial military goal, because if it lost superiority at sea it is probable that it would have lost the Cold War.

This highly expensive arms race cost the lives of several hundred submariners on both sides of the Iron Curtain as technology was pushed to the boundaries of operational safety. Each side continuously strove for superiority in equipment design and capability, and in operational performance at sea. By the late 1980s, despite committing massive resources, the Soviet Union remained unable to match the West's submarine capability and the costs of this undersea arms race directly contributed to its collapse. Faced with financial bankruptcy and a host of domestic problems, it was impotent to prevent the dissolution of its Eastern European empire and the demise of what had been its all-powerful Communist Party.

In 1955 the world's first nuclear submarine, *Nautilus*, became operational. Because steam was generated from a closed-cycle reactor system, steam propulsion was at last a practical system for the submarine. Indeed, the American-designed nuclear reactor system, in the decades since, has proved highly reliable and boasts an excellent safety record. *Nautilus* introduced a revolutionary change in submarine technology and capability. Fast, manoeuvrable, virtually unlimited in range and with no need to surface or snort, the nuclear submarine completely changed the face of naval warfare. In particular, it demonstrated great potency in the anti-submarine role, and was, therefore, accorded a high priority in both US and UK defence expenditure.

Nevertheless, the modern diesel submarine remains a potent weapon, especially in coastal waters and, of course, is much less costly to build and maintain than the nuclear version. A later chapter will reveal just how difficult it was for *Swiftsure*, at the time the RN's latest SSN, to detect and track a single Soviet 'Whiskey' class diesel submarine which was essentially of WW2 technology. Several classes of the West's modern diesel boats are now fitted with Air-Independent Propulsion (AIP) using fuel cell or other technologies. These can deliver several days duration at slow to moderate speeds without the need to surface or snort. Potential threat nations, such as China, have acquired AIP for their submarines, and present a highly challenging threat to counter.

The first Soviet nuclear submarines were commissioned in 1958 but their reactor plants, although more powerful, were of a much inferior design to their American counterparts. In particular the integrity of their reactor systems was poor and, due to inadequate shielding, their crews were exposed to high levels of background radiation. Another key difference from their Western counterparts was the large number of pressure-tight divisions within the Russian nuclear submarine. These made equipment access and maintenance much more difficult.

In expanding their submarine fleet, the Soviet Navy developed a number of specific types, each with a distinct purpose, all of which had to be countered by the navies of the Western Alliance. In particular, they built both nuclear and diesel submarines armed with anti-ship missiles (abbreviated SSGNs and SSGs respectively). These had the specific role of destroying the West's strike carrier forces. However, the earlier classes of these types had to surface to fire their missiles and, accordingly, were highly vulnerable to attack when preparing for weapon launch.

As the Soviet nuclear fleet expanded, there were numerous submarine classes and designs which paid little heed to achieving the benefits of commonality and standardisation. Quantity rather than quality was pursued and often equipment was sub-standard and poorly assembled, resulting in several incidences of serious fires. The first-generation boats were highly noisy and crude in design and their missiles used extremely hazardous liquid fuel propellant, essentially German V2 missile technology, always risky in a submarine environment. Additionally, their crews were mainly conscripts, often of varied ethnic and language backgrounds and, on the whole, were poorly trained. In summary, the Soviet submarine fleet was affected by a range of serious shortcomings which militated against safe operation and consequently a number of boat losses and major accidents were bound to occur.

In 1959 the United States Navy commissioned its first nuclear ballistic missile submarine (SSBN), the *George Washington*. She was armed with the solid-fuel Polaris ballistic missile system and was followed by forty similar submarines. These were built with an average construction time of less than two years. This starkly compares to the 14 or more years it now takes the UK to build this type of submarine. The US Polaris programme was a tremendous technical and engineering achievement involving large numbers of highly skilled technicians and craftsmen and numerous American companies, both large and small, which collectively successfully contributed to the monumental effort involved. Because the Polaris missile had a maximum range of 2,500 miles, the boats were based in ports which were relatively close to their patrol areas, with facilities being established in the Holy Loch (Scotland), Rota (Spain) and the island of Guam in the Pacific.

In 1962 the Holy Loch squadron of SSBNs deployed on a war alert to their weapon-launch positions in response to the Cuban Missile

Crisis. The establishment of American nuclear missile sites in Turkey was, to the Soviet psyche, a close pressing of its borders – a threat that it countered by beginning to put in place launch sites for nuclear-armed missiles in Cuba. The Soviets intended that these sites be established and achieve operational status undetected, but on 14 October 1962 a U2 reconnaissance aircraft, overflying Cuba, photographed several of the sites under construction. Analysis quickly revealed that these were intended for the installation of Soviet medium and intermediate-range ballistic nuclear missiles. The majority of the USA's eastern cities were therefore brought into their range, with a minimum warning time of attack. Two days later, President John Kennedy was briefed about this new, highly significant, strategic threat.

Despite bellicose advice from his senior military advisers, Kennedy decided upon the quarantine of Soviet ships entering Cuban waters, would be the 'Most probable action to have the best probable outcome'. Amongst other factors, he was very aware that an attack upon Cuba might, at the least, result in a Soviet take-over of West Berlin. At worst, it could invoke a pre-emptive nuclear strike upon the USA. Later evidence revealed that this was what the Cuban leader, Fidel Castro, strongly advocated to his Soviet masters.

On 26 October, the quarantine was put into effect and the US military alert was raised to Defcon 2 – 'Prepare for Nuclear War'. In response, the five Polaris submarines on patrol took up their firing positions in the Norwegian Sea. Two further boats, which were alongside the tender *Proteus* in the Holy Loch, prepared for sea and departed on a war footing within 24 hours. Once they had slipped, *Proteus* got underway and headed out to sea to avoid presenting herself as a possible target. Of note, one of these boats – the *Ethan Allen* – had, earlier in the year, fired a 600-kiloton nuclear-armed missile which travelled over 1,000 miles to a target area to the north-east of the Solomon Islands. This successful firing of a warheaded Polaris missile was the only one of its kind, and has not been repeated with the current in-service Trident missile system. Undoubtedly the Soviet leadership would have been briefed about this emphatic demonstration of US submarine-launched ballistic missile capability.

While the USN now had seven Polaris boats on station in the Atlantic, there were none in the Pacific. However, there were three Regulus missile-firing boats on patrol in the north-west Pacific. These had a total of eight nuclear warheads, targeting Soviet Pacific harbour infrastructure but the missiles were liquid-fuelled and required the boats to surface for launch. Commander William Gunn, Captain of one of these boats – *Grayback* – recalls receiving the alert to prepare for firing. 'We went to "Battle Stations Missile" and checked out all missiles. Then we remained on alert for the next two weeks, ready to shoot ... And you know we had the feeling that this is what we are supposed to do, and this is it, and we are here, and if it happens, we are the people who are going to execute it.'

On 27 October, Robert Kennedy, the US Attorney General and the President's right-hand man during the crisis, met with the Soviet Ambassador in Washington, and offered a top-secret deal to peacefully end the standoff. The USA pledged to withdraw its intermediate nuclear missiles from Turkey and not invade Cuba if the Soviets agreed to remove their nuclear missiles from Cuba. However, Kennedy issued a verbal warning that if the missiles were not withdrawn, the sites would be attacked.

The following day, Soviet Premier Nikita Khrushchev at last acknowledged the presence of the missiles, having previously denied this. Against the background of the USA's very robust stance, and aware of, at the time, the overwhelming strength of the USA's nuclear arsenal, he agreed to the withdrawal of the missiles and ordered his transport ships heading to Cuba to put about. Nuclear war had been averted and the world stepped back from the brink of many millions of its peoples being killed. Meanwhile, the USA's strategic forces remained on high alert until late November, by which time there had been incontrovertible evidence of the Soviet withdrawal of missiles from Cuba.

Of note, the USN deployed over 150 warships and support vessels in effecting the quarantine. However, by the time the quarantine was put in place, the majority of the missiles and their warheads had already been disembarked into Cuba. Until there was firm evidence of their removal, the US military continued with plans to attack and invade Cuba, if necessary, deploying tactical nuclear warheads in the process.

Prior to the detection of the missile sites, the Soviets had deployed four 'Foxtrot' class diesel submarines to the seas surrounding Cuba. Each boat's armament included one nuclear-tipped torpedo. Their Captains had discretion to use these weapons if attacked by US vessels. Three of the four boats were detected and tracked by US ASW forces during the enforcement of the quarantine. To coerce them to reveal themselves and surface, Practice Depth Charges (PDCs) were dropped onto them. Information had been passed to the Soviets regarding the use of these charges to signal that the submarine must surface. But this information was not passed to the submarines.

The PDCs contained only a small amount of explosive, but on detonating under the water they made a loud report. In the dreadful conditions onboard the submarines, with temperatures almost reaching 50° C, oxygen levels low and the propeller and sonar sounds of numerous anti-submarine warships above them, such explosions were bound to be extremely unnerving. Subsequent evidence has revealed that two of the 'Foxtrot' Captains, their stress levels almost at breaking point, seriously considered firing their nuclear torpedo at the harassing forces. In *B130*, the Captain was persuaded by his political officer not to do so. In *B59*, the situation was more serious, with its Captain ordering the weapon to be prepared for launch. Fortunately, onboard was the overall commander of the four boats, Captain Vasily Arkhipov, who overruled the instructions to prepare the weapon. No doubt self-preservation came into the decision-making process: the torpedo's 15-kiloton nuclear detonation could have caused lethal damage to the firing submarine. Nevertheless, had a nuclear weapon been used, and USN ships been destroyed, the inevitable American retaliation might have led to total war. Arguably, this was the closest the two Cold War superpowers came to a nuclear exchange.

It is difficult to establish why the Soviets did not deploy nuclear-missile armed submarines (the SSG 'Golf' class or the SSBN 'Hotel' class) to the Cuban area, but low machinery reliability and missile fuel instability may have been prohibiting factors. In the event, two nuclear-missile armed SSGs of the 'Zulu' class were deployed, pennant numbers *B75* and *B88*. The former was ordered back to Murmansk when on transit to Cuba, but the Pacific-based *B88* spent several days patrolling off Pearl Harbor.

To the Soviets, the crisis highlighted the limitations of their existing naval power and under the stewardship of the head of their navy, Admiral Sergei Gorshkov, they thereafter built a navy capable of global power projection, spearheaded by a force of nuclear submarines, which peaked in numbers and capability in the late 1980s.

Following the commissioning of *Dreadnought* in 1963 the UK began to build up a force of nuclear submarines which peaked at twenty hulls in the late 1980s. The development of the British nuclear submarine is described in the next chapter. This ambitious building programme absorbed a major proportion of the defence equipment budget and, contentiously, was at some cost to the remainder of the Royal Navy. In particular, there were limited resources available to expend on air defence for the Fleet, including its anti-aircraft missile systems and carrier-embarked fighter aircraft. This vulnerability was to be emphatically demonstrated in the Falklands War of 1982 when the fragility of the Royal Navy's air defences resulted in the loss of important ships. These losses severely prejudiced the conduct of the operation and much threatened its successful outcome.

By the 1960s the SSN, the nuclear attack submarine, had established itself as the West's premier means of countering the Soviet submarine threat. Stealthy, and fitted with first-rate listening sonars, they were to have marked acoustic superiority over their Soviet opponents. A further big advantage to the West was the highly classified Sound Surveillance System (acronym SOSUS). This consisted of listening and tracking acoustic arrays established on the seabed of those areas of the deep oceans which were of strategic importance. SOSUS exploited an acoustic phenomenon known as the deep sound channel. It was capable of detecting the presence of a potentially hostile submarine over immense distances, sometimes exceeding thousands of miles on early classes of Soviet nuclear submarines. Nevertheless, it had its weaknesses. It was not feasible to operate it in shallower or more confined seas, such as the Mediterranean, and it could have been easily destroyed or debilitated in war. Furthermore, its contact positional data normally covered a large geographic area. In consequence, precisely determining the location of a SOSUS contact by anti-submarine forces could take a long time, sometimes without success.

When in the 1970s the West's SSNs were fitted with passive listening sonars towed astern on long arrays, British and American boats gained the ability to make long-range acoustic detections of Soviet submarines, sometimes at over 100 miles. The towed array particularly utilised the detection of specific frequencies emitted by the latter's engines and auxiliary machinery. Theses emissions were known as frequency 'tonals'. On the other hand, the ability of Russian submarines to detect their American or British counterparts was very limited. This enabled the West's SSNs to follow or, in the jargon, trail, Soviet nuclear submarines for prolonged periods undetected, sometimes for weeks or even months. Trailing of Russian SSBNs was a priority because it both gathered intelligence on their mode of operations and, in the event of hostilities, gave the pursuing submarine the ability to destroy its quarry before it was able to launch a nuclear strike. But the boot was occasionally on the other foot. Soviet counter-detections did occur if the trailing submarine inadvertently got too close. In such situations the Russian submarine commander could become aggressive, turning directly towards the following submarine and making use of speed and active sonar to harass the hunter – now turned prey. Such a manoeuvre was known as a 'Crazy Ivan'.

For their own part, the Soviets explored different avenues of submarine technology. In the 1970s they introduced the 'Alfa' class SSN. Highly automated with a small crew (about 40 instead of the 120 typical in British or American nuclear submarines), the 'Alfa' was much faster than its Western counterparts. With its high-power liquid-metal cooled reactor, it had a maximum speed of over 40 knots, while its titanium hull enabled it to dive to more than twice the operating depth of the West's deepest diving submarines. However, the liquid-metal cooled reactor proved difficult to maintain and was to experience severe technical problems. There were also penalties in respect of safety and the quietness of the propulsion plant. Furthermore, the titanium hulls were immensely costly and, given all these shortcomings, this class of boat was not considered successful.

What they could not develop themselves, the Soviets sought through espionage. Notably a Soviet spy ring at the UK's Portland Underwater Research Establishment in the early 1960s acquired highly classified submarine sonar technology. Possibly the most damaging espionage was that gained through the Walker/Whitworth spy ring operating in the United States from 1968 to 1985. These individuals, being naval communications specialists, were able to select and pass highly secret signal traffic to the Soviets, in the process revealing the extent of the West's huge acoustic and anti-submarine superiority. In response, the Russians undertook a noise-quieting programme in their newest classes of submarines as a matter of the highest priority. Later Russian submarine classes were consequently much quieter and the West's marked acoustic advantage eroded from the mid-1980s onwards. Indeed, at the time of writing, the latest type of Russian SSBN, the 'Borei' class, is proving highly difficult to detect and track.

From the late 1940s, the United States Navy deployed submarines on intelligence gathering operations in the seas off the main Soviet naval bases in the Barents Sea and in the Western Pacific in the Sea of Okhotsk and off the port of Vladivostok. Very importantly, submarines operating covertly in the midst of Soviet naval forces provided hard intelligence which could not be gained by satellite surveillance. A priority objective was to record the acoustic signature of new classes of Soviet submarines or warships, highly important information in respect of designing or tuning the West's sonar systems to achieve maximum ranges of detection.

Another key factor was that, unaware of the intelligence-gathering submarine's presence, the Soviets undertook weapon tests which otherwise they would not have carried out in the overt presence of a NATO warship or aircraft. Besides gathering information on Soviet weapons and tactics, an overall objective of these operations, both in the Barents and Pacific, was to provide early warning of a military build-up which could be a precursor to hostilities.

During intelligence-gathering missions, some occurring at extremely close range, it was inevitable that collisions happened, particularly between two dived submarines. These may have amounted to no more than a glancing blow, but sometimes severe damage was inflicted. Despite these high risks, no submarine has been lost in this way, nor is it believed that any fatalities have been incurred. Nevertheless, an unexpected underwater collision is an extremely alarming experience to those involved.

The Royal Navy started to participate with the United States Navy in the Barents Sea operations in the 1950s and, in due course, extended their intelligence-gathering to Soviet naval forces in the Baltic and Mediterranean. Initially diesel boats undertook this task and found that the long snort passage to the Barents Sea had its own challenges. In the winter months their crews incurred the stress of prolonged periods at periscope depth conducting surveillance in conditions of near permanent darkness and living in damp, cold crew spaces. The control room watchkeepers worked in an almost totally dark environment, the only illumination being their faintly red-lit systems and equipment dials. To allow their eyes to quickly adjust to darkness, off-watch officers endured living in constant red lighting in their wardroom for weeks on end. Added to this, the seas in these northern latitudes were often extremely violent. This made depth-keeping challenging and constant severe rolling made life difficult and exhausting for the crew.

Events which occurred during these operations still remain highly classified, tightly controlled and not discussed even within the submarine community. However, inevitable leaks of information occurred from time-to-time, for example the already-related presence of *Sealion* off Nova Zemlya in the early 1960s to gather information on Soviet nuclear bomb tests. This data was used to determine the detonation yield and levels of radiation arising.

In 1968 a Royal Navy SSN was, for the first time, committed to Barents Sea operations. Unlike the USN, the Royal Navy designated a single specially-equipped submarine for the task, rather than rotating the role amongst the most modern SSNs. Fitted with specialist listening and observation devices, this practice allowed the nominated British submarine crew to build up expertise in intelligence-gathering in these Arctic waters, while avoiding the additional costs incurred in rotating the equipment fit between boats.

One of the first British SSNs on this task was *Warspite*. In October 1968, she was involved in a collision with a Soviet 'Echo' class missile submarine. This caused severe damage to her fin. After calling in to Lerwick in the Shetland Islands to make efforts to hide the damage, *Warspite* limped back to Faslane. The cover story was that she had hit an iceberg. Subsequently, at Vickers shipyard in Barrow for repairs, it was observed that it had been a strange iceberg as the fin damage revealed quantities of phosphor bronze, the material used to make submarine propellers.

In due course, *Warspite* was replaced by *Courageous* as the designated and specially-fitted submarine for operations in the Barents Sea. After *Courageous* there had always been at least one *Swiftsure* or, subsequently *Trafalgar*, class boat designated for Barents Sea intelligence gathering operations. No doubt the *Astute* class, now coming into service, will be continuing this role.

Apart from the gathering of exclusive intelligence, the experience gained in these patrol operations provided NATO nations' submarine crews with invaluable training, while demonstrating the West's will and ability to successfully confront Russian naval forces in war. Indeed, it is remarkable to consider that the West's submarines were the only element of its military forces which, during the Cold War, operated so close to Soviet forces, in some cases within 15ft while undertaking underwater hull surveys. These procedures required absolutely precise depth keeping and stationing underneath the intelligence target ship or surfaced submarine. Needless to say, they demanded nerves of steel on the part of the submarine's control-room team. At post patrol debriefings, dramatic film footage such as close-range observations of Soviet missile firings or views of the underwater hull fittings of a new class of Soviet warship, had British senior officers and Government Ministers absolutely spellbound. However, the lack of a capable weapon to destroy the warships or submarines filmed was conveniently forgotten or not discussed.

By the 1970s the Soviet Navy was much larger, more capable and had truly global reach. Besides maintaining a substantial permanent naval force in the Mediterranean, with normally a large number of naval warships anchored off Libya, the Russians periodically deployed significant numbers of submarines into the Atlantic. These operations demonstrated projection of seapower and potentially sought out NATO SSBNs. The Soviet Union also established a network of intelligence-gathering auxiliaries, known as AGIs, stationed off naval bases of interest. These invariably shadowed Western naval forces when they were undertaking major exercises. As mentioned previously, one such auxiliary was normally stationed on the likely SSBN transit routes off Malin Head, the most northern point of Ireland.

The Russians also embarked upon a comprehensive oceanographic research programme gathering extensive hydrographic and ocean features information, constructing and operating a large number of oceanographic research vessels to achieve this. Besides enhancing the ability of their own submarines and ships to exploit the environment to the best strategic and tactical advantage, the programme potentially offered methods of detecting the West's submarines other than by acoustics, including wake detection or disturbance of the sea's micro-organic structure. However, achieving successful detections using such methods was to remain elusive.

With the advent in the 1980s of the massive 26,000-ton Soviet 'Typhoon' class SSBN, armed with missiles of greater range, the Soviets started to withdraw their ballistic missile submarines from the Atlantic to home waters into so called bastions – specifically protected areas including under the Arctic ice pack. On the West's part, with the introduction of the much longer-range Trident missile, America began to close its forward SSBN bases and, in 1992, ended its presence in the Holy Loch.

These changes marked a new period of Cold War submarine operations. An expensive nuclear weapons strategic stalemate seemed to guarantee the peace of the world as the post-WW2 submarine pioneering days passed into memory. Nevertheless, these had been remarkable.

Throughout the Cold War, both sides were pushing the bounds of technology and submarine crews were often operating under great pressure. Consequently, serious accidents were bound to occur, either through material failure or human error. As stated earlier, in 1950 *Truculent* sank after a collision in the Thames Estuary with heavy loss of life and in 1951 *Affray* sank in the English Channel taking with her the entire crew. In August 1949 the first of the American intelligence-gathering operations in the Barents Sea ended with loss of life when the diesel boat *Cochino*, in stormy seas and in company with her sister vessel the *Tusk*, suffered a battery explosion. *Cochino* subsequently sank and seven crewmen died during the rescue operation by *Tusk*.

The incident emphasised the unforgiving environment of the stormy North Norwegian and Barents Seas.

The United States Navy lost two SSNs and their entire crews in the 1960s – *Thresher* in 1963 and *Scorpion* in 1968. *Thresher* had emerged from refit, and was undertaking trials in the Western Atlantic, when she suffered a major flood from a fractured seawater pipe in the engine room. With the reactor out of action and no propulsion available, the submarine sank well below its safe operating depth and imploded at a depth of over 2,000ft. Mercifully, the hull collapse would have occurred within a fraction of a second and the crew would have not suffered.

Although the wreck of *Scorpion* has been located in 9,000ft in mid-Atlantic, the cause of her loss remains uncertain. The most likely explanation is that a battery explosion caused disablement of the control room team. This would have resulted in loss of control and the hull of the boat imploding as it sank below its collapse depth of 1,500ft. Similar to the *Thresher* loss, those of her crew who had survived a battery explosion would have died instantly at the point of implosion.

As stated above, the Soviet submarine force was large and had many different classes of submarine, most of which embarked weapons which had hazardous features. Furthermore, its crews were often poorly trained and inexperienced. In November 1970 the Russians lost a 'November' class SSN in the Bay of Biscay. This was the first of several of their nuclear submarines to sink, adding to the post-war loss of six diesel submarines.

As well as outright losses of Russian submarines, sometimes involving the death of the entire crew, many serious accidents occurred where considerable numbers of the crew perished. Often these accidents involved many of the crew being subjected to high levels of radiation and, owing to the onset of radiation sickness, subsequently becoming seriously ill or dying. Evidently the life of the Russian submariner was considered to be somewhat cheap.

Perhaps one of the most dramatic losses was that of the SSBN *K219*, some 600 miles north-east of Bermuda in 1986. *K219* suffered a missile explosion when fuel leaking from one of the missiles came into contact with seawater. The missile effectively ignited in its tube, blowing the hatch open, spilling out its nuclear warheads, and killing several of its crew. The submarine subsequently surfaced but it was so badly damaged by the explosion that it sank a few days later in deep water, taking its remaining fifteen missiles and warheads with it. Two years after *K219*'s sinking, the Russians dispatched a survey ship to investigate the wreck using a deep-dive mini-submarine. *K219* was discovered sitting upright on the seabed but it is rumoured that the Americans had got there first and its missile hatches were open, the missiles and their warheads gone.

With the break-up of the Soviet Union, the Russian Federation submarine-building programme all but halted. However, since 2000 Russia has been constructing high-quality submarines and warships, although its navy is a shadow of its former self in terms of numbers. The old Soviet submarine force is now a big environmental hazard, with nuclear-contaminated submarine hulks dumped in many places including the Kara Sea. At the time of writing, Russia operates about 60 submarines – down from the 350 or so at the height of the Cold War. Nevertheless, capable and potent vessels are being commissioned and they do offer a serious threat to the West's naval forces.

The Royal Navy also now has a much smaller planned submarine force of four SSBNs and seven SSNs, compared to the thirty boats it had in 1989. This small force is still highly capable and the Tomahawk cruise missile has given British SSNs a new role of land attack in recent conflagrations such as Iraq, Kosovo and Libya. Meanwhile, the British Government is committed to replacing the four current Trident-armed SSBNs as they come to the end of their lives in the early 2030s. However, for a variety of reasons, including significantly protracted build times, construction costs are increasing almost exponentially.

On the American side, many submarine bases have been closed or downsized. From its peak level in the 1980s of forty SSBNs and ninety SSNs, at the time of writing the United States Navy has contracted to fourteen *Ohio* class SSBNs and about fifty-five SSNs including four *Ohio* class boats converted to launch Tomahawk missiles. As in Britain, submarine construction and equipment costs have risen significantly and issues of affordability cast doubt on whether even this force level will be sustainable in the future.

For the foreseeable future, the West's nuclear deterrent will primarily be vested in SSBNs. In addition, its submarine forces continue to conduct operational patrols, monitoring and intelligence-gathering among the naval forces of potential threats, such as Iran and China, as well as maintaining a watch on Russian activities.

For myself, during my submarine career, I was to experience being in sonar contact with over twenty Soviet submarines and was in relatively close proximity, undetected, to more than a dozen of these. However, I was to have no visual sight of their hulls, let alone members of their crew. My experience was confined to the view of vertical lines on a sonar screen or, at closer range, listening to their machinery or propeller noises on a set of headphones. It was only late in my career, that at a reception in the British Embassy, Havana, Cuba, I actually met a Russian submariner. He had been Captain of a 'Victor' class SSN and, in conversation with him, I learned that he had undergone many similar problems and challenges to those I had faced. During my career, I had developed a degree of respect for the Russian submariner's courage and resilience in going under the sea in unreliable and sometimes dangerous vessels.

Chapter 11

The British Nuclear Submarine

In 1958, three years after the commissioning of USS *Nautilus*, the USA agreed to provide nuclear submarine technology to the UK. Admiral Hyman Rickover, who had very much driven the introduction of nuclear power in the USN's submarine force and who headed the USN's naval reactors programme, took a lead in delivering this commitment. Subsequently, in 1963 the Royal Navy's first nuclear submarine *Dreadnought* completed build and was commissioned at Vickers Shipyard, Barrow-in-Furness. Incidentally this was the same year that I joined the Royal Navy.

Displacing 3,500 tons, *Dreadnought*'s hull design was based upon the USN *Skipjack* class, and her SW5 Pressurised Water Reactor (PWR) and propulsion plant was provided by the US company, Westinghouse. Her turbines delivered 15,000 Shaft Horse Power (SHP) which gave her a top speed of 30 knots. Notably, this type of reactor has been operated for many decades by the USN and Royal Navy, without a serious accident occurring. *Dreadnought*'s commissioning officers and crew had been hand-picked and many of the key personnel had been trained in the USN, including sea-time in boats of the *Skipjack* class.

However, after *Dreadnought* commissioned, Rickover pulled down the shutters on any further exchange of nuclear propulsion technology to the UK. His reasoning was that this would ensure the Royal Navy developed its capability to independently maintain and operate its submarine nuclear plants, without continued reliance upon the USN. Nevertheless, the Admiral's subsequent rigorous enforcement of this policy contrasted markedly with the USN's very strong support and cooperation in the delivery of the Polaris, and subsequently Trident, ballistic missile systems to the UK.

As *Dreadnought* began to participate in Fleet exercises, despite being noisy at speed, she emphatically demonstrated that she was extremely difficult to detect and track. In particular, her speed gave her the ability to repeatedly conduct successful attacks on a force of surface ships with almost absolute invulnerability. This demonstrated clearly to the Board of Admiralty that the Royal Navy and NATO were confronting a major threat from the growing numbers of Soviet nuclear submarines. Subsequently the UK embarked on an SSN building programme which, by the Fall of the Berlin Wall in 1989, had culminated in a force level of seventeen SSNs, in addition to four SSBNs and about a dozen diesel boats in service.

In 1962 the first all-British designed SSN, *Valiant*, was laid down at Vickers and, four years later, commissioned. She and her successors were powered by the British PWR1 reactor which closely resembled the SW5 in design and characteristics. She was fitted with arguably the most advanced sonar system in the world, which had an excellent passive listening mode complimented by a powerful active transmission facility. Her primary navigation method relied upon the Ships Inertial Navigation System (SINS). This is a complex gyroscopic platform which provides a continuous accurate position of the submarine, albeit it does require periodic updates using satellite or seabed contour data. SINS has been installed in all subsequent British nuclear submarines with later versions proving more reliable and accurate than the first fits.

Valiant and follow-on vessels of her class were soon to demonstrate remarkable operational achievements. Unlike *Dreadnought*, her main machinery was mounted on insulated rafts to reduce emitted noise and, for the times, she was considered quiet, with radiated noise levels similar to contemporary US SSNs such as the *Sturgeon* class. However, her machinery spaces were much more complex and cramped than *Dreadnought*'s, making access for repair difficult. She and the four other boats of this class would in the future prove challenging to refit, maintain and operate.

In the event of a reactor shut down at sea, known as a 'Scram', in the *Valiant* class, a large battery provided power to enable re-starting of the reactor and to drive an electric motor fitted on the main shaft which could deliver speeds of up to 6 knots. When the boat reached periscope depth or surfaced, two diesel generators would deliver electric power to take over from the battery. If the shaft or propeller were rendered inoperable, then a small trainable propulsor, known as the 'egg-beater' could be lowered, but it could only deliver about 3 knots of speed. In practice, its main benefit was to assist berthing alongside.

Dreadnought had a safe operating depth of 750ft which left little scope for error. In any severe bow-down situation, arising from a plane jam or other such emergency at speed, she could exceed her safe depth within 20 seconds. Furthermore, when large amounts of rudder were applied at higher speeds, she was liable to the severe effects of a phenomenon known as a 'snap roll'. This was as much as 40 degrees of lean into the turn caused by the relatively large fin (known as the 'sail' in the USN). As rudder was applied, as a matter of course, the after-planesman had to apply full rise on his planes, to keep the now-canted fin from having the effect of a huge hydroplane set to dive, causing a big down angle. Snap roll would remain a characteristic in future British SSNs.

During early high-speed manoeuvring trials to assess the effects of 'snap roll', the US submarine *Scorpion* developed more than 50 degrees of simultaneous roll and down angle within a few seconds of maximum rudder angle being applied. This extremely dangerous situation required urgent action by the Captain who ordered emergency blowing of the main ballast tanks and full-astern power. One of the submarine's officers later recounted: 'Some people are alleged to have woken up in different bunks than they were in originally, and many bits of crockery smashed into the deck-heads. Don't know the maximum depth reached, but almost certainly it exceeded test depth.' This episode served to demonstrate that at speed, several thousand tons of nuclear submarine could adopt some of the characteristics of an aircraft without its normal significant margin of safety between it and the ground. On the other hand, during this particular event, the reactor did not miss a beat. *Dreadnought* was very similar in hull shape to *Scorpion*.

In 1960 the first American SSBN, *George Washington*, conducted a successful launch of Polaris ballistic missiles and later on that year deployed on its first strategic deterrent patrol. The nuclear submarine hereafter had a new role of delivering nuclear strategic deterrence. The West's SSBNs had the ability to hide in the deep ocean, virtually undetectable. This made the SSBN the ultimate invulnerable nuclear deterrent system, guaranteeing a counter-strike in event of a nuclear attack. Such capability significantly enhanced and reinforced the concept of nuclear deterrence, and the Polaris system, and its Poseidon and Trident missile successors, became the bedrock of US Nuclear Deterrence Strategy.

Shortly after the December 1962 Nassau agreement, the Royal Navy Polaris Executive was set up under the leadership of Rear

Admiral Rufus MacKenzie. Its great success in delivering the Polaris project on time was an absolutely outstanding British training, technical and engineering achievement. Amongst many challenges, including fending off the Air Ministry's demands to run the project, it required the two build shipyards, Vickers in Barrow-in-Furness and Cammell Laird in Birkenhead, to be dragged into the twentieth century in practising, for the first time, rigorous planning and project-management procedures. The procurement of high-quality steel for the submarine pressure hulls also required the inclusion of molybdenum in the steel production process. Curiously, this material had to be sourced from the Soviet Union.

To MacKenzie's great disappointment, the Labour government which came to power in 1964 cancelled the contract for the planned fifth hull (which was to be named *Royal Sovereign*) as principally a political rather than a financial savings measure. In later years, the fragility of maintaining one boat at sea with only two boats available for patrol out of a force of four, was to be starkly exposed.

From a standing start in 1963, when no RN nuclear submarines were in service, *Resolution*, the first British Polaris boat, set off on her first patrol in 1968. Despite being twice the displacement of the *Valiant* class, in this very short timescale she had been designed, built, completed sea trials and work-up. Moreover, both her crews had successfully completed Demonstration and Shakedown Operations (DASO) which included Test Missile firings at Cape Canaveral. Naturally this required the full cooperation and committed support of the USN to achieve this extremely demanding programme. The following three boats, *Repulse*, *Renown* and *Revenge*, were commissioned at yearly intervals and made up the Tenth Submarine Squadron.

Resolution's reactor was also of the PWR1 design, and her main machinery compartments were only a little more spacious that than of *Valiant*, making maintenance and upkeep similarly challenging. Each of the *Resolution* class boats had sixteen missile tubes loaded with the Polaris A3 missile, which could deliver three warheads to a maximum range of 2,500 miles. The submarines also carried a conventional torpedo outload consisting of the pre-WW2 Mark 8 anti-ship torpedo and the ineffective Mark 23 weapon system for protection against submarine threats. At 2024 prices *Resolution* had cost about £700 million to build – a fraction of the cost of the replacement Trident submarines, the *Dreadnought* class – which are likely to involve an outlay of more than £4 billion per hull.

By 1970 the four SSBNs were in commission, with fully trained strategic weapon system specialist departments and dual manned by eight crews. To meet this remit, a significant number of senior rating weapons and engineering specialists were transferred from the surface fleet. Many of them were not volunteers but invariably they became committed and enthusiastic submariners, although the eligibility for attractive rates of submarine pay, no doubt had a bearing. All the SSBN crews had successfully completed their DASO missile firings at Cape Canaveral, which certified the crews as being fully capable of operating the Polaris weapon system and demonstrated that it was comprehensively functioning to specification. As a follow-up, on commencing their routine operational cycle, the crews were subject to unannounced Nuclear Weapon Inspections when alongside. The identification of serious personnel failures in these inspections could lead to disciplinary measures, including dismissal.

During the seven years it took to complete the Polaris procurement project, four SSNs and seven *Oberon* class SSKs also came into service. Additionally, British shipyards delivered a further seven *Oberon*s to the Canadian and Australian navies. This substantial submarine building capability has long since markedly diminished.

In the same timescale, over 100 engineer officers had to be trained and qualified to operate and maintain the nuclear steam plants. In parallel, much greater numbers of nuclear systems specialist senior rates also needed to be trained. This requirement posed a significant challenge from both a manning and training perspective but also demanded a dramatic – and sometimes painful – culture shift away from the somewhat buccaneering approach of the old conventional submarine days. Notwithstanding, the technical challenges of this new fighting arm attracted many and there was no shortage of high-quality volunteers.

Across the Atlantic, the USN had met a similar scale of national challenge in building, manning and commissioning its forty-one Polaris submarines during the period 1958 to 1967. To achieve this, great pressures and tight disciplines were applied to the build programme and, remarkably, one boat – the *Casimir Pulaski* – was completed at Electric Boat, Groton, Connecticut, in 18 months from laying-down to commissioning.

Swiftsure commissioned in April 1973, some six months before I joined her. First of a class of six SSNs, she was considerably more capable than *Valiant* and her sisters. She more than matched the contemporaneous USN's *Los Angeles* class which was delivered in large numbers from 1975 onwards. The *Swiftsure*s were designed to have much less pipework exposed to seawater pressure. In addition, a powerful emergency ballast tank blow system was fitted with features which were derived from the lessons learned in the tragic loss of *Thresher* in 1963.

Swiftsure was the first British submarine to be fitted with a digital data handling system, known as DCA. Limited in storage capacity to a paltry 64K, this system nevertheless was a step change in capability allowing the Command Team to track multiple sonar targets and derive target solutions which would support a successful approach to and attack of a submarine target. In 1978, the third of the class, *Sceptre*, was fitted with system DCB which, with a doubled storage capability, was for the first time capable of digitally controlling wire-guided torpedoes and setting anti-ship missile fire-control data. The *Swiftsure*s were succeeded by the *Trafalgar* class, the first of a class of seven, *Trafalgar*, commissioning in 1982. They were essentially the same as the *Swiftsure*s in hull design and propulsion system, but were modestly larger in displacement and the internal layout in the forward compartments was significantly different. By 1989, the year the Berlin Wall came down, six of the *Trafalgar*s were operational and the nuclear element of the Submarine Flotilla had increased to twenty-one hulls.

Four years later in 1993, *Vanguard* commissioned, the first of a new class of SSBN to replace the *Resolution* class. At 14,000 tons surfaced displacement, she is about twice the size of the latter class and can carry up to sixteen Trident D5 missiles. These have a range in excess of 6,000 miles and each can deliver up to twelve nuclear warheads. In sum, the awesome potential firepower in each of the four *Vanguard*s delivers a totally credible nuclear deterrent.

Chapter 12

Life in a British Nuclear Submarine

For the crew, life onboard a British nuclear submarine was much more comfortable than that experienced in an 'O' or 'P' class diesel boat. In the forward part of the submarine, the layout of the *Valiant* class was based on three deck levels, with the control room and wardroom on the first deck level and, on two deck, crew accommodation. The lowest, third deck, contained the main battery and auxiliary machinery spaces. For the first time, the crew benefitted from messdecks which were separate from the bunk spaces, and it was there where they had meals, watched movies or relaxed. While individual bunks tended to be more spacious and comfortable than those on diesel boats, inevitably there were not enough of them for all crew members and embarked trainees. Therefore, a number of crew would be required to sleep in the torpedo compartment on pallets beside the weapons or in camp beds in suitable equipment compartments. Alternatively, for those crew working on a two-watch system, some might have to 'hot' bunk, sharing one bunk with a member of the opposite watch.

Crew numbers in the British SSN are about 115, with the SSBNs having a complement in the order of 135. The latter operate a two-crew system with changeovers occurring after each patrol, which was originally planned to be about 60 days in duration. The SSN's complement is augmented by an additional watch of engineering staff which takes leave when the boat is at sea, allowing them to provide uninterrupted maintenance support when in the boat is in harbour. The complement of nuclear engineer officers is normally five. In the case of SSBNs, they additionally embark a doctor and, in their early years of operating, an officer who was a specialist in strategic weapon systems.

Nuclear submarines spend the majority of their time dived, and time on the surface tends to be confined to the transit of shallow water on the continental shelf which restricts their ability to be safely dived. With no need to snort, and its consequence of sucking cold, damp air into the boat, together with its characteristics of variations in atmosphere pressure, the temperature in the nuclear submarine's accommodation spaces is able to be maintained at a comfortable level. Much lower levels of humidity are also experienced and it is easier to keep the boat clean. Oxygen is generated by the electrolysis of pure water, with the arising hydrogen being ejected to the surrounding sea. Carbon dioxide is removed from the atmosphere by specialist equipment and there is additional apparatus to get rid of other noxious gases. In the event of failure of the atmosphere control equipment, then the boat can be ventilated through an induction system from the atmosphere but, of course, this requires the boat to be at periscope depth. There is also emergency air-purification and oxygen-making equipment which can be resorted to for a limited period of time should the exposure of the induction mast risk detection.

In a well-controlled and comfortable atmosphere and a placid ambience when deep and stable perhaps it is too easy for the individual crew member to lose awareness that he/she is within a steel tube under many hundreds of tons of sea pressure. The ear-piercing sound of even a small leak of highly pressurised seawater acts as a reminder to the crew that they are operating in a highly hostile environment.

Food is an important aspect of life for the submariner and it does much to alleviate the monotony of a patrol. Therefore, the galley team of four chefs in a nuclear submarine have to work hard to deliver three cooked meals, with choices, daily for each member of the crew. Normally one chef will be tasked to bake bread and rolls overnight, fresh for breakfast the following morning. The quality of the food served is almost always highly satisfactory, if not on occasions excellent. It is forbidden to consume food in the engine room spaces, but it has been known for engineering watches to enjoy soup heated up from the use of steam drains and jacket potatoes baked on the main turbine lagging.

Sunday lunches, by tradition, are a choice of roast and are normally preceded by a brief church service in the wardroom conducted by the Captain, as is his duty to do so under Navy Regulations. The service is likely to be sparsely attended by members of the crew but the prospect of some nibbles and a glass of sherry afterwards no doubt still tempts the odd individual to join in. In some submarines there might be instrument players who, by providing live music, add to the occasion. SSBNs in the past carried a small portable organ operated by foot bellows, or in one boat by the ingenious use of an adapted vacuum cleaner, to provide air pressure.

The capacity of the water distillation process on a nuclear submarine far exceeds that of a diesel boat and, while there has to be a degree of care exercised in the use of water, it is adequate for regular crew showering and for the running of a laundry service. Therefore, 'pirate rig' has never been worn in British nuclear submarines.

During the era 1970 to 1990 there was an increasing number of Soviet submarines passing to the west of the UK, on route to the Mediterranean or heading out to SSBN patrol areas off the USA's Eastern Seaboard. Consequently, SOSUS data became of increasing value in greatly assisting the UK's SSBN on patrol avoid the areas where threat submarines were likely to be present. It was also key to the success of the SSN or SSK in seeking out and locating the Soviet nuclear submarine.

On patrol, the SSBN has three primary objectives: to remain undetected; to maintain constant reception communications with HQ; and to be at all times ready to respond to a weapon launch signal. Remaining undetected means staying deep for the majority of the patrol, maintaining a quiet state and returning to periscope depth on the minimum of occasions. The SSBN's navigational position is calculated to a great degree of accuracy by specialist equipment, but only the Captain and a small cadre of the crew have knowledge of the boat's actual location. The Very Low Frequency (VLF) radio broadcast is the primary method of the SSBN receiving communication from shore HQ, with reception via a wire antenna which floats up to the surface from the patrol depth. However, this arrangement requires the submarine to proceed at slow speed to maintain continuous signal reception. Communications buoys developed from the version trialled by *Sealion* (see Chapter 5) can be used as a back-up, but their deployment to near the surface can be a relatively noisy procedure. Consequently, as stealth is a prerequisite in avoiding detection, their use is normally avoided. In situations where there is threat submarine activity in the vicinity of his patrol areas, the SSBN Captain needs to take prompt action to proceed slowly away from the threat direction, while maintaining constant communications. He does not have the luxury of opening range at speed.

The imperatives of remaining within target range, maintaining constant communication and avoiding detection by Soviet submarines on passage to the west of the UK, became of utmost concern to the British Polaris submarine Captain. In addition, there was the continuing threat of those Soviet SSNs tasked specifically to seek out patrolling NATO SSBNs. SOSUS provided regular reports on the location of Soviet submarines but it was not infallible and, as stated previously, often threat positional information covered a substantial area. Therefore, the SSBN on patrol always had to be constantly alert to a previously undetected submarine threat.

The UK's Nuclear Deterrent is committed to NATO, and its targeting plans are integrated into the US nuclear weapons strategic targeting plan (originally known as the SIOP – Strategic Integrated Operational Plan). In addition, there is a suite of exclusively national plans available. These are rigorously and meticulously developed by a nuclear targeting cell in the MoD, which is supported by intelligence and mapping agencies.

To effectively demonstrate its ability to attack these targets, while on patrol the SSBN must respond to Weapon System Readiness Tests (WSRTs) which occur about once a week, at any time of the day. These are initiated by receipt of an exercise firing signal, which requires the SSBN crew to execute a two-man authentication process and to undertake the full firing procedures, including hovering the boat, virtually stationary, at the missile launch depth, up to the point of opening the missile tube hatches. This exercise of simulated missile launch is completed within 15 minutes. In storm-force sea conditions, when in the hover, there is the additional challenge of maintaining depth and avoiding inadvertently broaching the surface. Of course, broaching markedly increases the risk of counter-detection.

After the patrol, the WSRT data is carefully analysed to ensure there are no crew errors, systems failures or defects evident. This and other weapons system data, together with the patrol navigational and sonar records, are analysed rigorously to evaluate total weapon system effectiveness which, for Polaris, was consistently in the high ninety percentages. Such levels of effectiveness could not nearly be matched by the RN's conventional weapon systems during the 1970s and 1980s. Notably, evidence of serious human error could result in censure or even dismissal, at a senior level.

As the Tenth Submarine Squadron boats settled into their routines, the benefits to Ship's Companies of a two-crew system with, in general, predictable leave and stand-down periods, became very evident. A friendly rivalry developed between the SSBN crews and those manning SSNs, where invariably programmes were changeable and, although their crews were augmented, this arrangement did not extend to the seamen officers. The SSN officers joked about the unofficial Tenth

Submarine Squadron motto of 'Hide with Pride'. However, I and many of my peers in SSNs undoubtedly underestimated the challenges and demands placed upon the SSBN command team. They had the onerous responsibility for safely and efficiently stewarding their load of sixteen Polaris missiles with their total of forty-eight 200-kiloton warheads. As the boats aged and incurred more frequent ship systems and propulsion plant defects, and the Soviet submarine threat increased, the SSBNs' crew challenges were more daunting.

Once settled into a Polaris patrol, a three-watch system allowed scope for frequent exercises and evolutions to keep the crew on their toes. These included the submariner's dread of having to tackle a fire or dealing with a major propulsion failure such as the reactor inadvertently shutting down. If a noise defect or piece of loose equipment was detected on the exterior of the submarine, there was the facility to deploy a ship's diver from one of the two escape towers to search for and hopefully rectify the problem. This procedure required the SSBN to come to a relatively shallow depth and to remain absolutely stationary while the diver was outside the hull. It was not without significant risk to the diver and was rarely conducted.

In event of an emergency, the patrolling SSBN does not have the luxury of returning to harbour to land a casualty or receive assistance to repair a serious defect. Should a crew member fall ill he or she will be treated with drugs by the Ship's Doctor in the hope that the illness can be held at bay until the patrol is complete. Surgery would involve a high risk of sepsis arising from the relatively high levels of bacteria in the submarine's atmosphere.

As the Polaris submarines aged and more defects arose, crews demonstrated great ingenuity or resilience in rectifying defects. As an example, the hull valve of the sewage tank jammed shut on one boat thus posing the highly unpleasant scenario of the heads being out of action until back in harbour. The defect was rectified by one of the engineer officers courageously entering the full sewage tank with a breathing hose and somehow making his way to the defective valve and successfully freeing it up.

Considerable effort was made to entertain Polaris crews when they were off watch. Besides movies, boat-wide quizzes and inter-mess games competitions were favourites and many individuals pursued hobbies such as model-making or artwork. Also, there was a limited range of gym equipment for crew members to use. One of the Doctor's ancillary tasks was to run the education programme for those crew members who wished to study for an educational qualification.

About once a patrol, when the operational situation permitted, the wardroom and senior rates mess enjoyed their own individual semi-formal mess dinners and there was always the opportunity to organise a picnic in the so-called 'Forest' – the missile compartment. Undoubtedly on occasions there was over-consumption of alcohol by a small element of the crew but this was never a serious problem in a well-led boat, where any evident excesses were quickly clamped down on.

During a Polaris patrol there would be occasional crew concerts in the junior rates mess, known as 'Sod's Operas', where comedy acts or song recitals were staged by all levels of the crew. These invariably demonstrated a lot of initiative in producing costumes from the boat's rag supply. The spectre of crew members dressed in rags performing comedy acts probably does not conform to the public's image of steely, serious individuals concentrating upon their gauges and instruments. Nevertheless, these events broke the monopoly of patrol and undoubtedly buoyed crew morale. On a Christmas patrol the 'Sod's Opera' would take the shape of a pantomime and a carol service would be well attended in the junior rates mess. On Christmas Day, many of the crew would open up Christmas presents which had been collected from their families before the boat sailed.

Once a week each SSBN crew member is entitled to receive a 'Family Gram' – a signal message, limited to forty words, from a designated family member. These are administered and vetted for sensitivity or security by the Off-Crew Officers prior to transmission and are subject to a final check by the Captain before being released to the individual. If their content, such as informing of the death of a relative, is considered likely to significantly affect the recipient's performance, it is withheld until returning to harbour. When the patrol has been completed, the Captain might well have the unpleasant task of relaying bad news to several of his crew.

In contrast, life onboard an SSN at sea is much more frenetic. It is a lot less structured and more varied than that of an SSBN: programmes are subject to change at short notice and, in general, periods at sea are significantly shorter than the duration of the average SSBN patrol. A typical SSN operating cycle will include individual boat training, exercising with other units – submarines, surface ships and aircraft – and trialling new equipment or systems. The latter activity inevitably means more time on the surface to embark trials staff and equipment and more frequent returns to harbour. Rather than a three-watch system, a two-watch system of six hours on and then six hours off might well be implemented in the forward part of the submarine if the operational tempo dictates more people being closed up. All these factors, and less available space, mean that there is less opportunity, and indeed requirement, to provide entertainment for the crew. Sadly, the personal stresses of a two-watch system mean there is much less time off-watch to allow social interaction in the wardroom and messdecks. Life can become somewhat a slog of watchkeeping, eating and sleeping.

Paradoxically, while on patrol conducting intelligence-gathering operations against potential threat forces, including trailing Russian submarines, there is the prospect of a more settled routine for the crew. Nevertheless, operating close to Soviet or other territorial waters limits or conducting certain, specialist intelligence gathering operations, demands the whole crew to be absolutely alert and on their toes. They need to able to promptly respond with precision to ship control orders such as a change of depth or speed. Therefore, in such situations key individuals might well experience prolonged periods of high levels of stress.

I never served in an SSBN on patrol and, consequently, I am indebted to the contributions of colleagues for the descriptions of the patrol activities related above. Although I have here only briefly touched on the essential differences for those serving in SSNs, future chapters will, I hope, give a more detailed picture of life in these submarines, with which I am much more familiar.

Chapter 13

Serving in HMS *Swiftsure*

Late October 1973 found myself as OOW on the bridge of the nuclear attack submarine *Swiftsure* in the English Channel heading out to a diving area in the deep water of the South-west Approaches. The destination was Gibraltar for a short port visit, with various trials being conducted on route. Making a comfortable 15 knots, I could sense the power of the submarine's propulsion system with well over 20,000 shaft horsepower available. This was many times that which *Oberon*'s diesels could generate. I had truly gone from the Morris Minor to the Ferrari. I had joined the boat in Plymouth on completion of its post-build work-up and had taken over as sonar officer, relieving Lieutenant Edwin 'Arkle' Atkinson. Handover complete in Gibraltar, I was now responsible for the operation of the submarine's suite of new, advanced types of acoustic sensor.

Since leaving *Oberon* in the summer of 1972, I had undertaken a series of professional courses. The most important of these was a five-month course learning about the sonar and torpedo systems fitted in nuclear submarines. A key element of the course content was getting to grips with the principles and complexities of underwater sound propagation. This was taught in parallel to learning about the new techniques and procedures in the analysis of the discreet sounds emitted by the Soviet nuclear submarine. These discreet 'tonal' emissions, if of a low frequency (typically less than 500 Hz), in favourable acoustic conditions could be detectable at very long ranges. However, it would take considerable skill and experience to exploit these tonal sounds in order to make a successful detection on a Soviet submarine, close its range and achieve an accurate fire-control solution. Little did I know at the time that these challenges would feature prominently during most of my future appointments.

During this period between sea appointments, I attended two other professional courses, both at the Royal Naval College Greenwich which, of course, had many attractions for a bachelor, not least its easy access to the delights of Central London. The first of these courses was the 'Lieutenants' General Course' which focused on the fundamentals of naval staff-work protocols and included instruction about the UK's key institutions and government organisations. How hosting a lunchtime drinks reception for about sixty 'Miss World' contestants fitted into the agenda, I cannot recall, but it was most certainly one of the most memorable course highlights.

The second course was nine weeks of instruction on nuclear energy theory and its practical application in submarines. The course was designed to give those officers who were not engineer specialists, a firm grasp of the workings of the PWR nuclear steam raising plant and its secondary, non-nuclear, machinery. Our engineer officers who would operate and maintain the plant, received much more extensive and intensive training including undergoing practical operating experience at the Royal Navy's prototype plant at Dounreay on the north coast of Scotland.

One of the key features of the PWR is that, as the coolant water in its nuclear core increases in temperature, the system's reactivity decreases and vice versa when the temperature drops. Consequently, it has the significant safety feature of being essentially self-regulating. However, when any nuclear reactor is shut down, there remains substantial decay heat, especially if it has been running at high power. There is a risk of a major accident if the cooling system totally fails and this heat increases to dangerous levels causing, in exceptional circumstances, the radiation shielding to fail. Therefore, the submarine PWR incorporates emergency cooling systems to prevent such a critical event occurring. The course instruction emphasised the imperatives of maintaining the integrity of the reactor cooling system, which is achieved by heat being removed from the core by a series of Main Cooling Pumps. As stated earlier, no serious accident has ever occurred on a US or UK designed submarine PWR.

The College's nuclear training facilities included a small nuclear reactor situated in one of the ancient basements. Known as 'Jason', its output was only a few kilowatts but it could be used for practical experiments to reinforce aspects of nuclear theory, such as reactivity decay rates. Ironically Greenwich Borough Council was sometime later to declare itself a 'Nuclear Free Zone'.

This period of over 12 months of training and leave between sea appointments had proved highly enjoyable and relaxing, providing me with a welcome break from the rigours of life at sea in a submarine.

Ahead of me lay almost five years of continuous sea-service including the challenges of getting to grips with a nuclear submarine's systems and procedures.

I joined *Swiftsure* at the same time as my mentor and friend, Geoffrey Biggs ('GB'), was taking over as XO and second-in-command. True to past form, he quickly delegated several of his more mundane responsibilities, such as maintaining the cleanliness of the forward part of the submarine, to myself. The Captain, Tim Hale, was a charismatic, flamboyant individual who was highly experienced in SSNs. Notably he had arrived for *Swiftsure*'s launch driving the steam train that Vickers had laid on to take VIP guests from Euston to Windermere. He had been a member of *Dreadnought*'s commissioning wardroom and had initially trained in the USA, undergoing sea time in USS *Scorpion*. Prior to the commissioning of the SSN *Warspite*, as its XO, he had featured in a prominent advertisement for the Triumph 2000 saloon, comparing its acceleration to that which could be achieved in his submarine. More seriously, he had experienced the previously related *Warspite* underwater collision with a Soviet 'Echo' class nuclear submarine which had occurred during an intelligence gathering operation in the Barents Sea. In this incident, the submarine had rolled 65 degrees to starboard, an extremely alarming experience for its crew. Naturally this event, where it was momentarily thought by all crew members that they would perish, was to temper his willingness to get into close range of dived Soviet submarines.

The wardroom totalled fourteen officers and were of very mixed backgrounds. Two Old Etonians were serving as forward watchkeeping officers, and one of the engineer officers was Cambridge educated. Another Oxbridge graduate was soon to join, Lieutenant Guy Warner, a brilliant mathematician and computer programming expert. He had been appointed as a forward watchkeeper but his prime responsibility was to steward the introduction of the DCA tactical data handling system. As DCA was the first such computer system at sea in submarines, unsurprisingly it suffered from frequent crashes or programming aberrations. Consequently, Guy was to be fully occupied in working with programmers to both rectify faults and introduce improvements.

Soon after joining, I observed a lack of social cohesion between the engineer officers and the remainder of the wardroom. The former were much more senior and experienced in operating a nuclear submarine than the junior seamen officers, but this was no justification for their clearly evident haughty standoffishness towards the latter. Thankfully, as in due course these individuals were relieved, the wardroom ambience became more convivial and friendly.

Designed to take on second-generation nuclear submarines which were emerging in large numbers from Russian shipyards, the 4,500-ton *Swiftsure* class was a significant improvement on the *Valiant*s, being faster, deeper diving, quieter and more manoeuvrable. Furthermore, its machinery spaces were much better designed, with a layout conducive to easier maintainability and improved access to individual pieces of machinery. The class had a safe operating depth of 1,250ft and their hulls could sustain the almost two million tons of pressure which would be exerted on them at a depth of 2,000ft. Although limited to about 16 knots on the surface, under the sea, where their propellers or propulsors were more efficient, they could almost double this. However, there were inevitably going to be initial teething problems in such a complex machine and, of course, the designers and constructors wanted to test it to the boundaries of its capabilities. This sometimes made for challenging times for the crew.

Swiftsure's sonars and sensor equipment were very much cutting-edge technology. However, on the downside, her torpedo armament consisted of the obsolescent Mark 8 anti-ship and the ineffective Mark 23 anti-submarine weapons. It was to be several years before *Swiftsure* received an effective, capable torpedo system.

During Vickers Contractor's Sea Trials *Swiftsure* more than met expectations regarding her performance, but on surfaced passage it was evident there was a need to flood the aftermost of its four main ballast tanks, increasing the depth of the stern to provide acceptable steerage and better bite for the propeller. *Swiftsure* was fitted with a large skew-bladed propeller but most subsequent Royal Naval nuclear submarines would have pump jet propulsors (a shrouded rotor arrangement) which are quieter and more efficient than conventional propellers. The stern ballasting measure effectively removed 25 per cent of the surfaced reserve of buoyancy. This contributed to making the bridge, which was much lower in height than the *Valiant*s, very wet in heavy weather. During *Swiftsure*'s Contractor's Sea Trials she had shipped an exceptionally large wave over the top of the fin. The OOW, a contemporary and friend, Lieutenant Roger Chapman, suffered several cracked ribs as he was thrown against the side of the bridge by the impact of the wave. He was the first of many bridge watchkeepers on this class of submarine to experience an extremely wet and uncomfortable watch in rough weather.

During these trials, the deep-dive to her maximum safe depth had gone well and all systems had proved pressure-tight and well-founded. However, there had been a nerve-jangling event in the first attempt at the deep dive. One of the team of Vickers engineers embarked for this test inadvertently triggered the engine room flood alarm when trying to free a jammed length of hose. The immediate control room response was to execute the emergency surfacing procedure, initiating the high-pressure air emergency blowing system and promptly increasing speed. Although proving the capability of this system, the event undoubtedly frayed a few nerves.

The first major series of *Swiftsure*'s first-of-class trials took place in early 1974 in the tropical environment of the Atlantic Underwater Test and Evaluation Centre (AUTEC) which has its shore facilities in the Bahamian island of Andros. Completed in 1966, AUTEC provides excellent 3-D tracking facilities of ships, aircraft and submarines. Its main tracking range is about 20 miles long and 15 miles wide and with Andros to the west and un-navigable reefs and shoals to the east and south, AUTEC benefits from unique deep-water acoustic conditions. This, and the absence of interference from passing shipping, make it an ideal place to test sonar and underwater weapons.

During the deployment, *Swiftsure* used the USN's modern, well equipped Port Canaveral as a base and, after enduring a Scottish winter, the crew naturally very much appreciated the sunshine of Florida and the motels of nearby Cocoa Beach where they lived when off-duty and in harbour. With the ending of the Apollo moon landings in December 1972, activity at Cape Canaveral had markedly reduced, and Cocoa Beach, developed in the 1950s, was already looking tired. Its motels, which had sprung up in the heyday of the space race, looked distinctly run-down. Nevertheless, for the crew there was plenty of nightlife and a particular favourite of the officers was a restaurant which had been frequented by astronauts and consequently displayed a large and unique collection of their autographed photographs.

Inevitably, as the crew imbibed warm local hospitality and cold American beer, there were to be problems when they were ashore. A particular hazard was the temptation to return from Cocoa Beach to the submarine's berth by walking along the side of the linking dual-carriageway. One junior rate ended up in hospital with a badly broken leg when hit by a passing car on this road. Fortuitously for him, the car driver was subsequently arrested for drink driving and in due course the sailor received substantial compensation. There was no compensation for two Petty Officers who decided to take the shortcut of swimming across the harbour. They were both swept out to sea and were fortunately found by the US Coastguard clinging to a buoy in the entrance channel.

Another revelation at Port Canaveral was specific to *Swiftsure* herself. The AUTEC trials had been preceded by a docking in Faslane. Included in the work undertaken was the adhesion of 1,000 rubber noise-reduction tiles to a section of the outer pressure hull. This was the first attempt to fit acoustic baffling to a British SSN. However, as the tiles were applied in Scottish winter conditions of wind and driving rain, it was no surprise that on arrival in Port Canaveral only about half a dozen had survived the submerged passage across the Atlantic. A more serious worry was the SOSUS detection during the crossing of a strong, discrete noise emission. This was established as coming from the main engine cooling water inlets on the after stabilisers situated either side of the hull, forward of the propeller. Eventually this noise problem was to be solved, but not before the complete failure of trial stabiliser fairings which fell off while manoeuvring at sea, temporarily exacerbating the noise problem by exposing the cooling water inlet pipes.

During the AUTEC trials period, numerous senior visitors were embarked for a day at sea to witness the handling and capability of Britain's latest SSN. All were highly impressed, including those from the United States Navy. To establish its handling and noise characteristics the boat was put through extremely demanding manoeuvres while scientists and engineers, both onboard and ashore, made acoustic measurements and collected data. One noise measurement trial involved the submarine being held stationary in a dived condition, in tidal conditions, at close proximity to a large acoustic array suspended from a buoy and attached to the seabed. Already one American SSBN had wrapped itself around the array with predictable consequences, becoming entangled in a mass of wires and hydrophones.

The tests to determine the dynamic manoeuvring characteristics of the submarine were often highly dramatic, with the embarked trials scientists trying to push the boundaries of the boat's safe operating envelope. Consequently, severe angles were experienced in both the horizontal and vertical planes. In one such trial, the lead scientist asked the Captain to increase speed and then put the planes to full dive. This resulted in the expected steep bow-down angle, at which point the scientist requested that the rudder be put hard over, whereupon the bow-down angle increased alarmingly. Plates crashed, people slid on the decks and hung onto whatever they could, at which point the

Captain took charge and by applying stern power and ordering the planes to full rise, got the boat back level. This was not before we had observed the scientist firmly hanging by one hand from overhead pipework, scratching his head with the other and saying, with no trace of panic in his voice, 'very interesting, that was not supposed to happen!'.

About a year later, another unexpected severe angle occurred when *Swiftsure* was at periscope depth in the North-west Approaches, proceeding at 6 knots, clearing signal traffic. Although the sea-state was only about Force 5, there was a significant swell running and the boat was rolling quite a bit. The incident occurred just after lunch and I was in the control room studying the chart before taking over the watch. Daily routine equipment checks were ongoing.

Suddenly there was a loud crash from the vicinity of the fin. The boat shuddered and rapidly took on a very steep bow-down angle of about 30 degrees. A second heavy crash followed and my immediate thought, shared by others, was that we had collided with another submarine. Looking down into the wardroom from the control room, I had almost a bird's eye view of the occupants at the second lunch-sitting, grimly clinging onto the table while their plates headed en masse down to the far end of the table where 'GB' was firmly clutching onto its edges. He deftly avoided the main avalanche of crockery and cutlery but one lone apple crumble and custard, bringing up the rear, ended up on his lap.

Meanwhile the down angle increased, despite the planesman pulling hard-back on his control stick and both forward and after planes indicating full rise. I was not alone in thinking we were heading for the depths with severe damage forward. My fears were increased when 'Full Astern' was ordered and I watched the propeller shaft revolution count increase in response, then suddenly fall off to zero. Had we also lost power on the main engines?

It then became clear, that we were going nowhere as the depth gauges were registering only about 110ft and were not moving. It soon became evident that, during the equipment checks, the control room systems operator, his attention distracted elsewhere, instead of raising the diesel exhaust mast had activated the wrong switch and had blown number four, the aftermost ballast tank, totally empty. The boat was effectively in suspended animation with its stern and propeller sticking out of the sea and the engines had tripped out on over-speed. The loud crashes we had experienced had been heavy waves hitting the fin as the boat initially broached the surface.

The main ballast tank vents were opened, a dived trim was quickly regained and a stiff admonition administered to the system operator. Getting underway again, a quick check revealed that there had been no damage done except for the apple crumble clinging to 'GB''s trousers.

Returning to the AUTEC manoeuvring trials, the *pièce de résistance* was a full-power run at depth where the boat's massive rudder was to be put hard over to port at her maximum speed of 30 knots. This test had been worked up to gradually, speed and rudder angle in both directions being increased in stages and the boat's attitude measured both onboard and by the range instrumentation. It was soon demonstrated that the amount of roll was greater when the rudder was applied to port. This was because of the horizontal thrust of the propeller's clockwise rotation. Therefore, the ultimate test would be putting the rudder hard-to-port.

This final trial took place in the late evening at a comfortable depth of 300ft. All compartments and the galley, in particular, had been fully secured and the crew closed up in maximum readiness at Diving Stations. The control room was illuminated in red lighting in case there was a need to rapidly surface. My diving station was on the DCA computer console in the control room directly behind the ship control panel and the one-man hydroplane and rudder operator. Therefore, I had an excellent view of the submarine's control systems. As the boat's speed was increased to 30 knots, there was no discernible tension in the control room as the prior tests had resulted in only a moderate degree of roll. However, at the order 'Port 30!', as the rudder went over, the boat rapidly listed to over 40 degrees. The dreaded 'snap roll' phenomenon had occurred where the fin was acting as a huge hydroplane causing an alarming roll to port and down angle. Everywhere the crew clung onto anything which was secure but, before the Captain could order stern power to drastically slow down the boat, the shrill report came from aft 'Reactor Scram! Reactor Scram!'. I then witnessed an absolute array of alarms simultaneously registering on the ship control panel. At the same time the Captain shouted 'Good God, we have lost the reactor!'.

Back aft, engineering mayhem had occurred as both of the vital electrical turbo-generators in the engine room simultaneously tripped out on low lubricating oil pressure. The consequent loss of electric power to the reactor's cooling pumps caused it to dramatically shut-down and start progressing into the safe, but drastic, emergency-cooling mode. Main propulsion was lost but the residual steam in the system allowed stern power to be applied for a short time, while the engine room watchkeepers quickly engaged the emergency propulsion system. Although very limited, this allowed control of the submarine to be regained. Highly expert and rapid reactions by the manoeuvring room team in getting the reactor cooling pumps restarted saved the day. If emergency cooling had initiated, it would have required the boat to be surfaced and the engineering staff to undertake complex procedures to restore the reactor to its normal operating mode. At worst, it could have meant an ignominious tow back to Cape Canaveral.

Fortunately, this situation was averted and within an hour the reactor was restarted and main propulsion restored. No damage had been caused and, in due course, the turbo-generator lubricating oil system of the *Swiftsure* class was modified to be more robust. But, again, such an experience had frayed a number of nerves. Later boats of the class were also fitted with a smaller-sized rudder. As for myself, it was not to be the only time in my career that the skill and knowledge of the Royal Navy engineer were to come to the fore in preventing a catastrophic situation.

This incident yet again demonstrated that events can rapidly get out of control in a nuclear submarine at high speed, with its potential to increase depth at over 1,500ft per minute, making safe depths of around 1,000ft look modest. Several years later the crew of the *Valiant* class SSN *Churchill*, coincidentally also conducting manoeuvres at AUTEC, briefly lost control of their boat. Before control was regained, her bows reached a depth of over 1,200ft, close to her theoretical pressure hull collapse limit.

During one of the return visits to Port Canaveral, I and a few of my fellow officers shared a rental car and paid a visit to Disney World which had recently opened near the city of Orlando. This proved a bit of a strange experience as there was an ongoing petrol shortage caused by strife in the Middle East. Consequently, there were very few visitors to this popular resort. Most unusually there were no queues at its many different attractions. Another diversion during the final few days at AUTEC was the holding of a cocktail party on the after casing of the boat where a number of the range staff were invited. In calm sea conditions, with a bar set up on the casing, the surfaced boat slowly circled off the range headquarters landing site and our US visitors enjoyed the unique experience of sundowner cocktails on the casing of a British nuclear submarine. It is highly unlikely that today's authorities would allow such a happening.

The AUTEC trials were followed by an eastward passage across the Atlantic to conduct torpedo discharge-system proving trials in sea areas near to Gibraltar. The location was chosen for the easy access of deep water and reasonably benign sea conditions which enabled recovery of the discharged practice torpedoes. Weapons were launched down to 1,000ft, an unprecedented launch depth for a British submarine. Here, over a hundred tons of sea pressure is exerted on the few square inches of torpedo tube rear door retaining clips, all that stood in the way of the Atlantic. Fortunately, few, if any, of the crew would have undertaken this calculation; some information is best kept to oneself.

For much of the duration of these tests, *Swiftsure* had the company of a smart and apparently businesslike Russian 'Kashin' class missile destroyer, stationed to gather what intelligence her operators could gather about this new British nuclear submarine. Both vessels exchanged the occasional friendly message by light using the International Code of Signals. On proceeding on the surface back to Gibraltar on a Friday evening for a two-day break, the destroyer requested *Swiftsure* to 'please stay at sea and keep me company'. This little cameo struck me as an example of the contrast in lifestyles between the West and the Soviet Bloc. There was no run ashore awaiting the Russian sailors and, even if they had managed to land in Gibraltar, they would have had no money to spend in its shops or bars. Instead they were confined onboard, with neither good food nor quality movies available to alleviate the monotony while the enticing lights of Gibraltar and its fleshpots twinkled on the horizon.

The torpedo discharge tests involved launching inert Tigerfish torpedoes with their rear-mounted guidance wire dispensers. The dispenser was a cylindrical container which held a reel of 5,000 yards of guidance wire intended to allow the firing submarine limited movement after launch. The torpedo itself held another 15,000 yards of wire for its controlled run-to-target which could take up to twenty minutes. After leaving the torpedo tube, the dispenser disengaged from the weapon but remained connected to the submarine by armoured cable. When Tigerfish started coming into service in 1976, this crude arrangement proved to be highly unreliable and, a considerable time later, was replaced by a more robust system.

After the torpedo was fired, the deployed dispenser restricted the submarine to a maximum speed of six knots and, normally at the end of the torpedo's run, would be cut loose. However, the wire dispensers used in these trials had special recording gear fitted and consequently had to be recovered. Slowly returning to periscope depth in one of the world's busiest shipping lanes with a bowcap open and dragging a guidance wire dispenser was a manoeuvre fraught with risk and engendered much nervous tension. I remember that on one occasion, while I was on watch, the submarine reached periscope depth almost underneath a passing merchant ship and only narrowly averted a collision. Once the boat had surfaced, divers were used to bring the dispensers onboard.

Meanwhile, I was getting to grips with the submarine's complex systems and operating modes. This had been a rather painful process and, for a period, I found myself less competent and knowledgeable as a control room watchkeeper to those junior to me. They had, of course, benefitted from the experience of Contractor's Sea Trials and the work-up phase. Furthermore, my less-than-satisfactory handling of a couple of minor ship-control incidents, in the beginning had quite knocked my self-confidence. Nevertheless, I gradually built up an extensive systems knowledge which, together with the first-hand experience of a number of incidents at sea, was to stand me in good stead in the future.

On completion of the evaluations in the Caribbean and Gibraltar, it was back to Scotland for more noise trials. These included a unique first-of-class noise ranging in a 'dead ship' condition, all machinery being shut down in stages to a state where absolutely nothing was running. The measurements were conducted over a period of several nights with the boat in a neutrally buoyant, static condition, suspended at 150ft depth between four buoys, one on each quarter, at a noise range situated in Loch Goil in Argyllshire. The reactor had to be shut down for several days prior to the trials to ensure the decay heat in its core had reduced sufficiently to enable its vital cooling pumps to be stopped for a period. This meant a miserably slow tow by tug from Faslane with the submarine's diesel engine providing power for its basic machinery load. As the navigator, Lieutenant Tom Morton, was on leave during this evolution, I undertook the pilotage on the bridge and for several hours was immersed in an extremely unhealthy cloud of diesel fumes from the exhaust mast at the rear of the fin, augmented by a spray of the mast's cooling seawater. To this was added a dash of relentless Scottish drizzle. Balmy bridge watches when on the surface on the AUTEC range seemed a long time ago.

On the final night of the trials the plan was to switch all machinery off, having only a bare minimum crew onboard the boat, which was in conditions of near darkness with only emergency lighting providing dim illumination. In the eerie silence, with the ventilation shut down, scientists and technicians scuttled around the various compartments, excitedly taking readings while at shore facilities technicians measured the external radiated noise. The Captain and I were in the control room as the final pieces of running machinery, the hydraulic pumps, which supplied pressure to the submarine's vital hydraulically operated systems, were switched off. As hydraulic pressure was an essential element of operating the submarine's many valves and control components, this was the last plant to be shut down. A minimum level of pressure was sustained for a short period by a number of pneumatic accumulators, filled with high-pressure air, which were incorporated into the hydraulic pipework.

After the hydraulic pumps were switched off, complete silence followed for a few minutes but soon all onboard became aware of an ominous gurgling sound which grew progressively louder. Staring through the gloom at the hydraulic oil header tanks at the rear of the control room, I became aware of great quantities of heavy, brown oily vapours spilling out. These rapidly engulfed the control room personnel to waist level. Before catastrophe struck as a result of either the crew being disabled by breathing the thick fumes or, being highly inflammable, they ignited, the trials were hastily terminated and *Swiftsure* was immediately surfaced using emergency hand control to work the compressed air valves. Once on the surface, machinery was restarted and the boat was quickly ventilated to get rid of these exceedingly dangerous hydraulic vapours. As surfacing OOW, I opened the upper conning tower hatch and arrived on the bridge to witness the sun rising over the loch's mountains on a glorious still spring morning with an accompaniment of cheerful birdsong, a vivid contrast to the stygian gloom below decks.

Subsequent investigations revealed that, on the hydraulic pressure reducing, some of the internal fittings of the accumulators had ruptured. This caused high-pressure air to course round the system ending up in the header tanks, which then generated the vapour cloud. After this escapade, the Captain and some members of the crew were clearly becoming increasingly stressed by the demands of the trials and their unpredictable outcomes.

Having completed further trials and exercises and a second call into Gibraltar, *Swiftsure* headed for a few days informal visit to the port of Barry, situated a few miles to the west of Cardiff. In the 1970s this former coal-exporting port was one of a large number of smaller British ports in terminal decline due to changes in trade and industrial patterns and restrictive labour practices. Furthermore, the advent of container ships required larger, deeper water facilities than those offered by many of the existing older tidal harbours. As activities in these ports ramped down, pilotage and tug provision also declined, thereby making *Swiftsure*'s entry into Barry, with her deep displacement draught and sluggish surface handling, a difficult one.

First impression of the harbour with its redundant coaling wharves was one of dereliction. Only one other ship was alongside, the regular Fyffes-owned specialist refrigerated cargo vessel unloading her cargo of bananas from the West Indies. The perception by some of the locals that nuclear submarines were hazardous was reinforced by the local Royal Navy liaison officer distributing potassium iodide tablets to the port employers with the advice that their staff swallow these radioactive material blockers if a nuclear accident should occur onboard the visiting submarine. This, of course, was complete nonsense. In the highly unlikely event of a serious nuclear incident onboard, the harbour area would have been evacuated long before there was the remotest risk of contaminants getting into the atmosphere. That said, the crew were soon immersed in generous local hospitality which compensated for them being billeted in the rather shabby local Butlins holiday camp. This, however, proved to have some unexpected benefits in the friendliness of the female staff. Shortly after *Swiftsure*'s visit, Barry was deemed unsuitable for berthing nuclear submarines and today it is no longer an active commercial harbour.

The late summer of 1974 saw *Swiftsure* for the first time being deployed on an operational patrol, setting up a sonar search barrier between the Orkney and Shetland Islands. Her quarry was the Russian 'Whiskey' class diesel submarine which regularly patrolled the seas to the west of the United Kingdom. This submarine normally deployed from the Baltic and was tasked with the training of prospective Soviet submarine commanding officers in potentially hostile waters, sometimes conducting submerged passage between the Mull of Kintyre and Rathlin Island to enter the Irish Sea. Besides training submarine commanders to operate in the potential enemy's backyard, these boats attempted to monitor NATO warship and submarine traffic in the North-west Approaches. Despite being typically about 20 or more years old, when running dived on main motors the 'Whiskey' was anticipated to be difficult to detect using passive sonar – listening as opposed to transmitting an acoustic pulse. It was *Swiftsure*'s task to covertly detect and track a deploying 'Whiskey' and to establish exactly where it patrolled and what it got up to.

Despite *Swiftsure* being Britain's most capable SSN and having the support of MPA, the patrol was not a great success. The specific target submarine was lost by monitoring forces as it dived on leaving the Skagerrak, north of Denmark, to commence its passage to its patrol area. However, quite by chance, we did achieve a short period of passive sonar contact at close quarters on the elusive Russian in the Orkney/Shetland gap. Unfortunately, the command team was unskilled in dealing with the short-range situation and this contact was soon lost. A few mornings later, the Russian boat was again detected, this time at about 15 miles range snorting to the west of the Outer Hebrides. However, the Captain was not keen to get close to him. Consequently, when the Russian stopped snorting shortly after sunrise, contact was again lost and not confidently regained despite a subsequent active sonar search which would have given the game away to the opposition that a British submarine was looking for him.

The patrol highlighted to me that, even when an SSN was equipped with the most modern of sonars, it was difficult to detect a diesel submarine when she was battery-powered. Also, once contact had been achieved, there was an evident need to develop specific tactics to deal with this type of target.

Tim Hale was replaced as Captain in due course in August 1974, during a second home-port visit, this time to Liverpool. His successor, Commander Keith Pitt, was a friendly and cheerful individual but a bit of a workaholic. While not having the same nuclear propulsion systems knowledge as his predecessor, he was to prove both more tactically aware and capable of improving the crew's fighting efficiency which undoubtedly was somewhat patchy. Moreover, *Swiftsure* had been designated to start undertaking the Barents Sea intelligence-gathering operations from the following year and the new Captain needed to significantly raise the operational sharpness of the command team to meet the unique demands of this task. As part of the training for these patrols, a number of exercises would be undertaken with other Royal Navy SSNs where the skills of covertly following another submarine would be honed.

As the crew efficiency improved, I recognised that the Ship's Company of *Swiftsure* was much more professional and better disciplined than the crews which I served with in diesel boats. Indeed, it was evident that several key individuals had been hand-picked to bring this world-leading nuclear submarine into operational service.

Meanwhile the boat had changed her operational base from the Clyde Naval Base in Faslane to the recently re-formed Second

Submarine Squadron in Devonport. This squadron, which eventually would be the home to all the newer *Trafalgar* class submarines, provided the opportunity for nuclear submarine crews to be posted to the South West of England. It was disestablished in 2019 when all Royal Navy submarine basing was moved to the Clyde Naval Base.

During an extended docking period in Devonport in late 1974, there being no shore accommodation available in the base wardroom, I and several wardroom colleagues rented a farmhouse in the Devon village of Cornwood on the edge of Dartmoor. Life in the farmhouse and Devon countryside was far removed from the stresses and strains of nuclear submarining and, over the three months of our stay, several lifelong friendships were cemented. We were particularly fortunate that Lieutenant Mike Allen, one of the boat's engineer officers, was joined in the farmhouse throughout by his wife, Helen. We were to be spoiled by her delicious meals which were well above our bachelor standards together with the semblance of order she brought to the house.

Meanwhile other new officers joined, including Lieutenant John Knapp as Torpedo Officer. Endowed with a great sense of humour and not afraid of friendly mischief, he much contributed to making the wardroom a less serious place. During a post docking work-up period, one evening when alongside in Faslane, several of us accompanied Tom Morton on his stag night, visiting several local pubs. On return to the base wardroom bar, all of us pretty inebriated, John Knapp ran out a mains fire hose which Tom playfully pointed it at the Base Duty Officer who had arrived on the scene to find out what was happening. Suddenly there was a full bore of high-pressure water coming out of the nozzle which immediately saturated the Duty Officer. However, even worse, Tom lost control of the pressurised hose which snaked around the bar spraying the occupants of several tables enjoying a quiet nightcap. No one was certain of the identity of the miscreant who turned on the hose full bore but, of course, we *Swiftsure* officers were blamed. After the fire hose incident, Tom managed to avoid any significant disciplinary sanction on account of his impending wedding, but we all were given a stiff dressing-down by the Base Commander. Incidentally, John Knapp subsequently transferred to the Royal Navy of Oman where he served for a short period before transferring to Oman Royal Yachts which he was to eventually head in the rank of Commodore for many years.

Another two new faces in the wardroom, as trainee seamen officers, were Cambridge graduates. Lieutenant James Burnell-Nugent was a somewhat serious officer who duly rose to the rank of Admiral and became Commander-in-Chief Fleet. Lieutenant Andrew Boyd possessed a brilliant intellect but he did not serve in submarines for long before being recruited into the intelligence services.

Back at sea, in February 1975 I found myself in the control room preparing to take over OOW on the bridge at night, in extreme storm Force 10 conditions. *Swiftsure* was making a surface passage down the Minches between the Inner and Outer Hebrides towards a dived rendezvous with the SSN *Conqueror* in the North-west Approaches. Constrained to the surface until reaching sea areas where the submarine was cleared to dive, the Captain was concerned about making the rendezvous on time and was keen to press on. This was despite the heavy seas battering the boat, driving large quantities of spray over the two crew members on the bridge and causing it to roll heavily. In the relative calm of the control room, as I checked the submarine's charted position and donned safety harness, I braced myself for a very wet and cold watch.

As I locked out of the upper conning tower hatch, well wrapped up in foul-weather clothing, there was a shudder as the boat hit a particularly large wave. This was followed by a torrent of water filling the space around the bridge access ladder and propelling me upwards. Fortunately, on the bridge, Tom Morton, in the near pitch-black darkness, grabbed hold of me as I was washed into the bridge cockpit and quickly secured my safety harness. I thought: not a good start to the watch. After a brief handover, Tom disappeared below. As I scanned what I could observe of the horizon, all I could see, in the near pitch blackness and violent wind conditions, were large breaking waves and wind-blown spume.

I and the lookout were frequently deluged by the solid crest of a wave as, unlike ships, submarines tend to go through waves rather than ride over them. Having rounded Barra Head and left the lee of the Outer Hebrides to head south-west, conditions got worse as the size of the waves increased. In the darkness and fury of the storm, I saw ahead an exceptionally large cresting wave and just had time to yell to the lookout to duck. There followed a heavy blow to the upper part of my body and several seemingly interminable seconds of darkness as the wave engulfed me. Undoubtedly, the lookout and I would have been swept overboard had it not been for our safety harnesses. As the effects of the wave passed, we were left reeling and choking, with for a brief period, water up to our waists. The bridge lifebuoy had been knocked over and its light actuated under the receding water in the bridge well and, in my now-illuminated surroundings, cold and very wet, I pondered on the strange way I had chosen to make a living. The watchkeepers in the control room reported that their depth gauges had momentarily read 80ft as the wave passed over *Swiftsure*. With the 60ft between keel and bridge, this meant that, even allowing for the gauges' dial fluctuation, for a few seconds there was at least a dozen or so feet of solid water above our heads on the bridge.

A few years later, Lieutenant Mark Stanhope, later to be First Sea Lord, was on the bridge of *Swiftsure* in storm conditions in the South-west Approaches. The boat had been on a Barents Sea intelligence gathering mission and, as part of her special equipment fit, the normal radar mast had been removed and replaced by a specialist intelligence gathering mast. As a consequence, the conning tower hatches were open with a cable running through them up to a portable radar set on the bridge. Yet again, an exceptionally large wave hit the bridge and, on this occasion, many tons of water poured into the control room through the open hatches. On the bridge Mark and his colleagues were submersed for so long that, with lungs bursting in desperation, he considered unfastening his safety harness which would almost certainly been fatal. Meanwhile, prompt action by the control room watchkeepers saved the situation by their blowing main ballast to gain full buoyancy and getting the lower conning tower hatch shut. However, the boat had taken on large quantities of seawater into the control room and below decks, causing damage to a number of control systems and other equipment. It was to be sometime before the conning tower airlock was pumped out and the bridge personnel could be relieved.

Returning to my own experience, on recovery from being swamped by the exceptionally large wave, I reported to the Captain that either the submarine be drastically slowed down or we bridge watchkeepers risked being drowned. In response he ordered that the lookout and myself be brought below and the bridge shut down. Having changed into dry clothes, I found maintaining watch below, with visual lookout on the powerful periscopes fitted with image intensification, both much more comfortable and safer, a world away from the exposure of the bridge. However, it engendered a false sense of security and soon the Captain increased speed, although the boat was still taking a real pounding.

In *Swiftsure*, unlike previous types of British submarine, the fore-planes were retractable into the hull and the initial practice was to have them extended when on the surface with rise applied to help to get the stern deeper. This feature resulted in yet another surprise for her crew. On diving a few hours later, it soon became apparent that all was not well. All the signs were that the boat was massively heavy forward and it was proving highly difficult to control her depth. After an hour of trying unsuccessfully to gain a reasonable buoyancy trim, concerned that *Swiftsure* was already late for her rendezvous with *Conqueror*, the Captain ordered the boat deep and fast, directing the trimming officer, Guy Warner, to continue to sort out the apparent excess of ballast water which was being carried forward. A very significant quantity of forward ballast was removed, but a few hours later, on being slowed down to check the state of the trim, the boat rapidly headed out of control to the surface with a steep bow up angle. Speed was applied just in time to avoid broaching the surface in the storm which was still raging. A hastily gathered investigation team soon reached the conclusion that, while the fore-planes' angle indicators were displaying 'normal' operating, the planes had been bent on their drive shaft to the full dive position by the exceptionally heavy seas. An immediate return to harbour and docking confirmed this to be the case and thereafter the *Swiftsure* class boats kept their fore-planes retracted whilst making passage on the surface in heavy weather.

In March 1975, I married my longtime sweetheart Linda, a Communications Officer in the Women's Royal Naval Service (WRNS). For Linda, it was to mean inevitably giving up her successful career to be with her new husband along with facing a future of frequent family moves which typify Service life. Our honeymoon was even put in jeopardy owing to the unplanned docking to fix the fore-planes problem but at the last minute it was agreed that a temporary relief would join, allowing our wedding arrangements to stand.

Meanwhile, the new Captain continued to train the crew to meet the challenges of the impending Barents Sea patrols. It was notable that he spent prolonged periods awake in the control room to train his body to cope with very little sleep for days on end. Apart from indicating perhaps a weakness in his ability to delegate, when he did eventually turn-in, he proved almost impossible to wake up. Another eccentricity of his was the introduction of the 'buggy box', a little low-level padded seat with castor wheels which enabled the periscope watchkeeper to look through the 'scope at a much lower level than normal. This ensured that the periscope height above the sea, matched that of the shorter electronic surveillance mast. Accordingly, this reduced the amount of mast exposure when intelligence-gathering in the vicinity of Soviet vessels. However, the downside was that it was difficult to keep a satisfactory periscope watch when sitting on the buggy box, especially if the boat was moving around a bit as it was inclined to slide around of its own accord.

My last period of sea service in *Swiftsure* involved major sonar trials in deep water off the Canary Islands, in May 1975, with a diesel submarine and consort ship. Much to my dismay, once the trials had started, the sonar departmental Chief Petty Officer reported to me that, in error, inadequate stocks had been embarked of the photographic chemicals required to operate the main active sonar display. Normally this would have not been an issue as active sonar was not often used but, on this occasion, a key element of the trials was testing this mode of operation and display. While pondering the best time to break the bad news to the Captain, the Russian Navy came to my rescue. Intelligence reports indicated that a large Russian naval force had deployed into the Eastern Atlantic and, consequently, being a far higher operational priority, the trials were terminated immediately and *Swiftsure* was dispatched to shadow the Soviet vessels. The latter were successfully detected but, because of *Swiftsure*'s after stabiliser noise problem, which remained unsolved, the Captain was reluctant to get in close and little intelligence gathering or crew-training were achieved. Having been spared the wrath of my Captain by the fortuitous Russian intervention, on return to harbour I handed over to my successor and bade farewell to the *Swiftsure* wardroom and my sonar team.

As the officer responsible for the sonar outfit, during the extensive evaluations of its systems, I had started to build up a substantial level of knowledge of the operation of sonars and of 'the acoustic environment'. However, I had been selected to undertake the Perisher Course and consequently had to accept that I would not be present to hone these skills during *Swiftsure*'s first Barents Sea operation planned for later that year.

I had learnt a great deal during my 20 months onboard *Swiftsure* and, in particular, I had developed an excellent knowledge of the nuclear submarine's many complex systems. Moreover, the nerve-wracking engineering events and ship control problems which had occurred during my time onboard, were to give me the experience and ability later in my career to confidently handle the nuclear submarines which, in due course, I would command. For me, it had been a highly exciting appointment where I had enjoyed immense job satisfaction. However, the major career hurdle of passing the fearsome Perisher Course was now my immediate goal.

Chapter 14

The 'Perisher' Course

In June 1975, aged 28 years and newly married, I arrived at HMS *Dolphin* to start the five-month Submarine Commanding Officer's Qualifying Course – 'Perisher'. The course, originally known as the 'Periscope' course, first took place in 1917 as a prerequisite to submarine command in the Royal Navy. However, as failure meant the abrupt end of one's submarine career, it became known as the 'Perisher'. I was well aware that if I 'perished', it was not only the end of my submarine career but, most likely, my future elsewhere in the Royal Navy would be pretty limited. In view of the latter, I would almost certainly have left the Service and pursued a civilian career. Consequently, I was determined to do my best to pass.

In my time the Perisher training focused upon teaching its candidates to conduct a successful periscope attack by a diesel boat upon surface ships. There had been only modest changes to this format during the 58 years of the course's existence. Indeed, the Mark 8 torpedoes still in service in 1975 as the only available anti-ship weapon had not changed much in the intervening period either. Unfortunately, there had been a degree of inertia in adapting the course structure to match the most likely combat scenarios should there be an outbreak of hostilities with the Soviet Union.

I joined eleven other prospective commanding officers, of average age about 30. Four were from the NATO nations of Norway, the Netherlands and Denmark. We were split into two sections, each under the instruction of a 'Teacher'. Myself and the three fellow countrymen on my course, Gordon Leverett, Nick Crews and Neil Robertson, were joined by a Dane and a Norwegian. Our teacher was Commander Rob Forsyth. Seven years earlier, I had encountered him during my early trying times as navigator of *Sealion*. I remembered well that, while I was undertaking a difficult dived navigation in a narrow channel,

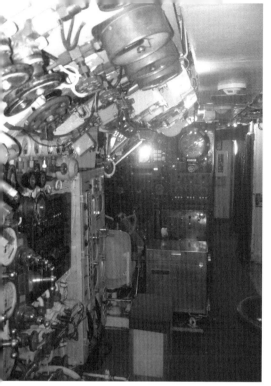

Left: *Odin* control room featuring the One Man Control (OMC) system.

Above: *Sealion* in the River Avon at the entrance to the Bristol dock system.

Below: 'Manny' Scicluna, the redoubtable coxswain of *Sealion*, manning the after hydroplanes.

Above: *Oberon* Crossing-
the-Line ceremony – the
Captain receives his shave
from King Neptune's
consorts.

Right: *Oberon* in heavy seas
off the South African coast
about to undertake a
helicopter transfer.

Below left: The loneliness of
command – the Captain of
Oberon contemplates the
Indian Ocean horizon with
the boat trimmed down
forward.

Below right: Pollyanna the
reindeer with the Captain of
Trident, Commander
Geoffrey Sladen.

Above: The Cuban Missile Crisis – one of the Soviet 'Foxtrot' class submarines forced to surface.

Above: Three *Resolution* class SSBNs on the surface in the Clyde – the fourth was somewhere on patrol.

Below: A 'Sods Opera' performance being staged in the Junior Rates Mess of an on-patrol Polaris submarine.

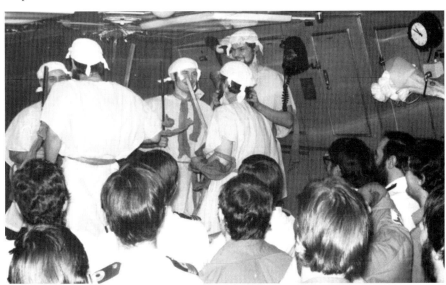

Left: *Swiftsure*'s control room.

Right: Setting up the bar for cocktail sundowners – *Swiftsure* on the AUTEC range.

Left: 'Whiskey' class Soviet diesel submarine.

Right: *Otter* paying off at HMS *Dolphin* April 1977.

Top: *Spartan* proceeding down the Gareloch in exceptionally calm conditions.

Above left: Preparing a Wardroom movie in *Spartan* – author in the background.

Above right: *Courageous* in the Falkland Islands, San Carlos Water – volunteer sentries!

Below: The 688 class SSN USS *Philadelphia*.

Above: *Valiant* at speed on the surface.

Below: *Valiant* trimmed down forward to check the propellor.

Above: Soviet 'Victor' class SSN.

Left: The author on the bridge of *Valiant* departing Bergen.

Below: Exercising fire drills in a *Vanguard* class control room.

Above: ICEX-18 – USS *Hartford* in the foreground, on the horizon USS *Connecticut* to the left, *Trenchant* to the right.

Right: The Deep Submergence Rescue Vehicle *Avalon* secured on the stern of USS *Batfish*.

Below: Preparing a recovered Tigerfish torpedo for air shipping at the Ice Camp – ICEX-88.

as a Squadron sea-rider he had assisted me to accurately determine the submarine's position and consequently I avoided a severe tongue-lashing from the Captain. Rob Forsyth clearly relished his role in developing the command qualities of his students and getting the best out of them. His style of tutoring and mentoring was characterised by lots of enthusiasm, energy and encouraging advice. Very evidently, he wanted none of his team to fail. The instructional style of the second and more senior Teacher, Commander Toby Frere (later Vice Admiral Sir Toby Frere), was much more reserved and measured, but probably equally effective.

The student's Teacher would be the ultimate arbiter of whether he should pass or not. Nevertheless, throughout the course, there would be discussion between the two Teachers regarding the progress of the individuals in their respective sections. Historically there had been an average pass rate of 75 per cent, but we were all too aware that the attrition rate in a few recent courses had been over 50 per cent. After almost two months at sea assessing the student's capability to be a submarine Captain, the Teacher's final judgement was almost always very fair and balanced. However, inevitably there was the odd individual who passed, but when actually in command, was found to be not up to the mark.

Following several weeks of induction and training in a shore-based attack training simulator, my Perisher course was structured around two sea phases: five weeks of periscope training in the Clyde Estuary, followed by two weeks of operational exercises in both the deep ocean and inshore areas. During the periscope training phase, each of the students would take turns at undertaking the role of Captain for one attack on a specific target, while his colleagues would fulfil the supporting roles of the command team. My course would be embarked in *Finwhale* and the other group in *Narwhal*. Each boat remained fully manned by her own Captain and crew.

The periscope training phase took place in the sea areas between the mainland and the island of Arran. The attack runs took place on a north/south axis with each of the submarines allocated its own separate area and the target warships reversing course at the end of each specific run. This training phase began with visual attacks being made on a single warship, gradually working up in the final week to the penetration of a defensive screen of four high-speed, manoeuvring escort warships protecting a Fleet tanker. This, of course, involved several weeks of expensive frigate or destroyer time which was of limited training value to their own respective crews. This was because many of the runs were conducted with the warships proceeding at a high speed where their sonar would have been ineffective. The two boats operated a daily running routine, returning in the evening to moor to a buoy at Rothesay where the course staff and students would disembark to stay overnight in the small, friendly Craignethan hotel.

While the human eye has a field of horizontal view of over 180 degrees, the horizontal vision through a submarine periscope is much smaller, normally less than 40 degrees. This constrained view requires the skill of rapid target location and, particularly where several escorts are in the vicinity, of retaining a mental picture of where all enemy units are and what they are doing. There also is the importance of conducting a 360-degree visual sweep every few minutes to ensure no threatening ship or aircraft has been missed.

The visual attack involves a number of constraints which markedly increase its complexity and difficulty. The most obvious is that the exposure of the periscope must be limited to a few seconds for each viewing, keeping its elevation above the sea-surface as low as possible. This, of course, risks even small waves blurring or obscuring the target image. Furthermore, to reduce the amount of telltale periscope wake, the speed of the attacking submarine has to be kept low, ideally 4 or 5 knots.

The periscope course phase ran from Monday to Friday with weekends spent in the Clyde Submarine Base, Faslane. Here the students could relax and prepare for the following week's challenges but few, if any, took up the option of travelling home. During the week, the daily routine would involve a 0700 boat transfer out to the waiting submarines, which had already slipped their moorings. The day's first Duty Captain would then take the boat to sea and dive it under the supervision of the submarine's actual Captain.

Once underwater at around 0830, the attacks would start at intervals of approximately 45 minutes. They would be relentless throughout the day, stressing not only the students – whether they were in the command role or in the supporting team – but also the submarine's own Captain and, in particular, his Ship's Company. Needless to say, operating at periscope depth extremely close to high-speed warships, both ship control and depth keeping had to be exact within tight safety margins. This required, on the part of the crew, intense levels of concentration and immediate response to orders.

Each of the runs was conducted in a specific formation which was designed to train the students in different facets of the visual attack. Some were carried out with the warships proceeding at maximum speed, with instructions to head directly for the periscope if sighted. Even in exercise conditions, the unexpected close-range sighting of a destroyer's angry bows heading straight towards him at high speed, drastically raised the adrenalin of the person at the periscope

The student would be expected to keep track of each of the approaching warships using mental arithmetic to calculate closing ranges and stopwatch timings of when to next look at a given vessel. There also would be the need to monitor ever-present fishing vessels and passing commercial traffic. On occasions, there were the additional pressures of mentally calculating the angle the torpedoes would be fired on (known as the 'Deflection Angle') without the aid of the torpedo course calculator.

A key aspect of the Perisher visual attack was to remain at periscope depth until the range of an oncoming escort closed to 1,200 yards. This allowed time to dive the submarine to a depth of 90ft, leaving plenty of clearance between the top of its fin and the keel of the approaching ship. In the confines and noise of the cramped control room, such 'go-deep' runs were highly intense, with the vibration and noise of fast revolving propellers passing directly overhead reminding all on board of the very real risk of collision. Periodic practice torpedo firings added further complexity, with the student having to deal with internal weapon readiness reports and tube launch preparations, and the imperatives of making certain that the range was clear. The latter involved ensuring that the torpedoes did not threaten fishing boats or shipping in the area, adding another challenge. Finally, there was the physical exertion of operating the periscope, crouching down to meet the eyepiece as it emerged from the deck, lowering the handles and then, once the top of the periscope broke the surface, rapidly swinging it onto the predicted bearing of the point of interest – the target or another threatening vessel. This was followed by determining the target's range and bearing, then snapping up the periscope handles and ordering it smartly lowered.

Clearly the Teacher had to be on his mettle as he monitored and assessed the student during each attack. His intervention of ordering the submarine deep had to be delayed until the precise moment when the student had missed the 'go deep' point and the submarine had then to be rapidly taken below periscope depth for safety reasons. At the same time, he was seeking evidence that a student – having made an error – could quickly recover the situation, demonstrating a key quality of the potential submarine Captain. During each attack, the Teacher constantly assessed how the individual student could cope with all the stresses and pressures which the submarine commander could be expected to deal with. He also would be seeking to identify the student's weaknesses and, in particular, whether his control of the submarine was safe. Unfortunately, during the periscope attack training phase, a student occasionally would completely lose his nerve and for his own wellbeing, would promptly be removed from the course.

Once an attack was over, the Duty Captain would collect up his records and receive a debriefing in the semi-privacy of the Captain's cabin. Rob Forsyth did not over-labour mistakes, such as the missed look on a threatening warship or mental arithmetic which had gone awry, most of which the student would be aware of anyway. Instead, he concentrated on advising how improvements could be made – a subtle and effective way of encouraging greater effort without undermining self-confidence.

For myself, I felt nervous and on edge before I assumed the command role, but once the attack run was underway, my apprehensions were replaced by focus and concentration as I took control of the periscope and manoeuvred the submarine. Paradoxically, during each of my attacks, I cannot recall feeling a significant degree of stress despite my actions being very closely monitored by the Teacher. Inevitably, I made comparisons with my fellow students' performance and gradually came to the conclusion that, whilst not the best candidate, I was not the worst.

The day's attack sessions over, tensions eased and the evening meal would be eaten in the submarine's cramped wardroom on her surface passage back to Rothesay. Finally, having returned to the hotel, both groups of students and the two Teachers would gather in the hotel bar, where we convivially mixed with the local regulars, who viewed us with a degree of bemusement. Coincidentally, one of the most popular tunes being played in the bar was Abba's 'The Teacher'. Drinking was moderate and there was no implicit requirement for a student to join the gathering, but his Teacher would have thought it a bit odd if a student elected to be alone in his room.

By coincidence, Geoffrey Biggs joined the Teachers for several days course familiarisation as, now in the rank of commander, he was designated to take over from Toby Frere. His quietly confiding that I was doing alright really boosted my confidence. Despite making the occasional mistake, such as missing a look at an escorting ship, during the closing stages of the periscope training, I knew that I was doing OK when Rob Forsyth started staging theatrics while I was looking through the periscope in the command role. These including a terrified-looking rating running through the control room pursued by a ranting cook wielding a carving knife, dramatics that must have eased the tension for the Ship's Company. However, while feeling reasonably confident and competent, I did not rate myself as a natural in handling visual attacks and having a good 'periscope eye'. I tended to rely upon stop-watch timings rather than trusting my innate instincts that it was time to look again at a threatening vessel. Although no one in my group failed the periscope phase of the course, twice, on arrival at Rothesay in the boat bringing us ashore, it was noted that there was a missing face in the *Narwhal* section. These occasions rather dampened the evening's relaxation in the hotel bar.

On completion of the periscope attack training weeks, the ten of us remaining enjoyed dinner at the well-known Glasgow seafood restaurant, Rogano, before heading south on the overnight sleeper. It was a relaxed, convivial gathering but we were all well aware that we had only passed the first hurdle and there were great challenges ahead in the operational phase.

There followed several weeks ashore participating in a joint maritime warfare course at the Maritime Warfare School in HMS *Dryad* near Portsmouth, where we trained in Fleet tactics and procedures. For myself it was a good opportunity to work again with my peers from the surface and air communities However, in an era when the Royal Navy was running down its fixed-wing aircraft capability, the vulnerability of our surface fleet to air attack once again struck home to me.

This course completed, the Perisher candidates started the final two-week operational phase. My section joined *Onslaught* at Devonport in early November. Travelling west by car, I became aware of my Irish Setter defecating over the navigational charts in the rear of the car but, thankfully, he missed my officer's cap. The charts had been painstakingly prepared for various anticipated operational scenarios, such as exercising minelaying techniques and photo-reconnaissance of shorelines of interest, during which I would assume the role of Duty Captain. As there was no opportunity to undertake a re-work with new charts, I cleaned the charts off as best I could. I did mark the resultant brown stains with an indication of their origin.

On her departure from Devonport, *Onslaught* headed to the South-west Approaches to participate in a major exercise where the opposition was a multinational group of NATO ships supported by anti-submarine aircraft and helicopters. I found this phase to be a marked change from the highly structured weeks of periscope attacks.

Attacking ships at night in heavy seas was particularly difficult. Nevertheless, this element of the course passed without any serious mishaps on my part and was followed by the final inshore phase in the Clyde Estuary. This was the Perisher course's culmination, with each student taking it in turns to command the boat for a whole day. Operating in highly confined waters, there were the imperatives of avoidance of detection by aggressive patrol craft and anti-submarine helicopters. In these vital closing phases, I knew that I was being over cautious in handling the submarine when in proximity to surface craft. Nevertheless, I was aware this would not cause me to fail but putting the boat into a distinctly unsafe situation would. With hindsight, I probably did not get the full benefit offered by this final fortnight at sea. Sadly, the course concluded with one failure occurring right at the end – the Norwegian officer clearly could not safely handle the inshore situation.

The final exercises completed, *Onslaught* headed for Faslane. We were individually called to the Captain's cabin to learn from Teacher whether we had been successful and passed. My elation on being informed that I was about to be Captain of *Otter* was somewhat tempered by the unexpected news that I was being appointed to the one Faslane submarine available, and not one of the six *Dolphin*-based boats due for a change of Captain. In anticipation of a Portsmouth posting, Linda only recently had been appointed to HMS *Mercury*, the communications training school near Portsmouth, and we had set up house in the nearby town of Petersfield. In an era where alignment of spouses' careers was not a consideration, it meant an end to Linda's successful career in the WRNS. However, I was not to know, that command of *Otter* would set me on course for a unique and highly rewarding career path.

The Perisher course equipped me to be a competent, safe submarine Captain, confident in my ability to handle the most demanding of inshore situations. However, it did not equip or train me to deal with the submarines of the Soviet Union, as little time was spent during the course learning how to successfully approach and attack a submerged target. Indeed, there was little reference to the Tigerfish torpedo which was coming into service and would soon replace the Mark 23 anti-submarine torpedo.

I was well aware that a submarine Captain engaging an underwater opponent had to be able to analyse information from all his acoustic sensors, some of it imprecise or conflicting. He would need to make rapid and complex assessments of the developing situation and, especially in the close-range, 'dogfight' scenario, he would have to counter the opposing submarine's manoeuvres. Most importantly, he needed to keep his team well appraised of his thoughts and intentions at the same time as evaluating his team's target parameter assessments. It was all about outstanding teamwork and trust between those in the sound room and the control room and was much less individualistic than the periscope attack as practised in the Perisher course. It required a significant degree of training and experience to gain competence in assimilating a target's parameters using only sonar bearing information and using this data to achieve a successful, undetected weapon firing position. Indeed, it was a real art which not all successful Perishers would, or could, master.

The course over, I concluded that there was a complete lack of commitment of resources to the underwater scenario, in what was an extremely expensive course to run. The key issue was one of culture. At that time the Royal Navy's Perisher course had acquired a myth-like status and its format had been developed by highly accomplished Teachers such as Sandy Woodward who, as a Rear Admiral went onto successfully command the Falklands campaign naval task group. In assuming command of *Otter*, I was to be fully occupied getting to grips with my immediate challenges as a new Lieutenant-in-Command. It would have been unwise of me to overtly criticise the Perisher course conduct and its validity in the era of Cold War. However, in later times, I gained much professional satisfaction in being able to significantly contribute towards improving the underwater combat skills of our submarine command teams.

Across the Atlantic, the USN's Submarine Prospective Commanding Officers course, committed much more effort and time in training for the ASW scenario. It routinely culminated in realistic submarine versus submarine engagements on the range at AUTEC where there were actual Mark 48 practice torpedo engagements. This aligned with the USN submarine's primary role of confronting the Soviet submarine force in peacetime and, in war, forward deploying to engage it in its own backyard. Nevertheless, the American submarine Captain's prowess in periscope attacks could be less than refined and, in general, he was not so skilled in handling the shallow water, coastal situation.

During the late 1980s and early 1990s, the Perisher course was increasingly conducted in SSNs. Indeed, the last Royal Navy Perisher course where the periscope phase was conducted exclusively in a diesel submarine, occurred in 1994. This coincided with the paying-off of the last Royal Navy diesel submarines in service, the four *Upholder* class (see Chapter 25). There was nevertheless high-level criticism that the course was being slow to adapt to the requirements of those students who had never served in a diesel boat nor would be likely to command one either. Accordingly, as the diesel boats were phased out, increasingly the course focused upon determining the suitability to be XO and thus Second-in-Command of a nuclear submarine.

There had been few, if any, serious accidents in the post-war, diesel boat Perisher. This was not the case when SSNs started to be used as the training platform. In 1990 while conducting Perisher exercises north of Arran, *Trenchant* ran into the nets of the fishing boat *Antares*, causing her to capsize. Tragically her crew of four perished. *Trafalgar* in 2002, conducting dived navigation west of Skye and operating under the Teacher's instructions not to use the primary ship inertial navigation system, ran aground incurring significant damage. Thirdly, in 2016 the *Astute* class boat, *Ambush*, hit the hull of a merchant vessel while Perisher operating in the Gibraltar sea areas, resulting in serious damage to its fin which took many months to repair.

At the time of writing, the Perisher course has been completely restructured and the periscope phase is now entirely carried out in a shore simulator trainer. Notably, in the case of a student failing this part of the course, given more sea experience, he or she may be given the opportunity to undertake it a second time. The operational phase continues to be conducted in highly demanding and testing scenarios at sea. Quite correctly, the days of conducting WW2-style attacks against a force of surface ships have long since gone.

Chapter 15

First Command – Difficult Times

On a bleak winter's day in early December 1975, I boarded *Otter* to take over as her Captain. As was traditional in the Submarine Service, the handover was brief and took less than two hours. Having met those officers who were not on leave, I mustered a small quantity of highly classified commanding officer 'Eyes Only' material and codes. I then checked out a small stock of securely-held medicinal drugs and declared I was happy to take over. The departing Captain, Lieutenant Commander Toby Elliot, was then 'piped over the side' for the last time and *Otter* was mine.

The submarine was in a floating dock and a quick walk-through revealed her to be in a state of engineering upheaval as the main work while in dock involved replacing a number of hull-valve casings which were suspect. Part of a Flotilla-wide rectification programme, this was a messy job which involved a considerable amount of restorative work after the base repair staff had finished. First impressions were that the machinery of the 13-year-old boat needed a refit and a thorough overhaul. Altogether she was rather tired in both mechanical condition and appearance.

At the time *Otter* was unique in the Royal Navy, being the only operational submarine modified to act as a target for torpedo tests and evaluations. To be able to withstand hits from practice weapons, the fibre-glass fin, standard in *Oberon* class submarines, had been replaced by a steel version. She also had protective shielding fitted to those small areas of her pressure hull which were directly exposed to the sea and to the vents on top of the main ballast tanks, which were vital to the boat's ability to dive and surface. These measures created additional top weight which reduced the boat's righting stability and I was to discover that, in heavy weather, she rolled much more than others of her class.

In *Otter* I had inherited a boat containing much obsolescent equipment; even her outfit of ancient Mark 8 anti-ship torpedoes were of a particular type which had been phased out elsewhere in the Flotilla. Her sonar was similarly antique, essentially the same technology as fitted in WW2 boats. Of particular concern, the long-range wireless communication equipment relied solely upon hand-keyed Morse for both the reception and transmission of signal traffic. I was only too aware that the number of shore radio stations competent to handle this slow, out-of-date mode of transmitting messages was diminishing. Clearly, handling signal traffic was going to be high on my list of potential problems.

Otter's officers seemed a mixed bunch in terms of ability, and the same could also be said of the Ship's Company. In the event, the latter were to prove a lively, high-spirited group of individuals, and they were sometimes to be a problem when on shore leave.

Otter's first major assignment in 1976 was to deploy to the Caribbean to the AUTEC range in the Bahamas to act as a target submarine for a series of sonar and torpedo trials. First, however, was a short post-maintenance work-up, allowing me to get to grips with the boat, her equipment and her crew. With Christmas leave over and repairs completed, I took the boat to sea for the first time proceeding to exercise areas in the Clyde Estuary.

On the second day at sea, I conducted practice torpedo firings using the torpedo recovery vessel as a target. The results were disappointing: the two Mark 23 ASW weapons fired stubbornly refused to run, emphasising the uselessness of this weapon, and one of my salvo of four Mark 8s failed to surface for recovery at the end of its run. The deputy Squadron Commander was embarked for the day and I could well have done without his presence in the control room on only my second day at sea in command. On the other hand, the Squadron Staff would have wanted to assure themselves that the submarine was in competent hands before it crossed the Atlantic.

Exercises over and returning to Faslane in the evening, I had to make my first alongside into a tight berth, with the sterns of the SSN *Courageous* and the SSBN *Resolution* ahead and astern respectively. The former was about to deploy on a highly classified intelligence gathering mission, and the latter was a key component of the UK's nuclear deterrent. I was therefore understandably rather nervous about executing the alongside. Bringing *Otter* to a minimum speed in the final 200 yards of the approach, I ordered the motors astern and, much to my surprise and consternation, got an ahead movement.

As *Otter* lurched forward towards *Courageous'* propeller, I ordered 'Full Astern!' which resulted in making strong sternway towards *Resolution*. This was checked by a 'Full Ahead!' order and eventually, after a series of further urgent telegraph movements, the ahead and astern oscillations diminished and I got the boat under control and somehow completed the berthing without causing damage to either of the two highly important neighbouring submarines. Meanwhile, the Squadron greeting staff caught their breath having sprinted back and forwards up and down the jetty towards where they thought impact was about to occur.

Once alongside, a quick investigation revealed that the junior rating working the telegraphs in the control room was an inexperienced trainee, who instead of putting the telegraphs to the 'Astern' position, in error placed them 'Ahead'. He should have been under the supervision of an officer but the latter was fairly inexperienced, and was absent changing his uniform as he was about to assume Duty Officer responsibilities on arrival.

While no damage had been done to the two other submarines, *Otter* had hit the jetty's berthing catamaran with a fair degree of force and as a result had bent several steel stanchions. I was bemused the following morning to observe a MoD policeman with notebook out, recording the damage.

My next task was to take the boat into deep water in the North-west Approaches in order to conduct a dive to its maximum safe depth of 600ft. This would test out the new hull valves and allow other proving trials before heading across the Atlantic. During the deep dive the radar mast flooded, rendering this navigation and ship safety system inoperative, the first indication that defective radar was to plague my time in command of *Otter*.

The return surfaced passage to Faslane, north of Ireland, took place in Storm Force 10 conditions. During the night, a major electrical earth registered on the forward battery-section and an inspection of the battery compartment revealed that the heavy rolling of the boat in the storm conditions was causing acid to spill out and track across the tops of several defective battery cells, creating sparking and arcing. With a real risk of a fire or an explosion, this was a highly dangerous situation which immediately required the submarine to be altered to a course which reduced its movement, while electrical maintainers entered the tight confines of the battery compartment to effect repairs and clean up the acid. This was a risky process which revealed to me the spirit and courage of some members of the crew.

Otter left Faslane at the end of January 1976 for a transatlantic surfaced passage. The first commitment was to act as target for sonar trials with the newly commissioned SSN, *Sovereign*, in an area to the north-east of Bermuda. The planned speed to make the rendezvous with the SSN, was faster than I felt comfortable with, given the highly likely severe weather which would be encountered. Five days out, in mid-Atlantic and in severe Gale Force 9 conditions, the boat started suffering from a series of main engine problems and a reoccurrence of battery earths due to her heavy rolling. As if this were not enough, the starboard engine's exhaust hull valve had begun leaking and seawater was entering the submarine at a worrying rate. With the obsolete wireless equipment, severe difficulties were also experienced in both sending and receiving signal traffic concerning the engineering problems. As I sat in my cabin, my ears alert for the increasingly familiar sound of an engine stopping, the possible prospect of breaking down in the middle of the ocean with inadequate communications to call for assistance alarmed me. For the first time I appreciated the meaning of that phrase 'the loneliness of command'. However, somehow the engineering team managed to keep the engines running and, when the storm eventually abated and the sea conditions moderated, the battery earth problems disappeared.

Having made rendezvous with *Sovereign*, a radio conversation with her Captain revealed that she, too, had had her own technical problems during the crossing which were still being worked on. However, despite all this and after a slow start, the sonar trials were successfully completed. Owing to the leaking hull valve, *Otter* was limited to periscope depth where the rate of ingress of seawater could just be coped with. Anything deeper was out of the question. The trials over, we headed for a short port visit to Hamilton, Bermuda, where I was very glad there would be an opportunity, most importantly, to repair the leaking hull valve and rectify at least some of the growing list of defects.

Whilst strolling through the centre of the city on the second day of the visit to the Bermudan capital, I spotted a local newspaper with the front-page headline – *SUB RUNS AGROUND*. On buying a paper to find out which unfortunate boat had had a mishap, I soon realised the headlines referred to *Otter*. As I had turned the boat round to make the final approach to the berth in the shallow, pristine, azure waters of Hamilton harbour, the propellers had stirred up a cloud of sand which an observing reporter assumed was caused by the submarine hitting the bottom. This was not to be the first time in my career that media misreporting would make life uncomfortable for me. A signal was sent to Flag Officer Submarines and the Squadron, refuting the newspaper article but I knew that the communication of bad news, no matter how unfounded, tended to have an adverse effect.

Shortly after departing from Bermuda, I received a personal signal from the regional Admiral expressing displeasure that the crew had caused some damage to the hotel they had been billeted in. With the engineering problems during the Atlantic passage, the reported grounding and crew misbehaviour ashore, I reflected that the deployment had got off to a rather dismal start.

Otter was next bound for Charleston Naval Base. Here, during a ten day stay, many much needed repairs were undertaken by the helpful and highly competent engineering team of the submarine tender USS *Orion*. As was the experience in most American ports, *Otter*'s Ship's Company received immense hospitality and, in particular, the crew of the host submarine, the SSN *Grayling*, excelled themselves. The local Submarine Squadron Commander, the redoubtable Commodore 'Al' Baciocco, hosted a reception for the wardroom, and Rear Admiral Julian Burke, Commandant Sixth Naval Division, was welcomed onboard for a tour of *Otter*. In all, my spirits were lifted by the warm welcome and support which *Otter* had received in Charleston. As an aside, I was to make enduring friendships with *Grayling*'s Captain, Commander Ken Cox, and the Captain of the SSBN *Mariano G. Vallejo*, Commander Jim Collins, the latter a host at one of the several receptions organised for the crew.

Our next port call was Port Canaveral, arriving there in late February for the fitting of range tracking gear and special noise augmentation equipment. This was required for those trials where the Tigerfish torpedo would be tested. On 1 March I celebrated my promotion to Lieutenant Commander, sharing a glass of champagne with my officers.

On the following day, *Otter* left Port Canaveral for six weeks on the AUTEC range. Here she would predominantly act in the target role at varying depths for sonar and weapons trials. Her trial consorts were again the SSN *Sovereign* and the *Leander* class frigate *Cleopatra*, the former firing Tigerfish heavyweight torpedoes and the latter launching lightweight Mark 44 and Mark 46 weapons either from her torpedo-tubes or from her helicopter. *Otter*'s equipment problems continued, with the reliability of the diesel engines and their associated electrical generators a constant source of worry. Conditions onboard when submerged, with sea temperatures of around 28°C, were stifling. The air-conditioning system proved totally inadequate in both maintaining reasonable temperatures and reducing humidity, and consequently the deckheads dripped with condensation.

During the weapon firings, the boat's watertight compartment bulkheads were shut down as a precaution against the effects of damage from an inadvertent hit. This meant that ventilation had to be stopped, making the air temperature soar into the high forties. On leaving Port Canaveral, several members of the crew had reported that they were suffering from symptoms of influenza and this soon swept through the Ship's Company, its effects exacerbated by the very high humidity and the temperature differentials of up to 30°C between the interior of the submarine and the bridge, when the submarine was running on the surface.

Shortly before arriving at the AUTEC range, I succumbed to the bug and was to feel awful for the next week or so. To give the crew a break and to enable them to get away from these highly unpleasant conditions inside the boat, two short port visits took place to nearby Nassau. The first harbour entry, at night and arranged at short notice to allow proper medical care for the worse infected members of the crew, was extremely challenging. Feeling very much under the weather, and again with no operational radar, I maybe should have delegated the harbour entry to the First Lieutenant but a number of factors led me to lack confidence in his ship handling ability. Therefore, I pressed on, increasingly worried on observing the dimness of the lights on the buoys marking the channel entrance. Furthermore, the beacon lights on shore marking the approach were either extinguished or displayed totally different characteristics to those described on the charts.

This fraught situation might have been eased by the early boarding of the pilot, but this individual boarded when just off the berth in an inebriated state and foul temper having banged his head on the way up to the bridge. He, therefore, was of little assistance.

The berth itself was situated between and at the end of two cruise-liner piers, and only 200 yards in length, allowing a mere 50 yards of leeway ahead and astern. An approach at right angles to the berth was called for, passing a berthed liner close to port, and hopefully tightly swinging the boat to starboard using the motors ahead and astern. Somehow, someone was looking down on me, and as I watched the bow swing down the length of the jetty, ropes were passed and the boat eased itself alongside with minimum manoeuvres. The Bahamas Naval Liaison Officer on boarding related that the foreman in charge of the shore berthing party was convinced there was going to be a collision and had cleared his people from the pier edge. The foreman was astounded when quickly the submarine was neatly berthed alongside. For my part, feeling really quite ill and run-down, I felt at last I had been endowed with a bit of good luck.

Once alongside, two of the crew who were showing signs of developing pneumonia were landed into a local hospital where they were to make a rapid recovery. Two days later heading back to sea in daylight, viewing the harbour entrance with its various reefs and hazards, I counted my blessings that *Otter* had not come to grief.

Back at sea, engine and other mechanical problems persisted. Often, only one of the two diesel engines was in working order, parts of the defective engine being repaired ashore in the AUTEC workshops on Andros Island. The wireless mast was also unreliable due to seawater ingress, making communications with the AUTEC staff and Squadron difficult. On one occasion, after surfacing in the evening at the end of a day's evasive manoeuvres against torpedoes, with the main battery absolutely exhausted, the one available engine could not be started. With the submarine stationary, wallowing in a long swell, with little power available other than for a few lights and essential equipment, internal temperatures climbed into the fifties from the heat exuding from the exhausted main battery. Wearily sitting, perspiring in the near darkness of my cabin, the two hours it took to get the engine going seemed interminable. The roar of the diesel starting, and sucking relatively cool fresh air into the boat's interior, was one of best sounds I had ever heard.

Added to the myriad of electro-mechanical problems onboard was the external damage caused by several practice torpedo hits. Shortly after the trials had started, it became evident that the Tigerfish torpedoes were performing badly. There were many delays and aborted runs and I sensed a degree of frustration onboard the firing submarine, *Sovereign*. Eventually one good run was achieved with the weapon using its active sonar to home but, perhaps overcome by exuberance, the *Sovereign* command team failed to heed the range control instructions to turn the weapon away from *Otter*. The high-pitched whine of the approaching 2-ton, 36-knot torpedo was clearly heard through the pressure hull, and was followed by a loud bang as the weapon struck forward in the area of the torpedo tube bow-caps.

I immediately surfaced the boat and the range staff quickly flew out divers by helicopter to inspect and assess the damage. Braving a school of hammerhead sharks which were not too far away, the divers checked out the forward part of the submarine and when they surfaced, clutching small fragments of torpedo, reported that a starboard tube bow-cap was badly stove in but otherwise there was no other damage. A few days later, a second inadvertent Tigerfish hit damaged the starboard battery cooling intake arrangement, followed by a *Cleopatra* tube-launched Mark 44 making an impact on the starboard propeller shaft. *Otter* was taking a battering.

In early April the trials were over and *Otter* headed back across the Atlantic on the surface to Faslane. Despite a series of mechanical problems, because of Herculean efforts on the part of the engineering staff the boat had met all her commitments and was always at the right place at the correct time. On returning to Faslane, the submarine was taken in hand for a docking and several weeks of repairs. It was cold comfort to me that, on inspecting the main generators, the shore maintenance staff expressed surprise that they had kept running and the boat had made it back across the Atlantic at all.

On return from the Caribbean, two new officers joined. Lieutenant Jim Boyd assumed the role of Navigation Officer and Lieutenant Johnny Milnes took over as XO. Cheerful and enthusiastic, Johnny immediately set about improving the morale and efficiency of the Ship's Company and was to prove a well organised and highly reliable Second-in-Command.

Meanwhile Linda, serving in the Portsmouth area, had resigned her commission in the WRNS, the outcome of my unexpected appointment to a Faslane-based boat. If she had remained unmarried, no doubt she could have reached the higher ranks of this Service but in the era of the 1970s there was no consideration afforded to appointing serving couples to the same base port. Therefore, for her to remain in the WRNS would have been impractical. However, she had had the compensation of being awarded extended leave at the end of her service and this enabled her to be with me during the majority of the port visits during the AUTEC deployment.

We temporarily set up home in one of the officer's married quarters in the village of Rhu, near the base, while we set about house hunting in the area. Linda soon got a job as a sales executive in Rank Xerox, at the time the UK's leading photocopier company. She was the first woman in Scotland to hold such an appointment. She evidently had impressed the interview panel, the more so as coincidentally its chair had recently lost his wife to a dashing nuclear submarine commander. Linda was to prove highly successful in selling photocopiers in the Glasgow area and indeed her salary and commission during the next four years were to significantly exceed mine. We thus had the good fortune of enjoying a lifestyle which most of my peers could not afford.

During my time in *Otter*, while alongside in Faslane, there was a visit from members of the Armed Forces Pay Review Board (AFPRB). This body has the remit of recommending to the Government the levels of pay and allowances within the Armed Services. Tour of the boat completed, during an informal chat in the wardroom I pointed out to the representatives that the civilian skippers of auxiliary craft delivering stores off-shore to an SSBN, were with overtime, better remunerated than the nuclear boat's Captain. I added that as a submarine Captain, my annual salary of £4,000 was less than that of a London bus driver. Their unsympathetic response was that naval officers had much better future career and salary expectations than the average public employee. The late 1970s indeed were an era where Britain's military personnel were significantly underpaid compared to their civilian counterparts.

After a few months searching, eventually Linda and I had our offer accepted on a house which we could afford and suited us. Situated in the village of Cardross, which borders the Clyde Estuary to the west of Dumbarton, one of the main attractions of the house was that to the rear was the local golf course. We soon joined it as members and took up golf.

After the post-AUTEC maintenance period alongside, in June *Otter*'s next major tasking was participation in a Submarine Flotilla training period in sea areas around Gibraltar. This involved the participation of a significant number of submarines. Before departing the English Channel for the passage south, my Squadron Commander, Captain Barrie Wallace, embarked. He remained onboard for both the passage and the first phase of the training period. This included torpedo firings against the frigate *Mermaid* and acting as target for torpedo firings by the SSN *Courageous*. In the middle of the exercises we were visited for a few hours by Flag Officer Submarines – Vice Admiral Iwan Raikes – who arrived and departed by helicopter. I sort of got the sense that *Otter* and, in particular myself, were under a bit of scrutiny.

The training period was one of intense activity involving varied and demanding crew exercises. The highlights included the night landing and recovery of a number of Special Boat Squadron (SBS) Marines and a successful 'underwater look' upon the submarine *Cachalot* when she was on the surface. The latter exercised the intelligence gathering technique of precise stationing a few feet under a target vessel, accurately matching its course and speed. Once in this position, the submarine is then manoeuvred to pass up and down the target's entire length while through the search periscope video shots or photographs are taken of its underwater hull and fittings. During this evolution the top of periscope is only about 10ft below the target's hull and consequently accurate depth keeping is a must. For us to bring back an array of good quality photographs of *Cachalot*'s hull and fittings was very much a plus.

Indeed, *Otter* conducted all of her exercise serials in a highly satisfactory manner and on entering Gibraltar for a few days alongside, I was quite relaxed. Gibraltar, with its combination of sunshine and cheap bar drinks, could be notorious for crews getting into trouble ashore with the local authorities and police. Just before entering harbour, I had received a signal from the commander of the First Submarine Squadron, who was in overall charge of the training period. The message informed me that on the previous evening there had been a lot of altercations ashore which resulted in several arrests of submarine crew members. I was therefore directed to warn my Ship's Company that instances of further bad behaviour ashore would not be well received.

Consequently, on the following morning, a Sunday, I was extremely concerned to be informed that one of my sailors was locked up in jail and had been charged with breaking into a house. In consequence, I despatched his Divisional Officer to the jail to find out what had happened. On his return, he reported that the sailor could not really recall what had happened but, worryingly, he had observed that the rating was badly cut and bruised around his face. The sailor in custody was a competent and well-behaved radio operator and I jumped to the conclusion that on his arrest he had been beaten up by the Gibraltar police. I therefore asked Johnny Milnes to go back to the jail to try and establish exactly what had occurred.

A few hours later I was relieved to hear from Johnny that our man had been released to be dealt with under my custody, on the strict understanding he paid for the costs of the damage he had caused to the house. Johnny also related the actual story leading to the sailor's arrest. He had been drinking in a first-floor upstairs terrace bar and had got into a pretty inebriated state. On deciding that he had had enough to drink, he had forgotten that he was not at ground level and had left the bar, weaving across the roofs of adjoining houses.

Soon he walked across one roof which was not substantial. It gave way and he crashed through the roof and ceiling of a bedroom occupied by a sole Moroccan woman wearing a long white nightdress.

She woke with a real start to see a dazed and battered sailor in her bedroom under a hole in the ceiling. Her immediate reaction was to scream and jump out of a window. The rating meanwhile had got a real fright at the sight of a white screaming apparition disappearing out of a window and, now in a state of terror, broke a door down to get out of this perceived house of horrors. His arrest by the local police followed.

A few days later at sea, at Captain's Defaulters, the offender was summoned and the charge of conducting an act 'To the Prejudice of Good Order and Naval Discipline' read out. He immediately pleaded 'Guilty' but keeping a straight face on hearing his Divisional Officer recount the mitigating circumstances, was very difficult.

The passage back to the UK was predominantly on the surface and, as again the radar was not functioning, I decided to stay well to seaward of the busy shipping lanes along Portugal's coastline. Unfortunately, during one night, thick fog descended and I found myself in the middle of a large deep-sea fishing fleet. Several times I had to take drastic action to avoid collision with a fishing boat suddenly looming out of the swirling fog at close range.

A month later *Otter* was at sea participating in a large-scale exercise in the North Sea. During one part of the exercise, she was required to surface and simulate a Soviet 'Juliett' class submarine firing her 'Shaddock' long-range anti-ship missiles. Two RAF Phantom fighters would represent the missiles and their flight profiles once the boat had surfaced in a simulated launch mode. I assessed that it would be difficult to do this undetected since the area was under intense radar surveillance by MPA. However, having sighted a Spanish fishing boat lying stationary as she hauled her nets, I reckoned, if approached close enough, she would provide cover against radar detection.

I surfaced within 200 yards on the side of the fishing boat opposite to that over which she was hauling her nets. I well recall sighting through the periscope the great surprise on the swarthy fishermen's faces as the submarine unexpectedly arose abeam of them. Within a minute, there was the further surprise of the roar of the two Phantoms streaking right over the top of their vessel at a very low height, before climbing near vertically as they assumed the profile of missiles heading for their targets many miles away. *Otter* was back under the water within another minute, totally undetected. Overall, it had proved a highly successful exercise for the boat, things were on the up and I was looking forward to the exercise debrief in the naval base at Rosyth.

However, on berthing at Rosyth, I noted the unexpected presence on the jetty of a grim-looking Deputy Squadron Commander who was to utterly suppress my elation. Once onboard in the confines my cramped cabin, he related that a well-known glamour model and pornographic actress, named Mary Millington, had approached the *London Evening Standard* and the *Sunday People* selling the story that, while *Otter* was in Nassau, she had been invited onboard by the crew where photographs had been taken of her in the nude. In addition, a salacious article had been written in a pornographic magazine, which she owned and published, which indicated the complicity of the boat's Captain in her invitation to board *Otter*. It was also alleged that she had then personally obliged several members of the crew. The Commander's first question was whether I or my officers knew of any of this, to which the answer was a definite 'no'. It was therefore agreed that a full ship's investigation should be conducted immediately. Meanwhile I prepared for a barrage of unwelcome publicity. It was also decided that there was no point in Flag Officer Submarines' Public Relations Officer attempting to refute Millington's claims, as this would risk putting the story on page three of the *Daily Telegraph*.

In due course, the investigation revealed that Millington had been staying in the same Nassau hotel as the crew. Meeting some of them, she had asked to visit the submarine. On her arrival at the pier the Duty Officer had granted permission for her to come onboard where she was given a tour by some junior ratings of the duty watch. When aft in the engine room and motor room areas, she produced a camera and invited her escorts to take pictures of her in various states of undress. I was relieved to learn that nothing else untoward happened onboard.

The story hit the front page of *The People* the following Sunday and included a rear shot of Millington in *Otter's* motor room wearing only a sailor's cap. It also featured to a lesser extent in several other magazines and newspapers. Shortly afterwards, a formal question about the incident was raised in the House of Commons and was responded to by the Secretary of State for Defence. The ratings involved were subsequently disciplined by myself but awarded relatively light punishments in line with the official view that it was a caper which went badly out of control. Perhaps the biggest casualty of the affair was my mother-in-law who was cold-shouldered by colleagues in her local Conservative Club on account of having such a disreputable son-in-law.

Across the Atlantic, a few months prior to Millington's visit to *Otter*, as the US SSN *Finback* departed from Port Canaveral, a topless Go-Go dancer performed a routine on top of the boat's fin. It was clear that the Captain had been complicit in this stunt and he was subsequently relieved of his command for being 'guilty of permitting an action, which could have distracted the attention of those responsible for the safe navigation of the nuclear-powered submarine maneuvering in restricted waters'.

For myself, the Millington incident was undoubtedly a significant blemish upon my time in command of *Otter*. There was never any issue of complicity from my officers and, at the time of the incident, Linda and I had been lunching with the British High Commissioner. However, questions were asked about why, after the event, the officers were never informed by those senior ratings who had known about it, but had not reported it up the chain of command. With an air of suspicion being sustained at Headquarters against *Otter*, the whole Fleet got to know about the story and, on occasions at sea on encountering other warships, I would be asked by signal if Mary Millington was onboard. However, as I settled into the command of the boat, I felt that somehow there were to be better times ahead.

Meanwhile, the infamous, but enterprising, Millington had undertaken a similar jape appearing topless with the policeman standing outside No.10 Downing Street. She was also rumoured to be having a relationship with a member of the Labour Cabinet.

Chapter 16

Better Times

On departing from Rosyth, with myself still digesting the news about Mary Millington, *Otter's* first tasking was to play the part of a distressed boat in a missing submarine exercise. This involved, in an area to the north of Dunbar in the Firth of Forth estuary, manoeuvring the submarine onto the seabed. Having achieved a stationary trim and having gently ballasted the boat in order for it to settle onto the seabed with minimum impact, an emergency indicator buoy was then released. Attached to the submarine by a wire, when it reached the surface it would start transmitting a distress signal which would alert the shore authorities that a submarine was in trouble.

A special exercise buoy had been fitted in Rosyth but, unfortunately, on reaching the surface its retaining wire parted and the buoy drifted away with the tidal stream. The result was that the group of warships despatched to locate *Otter*, on arriving on the scene and achieving recovery of the buoy, were searching several miles away. It was only with difficulty that *Otter* was eventually located when a series of the smoke flares which we had ejected were sighted. The exercise did demonstrate the imperatives of ensuring that submarine escape and rescue equipment was maintained in first-rate condition.

A few days later, on arriving back in Faslane very late at night, I found myself, not for the first time, in trouble with the MoD Police manning the main gate at the base. They demanded that they search my car. Both physically and mentally exhausted, I refused and drove out through the gate, knowing this would get me in to a spot of bother with the authorities. However, to me it was just another example of the MoD Police harassing submarine crew members rather than concentrating upon their prime responsibility of protecting the Base. As mentioned earlier, there were later to be several spectacular break-ins to the base where the MoD Police were very much found wanting.

As the publicity around the Millington affair gradually faded, *Otter* continued with a varied programme of tasks at sea. As the Royal Navy's only operational target submarine we participated in a number of torpedo trials at the British equivalent to AUTEC, the much smaller and more limited British Underwater Test and Evaluation Centre (BUTEC). This was situated in the Sound of Raasay, to the east of the Isle of Skye. Compared to AUTEC, as well as being much smaller in size and having considerably less capable facilities, at the time BUTEC was an unprofessional and inefficiently run set-up. In due course, I was to become intricately involved with this facility after I had relinquished command of *Otter.*

Many of these trials involved acting as target for a new variant of the Tigerfish torpedo. This wire-guided ASW weapon which, after a very long gestation, was coming into service as a replacement for the Mark 23. This new version, Tigerfish Mod 1, had also an anti-ship capability and a range of over 15,000 yards. This was a big improvement on the pre-WW2 Mark 8's maximum range of about 5,000 yards and, of course, no homing capability.

Early in August, *Otter* was tasked for one week to stand-in for the submarine conducting Perisher training. The latter had been withdrawn because of a serious defect. The course instructor was none other than my Perisher Teacher, Rob Forsyth, who at the end of the week was highly complimentary about the performance of *Otter*'s Ship's Company which had well exceeded all expectations. This did much to lift my spirits. Nevertheless, on return to Faslane I was required to explain to the Base Commander why I had refused to be searched by the MoD Police. Explanation delivered, no further action was taken.

During the autumn two home-port visits took place to the ports of Blyth and Birkenhead. Apart from crew rest and recreation, the aim of theses visits was to afford the local community an opportunity to visit a submarine. In addition to the usual crowded first-night cocktail party in the control room for local dignitaries and officials, open-to-the-public days were always very popular. Long queues formed of people eager to gain an insight to life under the sea and *Otter*'s young crew fully rose to the occasion.

Blyth was yet another coal port in serious decline but the crew enjoyed great hospitality from the locals, the older generation well remembering that the port was an operational submarine base during the Second World War. Indeed, I was invited to visit a local pub, the Astley Arms, which was a favourite of wartime submariners, where I was presented by a barmaid from the war era with a wartime bottle of Johnny Walker Scotch. This was an unclaimed raffle prize where the winner, a submarine Petty Officer, had failed to return from patrol to claim his prize. For many years the bar staff had kept the bottle in a safe place. The bottle, its contents now dark in colour, is on display at the Royal Navy Submarine Museum, Gosport.

In early December the continuing problems with our radar resulted in a hazardous passage into Birkenhead, the shipbuilding town situated across the Mersey from Liverpool. Having embarked a pilot at the start of the buoyed entry channel, thick fog descended. Within a few miles, the radar failed and I had no option but to abort the passage and extricate *Otter* from the narrow channel. While turning the boat around, despite warnings to all shipping in the vicinity that a submarine was manoeuvring in the middle of the channel, a small outgoing Danish freighter passed very close ahead, a mere 50 yards or less. Collision was only averted by applying maximum stern power. Alarmingly, clearly the bridge watchkeepers in the Danish vessel were completely oblivious of the close proximity of a submarine. My confidence in the pilot's ability was shaken as I was unconvinced that he had clearly relayed to the harbour control authorities the intention to turn the submarine around in mid-channel.

Having cleared the channel and left the fog bank, the radar fault was rectified, but although the visibility had improved considerably, the tidal window for entry into the Birkenhead dock system had been missed. Therefore, in late morning, having received a forecast of reasonable visibility, I made the decision to again head into the Mersey and to anchor off Cammell Laird Shipyard, Birkenhead, and await the evening tidal slot. This was achieved without difficulty and on this occasion the radar held up. However, having anchored, the visibility closed down and again my confidence in the pilot took a further knock when it became evident that having anchored in the position that he had advised, *Otter* was in poor holding ground. Consequently, we dragged anchor several hundreds of yards, right into the middle of the Liverpool/Birkenhead ferry crossing route: there was now a high risk of being hit by one of these vessels.

With visibility down to 100ft, I moved the submarine to a more secure anchorage just out of the main Mersey shipping channel and then spent several highly tense hours awaiting the rising tide. Unseen merchant ships passed only a few hundred yards away as I pondered how I was going to move into the locks when I could hardly see *Otter*'s bows and forward anchor light from the bridge. I reflected that my

decision to attempt an entry into the Mersey dock system had not
been the right one and I had been over-keen to meet my programme.
Now, confronting unpredicted and dismally poor visibility and with
the possibility of the radar failing again, my only option was somehow
to get into the safety of the Birkenhead docks.

At about 2000 the visibility improved a little, to about 200 yards,
and after discussion by radio with the Birkenhead dock authorities
it was agreed that they would place cars on either side of the dock
entrance with their headlights full on to assist identifying the entrance
through the murk. Having got underway once more, I found this
improvisation to be a great help in identifying the entrance and got
Otter safely into the harbour entry lock. Standing on the bridge
waiting for the gate astern to close and the one ahead to open once the
water level had matched that of the harbour, I was very relieved that I
had not hit the side of the dock. However, again the visibility plunged
to less than 100ft. Not trusting the pilot to competently direct the
tug standing by to tow *Otter* to her berth, it was agreed that the tug
would lead the way while I stationed the XO, Johnny Milnes, right
forward in the bows, in radio contact with myself on the bridge, to
give guidance on the helm and motor orders.

Gingerly moving out of the dock and just able to see the powerful
deck working lights of the tug which was only about 30 yards ahead, a
narrow swing bridge gap was safely negotiated. In the final approach
to the berth, I was totally reliant upon Johnny giving the engine and
rudder orders to get the boat alongside. The berth only appeared out
of the swirling fog during the final swinging in of the submarine as we
closed the dock wall. Once finally alongside, through the wet swirling
fog, I could see the welcoming party on the wharf and remembered
that the boat's cocktail party reception for local dignitaries and guests
had been cancelled a few hours earlier. However, that had been the
least of my worries in what had been a long and very tense day during
which I was highly relieved to have avoided a collision or grounding.

I later reflected that I had really earned my thirty-pence command
pay that day. However, since taking over *Otter* a year earlier, I had
experienced far too many near misses owing to a defective radar
system. Consequently, I resolved to coerce the Base maintenance
organisation into, once and for all, providing *Otter* with a reliable
radar. Meanwhile the non-duty watches cheerfully decanted ashore to
their hotels with no hint of them being aware of the risks encountered
in the previous 12 hours.

Otter was to have another period of 'Perisher running' towards the end of the year, on this occasion embarking a NATO course. Her participation involved one week of periscope training in the Clyde. This was followed by a final week of highly varied operational training where all the students were put through challenging scenarios with surface ship and helicopter opposition. The six students were from all from NATO countries, including three Norwegians. The Teacher was Commander Barrie Carr. However, as he could not operate the periscope ranging knob owing to an accident to his right hand, he was accompanied by Geoffrey Biggs ('GB') who supervised each of the student periscope attacks. True to form, he delegated a significant portion of these to myself while he enjoyed reading a book in my cabin. However, he clearly remained alert to what was happening in the control room.

One evening when *Otter* was secured to a buoy at Rothesay, the Captain of the target ship, the frigate *Salisbury*, Commander Hugo White (later Admiral Sir Hugo White), invited the Teachers and myself for dinner onboard his ship. I had been offered a cabin overnight and after the two other guests had departed ashore to their hotel, I was invited to share a bottle of Malt with several members of the *Salisbury* wardroom – a session which lasted well into the small hours.

Early next morning, on getting ready to transfer back to *Otter*, an anxious Hugo White informed me that the engines of both his sea boats would not start but he was pursuing the submarine, which was underway, towards the exercise areas. Eventually catching up with *Otter*, and with one boat now serviceable, I was successfully transferred when *Salisbury* was entering the designated exercise areas. 'GB' met me on the submarine's casing, took one look at me and ordered me to get turned in. It was payback time for the occasion I took *Otus* to sea. I was awoken by him at 1100 with a cup of tea and digestive biscuit and was curtly informed to take over the attacks for the rest of the day.

During the closing stages of the operational training phase, an exercise minelay having been conducted off the harbour of Lochranza, situated on north-west of Arran, *Otter* headed east into deeper water. However, in avoiding the opposing frigate, again *Salisbury*, we were much further north than planned. It was a cloudy, dark night and I was concerned that the navigational position was very much in doubt. Furthermore, I was a bit nervous, as earlier that evening it was evident that the frigate had passed as close as a few hundred yards away, unseen by either the Teacher or the Duty Captain. It had been understood that *Salisbury* should have been showing some lights. But when I checked the fine print of the exercise order, the instructions were for the frigate to be completely darkened.

The Duty Captain was on the search periscope looking for some navigational feature to help pin down where we were. Suddenly he yelled in excitement and ordered the rudder hard to starboard. Barrie Carr immediately enquired what had he seen. 'A cow Sir – I have just seen a cow!' Sure enough we were much further north than had been calculated and, as the moon came from behind a cloud, it had illuminated a lone black and white Friesian cow on the shoreline of Inchmarnock Island, staring out to sea.

The cow incident over and the operational phase completed a few hours later, *Otter* headed to Faslane to offload the course personnel. Happily, all of the students had passed. Much to my satisfaction, both Teachers commended *Otter*'s crew for being thoroughly professional and well prepared. Clearly *Otter*'s reputation was gradually being restored after the Millington affair.

One of the highlights of my time in command was the conduct of two short operational patrols where *Otter* was directed to gather intelligence upon a large ocean-going Russian tug bristling with radio antennae. It had been stationed for some time just outside UK territorial waters to the west of the Shetland Islands, near the island of Foula. Our task was to establish whether she was more than just a contingency tug, on station to provide assistance to Russian Navy vessels in the north-east Atlantic. This would mean conducting an 'underwater look' of her hull to confirm there were neither sonar fittings, nor exit facilities for a submersible craft.

During the first period on patrol in October 1976, we spent two days covertly monitoring the Russian through the periscope, but she remained at anchor throughout the period. This made it almost impossible in the murky visibility conditions and a strong tidal stream to obtain photographs of the underneath of her hull. First, closing to 1,000 yards astern of her, I checked that no one was fishing over the side. It was not unknown for submarines on surfacing after undertaking underwater looks on anchored Soviet warships to find their fins covered in fishing rods and line. What Russian sailors must have thought when their rods were suddenly snatched out of their grasp is a matter of conjecture.

Having taken a final accurate, visual set-up on the Russian vessel on its quarter at a range of about 1,000 yards, I set a course which offset the effects of the tidal stream, ensuring at all costs that the other vessel's anchor cable would be avoided. As I passed under it, I hoped there would be a few seconds glimpse of the underside of the hull, sufficient to capture detail on the periscope mounted cameras. However, in conditions of a strong tidal stream I found this extremely difficult to achieve without hazarding both vessels. If I had inadvertently got *Otter's* forward hydroplanes entangled in the tug's anchor cable there was the risk that we would drag the other craft under the sea. In hindsight, I wondered whether my superiors had thoroughly assessed the risks of the tug's crew being drowned and the international incident which would inevitably follow.

On returning the following February to the Shetland Islands to continue the intelligence-gathering task, I had better luck. Shortly after starting to observe the Russian, the latter got underway at slow speed heading out to sea, enabling a successful underwater pass to be conducted without worrying about the anchor cable. Achieving a good station under the Russian for about half an hour, this surveillance produced high-quality photographic shots of the vessel's bottom and her underwater fittings. These revealed that the tug had neither unusual fittings nor a sonar system.

In early March 1977, looking very smart and business-like, *Otter* departed from Faslane with a large paying-off pennant streaming from her wireless mast to her stern. She was heading on surface passage for refit in HM Dockyard at Portsmouth calling on the way for a visit to the port of Vejle, situated in south-east Denmark. After my Birkenhead experience, the base support staff had changed every component of the radar system from the aerial downwards and at last I had a reliable radar. This was fortuitous, as heading down the narrow channels of the Kattegat off the east coast of Denmark thick fog was again encountered. However, this time, the radar performed well and the crew conducted a flawless night navigational passage to arrive off Vejle where a pilot was embarked. In making the berthing, I was required to turn the boat in a highly confined basin and then to undertake a difficult stern-first approach up the port's narrow berthing channel. This I achieved with no tug assistance and a minimum of manoeuvring. My first, very ragged, berthing in Faslane seemed a lifetime away.

Soon after arrival at Portsmouth for de-storing and final pre-refit preparations alongside at HMS *Dolphin*, I relinquished command of *Otter*, having survived cases of bad publicity and a number of serious machinery failures. Notably the boat's radar was unreliable for most of my time in command and too often I was cursed by thick fog when on the surface in busy shipping lanes. The boat's low radar signature from a bow or stern aspect exacerbated the risks to ship safety and, on more than one occasion when the radar was defective, rapid collision avoidance actions had to be executed. On reflection, the base support organisation, notwithstanding its high priorities in maintaining SSBNs and SSNs, ought to have ensured that I had a reliable radar system.

Despite being high spirited and sometimes liable to serious disciplinary problems when ashore, nevertheless the crew had developed into a well-knit, happy, efficient team which had worked extremely hard to ensure *Otter* always met all her commitments in a timely, well prepared manner. If there had been moments that I felt they had let me down, there were other important occasions when they had risen unequivocally to my support.

The *Otter* experience was to prove an excellent apprenticeship for subsequent SSN command and, while in the future I was to encounter many demanding experiences, they were not to be as daunting as those I had to contend with in *Otter*. On my leaving call upon FOSM, Rear Admiral John Fieldhouse (later Admiral of the Fleet the Lord Fieldhouse) reassured, 'If you can survive the Millington affair, you can successfully meet all future challenges.' Privately, however, I was only too well aware that, no matter what the circumstances, the behaviour of his Ship's Company and the good name of his boat were ultimately the Captain's responsibility. A few years later I learned that Millington had committed suicide.

After leave, I was appointed to join the Submarine Tactics and Weapons Group (STWG) in Faslane. I was to take charge of the team responsible for training and certifying submarine crews in the use of the Tigerfish weapon system. Already this weapon had a poor reputation for reliability and performance and consequently, compared to other desirable shore jobs, my appointment was viewed by many as a bit of a poisoned chalice and most certainly, not career enhancing.

Chapter 17

Torpedo Problems

In late April 1977, I took up my new appointment to the Submarine Tactics and Weapons Group (STWG) at Faslane, heading up the Tigerfish torpedo crew certification team. I was certain that, in comparison with my Perisher peers, this was not the most prestigious of post-command appointments. Tigerfish had earned itself an unenviable reputation for poor reliability and performance and, indeed, its trials team had become known as 'Monty Python's Flying Circus'. It was now entering service and, in the next two years, most operational submarines would be required to undergo the certification process. This would demonstrate that their crews could safely and proficiently handle this new weapon system. The certification team consisted of a small number of officers and specialist ratings, whose role was to train and assess submarine crews in the competent handling and control of the new Tigerfish torpedo.

Prior to joining, I had been briefed by FOSM's staff that the overall certification process, which had been ongoing for just over a year, needed a thorough shake-up. The weapon firings were taking place at the BUTEC range and it was impressed upon me that too much time was being wasted due to range inefficiencies and a dilatory approach by the certification team. I soon learned there was much basis for these concerns and I would have many challenges ahead in improving the situation.

I took over from a Lieutenant Commander who was a functioning alcoholic. He had a brilliant intellect and, indeed, had been Teacher of the NATO Perisher course during my time in *Oberon*. Sadly, his addiction to alcohol had blighted his career and, with no possibility of promotion, he had elected for early retirement.

The certification process for each submarine was scheduled to take place over five days in the Sound of Raasay in the Inner Hebrides. After each day's torpedo firings, the certification team would be landed at Kyle of Lochalsh harbour. Their choice of accommodation, on the basis of cost, was local bed-and-breakfast houses which left plenty of balance from their daily accommodation allowance to be spent in local hostelries. A drinking culture pervaded the team, much encouraged by my predecessor. Of course, the longer the certification process took, the more time was available for evenings of drinking. This had become apparent to the submarine crews and was another factor which had done nothing to enhance the image or any sense of the importance of the Tigerfish weapon system. I quickly applied change and made it clear to my subordinates that the days of going onboard a submarine in a lethargic state, suffering from a hangover, were over. From now on, only the highest standards of professionalism would be acceptable. Supported by a highly competent Weapon Engineer Officer, Lieutenant David Waters, this shake-up soon paid dividends.

As described earlier, after WW2, the Submarine Service had become rather a backwater of the Royal Navy. Its first anti-submarine weapon was the electrically-propelled Mark 20 homing torpedo which was introduced in the 1950s. As stated previously it was unreliable. Furthermore, it had an unsatisfactory top speed of 20 knots and a maximum running depth of 800ft and its homing system was crude in design. Consequently, it was no match for the deep-diving Soviet nuclear submarines, nor their more advanced diesel type. In the 1960s, a wire-guided version, the Mark 23, came into service. However, this weapon proved even more unreliable than the Mark 20 and, as described earlier, would have proved absolutely useless in combat. British submarines also had a ground and moored mine capability but these weapons were all of WW2 vintage and, furthermore, there were no plans to update them.

In 1975, when the Tigerfish torpedo started entering service, the Royal Navy Submarine Flotilla possessed a total strength of eight SSNs and four SSBNs, together with more than twenty diesel submarines and a further three SSNs on the building slips. It was no longer a backwater, but the fighting arm which was attracting both the most talented officers and a large proportion of the warship building budget. Consequently, Tigerfish was the long-awaited anti-submarine weapon which was needed for the Submarine Service's growing nuclear submarine force. Unfortunately, not only was the new torpedo many years overdue, as stated above, it was rapidly acquiring a reputation for unreliability and poor performance. In consequence, some of the disdain being heaped upon it by submarine Captains was rubbing off onto the certification team.

I was soon dismayed by the apparent disinterest many senior submariners displayed in Tigerfish, few demonstrating much enthusiasm in acquiring an understanding of its characteristics, let alone its quirks. This was very much the antithesis of possessing detailed knowledge of submarine systems which had been the basis of my early training. Most of the Flotilla hierarchy focused upon its concept of operations at the time, which was – 'By confronting the Soviet today, being prepared for tomorrow's war'. In other words, if it was demonstrated that the Royal Navy's submarines could gather intelligence upon and covertly follow Russian warships and submarines in peacetime, somehow all would be well in war.

It was evident to me that many of my superiors were ignoring the lessons of history and, in particular, the severe impact torpedo failures had upon the effectiveness of both the German U-boat campaign against Allied shipping in the Battle of the Atlantic and the American submarine campaign in the Pacific War. In the case of the latter, if the USN's torpedoes had worked well from the outset of the war, Japan, confronting the loss of many major warships and the destruction of its merchant fleet, could have conceded defeat much earlier. Indeed, it could be argued that there may have been no need for America to use atomic bombs to bring about Japan's surrender.

Meanwhile, with an increasing amount of intelligence of Russian submarine movements and locations becoming available from Sound Surveillance System (SOSUS) chains in the North Atlantic, it had become vital to have central co-ordination for patrolling submarines and aircraft. This also ensured that British and American SSBNs were kept informed of any potentially threatening Russian vessels in their patrol areas. Accordingly, British submarines in the north-east Atlantic were now controlled from the Royal Navy and RAF MPA operational headquarters in Northwood, London.

Consequently, in 1978, the Flag Officer Submarines and his staff decamped from their old-fashioned offices and facilities in Fort Blockhouse, Gosport, to Northwood, a sure sign of the abandonment of its past image of a buccaneering sideline and its transition towards being the Royal Navy's primary strike force. With a marked increase in both capability and activity of Soviet submarines of the Northern Fleet this elevation of status was, of course, dependent upon having an effective anti-submarine weapon.

STWG was part of the response to this step change and combined the existing Flotilla tactical analysis group with the new Tigerfish weapons certification team. This organisational concept was unique in the Royal Navy and was based upon the American model of a single organisation which developed tactics alongside the assessment of both the effectiveness of weapon systems and the competence of crews trained to use them. The logic of this is inescapable but, remarkably, comprehensive analysis of weapon system effectiveness was new to the Royal Navy. Its initial introduction at this level of rigour had been established with the adoption of the United States Navy's Polaris system, where all facets of an SSBN's capability to launch and deliver a devastating attack upon the Soviet Union were thoroughly analysed.

The wire-guided Tigerfish was an electric torpedo which had a maximum speed of 36 knots and could home onto the target by transmitting sonar pulses (active homing) or passively listening on its miniature sonar system. A number of different commands were transmitted from the attacking submarine down its wire, but its Achilles heel was its highly unreliable arrangement for paying out its guidance wire. This was effected by a wire dispenser, fitted at the rear of the torpedo, detaching from the weapon once it was discharged. Apart from restricting the attacking submarine to a speed of about six knots, the outboard wire dispenser often 'tumbled' as it detached from the torpedo, causing the wire to break. Unlike the contemporaneous, much faster but noisier active-homing American Mark 48 torpedo, Tigerfish had to be 'command armed' after it had been launched and a broken wire meant that, even though it acquired its target and successfully homed in upon it, detonation would not occur. The Mark 48, which armed automatically, was normally fired upon a target intercept course, with its appropriate offset, making it much less reliant upon wire-guidance and, therefore, much more effective.

Tigerfish was also introduced into service at a time when British manufacturing was at an all-time low in terms of both quality of output and industrial relations. It was against this background that the torpedo was being manufactured by Marconi Underwater Systems Ltd. Poor component quality and manufacture, and its challenging advanced design features, had resulted in a serious delay in its introduction into service. Moreover, there was a lack of funding available to urgently rectify its shortcomings and, in particular, to remedy its poor reliability. This situation was convincingly hidden by the MoD behind the high priorities accorded to the SSN building programme, though in fact there appeared to be a perverse lack of impetus to ensure that the primary strike force of the Royal Navy was adequately armed.

There were other problems. The practice Tigerfish weapons used for the crew assessments and certifications used rechargeable propulsion batteries. These were different to the high-performance single-use units fitted to the war-shot torpedoes. The practice versions were prepared for firing by the MoD Armament Depot at Coulport, near Faslane, where the workforce was nicknamed the 'Coulport Bears' because of their strident militancy inherited from their antecedents, who worked in the Clyde shipyards. Their preparation of the practice weapons was often negligent, further and significantly compromising an already unacceptably low reliability.

The BUTEC tracking range, located in the Sound of Raasay, was completed in 1973. It was a poor second in comparison to the American alternative, AUTEC. Only about five miles by three in size, its depth of water was relatively shallow and, in its early days, its tracking hydrophones on the seabed were prone to damage by trawlers until an exclusion area was rigorously enforced around its boundary. The range vessels and equipment required to support the torpedo firings were also deficient, all of which further hampered the effectiveness of conducting the firings or testing the submarine crews. The situation was made worse by the poor quality of the range staff, many of whom also had a culture of excessive drinking, the curse of many communities in the West of Scotland.

At the end of run, the torpedoes would automatically de-ballast and broach the surface. There they would be secured by the crew of an inflatable boat, before being towed onboard the stern of a torpedo recovery vessel. However, these procedures were restricted to sea states of maximum Force 4, which were often exceeded, particularly during the winter months. Unlike AUTEC, where torpedo recovery was undertaken by a cage suspended underneath a helicopter, and therefore, far less weather dependent, much submarine time was squandered awaiting better recovery conditions.

During my early days at BUTEC, the shore and jetty facilities were still under construction and its senior naval officer was temporarily accommodated in the Kyle of Lochalsh station master's old office. The station platform was also used to transfer torpedoes on trolleys from the recovery vessels to the trucks which returned them to Coulport. This occasionally resulted in the unwelcome publicity of family holiday snaps featuring children astride a Tigerfish, the Royal Navy's new secret answer to the massive Soviet submarine threat.

I quickly made myself unpopular with the range personnel by shaking up the whole BUTEC organisation. Well aware that submarine time was at a premium, I required extended range operating hours lasting until sunset, instead of the cosy practice of ending activities at 1600. I also insisted on the instigation of rigorous daily checks to ensure the range equipment was properly functioning at the start of the day's firings. Too often a range vessel would arrive on station with defective target equipment. Its subsequent return passage to base to pick up functioning gear took at least three hours. Alas, wasted submarine time was not costed.

Prior to my arrival, the submarine crews undergoing certification only fired their weapons against unchallenging static noise targets which were a leftover from earlier development trials. I soon changed that by introducing mobile targets, both surface ships and submarines which, either by natural characteristics or by noise-augmentation, closely replicated the characteristics of Russian submarines. These were much more demanding for the crews to successfully engage and revealed a number of new problems such as that of the noise made by a running torpedo masking that of the target on sonar, making accurate guidance difficult. In addition to testing the crews in conditions as realistic as possible within the constraints of the range, these early firings started the process of developing tactics to achieve optimum use of the weapons, notwithstanding the chronic reliability problems. Another initiative was to start conducting firings away from BUTEC in suitable coastal areas in the West of Scotland, which gave the firing submarine more freedom to manoeuvre before weapon launch, thus adding further realism.

With the entire Submarine Flotilla being required to convert to Tigerfish within two years, the pace of certification was intense. My team and I took submarine crews through a comprehensive programme which included shore attack simulator training, instruction in the embarking and tube loading of Tigerfish together with testing and validation of the boat's weapon control equipment. During the sea phase, the team checked out that each submarine's crew was competent to use Tigerfish, usually firing up to eight individual weapons.

Apart from torpedo recovery weather constraints, there were plenty of other problems, both external and internal to the submarine, such as achieving clear range, which could delay weapon launch. It was hoped that, out of the eight torpedoes embarked as standard, there would be at least three reliable ones which would enable the certification process to be completed. Perhaps unsurprisingly, the occasional crew failed and had to repeat the whole programme. This was, however, an exception, as much effort was put in by the team to ensure the crews reached the required standards of expertise and capability first time round.

During my 16 months at STWG, I led the certification process for over twenty submarine crews. Experiencing well over a hundred Tigerfish firings, inevitably I built up a substantial expertise in this weapon system, the reliability of which remained doggedly low at about 40 per cent for an individual torpedo and its wire dispenser. However. I had the personal compensation of quickly finding a very pleasant hotel in the picturesque village of Plockton, a few miles from Kyle of Lochalsh. The surrounding countryside was absolutely stunning and the drive to the village an absolute pleasure, notwithstanding some summer evenings when I had to clear sheep comfortably settled on the warm surface of the single-track road. All were a very welcome contrast to the conditions of cramped, crowded submarine control rooms as crews struggled to master use of their Tigerfish weapons.

In September 1977, a few months into the job, I was tasked to lead a team to Hardanger Fjord in Norway, to fire a randomly selected in-service torpedo to demonstrate the reliability of the warhead. The outcome was to prove a low point in my experiences with Tigerfish. A remote spot on the west side of the fjord had been used for some time to test straight running torpedoes of both the Norwegian and British navies. With their limited range of a few thousand yards, these weapons were simply aimed at the steep sides of the fjord, exploding on impact with the sheer rock face. In the case of this first Tigerfish routine warhead proving shot, active homing was ruled out as, with multiple echoes likely from the rock face, the weapon's guidance could possibly go awry – perhaps even posing a risk to the firing submarine, *Ocelot*. Therefore, as passive homing was the only safe option, a noise source was suspended into the sea at a suitable point on the rock face. This was an essential prerequisite as the weapon needed to have strong target contact prior to detonation.

The firing did not go well. When the weapon was launched some 3,000 yards from the target, the wire dispenser failed to release. With the additional rear weight and drag caused by this imbalance, the Tigerfish careered on the surface across the fjord where our shore observer spotted it close to the aim point 'disappearing behind a clump of trees'. Not having been command-armed, on impact with the shore the torpedo did not explode, but *Ocelot*'s sonar team reported breaking-up noises which reassuringly confirmed that it had not actually come up onto the shoreline.

After reporting the failure to the Northwood headquarters, I soon learned that the Norwegian naval authorities were extremely displeased. Apparently, they had not been informed by the MoD that the torpedo being tested was an electric homing one with a maximum range of 15 miles, as opposed to the two or three miles of the straight-running types. They took the view that it could have been a danger to numerous settlements or vessels further up the fjord. I was consequently summoned to the Royal Norwegian Navy headquarters at Bergen to provide an explanation. I travelled there by one of two Royal Navy Sea King helicopters which had been hastily arranged to collect a specialist diving team intended to recover the wreckage of the failed Tigerfish. They had been urgently flown by commercial airline to Bergen airport. At a meeting with the local Admiral and his staff, I explained that there were a number of safeguards on the weapon which prevented it exploding other than at deep depth, but the Norwegians insisted that the Royal Navy make every effort to locate the warhead.

The helicopter flight from Bergen took us over the spectacular Folgefonna glacier before landing on the playing fields of the primary school in the village of Rosendal which, situated on the east side of the fjord, was the nearest suitable location to use as a base for the search. The school pupils, joyously pouring out from their classrooms, were thrilled at the noise and sight of the two unexpected aircraft which, having landed, decanted a team of burly divers and their equipment. I was more concerned about the bill for the evident damage the downdraft of the helicopters' blades had caused to the surface of their playing fields. Matters seemed rapidly going from bad to worse.

Meanwhile, a Royal Navy minehunter had been tasked to join in the search for the 300lb warhead and there was further assistance from a Norwegian Navy diving tender and its crew. Notwithstanding several days of search and the recovery of small fragments of the Tigerfish from a deep shelf on the side of the fjord, the warhead was never located. Accordingly, the search was terminated on the assumption that the warhead was lying in small pieces in several hundred feet of water.

On return to Faslane, I was required to conduct an investigation into the weapon's failure. The enquiry did not reveal much that we already did not know, and it was duly concluded that the dispenser had been defective, just one of many potential failures in a thoroughly unreliable weapon system. The whole incident, of course, had done nothing for the reputation of Tigerfish and left me feeling somewhat despondent about its many deficiencies.

The spring of 1978 found me back at AUTEC with the certification team. Our task was to conduct a series of Tigerfish tactical evaluation firings from the SSN *Conqueror* using the diesel submarine *Porpoise* as the principal target. David Waters and myself had designed each of the firing runs and my team were there to provide expert support to *Conqueror*'s crew to ensure, as far as possible, perfect preparations for each of the shots. Ashore in the AUTEC headquarters building on Andros Island, a small cell of STWG staff analysed the firings, providing rapid turnaround of the results, to highlight where improvements could be made on the weapon control.

Cape Canaveral was again used as a shore base and my team was allocated offices in a building in the NASA Space Centre. This location offered several benefits, including the local NASA staff putting on a tour of several redundant missile launch blockhouses. The visit to the Apollo launch control room proved very moving; all the instruments and control stations remaining virtually untouched, gathering dust as the programme of manned missions to the Moon faded to become just a remarkable memory. I also received an invitation to attend the launch of an Atlas Centaur rocket with a payload of commercial satellites. The night firing under a canopy of stars appeared almost surreal as the ascending missile quickly disappeared into the single cloud created by its venting fuel before lift-off, turning the cloud bright red before emerging and accelerating upwards into space in what had been a flawless launch. Ruefully I reflected – if only Tigerfish could have similar reliability.

There was a substantial cast of Tigerfish project civil servants and Coulport staff attending the weapon evaluations in a support role, many of whom had arrived in Cape Canaveral several weeks earlier and who were much enjoying the benign spring Florida climate. They were all under the charge of a senior submarine Commander, who I soon learned was of the old school and really out of his depth in terms of weapons systems knowledge. Although he had overall responsibility for the conduct of the trials, the purse strings for the whole operation were held by the civilian Tigerfish project personnel.

It soon became evident to me that, although the civilian staff of even the lowest status had been provided with rental cars for getting around Cape Canaveral and its environs, my own staff members were relegated to using a shuttle bus service. A firm representation to the senior Commander about the inequitable transport arrangements did not achieve any improvement. I was subsequently loaned a car by an American space engineer with whom I had become friendly, but this generous act did not improve the frosty relationship which had already developed between myself and the Commander. However, it was a lesson to me of the ultimate power exercised by those in the Civil Service who controlled budgets. As the trials progressed, I also gained a dispiriting insight into a culture of ambivalence within the project team about the firing results, whether they were successful or otherwise. I surmised that it was no wonder that it taken so long to get Tigerfish into service and, if this project was typical, the Navy's procurement organisation required a massive shake up.

During these evaluation firings, an unusually good streak of Tigerfish reliability was experienced and I was pleasantly surprised by the efficacy of the weapon's active-homing capability against *Porpoise*, even at a shallow depth where a lot of false surface echoes could be expected. As achievement of the run objectives was exceeding expectations, I proposed to the trials Commander that the weapon's active homing capability be explored further in more challenging scenarios. This would involve changing the authorised run plans but my superior, possessing little knowledge of Tigerfish, refused such a request on grounds that approval would be needed from headquarters and that would take too long. A heated but fruitless debate followed, with me emphasising that a great opportunity was being squandered. This added to my growing reputation of being quite a tartar who was not afraid to ruffle the feathers of my seniors.

On my return to the United Kingdom after completion of what had been a broadly successful series of AUTEC trials, I started considering my next job. The duration of my STWG appointment was always going to be a brief one as there was a shortage of command experienced XOs (Second-in-Commands) needed to man the SSBN squadron and the ever-increasing number of SSNs. Much to my concern, my appointer had indicated that I was most likely to be heading for an SSBN, an appointment I viewed with dismay. I saw it offering limited challenges on dull and monotonous deterrent patrols, not suited to my character and specific abilities. Furthermore, it did not make best use of my *Swiftsure* experience. To my relief, Lieutenant Commander Nick Ferguson, a Campbeltown colleague who was destined to join the SSN *Spartan* building at Vickers yard, asked to be appointed to an SSBN for personal reasons of family stability. Accordingly, I immediately seized the arising opportunity of the *Spartan* job to which my appointer agreed. Consequently, I prepared to go back to Barrow where the SSN was being completed.

Towards the end of my time at STWG, I was involved in providing support for trials of the 'Mod 1' variant of Tigerfish which had an anti-ship capability. Despite continuing problems of poor reliability, the new version started entering service in 1980. After the Falklands war the diesel submarine *Onyx* was ordered to sink the hulk of the landing ship *Sir Galahad* which had been badly damaged by an Argentinean air attack. The two Tigerfish torpedoes she fired were duds and failed to run and, therefore, *Onyx* reverted to using the venerable Mark 8 to achieve the sinking. These and other failed Tigerfish war-shot firings revealed a serious defect in the weapon's battery priming system. A procedure was developed as a short term solution to overcoming this problem. However, the weapon's warhead firing sequence should have been thoroughly tested before our submarines entered the Exclusion Zone set up around the Falklands Islands. The failed firings demonstrated just how weak and vulnerable the Submarine Flotilla would have been in any conflict with the Soviet Navy.

I had worked very hard in a so-called 'shore' appointment, spending a considerable amount of time at sea and, together with my team, working long hours, particularly when at BUTEC. Besides contributing to establishing high levels of crew competence in the use of their new torpedo, I had managed to initiate the development of optimum tactics to use it to maximum effectiveness. I also took every opportunity to hammer home the message to my superiors that significant resources needed to be accorded to improving Tigerfish reliability if the Submarine Flotilla was to be effective in war. This was a lonely challenge but gradually I fostered the whole-hearted support of some enlightened senior officers including Commander Michael Boyce the FOSM staff officer responsible for torpedo system effectiveness: this officer was destined to be Chief of the Defence Staff, heading the Armed Forces, at the time of the Second Gulf War. Such highly capable individuals were able to make the case for getting an improvement programme underway – but this was to take several years and would be far from plain sailing.

Chapter 18

HMS *Spartan* – Second-in-Command

I was extremely pleased to receive my new posting to HMS *Spartan* in September 1978, as her XO, Second-in-Command. She was the fifth and penultimate SSN of the highly successful *Swiftsure* class. For me, it was back to the Vickers Shipyard at Barrow-in-Furness where she was fitting out, with expectations of her commencing sea trials early the following year. *Spartan* had benefited from several significant class improvements, including an all-digital tactical data handling and torpedo fire-control system. Most notably, as a result of a serious fire two years earlier onboard the SSN *Warspite* alongside in Liverpool, the firefighting systems had been much enhanced.

The submarine had been launched that April by Emily, Lady Lygo, a charming and lively Floridian, wife of the Vice Chief of the Defence Staff Admiral Sir Raymond Lygo. As the traditional bottle of champagne broke against the hull, *Spartan* started a slow passage down the slipway. As she slid into the murky waters of the Walney Channel, she left behind the last of the class, *Splendid*, still in the early stages of construction. *Spartan* was then moved through the harbour lock system into a non-tidal berth for final fitting out and the testing of her machinery.

I observed, depressingly, that the productivity at the Vickers yard had not improved much since my earlier spell there in *Oberon* in 1972. There had been little significant change to the yard, a sprawling complex of shabby, soot-stained Victorian buildings, sheds and workshops, not in the least conducive to efficient build processes. Nevertheless, there had been some progress, including the removal of the old minesweepers *Pluto* and *Rifleman*, which had served as submarine crew accommodation and offices. Instead, a prefabricated building had been set up at the east end of the yard to provide the necessary crew facilities.

The slow decline of the British shipbuilding industry had provoked the Labour government to take this entire sector into public ownership in 1977. While this situation ought to have been a wake-up call to the management and workforce, the backing of the state had, unfortunately, merely encouraged the continuation of inefficient practices. The shipyard was badly in need of modernisation to improve its production processes and to update much of its obsolescent plant. I recall passing the 'Nuclear Pipe Workshop' each day, which was nothing more than a large wooden shack.

With a workforce of over 12,000, Vickers remained heavily overmanned but the management were hamstrung by strong unions which had an undue influence on how the yard was organised and run. While there was no significant industrial strife during *Spartan*'s building, this era marked the declining years of Jim Callaghan's Labour government and was a time of weak management throughout British industry. Therefore, on occasions, I got the impression that the workforce dictated their own terms to the management and there were many practices of evident inefficiency – for example, the so-called night shift was a misnomer, as, after midnight, the shift workers took to sleeping in the most innovative of places. Nevertheless, I soon became aware that many of the directors and senior managers were legendary in terms of their ability to build and deliver nuclear submarines and they exuded a great degree of pride and confidence that they would produce a first-rate ship for the Royal Navy.

Apart from the two SSNs, *Spartan* and *Splendid*, the only other vessel under construction in the yard was the aircraft carrier *Invincible*. A year earlier, a project to build three German-designed Type 204 coastal submarines for the state of Israel had been completed. Against a background of the loss of the *Dakar*, and increasing difficulty in maintaining its ageing former British submarines built in the Second World War, the Israeli Navy badly needed new boats. Acquiring replacements from German shipyards would have been politically unacceptable, so a contract to build under licence was awarded to Vickers, a construction programme that was accomplished under a shroud of secrecy.

Following a quick handover from one of my fellow-officers when serving in *Swiftsure*, Lieutenant Commander James Burnell-Nugent, who had filled in as XO on a temporary basis until my arrival, I assumed the responsibility of Second-in-Command. My superior was a highly experienced marine engineer officer, Commander Mike Waterhouse, who was *Spartan*'s senior officer until relieved by the appointed Captain. The latter was not due to join until the end of the year.

I found myself working from a stark, draughty office with the immediate task of preparation for *Spartan* Contractor's Sea Trials, only five months away. There was much to be done. A host of pressing problems was exacerbated by the absence of any other seamen officers, mainly due to the Royal Navy's Submarine Service going through a period of rapid expansion. There were simply no qualified officers to fill several of the boat's key posts until the pressure of approaching sea trials compelled the necessary appointments. Indeed, even the Captain did not arrive until after the trim dive in the yard basin in early December.

There was, nevertheless, no such shortage of ratings and I had the challenge of keeping an almost full complement of seamen occupied. They were thoroughly immersing themselves in Barrow life, well familiar with the local hostelries and billeted with landladies who, in general, looked after them very well. To keep them occupied, in addition to sport and training activities, they undertook considerable charity work, such as painting out rooms in community centres and assisting with Sea Cadet expeditions. One memorable highlight was a team being entered for the 40-mile Keswick to Barrow run/walk but alas, on the day of the race, although initially enthusiastic, the weather was hot and few made it past a pub at the halfway stage.

I quickly settled into the Vickers daily routine. Lunch for the *Spartan* officers was at the senior management level 'Silver Trough' dining hall. The 'Silver Trough' routine followed the convention of a buffet lunch, being served from 1230. At 1300 precisely, the BBC Radio Four news was switched onto loudspeaker and, when it ended, the assembled diners dispersed to their various workplaces. These protocols, of course, smacked somewhat of a bygone era.

I soon had a serious concern to address. Before joining, I had my doubts about the Coxswain, who was responsible for the boat's overall organisation and discipline. Although a charismatic and personable individual, he had been my Coxswain in *Otter* and, in hindsight, I was convinced he could have been much more forthcoming about the Mary Millington incident. Moreover, there had been rumours about him smuggling quantities of goods to the UK after the boat's Gibraltar visit. My worst fears were confirmed when, soon after I joined, I received a complaint about his handling of the billeting of the crew. It was alleged he had received kickbacks from some of the landlords of properties in which he had accommodated the junior ratings. Indeed, an investigation revealed that there had been serious irregularities and lodging funds had been diverted elsewhere. He was consequently quickly removed from post and subsequently was found guilty of fraud at court martial.

One of the Coxswain's responsibilities was the key task of drawing up the Watch and Quarter bill. This set out the manning of the submarine when it was in different states of readiness, such as proceeding to sea or preparing to dive. This was in addition to the prime role of managing the discipline and the administration of the Ship's Company. A relief was, therefore, urgently required. Needless to say, there was also a shortage of submarine coxswains and a replacement was not available until after the Contractor's Sea Trials. That said, the Chief Petty Officer who was appointed temporarily to fill the gap, did an outstandingly good job.

As was to be expected in operating a nuclear propulsion plant, the engineering department was provided with a comprehensive set of formal documentation including detailed reactor-operating and emergency procedures. However, remarkably for such a complex vessel, there were no equivalent instructions setting out the actions to be taken in the case of the failure of the general ship systems, or those specific to emergencies. For example, there were no properly documented procedures for what was to be done in the event of the after hydroplanes jamming. If this were to occur, vital actions would rapidly need to be taken. A drill by which the crew could swiftly and effectively deal with the problem should have been standard. It was clear to me that it was my high priority task to produce *Spartan*'s own procedures. This was made more complicated by changes in the system of valve numbering from that in the earlier *Swiftsure* class boats. Therefore, it was not just a matter of copying the documentation of *Spartan*'s predecessors. Without any seaman officers or a Coxswain to share the load, I had my work cut out. On top of the daily arising demands on my time and attention, I had to work late into many evenings producing the mass of operational and organisational documentation required before *Spartan* was ready to proceed to sea early in 1979.

Determined that the Ship's Company would be well prepared for the forthcoming sea trials and the work up which would follow it, I organised onboard training for the crew in the early evening, before the yard's nightshift clocked on. This was an unpopular initiative, disrupting the ratings' routines, most of whom found their unpressurised existence in the yard highly congenial and the pleasures of Barrow after work naturally far more attractive than onboard training.

In spite of these multiple tribulations, I experienced immense job satisfaction. During my time in *Swiftsure* I had built up a thorough knowledge of this type of submarine's systems and characteristics, which not too many of *Spartan*'s crew could match. Under pressure as I was, I felt very confident undertaking the challenges with which the preparation of *Spartan* had confronted me. To this, there was also the compensation of living in wonderful countryside in the Lake District. Having packed up my work for the day, I would head to the cottage I had rented near to the town of Broughton-on-Furness, situated close to Coniston Water. The journey of 20 or so miles of winding roads edged with dry-stone walls in peaceful moorland countryside, provided a pleasant relief to the industrial grime of the shipyard. Weekends were split between Linda joining me in the cottage, or myself heading home to Cardross – sometimes a challenging journey for both of us when snow affected the roads.

I experienced excellent cooperation between the shipyard managers and the submarine's staff who, once the reactor had been fuelled, had assumed responsibility for the nuclear plant and watertight integrity of the submarine. The Commissioning Manager, Stan Reeves – an ex-Chief Engineering Artificer (CERA) – was responsible for managing the daily build and test programme. Each morning he would chair the Plan-of-the-Day meeting, where the lead managers of the various disciplines would report progress and arising problems. I and the senior engineering staff attended these meetings which were held in a damp, uncomfortable, cigarette smoke-filled meeting room. All officers attending were much impressed by Reeves' grip on the build progress and his no-nonsense dealings with the odd manager who was not at the top of his game.

Specialist 'Naval Overseers' appointed by the Ministry of Defence ensured that the submarine's build progressed to the contract and design specification. However, they had some leeway to approve the crew's aspirations regarding unauthorised improvements and embellishments to make life more efficient and comfortable at sea. These improvements, known as 'rabbits', often focused on customising stowages for specific pieces of equipment, ensuring that, in rough weather, gear does not start flying around. I took quiet pride in the number of 'rabbits' achieved to meet the aim of making sure that the submarine's habitability was to the best of standards. When the submarine eventually commissioned, I was presented with a miniature rabbit hutch by the Shipbuilder.

Once the reactor core was installed, for reasons of nuclear safety, it became the submarine crew's responsibility for ensuring the boat's watertight integrity. This required one officer and a small watch of ratings to maintain a daily supervision duty. During the night, the duty watch slept in bunk spaces in the office block and again a meal was provided, for those of the crew who wished it, in the dock-side canteen at 2330. The Duty Officer was required to check on the integrity of the boat during the night and when, walking to the submarine's berth, I discovered the favourite places for the Vickers' night shift to sleep. This included a warm, covered alley full of steam-heating pipes but, unfortunately, this cosy location also attracted a fair number of rats.

Before the reactor was made to go 'critical' and start generating heat, a special barge secured alongside produced steam to test the main engines and the electrical generators. One wet Sunday afternoon, when I was duty and engrossed in the newspapers, I received a call requesting my presence onboard the boat as main steam turbine trials were about to commence. These had been referred to on Friday's Plan-of-the-Day meeting, but it had not been explained that the turbines would be clutched into the main shaft and the boat's propulsor. Accordingly, extra wires had been put in place to ensure no movement of the submarine. My role, grumpily standing on the wet, windblown after casing, was to ensure these securing arrangements did their job and that *Spartan* did not take off down the fitting-out basin.

The tests went well until stern power was applied. To my alarm, amongst other fitting-out basin floating detritus, I observed a large baulk of timber being sucked in towards the propulsor (a sophisticated, finely-engineered thruster arrangement). An urgent call on the temporary telephone system, which had been set up to the throttle operators, elicited no response. I, therefore, shouted down the engine room hatch for the throttles to be shut. Alas, I was too late and the timber disappeared into the shrouded propulsor. I immediately went below and explained to the throttle operators that a big bit of timber had just been ingested by the propulsor. To my concern, the supervisor's reaction was, without hesitation, to swing open the ahead throttles. I then spotted bits of wood being ejected to the surface but, fortunately, there had been no damage to the propulsor. At this stage, thankfully, the trials were concluded and I returned to reading the Sunday newspapers.

Meanwhile, the final fitting-out of the submarine progressed and the pace of individual machinery trials increased. It was satisfying to watch the final stages of the hull construction, albeit some pieces of equipment seemed of dubious utility. I often wondered the reason for two small glass windows in the front of Royal Navy SSN's fins, located just under the compass fitting on the bridge. In my experience, they were absolutely useless as little could be seen through them and they soon got smeared with paint splashes. It was, therefore, with some amusement that I spotted a fitter installing two metal plates under these windows. Questioning what he was doing, the knowledgeable worker responded that these were protective covers for the windows in case the boat was destined to operate under the ice. Evidently, during the construction of many submarines, no one had questioned the utility and cost of fitting these windows and their protective covers. This was but a modest example of redundant equipment which, if it had not been not installed, offered potential savings in the build process.

The first time the reactor went critical was an important milestone when the control rods were gradually raised to allow a chain reaction to be initiated, thus generating the heat which would be turned into steam in the two boilers inside the reactor compartment. From a monitoring station, which had been set up on the dockside as a safety measure, I observed the elation of the engineering staff as the reactor went critical for the first time.

Another important event in the progress to Contractor's Sea Trials was the trim dive in the dock basin. *Spartan* would carry both solid and seawater ballast to enable her to submerge without problems, taking into account a range of seawater densities and internal weight conditions. The easily removable liquid ballast allowed for the weight of additional equipment which would inevitably be fitted during the life of the vessel. The trim dive was a prerequisite to ensure there was the right quantity of both types of ballast and that the boat was properly balanced fore and aft. This evolution took place in the yard's fitting-out basin which, whilst adequate for the trim calculations, was not deep enough to completely submerge the boat, the top of the fin remaining above the surface.

It was my responsibility to ensure that, when the submarine submerged in the basin, it did so safely. Mindful that one of the previous *Swiftsure* class had ended up bow-down, stuck in the shipyard mud, I ignored the official naval architect's diving ballast calculations because, to me, they appeared unsound. Instead, I contacted other vessels of the class and got hold of their trim data and calculations. On the assumption that the Shipbuilder had built the submarine roughly the same size as the other *Swiftsures*, it was not difficult for me to work out an adjustment for the stores embarked, and the basin water density, to arrive at a safe trim condition for the dive. In the event, the trim dive was successfully completed without incident and, during the several hours under the water, the opportunity was taken to conduct some basic crew training. However, the naval architect concerned stuck to theory in directing the Shipbuilder to apply the final solid ballast corrections to the submarine. This was to have repercussions when the initial dive was undertaken during Contractor's Sea Trials.

The Captain, Commander Nigel Goodwin, joined in the middle of December and assumed the role of Senior Officer of the build crew. He had achieved relatively early promotion to the rank of Commander and it was soon evident that he was determined that *Spartan*'s Ship's Company should excel when the boat got to sea. While at times he could be a bit intense, I got on with him well and we developed a strong working relationship.

In early 1979 the two key lieutenants responsible for the navigation and sonar departments joined *Spartan*, Ian Whitehouse as Navigator and 'Tiny' Lister as Sonar Officer. Their unfamiliarity with the boat and her equipment required a great effort on their part to quickly get up to speed before the Contractor's Sea Trials. The trials would involve eight weeks of tests and evaluations, where the submarine was fully put through her paces to ensure all plant and equipment worked properly and that she had been built to the contract specification.

Late February 1979 saw *Spartan*, with tug assistance, move gingerly out of the dock complex into the open sea. The final culminating thrill of all my efforts, as the phrase had it, 'Getting Underway in Nuclear Power', was tempered by the Captain when arriving on the bridge for departure, declaring that his children had contracted mumps and that he feared he had caught the disease.

As *Spartan* moved past *Invincible*, the bow of which had been damaged earlier when she was being moved into the entrance lock, we were reminded of the risks of locking back into the dock system because it involved crossing a strong tidal stream. (Later, the entrance was significantly improved for the Trident submarines.) A shipyard joker had painted a large sign above *Invincible*'s damage, indicating the remedial work was going to be undertaken by the local car-body repair company. In the event, both *Spartan*'s departure and re-entry were achieved without incident.

Clear of the Walney Channel, *Spartan* moved out into deep water and, having discharged her tugs, headed north. Prior to her maiden dive, undertaken in the sheltered waters of the Clyde estuary, a junior mechanic popped his head into the wardroom and asked for some gin to clean the windows on top of the two periscopes. This was normal practice before diving, but whether the gin was applied to the windows or simply swallowed and breathed on the optics, was always a matter of conjecture. In the event, it proved difficult to submerge *Spartan* as she was evidently too lightly ballasted. As a consequence, the submarine was obliged to spend a weekend in Faslane while a number of the Vickers' shipyard workers attending the trials undertook the miserable task of securing tons of lead ballast under the casing in driving rain. With something of a sense of vindication, I saw the naval architect's theoretical trim calculations disposed of to the classified waste.

It was then back to sea in the Clyde Estuary to undertake work-up staff supervised safety training, prior to starting full power trials. This training ensured the crew would able to safely address a wide range of emergencies and equipment failures. Particular effort was dedicated to tackling that most serious of emergencies – fire when submerged. Smoke bombs and thunder-flash pyrotechnics ensured such exercises were as realistic as possible, with the added challenge of every member of the crew being required to don emergency breathing apparatus, while continuing to operate and, if necessary, fight the submarine.

A serious problem soon emerged in that several members of the crew had become ill, experiencing violent vomiting and dizziness. Fortunately, the symptoms, although very unpleasant, were short lived, and the cause was determined as contamination in a fresh water pipe. Meanwhile, the embarked shipyard personnel, who could be up to forty in number, had established themselves in the torpedo stowage compartment, nicknamed the 'casbah' because of the amount of coloured material separating their temporary bunks. Fitted out with a film projector and other comforts, this compartment was their sanctuary and was even out of bounds to the Faslane-based submarine work-up staff.

After several days of evolutions and emergency drills, the crew were cleared by the work-up staff that they were safe and competent enough to proceed with the trials. It was at this point that the Captain's concerns on sailing were realised. He started to experience the symptoms of mumps and quarantined himself in his cabin. The disease soon laid him out and I sent an urgent signal to HQ indicating that the Captain was poorly and that he should be landed as soon as possible. A boat transfer was promptly organised and he was escorted over the side by attendant medical staff, leaving myself temporarily in command. This might have seemed to be my moment, but with impending full power trials in relatively shallow water and a green crew, after two days I was relieved of the command burden when a temporary Captain, Commander Don Mitchell, arrived onboard by boat. However, he was to take very much a back-seat role and he let me get on running the submarine with minimum interference.

Prior to the acceptance of a new submarine into regular naval service – an important moment marked by the ceremonial hoisting of the White Ensign – she was still technically the property of her builders, regarded as a merchant ship and flew the Red Ensign. In recognition of my role of by default being their appointed ship master for two days, on commissioning Vickers paid me ten pence, a sum deriving from the old Board of Trade payment of one shilling *per diem* to a supernumerary aboard a British merchantman and reducing me – with something of an ironical twist of fate – to the equivalent status of a Distressed British Seaman. The Captain received his payment appropriately in Greek drachmas, which were mounted on a presentation plaque.

With the temporary Captain embarked, the next major element of the programme was to undertake machinery proving tests in the Irish Sea, working up to full power when dived. These were achieved travelling up and down the undersea valley known as Beaufort's Dyke which bisects the Stranraer to Larne ferry route. This relatively deep trench of water is about 30 miles long but just over two miles wide. Working up to a maximum speed of 30 knots when only a few hundred feet above the sea bed and executing a reversal of course at either end with an inexperienced crew, posed what, today, might have been an unacceptable risk, not least because over two million tons of explosives had been dumped in the bottom of the Dyke after the Second World War.

For myself, this proved a nail-biting period. During all the high-speed runs I stationed myself in the control room, closely supervising the operator of the boat's rudder and hydroplane control column, keeping an eye on the echo sounder and ready to react immediately to any equipment failure. The reversal of course was particularly tense and had to be undertaken gently to avoid the 'snap roll' phenomenon with the risk of a big down angle resulting in hitting the sea bed. Any loss of control of the rudder or hydroplanes, due to mechanical or electrical failure, could also have had catastrophic consequences. However, all went smoothly and, on reaching 30 knots, a fifty-pence piece was successfully balanced on its edge on the wardroom table: there was virtually no vibration – an excellent example of British engineering at its best.

The remainder of the sea trials were completed successfully. The Captain had rejoined, fully recovered, before the first deep dive to a maximum safe depth of 1,250ft. This was undertaken in deep water to the west of the UK. Such was the confidence that *Spartan* had been so well built, there was not the least bit of nervousness on the part of the crew as, in stages, the depth was increased. As a submarine goes deeper the hull compresses and there is the risk of doors jamming or compartment partitions bulging. To avoid this, the shipbuilder allows adequate margins of clearance on these fittings, and in the case of *Spartan*, Vickers had successfully achieved this.

During the majority of the machinery trials, the Commissioning Manager was at sea with us. Vickers was responsible for repairing equipment which had developed a defect and, if there was a problem with any mechanical equipment, the ever-enthusiastic Stan Reeves would disappear to help. He never wore overalls but seemed to have an inexhaustible supply of checked trousers which bore the brunt of the oil and grease he inevitably came into contact with.

Meanwhile the crew enjoyed the finest of cuisine because, although the catering staff decided the menus and ordered the food, the Shipbuilder was paying for it. Surprisingly the Faslane NAAFI food depot was not to be defeated by orders from *Spartan* when at sea, which included such delicacies as frogs' legs, lobsters and Alaskan king crab to support the cooks delivering the finest cuisine to the crew and the embarked civilian personnel. It was all a bit of a game to see how far Vickers could be pushed, including charging them corkage on their own beer and wine, the proceeds of which went towards the Ship's Company commissioning dance although, in reality, little of either was actually consumed at sea.

A key element of the Contractor's Sea Trials was the measurement of the boat's radiated noise. It was essential that, in approaching Soviet submarines, this should be minimal if counter-detection was to be avoided. Underway noise trials took place in a noise range located in deep water in the Western Isles. These were followed by static noise trials in Loch Fyne where *Spartan* was suspended on wires between four buoys and careful measurements taken of the noise of individual pieces of equipment.

The static trials took place at night, with a minimum number of personnel embarked. A shore facility undertook precise measurements of the radiated noise in various machinery running states, supplemented by a series of onboard readings. On diving each evening, I had to be careful to ensure the trim of the boat was not excessively heavy, or else there would have been a risk of damaging the buoys. The embarked technicians and scientists were always impressed how quickly we could get the 5,000-ton displacement submarine under the sea and placed within a few inches of the required depth of 150ft. However, they were not to know that this was easily achieved with the buoy wires taking some of the strain of the weight of the boat.

Near to the range building was the Creggan's Hotel, owned by the historian Brigadier Sir Fitzroy MacLean, an accomplished WW2 soldier, who took a prominent part in a number of special forces operations across several campaign theatres. Indeed, it is speculated that he was the inspiration for Ian Fleming's character, James Bond. Some of the officers dined one evening in his hotel and offered Sir Fitzroy and his wife Veronica lunch onboard *Spartan* followed by a movie in the wardroom. They readily accepted the invitation and, apart from experiencing a memorable Sunday lunch in an unusual setting, they enjoyed the additional extra of an ice cream between reel changes.

Returning to the shipyard in April, *Spartan* embarked on a normal three-month 'post sea trials build completion phase'. In the event, however, this was extended by two months for her to be fitted with special protection to a number of her vulnerable external fittings. This would enable her to undertake the role of a target, the first Royal Naval nuclear submarine to be so modified and indicating to me that, like *Otter*, she was destined to spend significant periods of time at the AUTEC and BUTEC ranges. The prospect of having a variety of practice and test torpedoes fired against her, sometimes intended to actually strike her, added zest to the future. Deployment to the AUTEC range would be very welcome to the crew who knew that this inevitably meant port visits to Florida.

Within a few months a full complement of officers had joined and, most importantly, the new Coxswain had arrived. Chief Petty Officer Harry Harrison was a larger-than-life character who soon won the hearts of the Ship's Company and, although sometimes a bit of a rogue, he proved a very loyal, competent and sensible assistant. Meanwhile I had commissioned a cartoonist to design a logo to reflect the boat's name. He produced the comic image of a Spartan warrior which was to feature on the crew's sweaters, a wide range of correspondence and, most conspicuously, on the fin and rudder of the submarine.

On a fresh, sunny September morning, the commissioning ceremony took place in a shipyard berth where a pavilion and stand had been set up. There was a substantial gathering of the families of the crew, Vickers' staff, local dignitaries and other guests with the shipyard band providing a jaunty musical accompaniment. There was also a welcome contingent of 'old Spartans', veterans who had served in *Spartan*'s WW2 predecessor. Their Vickers-built *Bellona* class light cruiser had been sunk off Anzio in January 1944 by a guided bomb. It was very much a humbling experience for the crew of the SSN to meet these stalwarts, several of whom had been severely wounded during the attack and, needless to say, they were delighted to be honoured guests and to be given a tour of a nuclear submarine. The crew were also extremely pleased that Lady Lygo was able to be present and, indeed, she was to maintain a strong interest in the submarine during its succeeding commissions.

The commissioning berth and everything around it had been spruced up and painted. This included the starboard side of *Spartan*, the side facing the commissioning stand, making it at least five and a half coats of external paint applied since the initial application. Indeed, the submarine had been completed to absolutely immaculate standards of finish and cleanliness, although I considered the employment of two women on their hands and knees using hack-saw blades to scrape off the piling from the wardroom carpet a bit over the top.

At the start of the commissioning proceedings, the Ship's Company proudly marched on led by Coxswain Harrison and formed ranks in front of the stand, their standard of marching and appearance absolutely outstanding. The commissioning ceremony was led by the Chaplain of the Fleet conducting a short service of dedication which culminated in the Captain reading out the commissioning warrant, which authorised HMS *Spartan* to join the Fleet. On completion of the reading, the shrill of a bosun's whistle was the cue for the White Ensign to be hoisted for the first time at the stern of the submarine and the Union Jack raised at the bows.

After the commissioning ceremony, the VIP guests were conducted round the submarine and ended their visit with a glass of champagne in the wardroom. This plan encountered a hitch when the Mayor of Barrow's well-built wife, nervous of descending the vertical ladder of the main access hatch despite much persuasion, proved a bottleneck. The situation was resolved when the Mayor himself threatened her with the deployment of the torpedo loading gear to get her below. All then progressed well and was followed in the evening by a highly successful Ship's Company dance in the Town Hall, concluding a happy and memorable day.

At 2024 values, *Spartan* had cost about £420 million to build, much less than the cost of the *Astute* class SSNs, commissioned from 2010 onwards, which at the time of writing are costing about £1.3 billion each. She nevertheless had her limitations. Although fitted with the latest sonar and weapon control equipment, against surface ships *Spartan* would have to resort to the pre-WW2 Mark 8 torpedo. She was also equipped with the Tigerfish anti-submarine torpedo which, although a marked improvement on the Mark 23, as mentioned in the previous chapter, initially suffered from several serious defects.

The seemingly interminable leaving parties now over, and the final modifications and improvements extracted from the Shipbuilder, *Spartan* prepared to leave her birthplace. During the forthcoming six months of work-up and trials she would join the Second Submarine Squadron, based in Devonport. However, the moment for *Spartan* to sever her connections with Barrow-in-Furness was not universally welcomed by the Ship's Company. A number of the crew had married Barrow girls and, characteristically, their young wives were not inclined to move out of the town and 'follow the drum'. Their influence encouraged an aspiration in their husbands to return to another submarine under construction as soon as possible.

As I waited for the passing of the order to close up at 'Harbour Stations' for leaving Barrow for the last time, I contemplated the moment of transition. I felt a strong attachment to *Spartan*, forged in part by the heavy but important work load that I had to deal with on joining. Moreover, I was convinced that she had been built to a better standard than any of her class and that we had achieved the best possible standards of crew accommodation. Furthermore, those two days of command during the sick leave of my Captain had, in some odd way, consolidated my affinity to the submarine.

Chapter 19

HMS *Spartan* – Operational Challenges

The post-commissioning work-up proved disappointing as, not for the want of enthusiasm and effort, we did not achieve above-average results in either the safety training phase or the operational work-up. The crew was assessed to have achieved a satisfactory standard in both, but tensions in the personal relationship between our Captain and the Captain heading the Faslane-based work-up staff (Captain Submarine Sea Training – CSST) undoubtedly contributed to not achieving the outcome that I had anticipated. The situation was not improved by the rather combative temperament of the two Lieutenant Commanders charged with the safety and operational training respectively. I viewed them to be over-critical and, on occasions, found their advice to me less than constructive, maybe because they were aware that my knowledge of the boat and its combat systems far exceeded theirs.

At the time, it was normal practice in our submarines to control a major incident, such as a fire or flood, from the control room. This had the drawback of an already crowded – sometimes noisy – space being further congested by the presence of additional crew, together with their system lay-out drawings or boards. *Spartan* was the first SSN to be fitted with a comprehensive internal communications system in the wardroom. Therefore, at our initiative, the wardroom was established as the Damage Control Head Quarters (DCHQ) during an incident. This arrangement proved a success and was subsequently adopted as standard practice in the Flotilla.

The crew proved to be high spirited and on several occasions some of them got into trouble when ashore in the Faslane base junior ratings club. No serious offences occurred, but the Captain and I became increasingly concerned that *Spartan* was earning a poor reputation with the shore regulation authorities. Therefore, when the boat arrived unexpectedly back at Faslane for repairs, I was given the task of dreaming up ways of keeping the junior rates occupied over a weekend. I suggested to the Coxswain that a naval bus be arranged to take the non-duty junior rates on a day's tour of the surrounding spectacular Argyll countryside. This was duly arranged but, again, the crew got into trouble.

In the event, the tour turned out to be a series of calls into a hostelry in each town or village visited. After the final pub visit in the village of Inveraray, there was an additional passenger in the bus: the tartan-clad mannequin which had been in front of the clothes shop in the high street. When the bus returned to the Base and the MoD Police checked the individual passes of the occupants, they were not amused by the presence of 'stolen goods'. The next day the Coxswain took the mannequin, together with a large bunch of flowers and box of chocolates, back to the shop owner. Fortunately, the latter saw the humour of the incident and did not take the matter further, but the bus trip had not been one of my better decisions.

In December 1979, having completed safety work-up, *Spartan* headed to Devonport, her new base within the Second Submarine Squadron. This SSN squadron had been established in 1974 and initially its staff was housed in temporary office accommodation. There was now a brand-new Squadron headquarters building next to the nuclear submarine berths. Nevertheless, these were situated on the north-west corner of the dockyard, exposed to the weather and the propellor wash from passing vessels. On several occasions, a frigate departing stern-first from one of the upstream berths got it wrong and passed far too close to an alongside SSN, posing a real risk of collision damage. Regarding my own family situation, when *Spartan* was alongside in Devonport for maintenance, Linda and I rented a comfortable cottage in the hamlet of St Ives Cross near the town of Callington, in Cornwall. To avoid significant separation and putting family life first, Linda had no option but to give up the highly successful sales career she had achieved at Rank Xerox when she left the WRNS.

A week after the submarine arrived, I was summoned to the office of the Squadron Deputy Commander, who was none other than my friend and mentor – Geoffrey Biggs ('GB'). A few days earlier some of the *Spartan* crew, evidently inebriated, had done a strip-tease on the table of a local pub. Unfortunately, a *Daily Mail* reporter happened to be present in the pub and the incident had subsequently featured in his newspaper. With a grin on his face, 'GB' asked what was the common denominator of 'All this nudity in the Submarine Service'?

I responded that I was not sure but his curt response was 'You!'. The ghost of the Mary Millington incident lingered on.

Early on the Saturday morning three days before Christmas, I received a very worrying telephone call from the Duty Officer informing me that two of the crew had been involved in a motorbike accident and were in the local naval hospital being treated for serious injuries. Immediately I headed to the hospital and, on arrival, was met by the surgeon who had worked all night to try and save them. From the grim expression on his face, I knew it was extremely bad news and he stated with great regret that he could not save one of them. The second, although badly injured, would survive. The dead sailor was Able Seaman 'Knocker' White, a real character and a highly popular member of the crew. With dread I awaited his parents' arrival from Norfolk later in the afternoon, knowing they were unaware that his injuries had been fatal. I was so glad that a Naval Padre was present to compassionately inform them that their son had died. For me it was an awful Saturday. As was Naval tradition, individual items of AB White's uniform and kit were auctioned amongst the crew and, reflecting his popularity, fetched a generous sum which went to his family.

After Christmas leave was over, *Spartan* headed north back to Faslane to conduct a series of weapons firings and to complete the operational work-up phase. Once again, I observed that, exactly as in my Perisher Course, the operational work-up programme was mainly geared towards fighting an 'enemy' who operated on identical lines to one's own or allied forces. I soon came to the conclusion that the Ship's Company had received inadequate training in the detection and trailing of Russian submarines.

The relationship with the work-up staff, which had not been good, reached an all-time low during the grand finale of the operational inspection, when *Spartan* was pitted against a number of surface units in the South-west Approaches. These included the anti-submarine carrier *Bulwark*, which had an embarked squadron of Sea King ASW helicopters. In perfect sonar conditions, the helicopters acquired and continuously tracked *Spartan* on their sonar and, despite drastic evasion manoeuvres, were proving very difficult to shake-off.

I was catching up with some sleep before taking over from the Captain at 0100 when, just after midnight, I was violently awakened by CSST who ordered me into the control room 'To take charge of the situation'. Entering the control room, rubbing the sleep out of my eyes, I noted with concern that the boat was below its maximum safe depth. To try and break off contact from the helicopters, the Captain had ordered the boat as deep as possible and at slow speed in order to minimise its sonar profile to the helicopters. However, this put the boat well outside of its safe manoeuvring criteria.

The Captain was sitting on his seat in the middle of the control room, arms folded and anger on his face. Evidently there had been a row between CSST and himself and he was refusing to acknowledge the latter's demands for the submarine to be brought back above the safe depth mark. To break the deadlock, I approached the Captain and whispered that it was time to take over from him. He said nothing but simply left his chair and went off to his cabin. I immediately ordered an increase in speed and brought the boat up to a shallower depth. There was no further discussion of the incident, but it cast a shadow over the remainder of the inspection. The overall outcome of the operational work-up was a 'Satisfactory' assessment but I was confident we had actually done a lot better.

In April 1980, seven months after commissioning, *Spartan* was on operational patrol in the Norwegian Sea up against Soviet submarines. In *Cold War Command*, jointly authored by myself and Captain Richard Woodman, details of the events during this patrol are described, but I have summarised the key incidents below.

For the first time *Spartan* was fitted with a towed acoustic array but the crew had no prior training in using it for Target Motion Analysis (TMA). TMA using towed-array data was, in any case, at this time in its infancy. Target parameters are derived from calculating range from observed changes in its bearing movement and carefully measuring changes in the frequency of its machinery noise tonal emissions. This data is used to calculate course, speed and range but the resulting answers exclusively using data from the towed array can sometimes yield just a general indication of a target's location and movement.

Spartan was reliant on Soviet submarine positional intelligence reports from the SOSUS system but, as mentioned previously, these provided a wide area for her to search. Notwithstanding these challenges, contact was soon made upon a 'Charlie' class cruise missile submarine (SSGN). Intelligence reports had indicated it to be participating in an exercise where it was tasked to trail and mark the Russian helicopter carrier *Leningrad* and its accompanying surface escorts. This group was replicating an American aircraft carrier strike force passing through the Norwegian Sea with the SSGN in the role of interdicting opposition. With its ability to launch lethal SS-N-7 anti-ship missiles whilst submerged and at short range – thus affording very little warning – the 'Charlie' class submarine at the time was the United States aircraft carrier's most dangerous opponent.

We patiently maintained trail of the Soviet boat for two days at a range of about 10 miles, but we never got close enough to generate an accurate fire-control solution. This would have marked the trail as a success but, in the event, only a rough range assessment was held on her. Meanwhile, above the waves, other intelligence sources recorded that the Russians had conducted simulated air attacks on the group, complete with gunnery exercises.

Eventually, during the final phase of the exercise, contact with the Russian force was lost amidst the noise made by shipping and fishing vessels off the Norwegian coast. Despite the disappointment in failing to achieve that fire-control solution, for our crew it was a good start; they had achieved practical experience in trailing a potential hostile submarine using their towed acoustic array. However, towards the end of the trail, in his enthusiasm to maintain contact, the Captain broke the cardinal rule of remaining within his allocated sea areas. *Spartan* had entered waters under the control of the Norwegian Navy and this resulted in an admonition from HQ.

Spartan was next ordered north to intercept an 'Alfa' class SSN, reported to be the first of this class which had deployed into the Norwegian Sea. Intelligence indications were that she had been partaking in the *Leningrad* exercise. Soon our towed-array sonar operators were in contact with the Russian at a range of over 100 miles to the east. She was heading east and our immediate concern was she would make it back to port for May Day celebrations before we caught up with her. If that occurred, the prize of achieving a highly desirable, close-range intelligence gathering approach would be eluded. Consequently, the Captain was very keen to close the range on the Soviet boat as rapidly as possible and ordered high speed towards its best estimated position.

Unable to maintain sonar contact while at speed, periodically we briefly slowed down to regain firm contact, but during these periods at slow speed were unable to establish the Russian's range. Twelve hours after the initial contact was made, on slowing down and regaining sonar contact, we soon realised that we had over-run the 'Alfa' and that she was now in close proximity. Indeed, now held on the hull array sonar, all the indications were that the Russian was rapidly moving aft. We quicky reversed course to maintain contact, but it was soon evident that the Soviet boat had skilfully manoeuvred to a position astern of us and that counter-detection had occurred.

A situation had developed akin to an underwater dogfight, the two opposing submarines manoeuvring less than two miles apart and risking collision.

Aware that there was to be no benefit in remaining in such a precarious situation, the Captain wisely decided it was time to break away from the 'Alfa' and to head west at maximum speed. The boot was clearly on the other foot, as the 40-plus knots capable Soviet submarine was managing to hold contact from astern transmitting on its active sonar. However, gradually after about an hour of the high speed chase in which we employed continuous evasion manoeuvres, the 'Alfa's' sonar transmissions became considerably fainter. The signs were that the Russian was finding it difficult to maintain contact and, indeed, the sonar transmissions soon ceased altogether, indicating contact had been broken. Meanwhile, I observed that the Captain, very much lacking sleep, looked absolutely drained and exhausted. He was clearly upset about the loss of tactical control and the counter-detection.

Having disengaged and continuing to head west, no further Soviet contacts were gained during this patrol and *Spartan* returned to her base in Devonport. There was no subsequent reproach for this incident, but there was a degree of concern expressed at headquarters that the Royal Navy's latest and quietest SSN had been detected by a relatively noisy Russian submarine. Close scrutiny of the results of a pre-patrol noise ranging indicated a noise short on a piece of machinery which could have given *Spartan*'s presence away. However, it was clear to me that tactical control had been lost and a detection at an impressively long range had developed into a less than satisfactory close-range encounter in which the advantage had swiftly and decisively passed to the 'Alfa' as *Spartan* stumbled on top of her quarry. It was also a lesson to me that the Russian submarine captain should be treated with a degree of respect and that some of them would excel in the underwater confrontation.

The summer of 1980 saw *Spartan* undertaking several torpedo trials at the BUTEC range, and in particular, she was the target for a new lightweight torpedo coming into service, known as Stingray. Entering service in 1983, this was to become the Royal Navy's main helicopter and ship-launched torpedo in the following decades. Additionally, sonar trials were undertaken in sea areas north of the Canary Islands, with the diesel submarine *Otus* acting as target.

A few days into the latter trials, a radio message was received from *Otus* indicating that they had a crew member with a suspected case of appendicitis. As they had no qualified medical staff onboard, they were seeking our assistance. Accordingly, both boats were surfaced but as neither carried an inflatable dingy, the challenge was to conduct a safe transfer of the patient. In the Force 4 sea conditions and with a substantial swell running, it was not possible to place the submarines alongside each other without risking significant damage. Instead, a berthing rope was secured between the two vessels, about 100 yards apart, with the plan that the patient would enter the water in an escape suit and haul himself along the rope to reach *Spartan.*

However, this option was abruptly abandoned when the sick sailor only managed a few steps out of his bunk before collapsing. Instead, our Petty Officer Medical Assistant (POMA), kitted out in a diving suit and with a waterproof bag of medical equipment strapped to his chest, bravely entered the angry-looking sea and pulled himself across to *Otus*. A few minutes later we received a message from the POMA that the patient was seriously ill and requesting that we urgently organise a helicopter to land him into hospital in the Canary Islands. All ended well and the sailor fully recovered.

Meanwhile at sea, the crew had settled into being a cohesive and happy Ship's Company where the officers had earned the full respect and confidence of the crew. Some officers did have their eccentricities. For example, the navigator liked to occasionally cook in the galley in the evening if things were quiet, adding the odd bottle of wardroom wine to improve the flavour of his casseroles. The heavily-built Sonar Officer, 'Tiny' Lister, sometimes took snuff, but after having wrecked several chairs when sneezing, he was banned from indulging in the stuff. Movies in the messdecks in the afternoon or evening remained highly popular, as were ship-wide quizzes or inter-mess game competitions.

In between trials, *Spartan* undertook a visit to Liverpool, her first home port call. During the dived transit south through the Irish Sea to the port, several visitors were embarked including the cartoonist Bill Tidy. He had been commissioned by the magazine *Punch* to produce a series of cartoons depicting the oddities of submarine life. He had already been to sea in *Dreadnought* but, while he was onboard, she had suffered a serious instrumentation problem which forced her to shut down the reactor, surface and be towed to Gibraltar. His trip in the almost brand-new *Spartan* was arranged to improve upon his only submarine experience of being in near darkness for several days and enduring a diet which included cold tinned vegetables. During his two days onboard, Bill proved to be an accomplished entertainer and raconteur, touring the messdecks, rapidly etching cartoons on the back of navigational charts, while at the same time delivering humorous stories.

When the boat departed from Liverpool, heading for Faslane, I had remained ashore in order to attend the wedding of a colleague. Unfortunately, things did not go well on departure from the Liverpool lock system. A tug wire, under too much strain, parted and struck the Casing Officer. It broke his arm – but it could have been a lot worse. As a result, he was hospitalised for several days in Liverpool and here Bill Tidy and his wife came to the rescue, visiting him each evening and supplementing his meagre hospital fare with an array of delicacies and more than one glass of wine.

In the summer of 1980 Commander David Burns relieved Mike Waterhouse as Senior Engineer Officer (SEO). Following the example of his predecessor, from his arrival David declared that despite being a Commander and, therefore, senior to me, we were of equal status onboard. He proved a highly supportive and competent department head and, when necessary, a strong counter to irrational directives from the shore support organisation.

Within the Devonport Dockyard complex, nuclear safety sensitivities were much more evident than in Faslane. In part this was because there was a housing estate only about a mile across the harbour from the nuclear submarine berths. The stationing of two ancient 'Green Goddess' fire engines on the pier adjacent to the submarine berths, was a visual reminder of the perceived possibility of a nuclear accident. In event of a loss of nuclear reactor coolant onboard a submarine, the plan was for these fire engines to spray water on top of its emergency cooling tank situated under the after casing. Such an accident has never occurred onboard a US or UK nuclear submarine and, as it is deemed highly unlikely to occur, this arrangement has long been discontinued. However, it was fairly symptomatic of an overenthusiastic nuclear safety regime in the dockyard.

Gold plating of nuclear safety procedures was demonstrated during an incident when *Spartan* undocked prior to deploying to AUTEC in the autumn of 1980. As the boat prepared to leave the dock early in the morning, the Dockyard electricians failed to arrive to disconnect the electrical shore supply, due to industrial action. Accordingly, David Burns instructed our own crew to disconnect the supply cables. Stationed on the bridge, as the tugs pulled the boat into the basin, I received an angry radio call from the Dockyard nuclear safety officer, an Engineer Captain. He remonstrated that nuclear safety had been compromised by not disconnecting the shore supply in accordance with the set procedures. Therefore, he demanded that *Spartan* re-enter the dock. Accordingly, I asked that the SEO come to the bridge to respond. On being handed the radio set, David quicky asserted to the safety officer that, as there were no procedures in place for docking the boat, the undocking must proceed. On arrival alongside, he was sent for but no doubt, at the subsequent interview, he would not have pulled his verbal punches.

The autumn of 1980 saw *Spartan* deployed to the AUTEC Range in the Bahamas, acting as both a target and firing vessel for torpedo trials. Port calls included Bermuda, Port Canaveral, Fort Lauderdale and Groton, Connecticut. Additionally, there would be opportunities for the crew to go ashore in the AUTEC headquarters island of Andros, enjoying the facilities of a beach bar and the opportunity for safe swimming. Also a few wives, including Linda, had flown out to Florida to be with their husbands during some of the port visits. In sum, the deployment offered the crew plenty of scope for relaxation and fun ashore and, as the case in most US ports, they experienced warm hospitality from local people. Crew morale was high and there were few disciplinary offences.

The trials of the Stingray lightweight torpedo and a new variant of Tigerfish, known as the Mod 2, were successful. Notably, a Tigerfish hit was achieved on *Spartan* when she was doing 28 knots down the range. During one of the Port Canaveral visits, loading trials of the USN Mark 48 submarine torpedo were successfully demonstrated. An advanced version of this torpedo, known as the Mark 48 Adcap, was being considered as a replacement for Tigerfish.

Before *Spartan* departed north to exercise with US submarines in sea areas off New England, the Cape Canaveral Navy League invited the wardroom, including wives, to a 'Sunset hay-ride into the interior swampland'. The envisaged hay wagon pulled by horses turned out to be a truck with bales of hay secured to its flat bed with sisal baling twine. The destination was a farmhouse about 40 miles north of Canaveral. After we climbed onto the rear and made ourselves as secure and comfortable as possible on the hay bales, the driver took off at breakneck speed along the freeway, not in the least concerned about his terrified dozen or so passengers clinging for dear life onto the bales. Leaving the freeway, for several miles the driver plunged the truck through swampy pools and bushland before coming to halt outside a farmhouse in the middle of nowhere.

Things got better thereafter with the lighting of a barbeque and being served up a hearty steak dinner by our Navy League hosts, who were fortunate in arriving by car. However, Linda and I were spared a return trip on the truck as one of our hosts kindly offered to give us a lift back to Canaveral. As we sedately headed back down the freeway, we were overtaken by the truck with its stream of bits of flying hay and its terrified occupants in the rear, again clinging onto the hay bales for dear life. No doubt our Navy League hosts meant well but this event will be always remembered as one of the more eccentric episodes of local hospitality I have experienced in foreign visits.

The final deployment port visit to the sprawling submarine base in Groton was preceded by a two week long tactical development exercise against USN submarine opposition. This exercise was aimed at improving and refining the use of the towed array and the opposition submarines had noise-augmentation equipment which replicated the acoustic emissions of a modern Soviet nuclear submarine.

Arriving into port in cold, snowy conditions, the crew were generously feted by the USN hosts of Squadron Twelve, known as the Tactical Development Squadron. Many were invited to the homes of squadron members to join the traditional family 'Thanksgiving Dinner' held on the last Thursday of November and where the traditional turkey was served.

My appointer had indicated that the following summer I would be posted to the Tactical Development Squadron on exchange service. Therefore, it was a good opportunity to meet my future Squadron Commodore, Captain Sam Ward USN, and several of his officers. There was also a chance to have discussions with the in-post exchange officer, Commander Rupert Best, Additionally, there was the opportunity to view the house in the nearby town of Mystic which he and his family were renting and where it was assumed we would continue the lease.

Before departing back across the Atlantic and rejoining our families for Christmas, there was one more bit of excitement for some of *Spartan*'s crew. It was observed that the tug that had helped secure us alongside was manned exclusively by female sailors. The same tug was berthed opposite *Spartan* on the other side of the pier and one evening, when it was conducting engine trials, the inside of its funnel caught fire. Flames belched from its top. For many of *Spartan*'s duty watch, this was the relished opportunity to tackle a real fire and seeing the tug's crew were finding it difficult to control the blaze, they rushed across the jetty to help, carrying bulk foam hoses. Soon they had put the fire out, but in their over enthusiasm had filled the tug's engine room with foam and had soaked several of its crew with water. Again

Spartan's crew came to the rescue, bringing the wet female sailors down into the senior rates mess where they were offered blankets and a large glass of warming rum. A friend dating back from *Otter*'s visit to Charleston, Captain Ken Cox, was now in charge of the base support organisation including responsibility for the tugs. He did gently tease me about the amount of foam in the tug's engine room.

On return to Devonport, Nigel Goodwin was relieved as a matter of due course as he had been two years in command, which was the normal duration for such appointments. We had worked well together and developed a firm friendship. Consequently, I was particularly sorry to see him leave as, no doubt, he considered that, during his time in command, *Spartan* had yet to achieve her full potential. He was relieved by one of my term-mates at Dartmouth, Commander Jim Taylor. He was an early promotion to Commander and had the reputation of being a pleasant, competent individual, but he had no significant prior nuclear submarine experience.

In early February 1981, *Spartan* was back on operational patrol in the North Norwegian Sea, on this occasion trailing a 'Victor' class SSN which was heading north-east towards her Northern Fleet base. The crew were now much better trained and prepared than they had been during the previous operational patrol. This greatly encouraged me and, even better, it was clear that Jim Taylor would let me take tactical control of *Spartan* whilst in contact with Soviet submarines.

The Russian SSN had initially been detected to the north-west of the British Isles. However, owing to the difficult acoustic conditions of the Iceland-Faeroes Gap caused by the noisy activities of fishing vessels and the confluence of ocean currents, the Gulf Stream meeting cold Arctic water, *Spartan* had lost contact. Therefore, we headed deep into the Norwegian Sea ahead of the Russian along his predicted track. This gambit paid off and, as anticipated, contact was regained and the trail resumed.

When about 100 miles south-east of Bear Island, hull sonar contact was achieved on the 'Victor' which was randomly manoeuvring within a certain area. Using the much more accurate hull sonar bearings, *Spartan* closed range to about three miles to the east of the 'Victor's' search area and waited as events unfurled. Soon there was great excitement in the control room as a 'Delta' class Soviet SSBN was detected and classified, heading on a south-westerly track. Maintaining a prudent distance, we observed on sonar the 'Victor' circling round the SSBN conducting not very effective so-called 'delousing manoeuvres,' aimed at detecting any trailing 'hostile' submarine. However, in this case, the inverse had occurred and the 'Victor' had acted as a lure to a more valuable quarry.

After several hours, having evidently completed his sanitising manoeuvres, the 'Victor' headed south-east. Contact faded on him shortly thereafter, but now we had established a trailing position on the port quarter of the 'Delta' class SSBN as she headed north-west. There was great excitement throughout the boat as word passed around that we had undertaken a unique piece of intelligence-gathering of a Russian 'Victor' class SSN sanitising a deploying 'Delta' class SSBN. Moreover, we were now following a strategically important contact; it was exactly what *Spartan* had been designed and built for, and for which our Ship's Company had trained so hard.

Just before midnight, it was evident that confusion existed in the sound room regarding the bearing of the 'Delta'. The operators could not determine whether *Spartan* was on her port or starboard quarter until it became clear that two distinctly separate sets of contact characteristics were being held on two different bearings. I quickly realised that we were now behind not one, but *two* 10,000-ton 'Delta' class SSBNs which were about ten miles apart heading deep into the Greenland Sea towards the ice edge.

For the next day we maintained trail of the two 'Deltas' as they headed towards the Arctic ice edge. However, due to the absence of an accurate navigational fix for some time, dependence upon navigational charts of limited detail and a lack of knowledge of the exact location of the ice edge, I felt somewhat uneasy. I was aware that neither of the 'Deltas' had been held on SOSUS, and consequently the Naval Headquarters at Northwood would have no idea where *Spartan* was operating in the extremely large patrol area designated to her. However, we were now approaching the limits of the sanctioned operational zone and, at the time having no secure method of radioing for extra operating space, reluctantly were obliged to abandon the two SSBNs and head south away from the ice. Despite this disappointment, we were satisfied that we had achieved a highly successful and unique trail and that *Spartan*'s presence had not been detected.

A few days later, when back in the middle of the Norwegian Sea, contact was made with a homeward-bound 'Charlie' class SSGN. However, it was of low intelligence priority and after trailing her for a day or so, contact was broken off and we headed back to base. For myself, about to leave the boat, it was a tremendously satisfying end to my time in *Spartan* from build at Barrow to a highly successful operational patrol. The submarine returned to Devonport to accolades from the headquarters staff for what had been an outstandingly creditable period at sea. Undoubtedly my performance and achievements in *Spartan* had erased the adverse difficulties of my time in command of *Otter*, and the ghost of Mary Millington had been finally laid to rest. This was reflected in my selection for promotion to Commander a few months later.

Spartan was to go on to conduct several exceptionally accomplished operational patrols and took an active part in the Falklands War. She decommissioned in January 2006, shortly after completing a five-month 30,000-mile deployment in the South Atlantic and Indian Oceans which included visits to ports in the United Arab Emirates (UAE) and a notably successful port visit to Rio De Janeiro. All in all, this was a fine way for this highly successful submarine to end her time in service.

Chapter 20

Serving with the United States Navy

In July 1981 I arrived in Connecticut, with Linda, to take up the post of Royal Navy Exchange Officer, Submarine Development Squadron Twelve, known colloquially as the 'Devron'. It was headquartered in the Submarine Base located in the town of Groton on the River Thames, opposite the city of New London. I was the fourteenth Royal Navy Officer to take up this appointment, the first arriving in 1955. Rather than be temporarily billeted in a hotel during the two-week handover period, we were fortunate to be accommodated with Captain Ken Cox who, as officer in charge of base support, was entitled to spacious married quarters. The handover from Commander Rupert Best completed, we moved into the rented house he and his family had occupied, in the pretty, historic town of Mystic, some 12 miles east of the submarine base. The house, a bit shabby and not terribly well maintained, had been occupied by several of my exchange officer predecessors. Built in the 1860s, it was old by American standards and we were soon to learn that, badly insulated, it was difficult to keep warm during the winter months. Nevertheless, the prospect of living in a delightful corner of New England for two years seemed a favourable exchange for the rain and midges of the Gareloch where the American officer, with whom I had exchanged places, was destined.

Mystic had been a leading whaling port in the nineteenth century and its old seaport area had been transformed into a world-renowned maritime museum which attracted a large number of visitors. The town's main street straddled the Mystic River and contained shops typical of small-town America, including an ice cream parlour, barber and newsagent. Most of the town's houses and major buildings were of white, wooden clapboard construction and it presented the image of an affluent, well-ordered New England community. We soon immersed ourselves in the local scene and were made thoroughly welcome by several families who over the years had 'adopted' the Royal Navy Exchange Officer. The Devron had been formed in 1948 as an elite submarine squadron which had the specific role of developing war-fighting tactics as a result of the United States Navy's experiences fighting the Japanese in the Pacific. One of the conclusions drawn from that submarine campaign in the Pacific, which virtually destroyed all Japanese merchant shipping, was that a relatively small number of Captains achieved the majority of sinkings. In the case of the German successes against Allied shipping in the Battle of the Atlantic, a similar outcome occurred. Those Captains who employed the optimum attack tactics were more likely to achieve sinkings and to survive enemy counter-attacks. This statistic assumed great relevance against the Cold War Soviet submarine threat, where the West's combat superiority was gradually narrowing and the consequences of failure could potentially have severe geopolitical implications. It was for these reasons that the United States Submarine Force senior officers placed a high priority on tactical development, particularly as an increasing number of SSNs – known in the United States Navy as 'Fast Attack Submarines' – were coming out of American shipyards.

When I arrived in America, its submarine force was expanding at an unprecedented peacetime pace, with a force level of ninety SSNs planned. Its workhorses of the 1970s, the thirty-seven '637' *Sturgeon* class SSNs, were being joined by the bigger and faster '688' *Los Angeles* class boats, of which there were twenty in commission and twelve under construction. (The numbers 637 and 688 were the hull numbers of the lead vessels of the respective classes.) There were also about twenty older generation attack boats in commission, predominantly of the *Skipjack* and *Permit* classes. At the same time, the United States Navy's SSBN force totalled over thirty submarines armed with the Poseidon and Trident C4 missiles, and the new 18,000-ton *Ohio* class boats were about to start commissioning. In due course the latter would carry the much more capable Trident D5 missile and be built up to a total force level of eighteen submarines to replace the older hulls. When I joined the Devron, it consisted of six modern SSNs – one of which, the USS *Dallas*, was fitted with the world's first all-digital sonar and combat systems.

The Devron's shore headquarters was situated in a building which once housed naval cells: indeed several of the offices still had bars on the windows. Its naval staff was augmented by a number of contracted civilian specialists, some of whom were exceptionally qualified mathematicians. I was fortunate in the various assignments

I was given to be supported by two particularly brilliant individuals, Doctor Bill Browning and Doctor Walt Stromquist. Both were highly innovative in their approach to solving submarine tactical problems, particularly in the realms of sonar search and developing the optimum use of contact data from towed arrays.

Elsewhere in the area, there were two other submarine squadrons – Squadron Two and Squadron Ten. The former consisted mainly of the *Skipjack* class SSNs in their final years of service and Polaris SSBNs, which had been converted to the role of training platforms. Also in this squadron was the highly classified deep diving 400-ton submarine, *NR1*. Nuclear-powered, and with a crew of only about ten, it was reputedly capable of depths exceeding 12,000ft and had been employed in a number of covert operations. Of note, in 1986 it had assisted in the recovery of parts of the *Challenger* space shuttle. Across the river Thames, the depot ship USS *Fulton* berthed on New London's State Pier, supported Squadron Ten. Its submarines were all of the *Permit* class, the predecessor to the *Sturgeon*s.

Anyone looking over the bridge which linked New London with Groton into the Electric Boat yard would be awed by the sight of several huge *Ohio* class hulls protruding from the building sheds with a scattering of 6,500-ton '688' class boats in the water at the fitting out berths. However, the '688' build programme at the yard had encountered severe problems because of faulty internal welds in several hulls. These required significant restorative work which incurred serious delays, causing a backlog in the shipyard. On being given a tour of one of the delayed submarines after it had eventually been commissioned, I observed that its final finish was well short of the standards achieved in *Spartan*. In particular, the accommodation areas were notably austere and there were most certainly no carpets to hacksaw the piling from. However, I reflected that this was a warship and rough edges and poor paintwork would not be detrimental to her fighting ability.

In terms of numbers of vessels, the American all-nuclear submarine force was bigger than the entire Royal Navy and the ongoing programme of expansion produced a positive buzz within the Devron, with numerous ongoing projects addressing most aspects of submarine operations and warfare.

Early in 1981 the energetic, ambitious 38-year-old John Lehman was appointed by the incoming President, Ronald Reagan, as Secretary of the Navy. In due course he went on to unveil an aggressive wartime maritime strategy of forward deployment of submarines and aircraft carrier battle groups into the North Norwegian and Barents Seas, the very backyard of the northern Soviet Union. It was also planned to deploy a large United States Marine force which could rapidly be landed in northern Norway to bolster NATO troops there, preventing the Russians from seizing the airfields that would be crucial in supporting the West's forward deployed maritime forces in case of a hot war.

One of the goals of this offensive strategy was to rapidly destroy all nuclear-armed Russian SSBNs on patrol in Arctic waters, and to prevent other enemy submarines from entering the Atlantic to attack shipping carrying crucial supplies and reinforcements to Western Europe. Any surface units of the Soviet navy at sea would also be destroyed, thus neutralising the enemy's submarine and surface fleets.

As part of this over-arching strategic plan, on the outbreak of hostilities, both British and American SSNs would be deployed well forward into the Barents Sea and Arctic Ocean, whilst ASW aircraft and helicopters would provide protection for surface forces operating in the Norwegian Sea. A barrier of NATO diesel submarines would be set up in constrained areas, such as the seas between the Orkneys, Shetlands, Faeroes, Iceland and Greenland, colloquially known as the Greenland-Iceland-UK (GIUK) gaps. In these chokepoints there would be less need for mobility and speed to successfully intercept and destroy Russian submarines trying to get into the North Atlantic. Therefore, they were allocated to the diesel boat forces.

The United States Joint Chiefs of Staff (JCS) and NATO High Command never formally approved the Lehman strategy, which drew its share of critics. Many viewed it as suicidal to consider operating carrier groups in the North Norwegian Sea in the face of the massive Soviet air and sea power concentrated in the adjoining Barents Sea and northern Russia. However, the strategy underpinned the United States Navy's aspiration in the 1980s to expand to a 'Six Hundred Ship' force and governed many of the tactical development projects of the Devron.

Soon after my arrival I was off to the Submarine School, joining a Prospective XO's two-week course to learn about USN submarine sonars and combat systems. Surprisingly, during the course I was not subject to any security constraints and I gained a comprehensive knowledge of the world's first all-digital sonar, the BQQ5 system. Also, I achieved a sound understanding of the latest combat system, the Mark 117 Torpedo Control System. These gave me an excellent baseline from which to work with my American peers.

After completing the course, I was sent to sea on a familiarisation trip in the six-year-old USS *Richard B. Russell*, the last of the '637' class to be commissioned. Prior to embarking, it had been made clear to me that its main machinery spaces were off limits to non-US personnel. Owing to the Rickover embargo on providing further nuclear technology information to the Royal Navy, I was prohibited from proceeding aft of the nuclear reactor bulkhead in the boats in which I went to sea.

The '637' class was capable of about 25 knots and had a maximum safe diving depth of 1,300ft, but had only four torpedo tubes compared to the six in the earlier *Skipjack* class and the British *Valiant* class. Nevertheless, they were quiet boats, handling well at all speeds and, accordingly, popular with their Captains.

Russell was armed with the Mark 48 anti-submarine torpedo, the Harpoon 60-mile range anti-ship cruise missile and the anti-submarine SUBROC missile with its nuclear depth bomb warhead. Similar to British submarines, the torpedo compartment was also used to accommodate some of the crew or visitors in removable bunks set up beside the weapon racks. In the case of the USN, some of the racks housed nuclear-warheaded weapons. However, I was spared the experience of sleeping alongside a nuclear bomb and was accommodated in one of the crew bunk spaces, where I enjoyed the comfort of sleeping between freshly laundered linen sheets. This was a new submarine experience, because as previously mentioned Royal Navy nuclear submariners normally slept in much less comfortable nylon sleeping bags.

Russell was in the middle of a post-deployment, extended maintenance period alongside to enable the crew to enjoy quality time with their families. Therefore, a week at sea in local exercise areas, spent undertaking crew training, was not popular with the Ship's Company and they showed distinct signs of lethargy. On completion of diving the boat and achieving neutral buoyancy, to shake up the crew, throwing caution to the wind, the Captain bravely ordered maximum depth and a 30-degree down angle. As the angle increased, all mayhem broke out in the decks below as loose equipment and stores careered down the main passageway. Books and tools came off shelves in badly secured offices and the galley became a mess of broken jars and food on the deck. As the boat levelled out at 1,300ft, any lethargy amongst the crew had been dispelled, as the clear up of multiple messes and properly securing equipment commenced. I reflected afterwards that, perhaps, there were safer ways of putting the crew on their mettle.

I quickly settled into American submarine routines and procedures which were in the main similar to those in the Royal Navy. The crew's normal routine was centred around four meals a day at six-hour intervals, starting with breakfast at 0600 and ending with Midnight Rations – 'Midrats' – at 2359. The latter normally consisted of pizzas or sandwiches but I rarely had appetite for food at such a late hour. The cooks delivered a greater proportion of pre-made courses than their RN equivalents and consequently, in my experience, the quality of the food was not quite up to the same standard. As ever, movies were enjoyed by the crew and book reading or physical exercise were popular off-watch activities.

Unlike the RN Submarine Officer fraternity, the majority of the officers were qualified nuclear engineers. Early in a junior American submarine officer's career, he/she would have to undertake the daunting double task of qualifying to keep watches both in the control room, supervising ship control and conducting the navigation and in the manoeuvring room, in charge of the reactor and propulsion plant. Although one of the more senior officers would have the responsibility of being the boat's Engineer Officer, the Captain ultimately made engineering decisions. Furthermore, the operation of the reactor was accorded the highest level of importance within a submarine's annual external inspection regime.

This was very different from the Royal Navy system of the Executive branch filling the warfare roles of command, navigation and sonar, supported by officers of the marine and weapon engineering specialisations. As a result, the Royal Navy Captain relies heavily upon the advice of his professional engineers and a key skill will be his ability to ask the right questions and to incisively, but diplomatically, probe the engineering advice proffered. I came to the conclusion that both officer structure systems had their specific advantages and had evolved to suit the culture and background of their respective officer corps.

My time at sea in the *Russell* might have turned out to be a long one as a Soviet 'Victor' class SSN intruder was reported to have been detected in adjacent areas. With the new SSBN *Ohio* conducting Contractor's Sea Trials, the Russian's task would have been an intelligence-gathering mission. To have measured the *Ohio*'s acoustic signature at that early stage would have been a real coup. However, as the *Russell* had only been intended to spend a few days carrying out independent exercises, she did not have an acoustic towed array fitted. Consequently, in the difficult environment of high levels of shipping noise and fishing vessel activity, it would be a tall order to make a detection on the opposition. Although there was a flurry of initial excitement on a possible detection of the 'Victor', the contact was soon classified as a merchant vessel and no further detections of interest were gained. Therefore, we arrived back in harbour on schedule.

Fourteen months later, in October 1982, in the same sea areas, the small SSN *Tullibee*, just out of refit, was unfortunate when shortly after submerging, she became aware of a 'Victor' SSN on her tail. She had probably been sighted by the Russian while on the surface preparing to dive and, because she had a similar superstructure profile to an SSBN, although much smaller than an *Ohio* class submarine, she could have been misidentified. The unfortunate *Tullibee*, due to her small reactor size and limited power, was only capable of 16 knots and found it very difficult to shake off her pursuer which had commenced aggressively harassing her with close-range passes. On hearing about this incident, I could only but imagine the alarming and unexpected situation the green *Tullibee* crew found themselves in, especially operating in waters close to the American mainland, which would have been considered generally free of Russian submarine intrusion. This event, and others similar, clearly indicated that the Russian Bear was confident enough to flex its underwater muscles.

My first project was to lead a small team of civilian contractors in developing tactics and procedures for SSNs to provide direct support to an aircraft carrier strike force. This concept was one of the key factors in the development of the '688' class with its high submerged speed capability. My work included the evaluation of an anti-ship version of the Tomahawk cruise missile which had a range of 300 miles. However, for a number of reasons the enthusiasm for direct support was waning, mainly because of the difficulty of avoiding 'friendly fire' in highly dynamic situations.

I soon found myself addressing a more pressing problem. To contend with the increasing threat of ever quieter and more capable Russian submarines, there was an urgent need to develop new methods of approaching these vessels, exclusively using data from the towed acoustic array. Detections were likely to be made on the latter at ranges well beyond those achieved on hull sonar arrays. Aware of the importance of this stealthy method of acquiring target information, I was equally concerned about the consequences of the towed array's contact vagaries and typical target bearing inaccuracies. This sensor urgently required evaluation and development before offering a real practical answer to the challenges faced by Western submarines when confronting the new generation of much quieter Russian boats. Needless to say, I leapt at the offer from my superior, Commander Mike MacLean, to take the lead in addressing this priority problem. I also achieved an agreement to put greater effort into improving short-range submarine encounter procedures through the mechanism of a jointly funded USN/RN project, which I would direct.

For me, these were heaven-sent opportunities. I would be provided with the research facilities to develop computer simulations which comprehensively replicated the submarine-versus-submarine engagement. From expert analysis of the results of these, my team and I would then be able to develop tactics and procedures for testing at sea. We went on to design and execute six tactical evaluation exercises at sea where those submarines acting in the Russian role were fitted with special noise-augmentation equipment. This ensured their acoustic characteristics would be as similar as possible to the opposition. A real benefit of the outcome would be that, although there were equipment differences between the two navies, the Americans were very willing to make the results and the tactics developed available to the Royal Navy.

One of the most enjoyable aspects of my job, was representing the Royal Navy at the commissioning of submarines completed at the Electric Boat yard. The first of these was that of the '688' class *La Jolla* conducted at the submarine base. Afterwards at a reception held in the base officers' club, I was introduced to the legendary Admiral Hyman G. Rickover, cited as the 'father of nuclear power' in the United States Navy. As the long-standing Director Naval Nuclear Propulsion, he governed the commissioning and operation of naval reactor systems with a rod of iron. Nevertheless, the octogenarian Admiral, blunt, abrasive and confrontational in character, had become an increasingly controversial individual. His reputation had received a significant dent whilst he was onboard *La Jolla* during sea trials: he had over-ridden normal procedures and gave orders which, by applying excessive stern power, resulted in a temporary loss of control of the boat.

Never a great friend of the Royal Navy, it was clear that Rickover was not interested in talking to me. After a brief exchange of words, he abruptly turned his attention to one of my American colleagues. This coolness was noted by a large bear of a man standing nearby who interjected, introducing himself as Takis Veliotis, Managing Director of the Electric Boat Company. Taking me aside, Veliotis, a Greek by nationality, expressed in emphatic terms his derogatory views of the Admiral. Very evidently there were extremely strong tensions between the two of them, particularly regarding the debacle of the '688' class faulty welds, the substantial costs of which eventually ended up being paid by the American taxpayer. At the time I thought it decidedly odd that a Greek national should be managing America's prime submarine building yard which was delivering the highly classified *Ohio* class submarines. The following year I was astonished to learn that Veliotis had fled America, wanted by the FBI on charges of taking kickbacks from subcontractors to the Electric Boat Company.

A few weeks after my encounter with Rickover and Veliotis, on Remembrance Day 1981, Linda and I attended the commissioning of the USS *Ohio*. We were the only foreign citizens present. A temporary stand to seat the four thousand guests had been set up on the berth alongside the truly awesome mass of the black painted SSBN. Inside her length of 560ft were housed twenty-four missile tubes containing Trident C4 missiles, each of which could carry up to eight thermo-nuclear warheads. The cold, overcast weather added to the sombreness of the occasion. Shortly before the arrival of the guest of honour, Vice President George Bush, the diminutive and somewhat lonely figure of Rickover, wearing a civilian suit and raincoat, walked up the gangplank and took up his position on the superstructure. He looked passive and nonchalant about the proceedings, as if unimpressed that his achievement of delivering the world's first nuclear submarine – the *Nautilus* – in 1955, had eventually resulted in the building of this single, terrifying vessel, capable of destroying all of the Soviet Union's large cities.

Whilst the ensemble awaited the arrival of the Vice President, I spotted numerous Secret Service agents and police stationed in the surrounding buildings and vantage points. When the Vice President arrived in a limousine with escorting cars ahead and behind, I was most impressed that, when the entourage came to a halt, all the car doors opened in perfect unison and the bodyguards instantly took up precise station round their ward as he left his car. The Americans were taking no chances even in a high-security area such as the Electric Boat shipyard. It was also noticeable that, if there had been any peace protests outside the shipyard, the protesters had been kept well away from public view.

In a short speech Vice President Bush declared that *Ohio* heralded a new dimension in national strategic security. In his own speech

Rickover summed up that *Ohio* had only one purpose which was 'to strike fear in the hearts of our enemies'.

The commissioning ceremony over, a large number of those present made their way to a spacious assembly hall in the base to enjoy a buffet lunch and a glass of wine. There was nowhere to securely place my Royal Navy Commander's hat, always an attractive trophy for the American sailor. I therefore hung onto it, albeit finding it increasingly difficult to juggle a plate of sandwiches and wine glass with it tucked under one arm. I soon spotted a hiding place for it. The Vice President and his entourage were ensconced in a curtained-off area in the corner of the hall and it could be tucked under the overlap at the bottom of the curtains. Bending down to slide the cap under the drapes, I spotted several sets of feet suddenly around me. Looking up, I realised that I was surrounded by serious looking men with ear-pieces and bulges under their jackets. Smiling meekly, I retrieved my hat.

Towards the end of my time in the USA, we were back in the Electric Boat yard attending the launch of the '688' class boat, *Minneapolis St Paul*, named after the two Minnesota twin cities, separated by the Mississippi. In a construction hall, facing the submarine's bow, seated under the hulls of three others of the class in various stages of construction, I was again awed by the scale of the USN submarine building programme. Unfortunately, poor visibility at the Groton airport had seriously delayed the arrival of the aircraft carrying the launch party of VIPs from the two respective cities. Tidal constraints dictated the launch could not await their arrival and we witnessed the city fathers rushing up the launch platform stairs with the boat already roaring down the slipway. On arriving onto the platform, they sadly confronted an empty void where the *Minneapolis St Paul* had been a few moments previously. At least they were treated to an excellent lunch in the shipyard.

During my early time at the Devron I realised that I would have to establish my professional credibility if I was to overcome the security constraints of being a foreign national. As the months passed, I gained the trust of my superiors. I was assigned more responsibility and the rules of security access were relaxed. I went on to undertake some of the short-range encounter work in the Submarine School attack training simulators, using the students of the Prospective Commanding Officer (PCO) course – the United States Navy's equivalent of Perisher – as testers of new trial tactics. This work was focused upon establishing a safe minimum range to trail Soviet submarines and so avoid the risk of counter-detection or, worse, a collision should the opposition do a 'Crazy Ivan' by suddenly reversing course. I could not help but observe that, compared to the Perisher, the PCO course placed much more emphasis on anti-submarine warfare training.

After a few months in post, the unexpected reappointing of one of my peers provided me with a priceless opportunity to get my teeth into some cutting-edge tactical evaluations. I was tasked with setting up an evaluation exercise involving an American SSBN and SSN operating in the Marginal Ice Zone (MIZ) to the north-east of Greenland. This exercise was given top priority as it was known that Russian SSBNs were increasingly making use of the high levels of ice noise in the MIZ to mask their presence. Its aim was to assess how difficult it was to trail another submarine in such conditions. As this task involved an American SSBN, by the security classification rules, I should not have been taking the lead in such sensitive areas. A British voice talking to Commander Submarine Atlantic operations staff about planning detail caused a bit of a ripple and questions were asked about my access to No Foreign Dissemination (NOFORN) information but, to the best of my knowledge, there were no consequences for my seniors. Nevertheless, on the down side, I was denied access to the results of the exercise.

In January 1982 I was back at sea on the AUTEC range onboard the *Richard B. Russell* running an evaluation to try out new underwater dogfight tactics my team had developed. Another Devron '637' class boat, the *Archerfish*, was acting as the target. It was planned to embark Navy Secretary John Lehman, who had a naval aviation background in the Reserves, and I was looking forward to the Secretary's visit, not least as he would get first-hand insight into joint US/UK cooperation at the cutting edge of SSN tactics. I was, therefore, personally disappointed when I learned that, at a few hours' notice, Lehman's embarkation had been cancelled.

In between the tactical evaluation serials, *Russell* carried out a Mark 48 attack at periscope depth against a manoeuvring frigate. The attack did not go well, in part because of the Captain's rather inaccurate visual target set-ups which caused confusion amongst the control room attack team. Unlike the then practice in RN submarines, a periscope image of the frigate after each look was also assessed by members of the team. The latter's varying calculations added to the Captain's uncertainty. The robust and energetic Vice Admiral Al Baciocco (last encountered by myself during *Otter*'s port visit to Charleston) was onboard, presumably to mind the Navy Secretary. Clearly, from his facial expressions, he was unhappy about the ongoing proceedings. At long last the Mark 48 was fired and thankfully headed in the general direction of the target. When the attack had completed and personnel stood down, the Admiral took me aside and assured me that the less than impressive attack I had just witnessed was not typical. However, notwithstanding my reservations about the format of the Perisher, very evidently RN Submarine Captains, in general, were much more accomplished in the use of the periscope than their USN peers.

It was only after the exercise completed that I learned the reason for the cancellation of the Lehman visit. On the day of the planned visit, he had been instrumental in forcing the resignation of Admiral Rickover. He saw the latter as being obstructive to change. On 31 January at a very tense meeting in the Oval Office between President Ronald Reagan, the Navy Secretary and the Admiral, it was made clear to the octogenarian Rickover that he should retire.

Lehman's criticism of Rickover coincided with the recovery of the United States, and in particular its armed forces, from the humiliations of the Vietnam War. The Rickover era of dominance in all United States Navy nuclear propulsion matters had ended, and Admiral Kinnaird McKee replaced him as the Director Naval Nuclear Propulsion. However, Rickover's legacy of the highest possible standards of nuclear plant operation, and the primacy accorded within the United States Submarine Service to nuclear systems, was to be perpetuated. Lehman's intention was to build upon this, to revitalise the United States Navy and to build it up to the 600-ship level.

In March 1982 Commodore Dean Sackett took over as Squadron Commander. He and Captain Jim Patton, his deputy, did much to support my work, contributing a great deal to the marshalling of innovative initiatives, together with providing submarine time at sea for tactical evaluation. They were also crucial to supporting the analytical effort that drew out the invaluable lessons learned in these sea tests. Enduring and strong friendships were formed with both men and Dean Sackett very enthusiastically accepted the role of godfather to my daughter, Faith, born in the Groton base hospital in November 1982.

On 2 April 1982 Argentinian forces invaded the Falkland Islands. Within weeks Great Britain had responded by dispatching a naval task force on a 6,000-mile passage to recapture the islands. As it became more evident that a diplomatic solution would not be forthcoming to resolve the crisis and war became more likely, I felt rather uncomfortable being in a foreign country when my peers and friends were going to war. Although the American national media were in general pro-British, there was an element which regarded the imminent conflict as yet another British colonial war, ignoring the uncomfortable fact that Argentina was ruled by a military junta with an appalling human rights record. However, it was evident that my USN colleagues, together with my civilian friends, were unquestionably on the British side and were sympathetic to my isolated situation.

I felt that, at the least, my expertise in the use of the Tigerfish torpedo and, in particular, the tactics needed to successfully take on a modern Argentinean diesel submarine, would be called upon. If my advice had been sought, I would have strongly advocated that each deployed submarine launch one of its Tigerfish war-shot torpedoes as a test exercise. This would both prove the weapon system and familiarise the crew in controlling a war-shot weapon which had a much longer endurance than the practice version; it would have been too late to discover latent problems when actually engaging the enemy. But, to my disappointment, there was no phone call or message seeking my advice. Indeed, as previously stated, later events proved there was a serious, undiscovered battery problem in Tigerfish which could have been worked round if it had been identified earlier.

In mid-April I joined the '637' class *Whale* for two weeks to evaluate approach and attack tactics in the comparatively shallow waters of the Gulf of Maine. The *Whale* impressed me as being a happy, efficient and well-led submarine, which had excelled in recent Barents Sea surveillance operations. Her Captain, Commander Emil Morrow, proved extremely cooperative and interested in the conduct of the various evaluation scenarios. Furthermore, he did his best to read signal traffic which contained Falklands crisis information and pass the contents to me. With the exercise successfully completed, *Whale* headed towards Halifax, Nova Scotia, for a port visit.

Meanwhile I had learned about the sinking of the Argentinean cruiser *General Belgrano* by the British SSN *Conqueror*. I speculated whether the submarine's Captain, Dartmouth contemporary and friend Commander Chris Wreford-Brown, had used Tigerfish Mod 1 torpedoes in the attack or whether he decided to fire a salvo of the much more reliable straight-running Mark 8 torpedo. In the event he had decided to use the latter on the grounds that its much bigger warhead would be required to severely damage or sink the former American WW2 vintage heavy cruiser. This decision was misconceived to the extent that the effect of a Tigerfish detonating underneath the target would be the equivalent of a direct hit by the Mark 8. Moreover, it would have been most likely that the Tigerfish would have homed onto the target's propeller noise, detonating under and breaking off the stern and almost certainly incurring less fatalities than the 321 crew killed by the two Mark 8s which struck the ship, one of which hit the hull amidships.

As stated earlier, almost certainly had *Conqueror*'s Captain chosen to use Tigerfish, the torpedoes would have not run. Tigerfish problems continued, but this monumental deficiency at long last galvanised the application of adequate resources and effort to rectify this weapon's chronic shortcomings.

The day after *Whale*'s arrival in Halifax, I was met by Linda as it was planned we would take several days leave to drive back to Mystic, stopping off at a small hotel in the scenic environs of Mount Desert Island, Maine. Linda cheerfully disclosed, that whilst I was at sea, because of small local pockets of pro-Argentinean support, the British embassy staff had suggested it might be a good idea to temporarily take down the large Union Jack which flew from a flagpole in the garden of our house. This she had done. However, on hearing of the good news of the re-capture of South Georgia on 25 April, she had swiftly re-hoisted the flag.

While enjoying the solitude, stunning beauty and peace of the Acadia National Park, I heard the grim news on the car's radio that the destroyer *Sheffield* had been hit by an Exocet missile. We knew *Sheffield*'s commanding officer, Captain Sam Salt, very well indeed and there was no news about whether he had been a casualty. Feeling utterly in the wrong place amid the green loveliness of the serene park which was such a contrast to the bleak environment of the South Atlantic, I felt gut-wrenching sympathy for the crew of the destroyer.

Hostilities in the Falklands ended on 14 June and, by coincidence, the following day we held a reception in the large garden surrounding our house to celebrate the Queen's Official Birthday. During each Devron RN Exchange Officer's period of duty, it had become traditional that he host such an event, inviting local senior officers, together with professional colleagues and civilian friends. We were lucky to be friendly with the leader of the Mystic Pipe Band and during the course of the afternoon, Mystic echoed to the sound of bagpipes and drums. As the band marched up our drive in striking white tunics and Stuart tartan, playing the uplifting tune, 'Black Bear', they made a highly memorable sight and sound. I reflected that this was a fitting way to also celebrate a successful outcome to the Falklands War.

At the end of June, my old boat *Spartan* returned to Plymouth from operations off the Falklands Islands. She was the first vessel to arrive in the area to enforce the 200-mile maritime exclusion zone promulgated by the UK Government. Shortly after her arrival, Argentine merchant ships were sighted mining the harbour at Stanley, but the Rules of Engagement in force did not allow an attack. This was partly due to concerns about escalating the war too early. With the exception of a short period in Gibraltar to embark additional torpedoes, stores and food, on arrival back at her base, she had been at sea for five months, having been diverted from a patrol in the North Norwegian Sea. She had been well built.

A few months later, Captain Jim Patton cheerfully dropped a large document on my desk which was clearly marked NOFORN. It was the American Defense Intelligence Agency (DIA) report of the analysis of the war. As the Falklands War was unique in being the only major maritime conflict to have occurred since WW2, its analysis had been awaited with interest. As was to be expected, the report indicated that the actual number of Argentinian aircraft losses was substantially less than originally claimed. Half of the kills in the air were attributable to the Sea Harrier and extremely few aircraft had been shot down by the short-range Seacat missile system or by gunfire (reportedly over eighty Seacats were fired for only one confirmed kill). This analysis reflected the lack of resources committed over the years to the self-defence of the Royal Navy's warships.

Along with the rest of the world, I also noted that after the sinking of the *General Belgrano* the Argentinean Navy remained in harbour with the exception of their modern German Type 209 submarine *San Luis*. I later learned that this submarine had conducted two attacks upon Royal Navy warships but their German-made SST-4 torpedoes malfunctioned due to a fire-control system defect. Evidently, defective torpedo systems were not the exclusive preserve of the Royal Navy. Added to the fuse failures of many of the Argentinean bombs, these factors significantly saved British ships and lives.

Some vessels appear to be 'jinxed' in that they seem to have attracted more than their fair share of accidents or incidents. One such submarine around my time in the Devron was *Greenling*, a Squadron Ten boat based across the Thames. During preparations prior to firing practice torpedoes, the depth gauges in the forward part of the boat were shut off in error. It was only when the Chief Petty Officer in charge of the torpedo tubes, reported difficulty in opening the bowcaps, that it was noticed she was well below safe depth. A subsequent check of the hull structure revealed no damage but another serious *Greenling* crew failing resulted in a Mark 37 war-shot torpedo being fired in error when alongside. Fortunately, its battery did not prime and it sank to the harbour bottom after a short distance. The gravity of this incident was exacerbated by the torpedo not being missed until the entire weapon load was landed and it was noted that the outload was one weapon short. A subsequent enquiry revealed that one evening, when alongside, the Duty Officer demonstrated to his girlfriend the firing of a torpedo tube full of water, known as a 'water-shot'. Unfortunately, he did not first check that there was no weapon inside the tube.

Another 'jinxed' submarine was the *Dallas*, a brand-new '688' class submarine. In the summer of 1982, I was at sea in her, to direct a new series of tactical evaluation exercises to the north of Bermuda. The previous year she had run aground on the reefs at Andros near the AUTEC range, damaging her rudder and she later had hit a navigational buoy when entering harbour.

This class (the lead vessel *Los Angeles* commissioned in 1976) had been introduced to contend with the increasing number of high-speed Soviet submarines then coming into service and, at the time, the role of providing anti-submarine support to carrier led battle groups. It was assessed that both tasks required a dived speed well in excess of 30 knots and a much more powerful propulsion plant than that fitted in the '637' class. Rickover offered the S6G reactor and machinery system which were based on the design of the plant fitted in the nuclear-powered cruiser *Bainbridge*. It would be capable of delivering over 35,000 shaft horse power and had several features which reduced radiated noise, but its installation required significantly greater space. Consequently, the '688' class boats, at over 6,000 tons displacement, were much larger and longer than previous SSNs.

Their long hull made them difficult to handle when manoeuvring under the water at high speed. Furthermore, their length of hull aft of the fin made them susceptible to broaching the surface when at periscope depth in rough weather. These deficiencies were improved upon in later vessels of the class by locating the forward hydroplanes in the bows, as opposed to the fin which had been standard in American nuclear submarines. Most of the class had propellers as opposed to the much quieter pump-jet propulsors being fitted to all British nuclear boats. Such a change had been resisted by Rickover, perhaps on the grounds of the propulsor's lesser stern power, but all new American SSNs are now being incorporated with this form of drive.

As stated earlier, *Dallas* was the first American submarine to be fitted with totally computerised sonar and fire-control systems. To assist in the evaluation of this new equipment, I was accompanied by Dr Bill Browning, an expert in target motion analysis. We were looking forward to continuing to refine approach and attack tactics using exclusively towed acoustic array data. However, the gremlins again struck *Dallas*. Shortly after the evaluations had started, while I was sitting in the wardroom late in the evening, a worried looking Captain entered and told me that the boat needed to be urgently surfaced and the reactor immediately shut down. Crew error had caused all the fresh water onboard to be contaminated, including the vital feed water for the boilers in the reactor compartment.

Continuing to use contaminated water in the boilers would have caused severe damage so *Dallas* temporarily had no effective propulsion. I recalled my own anxiety when *Otter* had been immobilised on the AUTEC range but this situation was worse: *Dallas* was a nuclear submarine in a very vulnerable state, a long way from assistance in mid-ocean to the north of the Bermuda Islands. However, there was copious expert advice and guidance from headquarters on how to recover the situation and get the plant back on line.

To clean up the fresh-water systems and to make new, pure water, required almost three days of running the boat's one back-up diesel generator providing all power while on the surface. Water was only available for drinking but surprisingly paper plates and tooth cleaning plugs were produced from the boat's stores. With the *Dallas* stationary and wallowing on the surface of the tropical Atlantic and the Fairbanks-Morse diesel generator roaring away under the wardroom, life onboard was uncomfortable. Nuclear submariners take for granted a plentiful supply of fresh water for daily showers and the crew felt the lack of it acutely. However, the clean-up progressed successfully, the plant was recommissioned and the embarrassment of a tow to harbour avoided. Towards the end of the reactor restart the Captain presented me with a large tinned fruit can full of hot water from the engine room (off limits to me). Grateful for this gesture, I made my best-ever use of a few pints of hot water to remove three days of grime and face stubble. Despite the restoration of normality, it took some effort on my part to persuade a rather shaken Captain to continue the evaluations. However, these were successfully completed with very encouraging results from the new tactics being tested.

In the first six months of 1983, prior to our return home in the summer of that year, I ran two further evaluations in '688' class boats. In the first of these, aboard the *Atlanta*, the larger-than-life Texan Captain, Commander Warren Lipscomb, made me an 'Honorary American Submariner'. In the crew's mess I was presented with a submarine badge and a set of blue, cotton coveralls (known as a 'poopy suit') which American submariners liked to wear at sea. By now I felt really at home in American submarines.

In *Philadelphia*, the Captain ignored the rules and invited me to witness drills in the engine room. This was a courageous decision on his part. I learned afterwards, at least in the Rickover era, if found out he could have been relieved of command. On entering the engine room spaces, I was struck by how much simpler the layout and instrumentation were in comparison with Royal Navy submarine nuclear plants. In particular, the machinery configuration was much more conducive to ease of access for maintenance and repairs. I was also impressed by the damage control and firefighting equipment available and, while I kept my engine room observations to myself, I did pass some of the damage control equipment details back to the Flag Officer Submarine's engineering staff. Some of these concepts were taken up by the Royal Navy and I was personally to benefit from the availability of American steam-leak repair kits when I went on to command Britain's oldest SSN, *Valiant*.

Meanwhile it was becoming more evident from operational reports that, owing to improvements in the radiated noise of Soviet submarines, in part a result of intelligence being passed by the Walker-Whitworth spy ring, the West's marked submarine acoustic advantage was shrinking. It was becoming more difficult to detect and trail the latest Russian submarines and the number of counter-detections, whilst remaining small, was increasing. Accordingly, a highly classified cell was set up within the Devron to analyse so-called 'events'. The introduction of the new tactics and procedures, in the development of which I had taken a lead, was very timely in respect of contending with the decrease in technical advantage.

In July 1983 my family and I bade a sad farewell to the civilian and naval friendships we had made in Connecticut. It had been a most enjoyable and professionally satisfying two years. Thanks to the support I had from an excellent team and the provision of a significant amount of submarine sea time, solid advances had been achieved in developing optimum undersea warfare tactics. On my return to the Royal Navy, Flag Officer Submarines, Rear Admiral Sandy Woodward, presented me with a personal commendation from US Navy Secretary, John Lehman. The citation read that I 'had developed tactics that will result in prompt and immediate improvement in the tactical readiness of US and UK SSNs, significantly contributing to the national security of each nation'.

Chapter 21

In Command of HMS *Courageous*

Before returning to the UK in the summer of 1983, I had lobbied hard to be appointed to the command of a *Swiftsure* class SSN. I had spent much time at sea in American submarines developing approach and attack tactics against Soviet submarines and naturally was keen to try them out against the real opposition. I believed commanding a modern boat to be my best opportunity to do so. Secondly, I would be able to move my family from Scotland to the more benign climate of Devon where the *Swiftsures* were based. However, my appointer had other plans and I was informed that I would be posted in November to the most modern of the *Valiant* class, *Courageous*, and, when she paid off into refit in the summer of 1984, I would then take over *Valiant* which at the time was the Royal Navy's oldest nuclear submarine.

Both of these boats were based in Faslane and, needing a bigger house, we bought a nineteenth-century Church of Scotland manse which, requiring considerable work to both the house and its large garden, was a bit of a project. Situated at the edge of the village of Garelochead, some two miles from the base, it overlooked the Gare Loch. The deeds of the house revealed two restrictions: it could not be used as a public house or betting shop. A third covenant – it could not become a 'House of Ill Repute' – was open to interpretation.

Whilst I was in America, *Trafalgar*, the first of a new class of SSNs, was commissioned in May 1983. Very much based upon the *Swiftsure* design, *Trafalgar* was slightly larger in overall size than the former, but had a reduced top speed. This new class arguably benefitted from an improved internal layout in the forward part of the boat, albeit in general the hull and the machinery were unchanged. Meanwhile, in the previous year, the British Government had made the decision to replace the four ageing *Resolution* class SSBNs with the same number of much bigger submarines which would be capable of deploying the longer-range and more accurate Trident D5 missile. Accordingly, the design of the new 14,000-ton boats was well underway and the long overdue modernisation of the Vickers shipyard, which would build them, was substantially progressing, funded by the MoD.

At the same time, the Naval Staff was seeking government agreement for the procurement of a new class of diesel submarine to replace the *Oberon*s, most of which were reaching the 20-year-old mark. The requirement called for a low-cost submarine which, in war, would be deployed to the Shetland-Iceland Gap and in peacetime would serve in an ASW training role. With increased use of automation, it was planned that the new class would have a significantly smaller complement than the *Oberon*s, in theory, realising significant through-life cost savings. In the event, the design chosen was the Vickers 2400 type (the number reflecting its tonnage) and eventually four of these were built, named the *Upholder* class. Notably Vickers had not produced the detailed design of a submarine for many decades as, historically, the submarine designers at the MoD in Bath were responsible for undertaking this task.

Meanwhile the *Oberon*s were being updated with new sonars and fire-control equipment, replacing obsolescent kit, much of which dated back to the 1950s. However, their hulls and machinery were becoming increasingly difficult to maintain. The Trident, *Upholder* and *Trafalgar* class build programmes were set to peak in the late 1980s and the Submarine Service continued to expand with a total force level of thirty-two boats envisaged – four SSBNs, eighteen SSNs and ten diesels.

The Trident programme required a significant extension of the Clyde Submarine Base to accommodate the much bigger submarines. New berthing, docking and training facilities were built, altogether a challenging and expensive project in itself. Meanwhile the shore infrastructure in HMS *Dolphin* would be modernised to support the *Upholder* class. Against a background of the continuing build up and capability of the Russian Navy with its increasing number of vessels deployed overseas into such areas as the Mediterranean, the Submarine Service was most certainly the place to be for any ambitious officer or rating. However, all these programmes would push to the limit the specialist technical resources available in the UK to manage such wide ranging equipment procurement and base modernisation projects.

Courageous had been completed at Vickers in 1971 and had been subsequently updated with the latest fire control equipment. It was now armed with the highly effective, 65-mile range, American supplied Sub-Harpoon anti-ship missile. This was a step change from the 50-year old short-range Mark 8 torpedoes which, finally, were being withdrawn from service. Against both submarine and surface ship targets, she also had the Tigerfish torpedo, which at long last had become increasingly reliable.

Although capable of 26 knots dived and reasonably quiet, as stated earlier, the *Valiant* class suffered from terribly cramped engine room and machinery spaces which made access and maintenance difficult. Furthermore, they had the vulnerability of a considerable amount of internal piping – even that providing toilet flushing water – being subject to full external seawater pressure. In later, deeper-diving classes, for safety and cost reasons, the amount of such piping was reduced to a minimum. The *Valiant*s' maximum safe operating depth was 750ft with a theoretical crush depth of about 1,300ft, compared to the well over 2,000ft of sea pressure the *Swiftsure*s could sustain. Within these margins, there would be less than one minute to take recovery action in event of a catastrophic plane jam while at depth and speed. Furthermore, the *Valiant*s lacked the benefit of a separate emergency, high-pressure, ballast tank-blowing system as fitted to the *Swiftsure*s.

Dreadnought and the *Valiant*s had the characteristic of, when at maximum speed on the surface, being effectively able to plane on a 10-degree rise angle. This was known as being 'On the Step' and raised the maximum surfaced speed by five knots to 20 knots or more. However, although it was exhilarating for those on the bridge, it involved flooding the aftermost ballast tanks and could only be achieved in benign sea states. Furthermore, for the crew below, working with a permanent rise angle on the boat could be tiring. I therefore ordered it on only a few occasions.

Prior to taking over *Courageous* from Commander Rupert Best who, coincidentally, I had relieved in New London, I undertook several courses to familiarise myself with its systems and equipment. These culminated in November 1983 by attending a two-week commanding officers' pre-joining course at sea, which by chance was onboard *Courageous*. Joining her at Faslane, sailing was delayed by about 12 hours because of a steam leak in the engine room, the first of many I was to experience in my time in command of both *Courageous* and *Valiant*. The training period centred upon a joint warfare exercise in the South-west Approaches, during which I was informed by signal that my father had unexpectedly died. However, like all seafarers, I had to contend with and contain such bad news, appreciating there was no practical way of being landed other than in extreme emergency.

Rather than the usual two-hour Captains' handover, I used the period at sea to take the measure of *Courageous* and her crew. First impressions were that the boat was in reasonably good mechanical condition and the officers were experienced and competent. After returning to Faslane in May 1982, from a three-month series of Sub-Harpoon trials based in San Diego, California, the crew had to make a difficult step change in preparing for a war patrol in the South Atlantic. This patrol got off to a dismal start when it was discovered that a bag of highly classified crypto codes had gone missing while alongside in the base. Furthermore, the towed array was severed by over-violent manoeuvring when *Courageous* arrived on station.

After two more South Atlantic deployments, most of the officers were mentally tired, having undergone the stress of both challenging operating conditions and much family separation over the past two years. Indeed, none of the crew was looking forward to a fourth patrol in the South Atlantic which was planned for the following March: the Falklands War was long over and such deployments, about three months in length, were characterised by tedium and boredom at a time when the war was fading in the national conscience. Nevertheless, for several years after the war, it remained MoD policy to deploy an SSN and several escorts to Falklands waters.

After Christmas leave and completion of a maintenance period, I took *Courageous* to sea for tests, trials and Tigerfish torpedo re-certification. I quickly settled into my new command and looked forward to cutting my teeth in *Courageous* before taking over *Valiant* for a full two-year appointment. Unlike *Otter* where the Captain's cabin was no more than a cupboard-size space, my cabin was well fitted out with a bunk, washbasin, a substantial desk and a wardrobe. I could, therefore, make better use of my time when in it. As was the tradition in submarines, I would breakfast in my cabin, but for lunch and dinner, I ate in the wardroom, albeit in the status of a guest. As was normal for the era, I had the luxury of being supported by a Petty Officer Steward, but most of his time was spent on wardroom duties.

This period at sea revealed that both of the boat's speed probes were defective which meant the submarine was without any indication of speed through the water. An emergency docking was arranged to fix the defects subject to *Courageous* immediately vacating the dock upon completion. This proved to be a contentious issue as the repairs were finished at 2200 on the evening of 28 February and, despite no pressing operational need to leave the dock overnight, the base organisation insisted that the undocking proceed. I was not happy with this decision as it meant bringing in additional crew overnight for the evolution and the 12-week deployment was only a few days away. Undocking at 0230, with the assistance of a tug, I undertook a few circuits off the berths to check out the one probe under the waterline. This appeared to function correctly. Eventually getting alongside about 0400 allowing the non-duty crew to get home about 0500, this was not a morale building episode. However, such operational pressures, be they justified or otherwise, were considered the norm at the time.

Courageous sailed from Faslane on Monday 4 March and started the 6,500-mile dived passage to the Falkland Islands to relieve *Warspite*. She was stored for 12 weeks, including over 100 movies and a large quantity of Austrian smoked cheese and digestive biscuits, a favourite delicacy of the XO, Lieutenant Commander Richard Peck. Soon after diving, again both speed probes proved defective but I pressed on despite having no speed indication, having been reassured by the Weapon Engineer Officer, Lieutenant Commander (later Rear Admiral) Peter Davies, that somehow repairs would be achieved on reaching the Falklands.

Arriving off Port Stanley on 23 March, after briefings from the Commander British Forces Falklands Islands (CBFFI) staff, *Courageous* undertook the first of three short patrols off the Argentinean coastline aimed at collecting general intelligence of air, maritime and military activity. This was achieved by cruising at periscope depth just outside the 12-mile territorial limit during daylight hours, which was the only time any military activity was detected. Two Spanish-speaking 'spooks' were embarked who, with their specialist equipment, were able to tune into Argentinean military radio circuits, particularly aircraft control frequencies. The first patrol's prime objective was to collect intelligence of aircraft activities at the air force base of Rio Gallegos, situated on the bleak, desolate coastline of southern Patagonia. Overnight, normally we withdrew to some distance offshore as the Marine Engineer Officer, Lieutenant Commander Vlad Cirin, was always keen to keep his engineering staff on their mettle by conducting drills. Naturally, before practising reactor shut-downs, I wanted to ensure plenty of sea room outside territorial waters.

Although the seabed around the Falklands Islands had been reasonably well surveyed, when off the Argentinean coast, navigation relied on charts which had been drawn up based on outdated surveys.

Many of these surveys had taken place in the 1920s using crude weighted lead-line sounding techniques. Therefore, there was always the risk of grounding on an uncharted shoal or pinnacle of rock. Already one submarine, the diesel boat *Onyx*, had badly damaged its bow when, after landing and recovering special forces during the hostilities, it had hit an uncharted pinnacle off the Falklands Islands. However, in the event, the charts used proved remarkably accurate, notwithstanding their dated surveys.

On patrol, *Courageous'* torpedo tubes were loaded with three Tigerfish Mod 1 torpedoes and three anti-ship Sub-Harpoon missiles. The extant Rules of Engagement directed that any submarine detected within a 150-mile radius Exclusion Zone around the Falklands should be attacked. Nevertheless, two years after the end of the war, I doubted whether the British government would have welcomed news of such an engagement. In the event, Argentinian military activity was at a low ebb and the only submarine detected was during the third patrol when the radar transmissions of a German-built '209' class boat were intercepted, firmly alongside in its base in the city of Mar Del Plata.

There was very limited combat air activity at Gallegos air base and it was clear from communications intercepts that the Argentinean Air Force was bent on enjoying a good long Easter weekend. Therefore, I decided, for the want of anything better to do, to follow the route of Sir Francis Drake on his voyage of exploration to the Pacific, swinging into the Bay of San Julian where the great English seafarer had made landfall after crossing the Atlantic. The civil airfield at the port of San Julian, the closest runway to the Falklands Islands, had been used during the war for combat operations and, therefore, it was also considered worth checking it out for any military activity, admittedly an extremely remote possibility.

Arriving at the bay in stormy weather as darkness fell, I was dismayed to sight a considerable number of Argentinean fishing boats emerging unexpectedly round a headland and effectively blocking exit out of the bay. In this situation, my Perisher training came to the fore. I carefully manoeuvred the submarine at periscope depth between the fishing boats to avoid getting anywhere near their nets. The difficulty of this was increased by heavy seas frequently washing over the periscope and the myriad of confusing lights the fishing boats were displaying. It occurred to me that this had been a foolish venture and, if I had got caught up in nets, this most certainly would not be welcome news at headquarters. On the other hand, such ventures during a tedious patrol kept myself and the crew on our mettle and ready for the unexpected. The fishermen, of course, thankfully remained blissfully unaware that there had been a British nuclear submarine in their midst. Needless to say, it was a relief to make my way out to the open sea without incident.

During the tedium of these patrols, food was an important morale factor for the crew and the cooks did an outstanding job in producing high quality, varied dishes. Each evening bread and rolls were baked, and it was a real treat to enjoy a fresh hot roll and butter early in the morning. Periodic meetings with surface ships enabled a top-up of some provisions, including vegetables and fruit. For recreation, the crew watched films, read books and there was the occasional quiz night or whole ship entertainment such as a horse racing game evening. A return-to-harbour lottery was also run to estimate the exact time of arrival back in Faslane and one lucky young crew member was to win over £1,000 on the boat's return.

In between patrols, anti-submarine exercises took place with the on-station surface group, consisting of four escorts and their Royal Fleet Auxiliary support ships. The first rendezvous I made with the ships was at night with *Liverpool*, the senior warship of the group. In accordance with orders, she was fully darkened. That said, at a range of five miles, through the powerful image intensified search periscope, I spotted a chink of light on the upper deck. After reporting this to *Liverpool*, I observed someone's torchlight making way to secure the loose fitting which had allowed the escape of light. Periscopes truly had developed into highly powerful surface surveillance tools.

Sonar conditions for the surface ships were generally poor and they found it difficult to make contact with their active sonars. As a tedium-busting diversion, on occasions I trained the control room officers to take up and maintain station directly underneath one of the escorts. This position was within the blind arc of the ship's sonar, so there was no chance of being detected. This was exhilarating and testing for the control room team, but I had to admit it was not good training for the escorts, struggling to gain contact.

Most of the time the weather was inclement. On more than one occasion at the end of a day's exercises with the ships, through the periscope I watched the surface ships being severely battered by an Antarctic storm. I and the crew were glad of the stable, secure environs of an SSN, as *Courageous* slipped down to the placid calm of the depths, to enjoy afternoon tea and a movie.

I was determined to make the best use of *Courageous'* time on deployment. For much of the time the surface ships had little to do, so

I initiated a number of evaluations to test the boat's long-range sonar and radar detection equipment's capability to develop a fire-control solution which allowed successful targeting of the Harpoon anti-ship missiles. These tests indeed demonstrated that the boat's sensors could support successful targeting out to 50 miles range or more.

However, despite such achievements, for me, time on patrol often weighed rather heavily. Frequently there were few command decisions or actions required of me and I found that reading for four or five hours a day was the maximum I could undertake. Besides a daily movie, I would sometimes pass the time away by playing chess on a simple computer, where inevitably I was the loser. I also had a stock of tapes of the BBC *Archers* programme which I routinely listened to at 7pm each evening if nothing more interesting was happening.

Most SSNs, when deployed to the Falklands Islands after the war, had strayed well outside their allocated patrol areas to give their crews the opportunity to see the southern tip of the American continent – Cape Horn. *Courageous* had been no exception and I, therefore, saw no point in breaking my area restrictions for such a venture as virtually all the crew had already experienced this. Instead, I swung by the Argentinian island of Isla de los Estados, situated about 18 miles off the south-east tip of the mainland, and considered to be the southernmost extreme of the Andes range. For those of the crew who wanted to, there were periscope views of a rugged landscape of snow covered mountains rising to almost 3,000ft.

But it was not all monotony. On one memorable sunny evening, a large number of dolphins and pilot whales, including their young, gambolled round the submarine for well over an hour. I ordered the boat to a depth where the periscopes were well below the surface. This enabled the crew to take turns to have a periscope view of their underwater activity, to an accompaniment of a sonar loudspeaker broadcasting the many chirps and squeaks emitting from the mammals who appeared highly delighted to have encountered a submarine to play with.

There was also an incident which could have terminated the deployment. While operating close to the Falklands, the opportunity was occasionally taken to embark some of the headquarters army personnel for a day's familiarisation at sea. Also, when with the surface ships, several personnel exchanges took place by helicopter transfer. Shortly after surfacing one morning, in darkness, to the south of the Falklands in preparation for a personnel transfer to the frigate *Penelope*, the boat's bows dipped into an exceptionally big wave.

With the submarine not in full buoyancy (achieved after surfacing by a blower passing low pressure air into the ballast tanks), this caused a substantial flood of water to pour down the conning tower into the control room.

Having handed over command to the Executive Officer, I was in my cabin getting ready for the transfer to spend a day in *Penelope*, when I was startled by a loud bang and vibration as the wave hit the conning tower. This was followed by the roar of several tons of water flooding into the submarine through the conning tower. On dashing into the totally darkened control room, I sighted the officer in charge of the control room, Lieutenant Neddy Kemp, courageously saving the situation by climbing up through a torrent of icy water and pulling the lower conning tower hatch shut to stop the ingress. A substantial amount of water was sloshing around the control room deck and flowing in the general direction of the wardroom.

For a few exceedingly anxious and stomach-churning moments I could not establish contact with the surfacing OOW, Sub Lieutenant Gerry Bernau, and his lookout. I feared the worst – that they had been swept over the side where there would be absolutely no hope of recovery. It came as a tremendous relief to hear the OOW testing his microphones when he had reached the bridge platform and completed the folding down of the steel flaps which covered the top of the bridge when dived. He had two years previously survived the sinking of *Ardent* during the Falklands War, and afterwards I considered that it would have been really tragic if he had been drowned at sea in the vicinity of the same islands. Fortunately, there was little damage to the submarine other than a soaked wardroom carpet and a few officers' clothing drawers which had topped up with water. A visiting officer from *Penelope* did sterling work in helping bail out the wardroom.

I reflected afterwards that I should have been paying more attention to the ongoing surfacing procedure. Notwithstanding the XO being in charge, I should have ensured the boat had gained plenty of buoyancy before the order to open the conning tower upper hatch was given. Command at sea sometimes requires a degree of luck and, instead of facing the situation of having a damaged boat wallowing on the surface in a very hostile sea environment, I got away with a damp wardroom carpet and a few sodden shirts and socks.

Midway through the deployment, I and some of the crew were lifted off by Chinook helicopter to spend a day in Port Stanley. From my vantage position in the Chinook's cockpit, on the final approach to Port Stanley airfield, I was bemused to spot two Phantom fighters flying at speed overtaking the helicopter from below. Air traffic control at the airfield was evidently rudimentary. The town was still showing the ravages of the war with the odd damaged building and much detritus everywhere. It reminded me of a neglected Scottish village. However, a few entrepreneurs had moved in, and one venture focused upon a 'lamburger' shop which also supplied trail bikes for hire and this was well supported by the local British forces who had little to do in their leisure time.

After receiving an operational briefing at the joint forces headquarters, I was taken to the Governor's residence to call upon Sir Rex Hunt. I found him to be a pleasant, avuncular man, highly interested in *Courageous* and her crew and happy to recount his personal experiences during the war. Official duties over, I and several of the officers headed to Port Stanley golf course, the most southerly in the world. This proved to be a highly demanding 18-hole challenge of rudimentary tee-off areas, extremely coarse fairways pitted with shell holes, and rough and ready greens. There were two unique local course rules: owing to the presence of mines, areas of the rough were out-of-bounds, and balls could be lifted out of shell holes on the fairways without penalty.

A few days later we embarked by helicopter half a dozen army personnel to experience a day at sea in a submarine. Included in the group were two army nursing officers who arrived in full battledress, complete with pouches of first-aid kit. I had no idea what they had expected to encounter in *Courageous* but, perhaps because they were in an environment well outside their comfort zone, they proved to be arrogant and abrasive towards the crew. Therefore, on surfacing in Berkeley Sound to off-load the visitors by helicopter, I was disappointed to be told by its pilot that, because of an ongoing lightning and snow storm, the transfer might have to be aborted. The thought of two of my officers having to give up their berths for the two really unpleasant nursing officers filled me with gloom, the more so when they indicated that they were not happy about staying in *Courageous* overnight. I was, therefore, highly relieved when a short time later the helicopter pilot reported the storm had abated and that he was happy to conduct the transfer. Needless to say, the two nurses were the first to be sent up the transfer wire.

Towards the end of her deployment, *Courageous* secured for two days at a buoy in San Carlos water. This gave some of the crew the option to go ashore to the local Army base at Kelly's Garden. The British supply tanker *Eagle*, moored two miles away, also provided much-welcomed hospitality. I and several officers took the opportunity to invite the San Carlos sheep station manager and other local civilians to lunch onboard. Sadly, they proved a rather uninspiring group who showed little genuine appreciation for the lives which had been sacrificed to remove the Argentinians from their land.

Shortly after securing to the buoy, the sentry who was stationed on the after casing was joined by two penguins who stolidly remained there for the next two days, enjoying titbits from the crew such as scones and jam. It was one of these penguins which featured in an iconic photograph standing guard by the White Ensign at sunset.

Courageous' return home was delayed for several days. The relief submarine, *Valiant*, was diverted to intercept and track a Soviet submarine which had been detected in the UK's North-west Approaches. It was with some joy that the crew eventually received the information that she was on her way south and *Courageous* was released on 10 May to head north back to Faslane, gathering intelligence outside the Argentinian naval base of Mar del Plata on the way. There we experienced anomalous visual propagation – a sort of sea mirage. Despite being more than 12 miles off the coast, buildings and cars on the sea front could be observed through the search periscope. It was a final opportunity for the crew to have a close look at Argentina.

By the time of the return passage, the highly energetic and innovative Peter Davies had achieved three working log speed probes, including a jury-rigged one mounted on the casing. On the passage south, his technicians had ingeniously built an underwater divers' platform to attempt replacement of the defective log situated at the base of the forward ballast tanks. Despite surfacing in benign sea conditions, this effort proved unsuccessful. Nevertheless, when the boat was on the surface in sheltered waters, Peter persisted with the repairs until there was a successful outcome.

In early July, *Courageous* left Faslane, paying-off pennant flying, base band playing and a large crowd of well-wishers gathered. She was heading on surface passage routed round the north of Scotland for a visit to the German port of Bremerhaven, prior to entering Devonport Dockyard for a long refit and nuclear core refuelling. Approaching the German coast, when still dark, I was urgently summoned to the bridge by the OOW who was extremely worried by a large container ship bearing down about a mile away on the port bow, and not giving way in accordance with the international 'Rules of the Road'. Over the VHF safety circuit, I heard a guttural voice, presumably from the container ship, demanding that the 'F … g fishing vessel get out of the way'. I responded that this was no fishing vessel on his starboard bow but was a nuclear-powered submarine. I was relieved to observe the container ship immediately alter course to pass well clear astern of *Courageous*.

Harking back to my time in *Otter*, I was again cursed by running into dense fog which delayed the planned arrival off the Bremerhaven channel entrance into the River Weser. Having embarked the pilot, he advised that I make maximum speed up the river to ensure the tidal window into the dock system was not missed. The fog had cleared and making 20-plus knots over the ground in a busy, narrow shipping lane was both exhilarating and concerning in equal measure. The German pilot, noting the worried look on my face, suggested I relax and enjoy the scenery. I curtly pointed out to him that if a mess was made of the pilotage resulting in a grounding, both of our pictures would feature in the worldwide press the following day. The pilot took the point and concentrated hard for the remaining part of the passage.

A successful and enjoyable visit completed, the submarine's departure was totally without incident, unlike the previous visit of *Courageous* to Bremerhaven, when she was involved in a minor collision with a tug on leaving the lock system. On this occasion the harbour authorities, with classic German efficiency, were taking no chances and an array of tugs awaited at the lock entrance, with a helicopter hovering overhead.

Arriving in Devonport, I reflected that *Courageous* had served me well in the last nine months of her second commission and it had been an excellent learning experience before moving to *Valiant*. There had been few serious problems with the plant or other equipment and the crew had performed magnificently, displaying great professionalism and outstanding commitment. The South Atlantic deployment had not proved operationally challenging, but there had been several events and incidents which had added to my command experience and confidence. Altogether it had been a less daunting challenge than the highs and lows I had experienced while commanding *Otter*.

A few days after arrival in the dockyard, I handed over to the XO who gathered the entire Ship's Company on the casing to bid me farewell. It was the end of my first SSN command and I very much looked forward to the new ventures ahead when I took over *Valiant*.

Chapter 22

In Command of HMS *Valiant*

In September 1984, on a date close to my 38th birthday, I assumed command of *Valiant*, attached to the Third Submarine Squadron. I was probably a little bit older than the average SSN Captain but, that said, I had cut my teeth in this class of submarine during my short command of *Courageous*. Moreover, I had copious SSN experience across a wide range of operations. Therefore, I was confident that I could meet the forthcoming challenges of commanding the Royal Navy's oldest nuclear submarine in service.

When I joined, the boat was undergoing extensive maintenance in dry-dock at Faslane following a three-month deployment to the South Atlantic. After an introduction to those officers not on leave, I completed a short handover from Commander Chris Wreford-Brown, who had been in *Valiant* since the end of 1982 following his critical period in command of *Conqueror* during the Falklands War. He introduced me to the Lieutenant Commanders who were heads of department: Simon Martin – XO, Andrew Miller – Marine Engineer Officer (MEO) and Philip Marsden – Weapon Engineer Officer (WEO). Reassuringly, all were highly experienced nuclear submariners and, indeed, proved to be very capable individuals.

Commissioned in 1966, *Valiant* was the first nuclear submarine of all-British design, though her propulsion system was based on the American model of two steam generators – or boilers – in the reactor compartment, providing steam to drive two turbines. These were coupled through a gearbox onto one propeller shaft. However, unlike her American contemporaries, as highlighted earlier, the machinery spaces were highly congested and maintenance was always challenging. This was exacerbated by the inevitable first-of-class problems and the poor design of some of the auxiliary systems. Accordingly, *Valiant* was all too often affected by serious engineering defects which had earned her the nickname of the 'Black Pig'.

During her first commission, a minor fire occurred in the reactor compartment while the submarine was at sea. The reactor was promptly shut down and Lieutenant Commander 'Tubes' MacLaughlin, the Senior Engineer Officer, immediately raced into the compartment well before the regulation ten-minute radiation cooling period had elapsed. Dressed only in pyjamas, he successfully tackled the flames with a hand-held extinguisher, preventing the fire from becoming serious.

During her second commission, while in the Mediterranean following a Soviet 'Victor' class SSN, a seawater pipe on a cooling system failed in the reactor compartment, activating a flood alarm. Rapidly brought to the surface, *Valiant*'s reactor was shut down and her diesel engines started to provide alternate power. The noise of these evolutions alerted the Russian boat and it returned to periscope depth to investigate what was going on. The bridge watchkeepers on *Valiant* spotted her periscope rapidly closing in what was assumed to be an aggressive approach and a nearby American destroyer was called in to ward her off. It was only years later that it was established the Russian Captain had no hostile intent and, having seen smoke pouring from *Valiant*'s conning tower, thought she was in trouble and was closing to offer assistance. The smoke was, in fact, the exhaust from the diesel generators. Subsequently all seawater piping was removed from the *Valiant* class reactor compartments.

Nothing in this respect changed during my time in *Valiant*. For example, when, proceeding deep off the coast of Portugal on 24 February 1986, my diary records the separate incidents of a serious flood caused by a fractured fully-pressurised seawater pipe, a major steam leak in the engine room and a temporary loss of propulsion. On the other hand, when *Valiant* was at sea with her propulsion plant behaving itself, she notched up some notable operational achievements which her crew could justifiably be proud of.

In 1981 *Valiant* took part in the Royal Navy's first tactical evaluation under the Arctic pack-ice. This exercise explored the problems unique to the approach and attack of an enemy submarine in this environment. The following year she played an active part in the Falklands War, stationed close to the Argentinian coast, blockading the enemy's naval forces and providing the British Task Group with early warning of air raids. During my time, I took *Valiant* on two patrols in the eastern Atlantic where her crew achieved distinct success in hunting for and tracking Soviet submarines. These operations are recounted in some detail in my earlier book – *Cold War Command.*

Before joining, I learned that *Valiant* lacked a modern digital data handling and torpedo fire-control system. Instead, situated in the control room were two large plotting tables of WW2 vintage and a mechanically driven torpedo control system which was unsuited to the firing of either of its two weapon systems – the Tigerfish torpedo or Sub-Harpoon anti-ship missile. The latter was controlled by rudimentary missile setting equipment located in a barely accessible corner of the control room. This equipment had been transferred from *Churchill* on completion of her Sub-Harpoon missile trials firings, which had taken place several years previously. The only piece of standard digital equipment was the Torpedo Guidance Control Unit (TGCU) which had been in service since 1968 and was basic in capability. That said, *Valiant* had two recently introduced long-range sonar detection sets, additional to the normal equipment fit. These would provide a distinct advantage when up against the Soviet submarine.

When at sea, the CEP was continuously manned and provided a display of the bearings of all sonar contacts, and their characteristics, against time. When close to a chosen target a large, clear Perspex plot, set up vertically, was used to display the target's bearings, also against time, from the most accurate of the sonar sensors. Both these aids were somewhat crude and manpower intensive but they were fool-proof and, in particular, the Perspex plot clearly displayed target movement and trends.

In early November, I took *Valiant* to sea for the first time for a few days shake-down after her extended period of three months alongside. Happily, there were no major technical problems and, on return to the Base, preparations were made for a visit to the boat by a high-level delegation of the Chinese People's Liberation Army Navy (PLAN). This visit was headed by its Commander-in-Chief, Admiral Liu Huaqing, who is acknowledged as being 'The Father of the Modern Chinese Navy', having greatly contributed to its modernisation. Just before entering the Base in the lead staff car, the nearby Peace Camp was pointed out to the 68-year old Admiral. On being asked by the accompanying British liaison officer, what would happen to such a set-up in China, the response was a slit-throat gesture.

I greeted the delegation as they boarded *Valiant* and began taking them on a tour of the forward part of the submarine. They were accompanied by Commander Mike Farr, the Deputy Squadron Commander, who fortuitously was an accomplished Mandarin linguist and acted as interpreter. Tour complete, while having coffee in the wardroom, the Chinese officers were very keen to know the levels of radiation they were being exposed to. In reality these were less than standing outside in strong sunshine. However, their questioning did indicate that the crews of their own nuclear submarines were subject to levels of radiation which would be unacceptable to their Western counterparts. They also insisted that they go aft to the engine room but Mike Farr emphatically refused their demands. At the evening dinner in the HMS *Neptune* wardroom, all present were provided with a set of chopsticks, but pork chops and baby carrots even defeated the Chinese guests.

My next significant task after taking command was also a diplomatic one, taking part in the extensive celebrations of the 75th Anniversary of the founding of the Norwegian Submarine Service. In November *Valiant* berthed in the Norwegian base at Haakonsvern, near Bergen where the crew were accommodated in local hotels. The USN was represented by the SSN *Batfish*, also berthed in Haakonsvern, and the diesel submarines of six other nations were moored alongside in the centre of Bergen. These celebrations culminated in a Sunday morning parade of the submarine crews and their inspection by Crown Prince Harald. Unfortunately, there was a conspicuous gap in the parade where the West German squad should have been. The bus that had been arranged to bring them from their boats to the parade ground had failed to materialise. This failure was initially seen by the senior German officers present to be a snub arising from Norway's continued sensitivity over German occupation during the Second World War. Fortunately, the threat of the German submarines and their support ship making an early departure was dispelled when it was made clear by the Norwegian hosts that the non-arrival of the bus was simply an administrative error.

Early in the evening I attended a reception onboard the German submarine support ship. On departure my Commander's cap could not be found in the temporary cloakroom which had been set up at the gangway. The ship's Duty Officer was extremely concerned about my missing headwear which he suspected had been acquired by one of the crew as a trophy. I was not too worried as I had a spare onboard *Valiant*. Shortly after returning to my hotel, I was informed by the receptionist that there was a German Navy contingent in the lobby who wished to see me. In the lobby, I was met by a Lieutenant and two Petty Officers, one of whom had my cap placed on top of a cushion. On my expressing surprise that the cap had been retrieved, the Lieutenant responded with a glint in his eye 'Vee haf vays of making zem talk!'.

Later in the evening, my boss, the Third Submarine Squadron Commander (SM3), Captain Mike Harris, arrived in Bergen to embark the following morning for several days of sea-time in *Valiant*. I had hoped for an early night, as departure was planned first thing the following morning. However, our Norway Naval Attaché had other ideas and, after accompanying SM3 and myself to dinner in a local restaurant, insisted that we move on to a well-known local hostelry. There, as the only British submarine Captain present, I was invited to take the stage and sing something. Thinking of nothing more appropriate, I resorted to several verses of 'Campbeltown Loch', much to the mirth of the gathered locals. It was in the small hours before I managed to return to my hotel room for a few hours' sleep before returning onboard for departure.

Next morning, in darkness and sleet, I manoeuvred *Valiant* out of a tight berth with not very effective tug assistance. Thankfully there were no mishaps and, nursing a bit of a sore head, I headed out to sea to take part in a short exercise with the other submarines which had been present in Bergen. Starting the exercise later in the day, *Valiant* did exceptionally well in detecting and simulating attacks on the diesel submarine opposition. Mike Harris was notably impressed by these outcomes and, when landed a day later at Lerwick in the Shetland Islands, he expressed that he was totally content with his *Valiant* experience. For my part, after several days of celebrations and partying, I would have appreciated a quiet few days at sea without the presence of my superior.

On return from Norway, *Valiant* continued a varied programme of exercises and trials at sea, including a number of trial firings of Spearfish torpedoes. This new heavyweight torpedo was planned to replace Tigerfish. The trials included weapon launches in the shallows of the Sound of Jura with only a few tens of feet below the keel. Even more demanding were a series of firings at BUTEC where *Valiant* would act as both firing vessel and target. Proceeding at depth and protected by a maximum depth setting on the weapons, *Valiant* carried out a number of attacks on herself, whilst conducting a variety of manoeuvres in the relatively shallow range area. Constrained to remain deep until the weapons stopped after about 20 minutes of running, I did not feel comfortable with two tons of 65-knot torpedo repeatedly passing just above the hull. Furthermore, tightly altering course in the shallow waters of BUTEC, set my nerves on end. In hindsight, I don't think adequate consideration was given to the effects of an inadvertent hit by a torpedo propelled by a highly explosive fuel mixture.

In March 1985 the *Sunday Times* defence correspondent James Adams embarked in *Valiant* for a few days at sea, undertaking an 'off-the-record' familiarisation passage. While submerged in the Clyde Estuary, a serious engineering problem occurred. In the early evening, Andrew Miller reported that a high-temperature alarm was registering in the reactor compartment. Consequently, the reactor needed to be shut down quickly and its compartment entered to identify this serious problem. However, the port main turbine and the port turbo-generator, the latter one of two vital steam-driven electrical generators, were already out of commission due to suspected seawater contamination of their cooling systems. Therefore, the status of *Valiant*'s propulsion system was highly precarious.

I vividly recall that, as the heavy entry door to the reactor compartment was opened, there was a gush of hot, damp air into the access area – not a good omen. On entering, the engineers quickly located a small high-pressure steam leak on the starboard boiler. Fortunately, it was on the non-radioactive part of the system, but it required the boiler to be shut down and isolated before the reactor was started up again.

All the intensive training of the nuclear engineering team came to the fore as they cross-connected the good port boiler to the available starboard turbo-generator and engine turbine. This provided sufficient limited power for *Valiant* to surface and limp back to Faslane for repairs. Getting alongside early the following morning was challenging as I had limited stern power available and the trainable auxiliary 'egg-beater' failed to respond. Furthermore, only one tug was available to assist manoeuvre alongside. Once safely berthed, a big weight was lifted from my shoulders.

For myself, this episode gave me great confidence that my engineering team, led by Andrew Miller, could contend with just about anything the 'Black Pig' could throw at them. While Adams could easily have published a story with sensational headlines along the lines of a British nuclear submarine having a hole in its reactor, happily he honourably disclosed absolutely nothing about the incident.

After several weeks of repairs, *Valiant* was back at sea and on a mission which I much looked forward to – a three-week operational patrol in the sea areas to the west of the United Kingdom. During the repair period Simon Martin had been relieved as XO by a

much less experienced individual who had only recently passed the
Perisher course.

As related earlier, during my time serving in the US Submarine
Service one of my key tasks had been to develop and refine the
approach tactics to a Soviet submarine using data from the towed
acoustic array. However, many aspects of these tactics were novel
in concept and had yet to be accepted and taught to our command
teams. Therefore, after joining *Valiant*, I had spent a considerable
amount of time training the control room team in these new methods.
I also had the towed array's cable length shortened and customised
for *Valiant*. This was to achieve a better balance between minimising
array stabilising times after course alterations, while ensuring the
boat's own noise did not reduce the detection capability of the array.
By very good fortune, I benefited from a highly experienced team
of sonar operators, most of whom had been onboard when *Valiant*
had encountered a Russian 'Victor' class SSN in the North-west
Approaches a year earlier. Altogether I was confident that *Valiant* was
well prepared for the forthcoming patrol.

The wartime role of *Valiant* was to seek out and destroy enemy
submarines, hence the 'Hunter Killer' term for the SSN. Paramount
to her success would be her stealth. Despite being of first-generation
design, for the era of the 1980s, she was quiet and, if well handled,
at slow speed would be detected at no more than two miles by an
alerted Soviet submarine. Stealth, or the emission of minimum
radiated noise, also is vital to achieving the optimum passive sonar
performance, maximising detection ranges on enemy submarines, at
the same time reducing the risk of counter-detection. To accomplish
this, it is vital that no transmission or avoidable noise should be made
by the hunting submarine. Accordingly, the sound room team will
have available several means of monitoring the noise emitted by the
boat's machinery. However, these internal monitoring systems are by
no means totally reliable and on setting out for the patrol, a serious
noise short located under *Valiant*'s after casing remained undetected

The towed acoustic array is capable of detecting the quietest of
noises emitted by opposition submarines at considerable distances.
Such emissions, interpreted by the sonar team, provide the submarine's
command team with the bearing and emission frequency data to
calculate the position and movement of an opposition submarine. This
enables covert approach to achieve a torpedo firing position on the
target, ideally on its quarter but remaining outside counter-detection
range. During peacetime operations, a noisy or revealing manoeuvre

during the approach could well result in an aggressive charge by the opposing submarine – the previously-described 'Crazy Ivan' – or an irrecoverable high-speed evasion on its part.

One of the key objectives of *Valiant*'s forthcoming patrol was to gather intelligence on Soviet submarines detected in the deep ocean sea areas immediately to the west of the UK. These areas would be where British and USN SSBNs were most likely to be patrolling. Most of these Russian submarines would merely be on transit to and from the Mediterranean. Alternatively, they could be heading out to the western Atlantic to take up strategic deterrent patrols off America's eastern seaboard, thereby bringing their nuclear-armed missiles within range of the majority of United States cities. However, there were those submarines, tasked with covert operations, which disappeared into shallow water out of SOSUS coverage or exploited oceanographic features to mask their presence. These included diesel submarines which continued to operate in the United Kingdom littoral waters and which, when propelling using electric motors, remained very difficult to detect. *Swiftsure*'s earlier problems in detecting and tracking an obsolescent Russian diesel boat demonstrated the inherent challenges.

Some Soviet SSNs were tasked with attempting to detect and track the Royal Navy's single patrolling SSBN. With only one SSBN maintaining the UK's independent nuclear deterrent, such contact, if achieved and maintained, could have severely prejudiced Britain's nuclear deterrence posture. To avoid an enemy SSN being in a position to strike pre-emptively if the Cold War turned hot, it was imperative that the patrolling SSBN at all costs avoided detection. During the early 1980s the UK's Polaris system was updated to incorporate a decoy package to enable the missiles to penetrate the Soviet Union's Anti-Ballistic-Missile (ABM) systems. In recent years these had been significantly improved. The decoy system, developed under the ambit of Project Chevaline, was extremely sophisticated and effective. However, it did reduce the range of the missile to 2,000 miles and notably restricted the size of the UK SSBN's patrol areas, making avoidance of Russian threat submarines more difficult. Thus, it was all the more important that *Valiant* seek out and promptly report the position of the latter.

Valiant's initial patrol area was north of the Shetland Islands. Soon SOSUS intelligence was received of a south-bound 'Victor' class SSN heading towards the North-west Approaches to the UK. Known to be fitted with non-acoustic submarine detection equipment, this vessel was of specific intelligence interest, particularly when it reached the

United Kingdom littoral waters. Indeed, in addition to RAF Nimrod MPA air cover, the towed array-fitted frigate HMS *Cleopatra*, commanded by Captain (later Vice Admiral) Roy Newman, was on station. She was positioned south-west of the Faeroes/Iceland gap, also on task to detect and track this vessel. This was clearly a high priority target.

My first objective was to use the SOSUS positional data, albeit characteristically covering quite a large area, to station *Valiant* right ahead of the 'Victor's' predicted track. A few hours later, we were rewarded with a faint trace on one of the towed array displays indicating long-range detection of the target. Highly relieved that firm detection had been made so quickly, I commenced a careful approach from ahead, allowing the unsuspecting Russian submarine to pass some distance to the west. That achieved, I took up a comfortable shadowing position on her quarter.

During the next five days we trailed the 'Victor' as she steadily headed towards waters to the west of the UK. But on reaching these, her mode of operations markedly changed from straight passage to that of frequently carrying out search manoeuvres. This made her much more difficult to shadow, while still avoiding risk of counter-detection. Consequently, the control room team had to be on their mettle at all times, ready to deal with any unexpected target course alteration. For myself, I shared the command role with the XO, who would normally relieve me about 0200, allowing me to get a few hours of sleep, augmented by cat-napping at other times.

Periodically range was closed to gain contact on our hull sonar array. This enabled the control room team to use precise target bearing and tonal frequency information to derive an accurate torpedo fire-control solution. From this information a simulated Tigerfish attack would be conducted and carefully recorded. This procedure was known as achieving 'Approach to Attack Criteria'. The close approach had the particular satisfaction of converting a faint line on a sonar display into a firm aural contact, characteristically machinery whines and propellor noises. Besides the intelligence gained, being so close to the opposition gave *Valiant*'s crew a real buzz, proving that, even in the UK's oldest SSN, her people could cut the mustard.

After one of these close approaches, I handed over control of the submarine to the XO, instructing him to proceed to the west to open range from the Soviet boat. A few hours later I was urgently summoned to the control room and quickly realised that a close-range situation had developed. Somehow *Valiant* had ended up to the south and directly ahead of the Russian submarine. Immediately I ordered evasion manoeuvres, altering course away from the 'Victor' and gradually increasing speed. No doubt the Russian had made a sonar detection on *Valiant*. This was confirmed by his coming to periscope depth and operating radar to check if, in the absence of a close contact, he had encountered a submarine. However, by the time he went deep to regain contact, we were well beyond his sonar detection range. *Cleopatra* later confirmed that the Russian had returned to periscope depth by detection of his radar transmission.

This incident shook my confidence in the new XO's ability to handle the underwater scenario, somewhat confirming my concerns regarding the shortcomings of the Perisher course. He had broken one of my cardinal rules by not frequently altering course to establish target range and had unwittingly got into an uncontrolled close-range situation which, in war, would have resulted in a lethal enemy counter-attack. Reflecting afterwards, I considered that maybe I should have spent more time training him in my ways and methods of trailing the opposition. That said, I was to come across other command-qualified officers, who although brilliant on the periscope, had not the aptitude to contend with the underwater situation. These individuals, no matter what training was offered to them, found it difficult to assimilate target bearing and emitted frequency information into a mental picture of the location and movements of the opposing submarine.

After this incident, I was ordered by HQ to hand over contact to *Cleopatra* and consequently, I withdrew *Valiant* to a stand-off position. However, it soon became apparent from signal messages that *Cleopatra* was experiencing problems in maintaining contact with the 'Victor'. Clearly Captain Newman was extremely frustrated about this situation. Based upon MPA reports of *Valiant* being a mere three miles astern of the Russian, he questioned why, during a covert operation, I had got so close behind it. This criticism did not concern me, as this incident was but one of several successful 'Approach to Attack' events. What did seriously worry me was HQ reporting that the MPA had detected a serious noise emanating from *Valiant*. This was most unwelcome news and utmost care would now be needed in making further close approaches to Russian submarine contacts. Despite extensive internal noise monitoring and a surfacing to check the casing and superstructure for loose fittings, locating the noise and its cause was to prove elusive.

Meanwhile *Cleopatra* continued to experience difficulties in gaining detection on the 'Victor'. In consequence, to my great satisfaction, I was directed by HQ to close the last known position of the Russian and to relocate her. Less than eighteen hours after breaking off contact, *Valiant* had again taken up a position astern of the 'Victor' which had now resumed his transit to the south-west, presumably having completed his search task. As the Soviet submarine was no longer a threat to patrolling SSBNs, I broke off contact and headed back towards the Shetlands/Faeroes Gap,

My next task was to intercept yet another southbound 'Victor' class SSN which had been detected on SOSUS. Meanwhile, *Cleopatra* had resumed her station in the Iceland/Faeroes Gap. Within two days this new 'Victor' had been detected and a trailing station taken on her quarter, with occasional close range fire-control solution and intelligence gathering passes being accomplished. This submarine proved to be on a straightforward passage to the Mediterranean and of limited intelligence value. Accordingly, when it reached a position to the west of Ireland, I made the decision to break the pursuit. Meanwhile, contact had been made on a homeward bound 'Yankee' class SSBN but, as it was of no intelligence interest, I did not close range on it.

A day or so later, in the area of an underwater feature known as the Rockall Trough, an outward-bound 'Echo II' class cruise missile submarine was detected and followed for a short period. Although one of the earliest, noisiest, primitive and most dangerous types of Russian nuclear submarine, this was something of a coup because *Cleopatra* had been unsuccessfully searching for her. The 'Echo II' was making about 11 knots in a south-westerly direction and appeared to be heading across the Atlantic. The contact stimulated some speculation aboard *Valiant* that, armed as she was with eight nuclear-tipped 'Sandbox' cruise missiles, she might well have been trailing her coat in response to the forward deployment in Europe of nuclear-armed Pershing cruise missiles by the USA. The loud whines and thumps of machinery in this ageing submarine of the Red Banner Fleet made fascinating listening. However, clearly again it was of no great intelligence value and after a few hours trail was broken off and the search resumed for contacts potentially threatening to the UK's on-patrol SSBN.

The final contact of this short patrol was a homeward-bound 'Victor III' class. At the time this type of SSN was the most capable of Russian submarines and with *Valiant*'s serious, unresolved noise problem, I did not want to push my luck. This contact was, therefore, marked from a reasonable range. His relatively transit high speed of over 12 knots meant periodic sprints at speed to catch up with it, during which contact was lost on sonar.

Meanwhile, lacking complete confidence in the XO, my sleep was light. One ear was cocked to the stream of sonar reports emanating from the sound room adjacent to my cabin, as *Valiant* carried out frequent ranging manoeuvres. During a short cat-nap, I was urgently called into the control room by the XO who sensed all was not well. I quickly scanned the sonar displays and from the target bearing movement and marked downward shift in target emitted frequencies, realised that, yet again, an inadvertent close-range situation was rapidly developing. Evidently the 'Victor' had slowed down and *Valiant* was overhauling him up his port side. I had to quickly decide whether to turn towards the 'Victor III' and gain an accurate fire-control solution, or to prudently turn away and return to a trailing position on his quarter. I decided upon the latter, regretfully foregoing the rare opportunity of conducting a successful simulated attack upon this most modern of Soviet submarines.

After two days of trailing in deteriorating sonar conditions, contact was broken off with the Russian. With no more encounters likely, *Valiant* was directed to head back to her base in Faslane. In just over two weeks, the 'Black Pig' had completed a successful patrol in the Western Approaches with, in such a short time, an unprecedented five submarine detections to her credit. The later analysis of the significant number of simulated attack approaches conducted, revealed a high success rate, earning the crew of the Royal Navy's oldest nuclear submarine strong accolades. However, I still had the difficult task of dealing with the XO's inability to contend with undersea operational scenarios.

Once back in harbour, after careful deliberation, it was amicably and mutually agreed between all concerned, including the Squadron Commander, that the XO would be better off serving in the surface fleet. This was a sound decision as he went on to successfully command a surface warship. His replacement was an extremely experienced officer who had commanded a diesel submarine and had been XO of the SSN *Warspite*, Lieutenant Commander Huntly Gordon. We were to get on well, making a strong team and developing a lasting friendship.

Two months later, in July 1985, *Valiant* was at sea in the North-west Approaches, taking part in a sonar trial, when intelligence sources indicated a significant Soviet submarine build-up to the west of the UK. In view of the potential threat posed to the on-patrol UK SSBN – *Revenge* – *Valiant* was directed to proceed at best speed to

Faslane to fit a towed array, then immediately return to sea to support the detection and location of the Soviet submarines. Coincidentally, *Revenge* was captained by my near neighbour in Garelochead, Commander Ian McVittie.

However, despite extensive efforts to locate and rectify the noise problem, it remained. Consequently, on arrival back in port, I was informed of the HQ staff's concerns that this would make *Valiant* vulnerable to counter-detection, potentially prejudicing the covert nature of the operation. Consequently, there was doubt whether or not to deploy her. Although I could see the sense in this, it was not good news. I was extremely frustrated that, despite commanding an excellent Ship's Company, I was being hampered by *Valiant*'s age and defects. In the event, however, I was directed to proceed to sea immediately and on route through the Clyde Estuary a quick noise-ranging would be undertaken to check the intensity of the noise defect.

Meanwhile the new SSN, *Trafalgar*, alongside in Faslane, was also preparing to proceed to sea to confront the Russian submarines. She was commanded by one of my contemporaries, Commander Toby Elliot. If *Valiant*'s noise defect remained serious, the fall-back position was that we would undertake a secondary supporting role to *Trafalgar*. I viewed the prospect of playing second fiddle to *Trafalgar* with a degree of gloom.

Just before getting underway late in the evening, I was summoned ashore to speak to the duty submarine staff officer at Northwood. Through a highly secure voice link, I received a rather garbled briefing of the Soviet build-up informing me that there were numerous submarines operating to the west of the UK. Back onboard, I was met by a smiling Andrew Miller, reporting that he had something to show me. Following him along the after casing, he took me to a spot where, on bending down, I heard a distinct rattling noise. Evidently this was coming from a defective pipe valve under the casing – he declared it was almost certainly the source of the problem. The good news was that it could be quickly and easily fixed.

Getting underway at midnight with the towed array attached and, thankfully, later having received the 'all clear' from the Clyde noise-range check, *Valiant* made a fast surface passage to the areas where Russian submarine activity appeared most intense. Events during the next three weeks at sea, during the summer of 1985, were to prove the most exciting and exhilarating of my submarine career.

Almost immediately after diving the submarine to an optimum search depth, less than 24 hours from leaving harbour a faint trace on one of the towed array screens indicated contact on a Russian submarine. I altered course to present the towed array at its best detection aspect and, soon, different frequency tonal lines appeared. classification of the contact revealed it to be our old adversary, the specially-fitted 'Victor' submarine we had encountered on the previous patrol. Evidently, it was now returning from the Mediterranean and, with its non-acoustic submarine detection equipment, was again on the hunt for SSBNs. My next step was to manoeuvre to calculate the Russian's range. Having done so, I returned to periscope depth and transmitted an urgent 'flash' signal by satellite communications, reporting the contact's position to HQ. The latter's encouraging response indicated relief that at least one threat submarine had been firmly located.

Over the next day, I carefully monitored the 'Victor', establishing its search pattern and periodically updating Northwood HQ of its position. Having gained confidence on what he was up to, I considered it time to close range and gain 'Approach to Attack Criteria'. I chose to do so just after midnight, when I reckoned the Russian crew would be at a low state of alertness.

Seated in the middle of the control room, I was in a good position to view the sonar screens and the two plotting tables where the control room team was methodically laying out the calculated track of the Soviet. At the same time the old-fashioned, clockwork driven Mark 8 torpedo calculator provided the team and myself with an excellent presentation of the target aspect and range, relative to own submarine. A quiet noise condition had been ordered, with all unnecessary equipment shut down and the crew made aware of the need to minimise noise. The control room team was at high alert with the XO, Huntly Gordon, quietly supervising the operation of the submarine's systems and depth control, whilst providing oversight of the calculation of the target's parameters.

As I started the final approach, I ordered 'Start an Event!' at which recording equipment was switched on and manual plots were annotated. Periodically altering course in order to refine the Russian's range, course and speed, I carefully closed range. My aim was to position *Valiant* at about three miles on its quarter, just after it had conducted a course change. This achieved, I awaited the report from Chief Petty Officer supervising the sound-room team that contact had been achieved on the bow array. This would provide the accurate bearings required for a successful Tigerfish attack. Suddenly over the control-room loudspeakers came the excited cry 'Target detected aural on the bow array, Red 50 degrees, machinery noise and other emissions!' 'Got him!' I declared excitedly – 'Standby Tigerfish attack'.

With the TGCU now being fed accurate sonar bearings and the Russian boat's parameters set on it – I ordered 'For exercise Fire!' The 'fire' button was then pressed and a simulated wire-guided Tigerfish torpedo then streaked across the TGCU's screen towards the target. As it closed the latter, it registered its progressive attack phases which culminated in a successful simulated hit. It was then time to withdraw before the Russian was alerted or undertook his next course alteration. When well clear, the event recording was stopped, the normal quiet state assumed and the non-essential control room members stood down. For my part, I welcomed a steward arriving with a cup of coffee and a freshly-baked, buttered bread roll. It had been a long 24 hours, but I could now relax and the post-event analysis of the attack could wait until the morning.

Meanwhile *Trafalgar* had arrived in her allocated areas to the east of us. She was not in contact with any of the opposition submarines. Furthermore, she was not to gain contact before being ordered to withdraw back to base a week or so later when it became evident the Russian submarine activity to the west of UK had returned to normal levels.

On the morning of the fifth day in company with the 'Victor', a second submarine of much quieter characteristics was detected and *Valiant* took up station behind them both. I suspected the new contact was a 'Victor III'. Whilst comfortably in the trail behind both submarines, a *Valiant* gremlin struck again. In the early evening a high-temperature warning in the reactor compartment required the reactor to be shut down and the compartment entered. I considered, gloomily, that this might be a repeat of the serious defect which had occurred earlier.

With the reactor shut down, we continued the trail on battery power, probably a first for a nuclear submarine. But speed was constrained to 5 knots and the battery endurance was very limited. As time passed, tensions rose while awaiting the emergence of the engineers from the reactor compartment to report the result of their investigations. The entry completed and the reactor access-door shut, Andrew Miller's smiling face was a sure sign that the news was good: the instrumentation warning was a false alarm.

Having dropped back to a prudent range, the relatively noisy recommissioning of the nuclear plant took place and, within an hour of the reactor being 'scrammed', *Valiant* was back in the trail with full power available.

Overnight both Soviet submarines were shadowed as they headed for the Shetland/Faeroes Gap. The next day strong Soviet surface ship sonar transmissions were detected and it was evident that the two Russian submarines were heading towards a small escorted convoy. Strangely there was no intelligence to support the presence of a Russian surface squadron of any size. *Valiant* clearly was right ahead of the convoy, in company with the two Russian submarines who appeared shaping up to conduct exercise attacks against it. Before it became dark, I decided to return to periscope depth, both to report what was going on and to take a visual look.

Raising the periscope in calm conditions, against a background of a glorious sunset, I spotted the masts of several ships and, in the middle of them, the upper superstructure of an *Udaloy* class destroyer. At the time, this was the Soviet Union's latest ASW warship and was fitted with a highly-powerful active sonar. The significance of these observations struck me forcibly. For all my experience in six operational patrols and several close encounters with Russian submarines, this was the first time during these that I had actually sighted a unit of the Soviet Navy.

However, positioned right ahead of the escorting warships, I could not afford to enjoy the luxury of dwelling at periscope depth to further observe the convoy. Heading back down to the sanctuary of the depths, we swiftly assessed that the surface force consisted of several Russian replenishment ships escorted by two or three destroyers. In all probability these vessels were simulating a NATO reinforcement convoy, providing Russian submarines the opportunity to make dummy attacks for evaluation and exercise purposes.

Over the next two days *Valiant* took station close astern of the convoy, observing repeated attacks by the two Russian nuclear submarines and as well as encountering a diesel submarine in its midst. Later I was to learn that above the sea, the Soviets were carrying out simulated air attacks while their anti-submarine aircraft played the role of their NATO counterparts. To this mix was added RAF Nimrod aircraft monitoring the effectiveness of the Russian MPA detection systems. I later reflected that this was real Cold War stuff – a Russian convoy playing the NATO role, a few hundred miles to the west of the British Isles, being harried by Russian aircraft and submarines. Meanwhile the surface force was being followed by a Royal Navy

SSN while Russian MPA were also simulating the NATO role, but being monitored by their RAF counterparts.

In such a complex, multi-contact scenario, *Valiant's* control room team had a real challenge in maintaining a handle on the overall tactical picture. Besides marking and evaluating the Soviet contacts on the manual WW2 plotting tables, the team heavily relied upon calculating target ranges using hand-held calculators or slide-rules. Nevertheless, these basic methods delivered good results. Meanwhile the sound room personnel were intensely occupied in simultaneous tracking and reporting of the surface ship and submarine contacts. At all times, there was the continuing imperative of avoiding being detected and becoming part of the action, or, at worst, risking collision with the Russian submarines as they made their high speed forays into the convoy. Despite the sterling support of Huntly Gordon, owing to the intense activity going on around *Valiant*, I slept very lightly. Indeed, after over a week of continuous contact with the opposition, I was slipping into deep exhaustion.

When the convoy arrived north of the Shetland Islands, it became increasingly evident that it had dispersed and the two Russian SSNs had headed away. Although contact with these had faded, two new Soviet nuclear submarines had been detected to the north at long range. However, these were not accorded priority status by HQ. Accordingly, I headed *Valiant* back to the west of the British Isles to seek out any Soviet submarine which might be still be lurking undetected off the North-west Approaches. This interlude, out of contact, gave me a chance of some welcome deep sleep which I felt all the better for.

When back to the west of the UK, I received information that two 'Delta' class SSBNs, homeward-bound from their deep Atlantic patrol areas, were about to enter our areas. They were about 24 hours apart and soon detection was made on both of them. I carried out a brief trail of the first but I hauled off shortly after detecting the second as they were of little intelligence value. Nevertheless, I recall wardroom discussion about what British public opinion would have thought about a pair of potentially hostile SSBNs passing a mere 200 miles off the British coast. Their thirty-two nuclear missiles had the destructive power to totally devastate the United Kingdom.

A few days later *Valiant* detected yet another SSBN but this event turned out to be rather unfortunate. I had received instructions to intercept a SOSUS-reported 'Victor II' class SSN which appeared to be heading for the Mediterranean. *Valiant* was again tasked to determine whether or not it had been ordered to search for on-patrol SSBNs and, accordingly, I established a listening search along its predicted track. Unfortunately, in the process we stumbled upon a US SSBN. It had been returning from patrol and as an engineering drill had been running its diesel engine. This noise was detected by our sonar team who initially found it difficult to resolve whether it was a fishing vessel or a snorting submarine.

There was depth separation between the two submarines, with the US boat allocated the shallower zone. Assuming any SSBN in the vicinity would have opened range from the 'Victor's' track, I broke the rules and returned to periscope to check out the fishing vessel possibility. A rapid visual sweep, affirmed that there was no surface vessel around and that the contact must be a submarine. Quickly returning to the depths, I was elated in thinking that we had detected that highly elusive threat Soviet SSN which we had been tasked to locate. However, it gradually became evident that the sonar characteristics of the contact were not those of a Russian submarine and that we were tracking a US SSBN. Accordingly, contact was rapidly broken off and a suitably contrite signal transmitted to HQ to the effect that *Valiant* had detected and for a short time tracked a US SSBN. The response was measured and there was a gentle reproach regarding the breach of depth zone rules. However, no doubt there was bemusement within HQ that *Valiant* had 'bounced' a US SSBN.

The 'Victor' was detected some hours later but, disappointingly, she was at some distance to the south. Nevertheless, she had evidently not slowed down into a search mode and was in straightforward transit to the Mediterranean.

Two days after the US SSBN event, there was yet another encounter with an SSBN. However, this one was fully authorised and involved closely searching around the UK's on-patrol SSBN, *Revenge*, to ensure that there was no undetected Soviet submarine in her vicinity. This operation, known as 'delousing', was successfully executed. But I did recall *Spartan*'s trailing of a 'Victor' SSN and its subsequent 'delousing' manoeuvres which led to the detection of a Russian SSBN. Nevertheless, on this occasion, there was absolute certainty that there was no opposition submarine anywhere near *Revenge*.

Valiant's patrol ended with the long-range detection and several days tracking of a missile firing 'Charlie II' class heading north. She was returning from the Mediterranean where she would have been tasked to shadow the aircraft-carrier battle-groups of the American Sixth Fleet. Should hostilities occur, her role would have been to neutralise such a potent surface force with her lethal anti-ship cruise missiles. With this intercept efficiently concluded, *Valiant* headed home, the Ship's Company in high spirits. Although we had been at sea for only a little over three weeks, nine Russian submarines had been detected, again a remarkable number.

The significance of this achievement was all the greater when *Valiant*'s run-down state was considered. With nine months remaining of her commission, some at Northwood HQ were keen to deploy *Valiant* on further operations against the Red Banner Fleet, but she was increasingly showing her age and the need for a major refit. Her engineers had to work extremely hard to keep the boat going and any time in harbour involved intense periods of repairs to her machinery.

On more than one occasion a minor fire had broken out onboard when alongside in Faslane, resulting in the arrival of the Dunbartonshire fire brigade. One of these incidents had occurred when I was playing golf at a local course with Mike Harris, Captain SM3. During the round we spotted a series of fire engines heading towards the Helensburgh area. Play over, on arrival back at the clubhouse, I was met by the club's professional who stated that he had received a message for me. He handed over a slip of paper with the alarming message 'Reactor Compartment on Fire'. My heart pounding, I immediately rang *Valiant*'s Duty Officer. Right away he put my mind at rest, informing that there had been welding ongoing in the reactor compartment when a protective welding blanket ignited, but it had been quickly extinguished. However, much smoke had been generated and it had been sucked up through the ventilation mast into the top of the fin. Smoke coming out of *Valiant*'s fin raised an urgent telephone call from the base command building enquiring where the fire was. The unfortunate response by a duty junior rating was 'The reactor compartment is on fire'. Immediately the alarm was raised and the Dunbartonshire fire brigade urgently summoned whilst the base firefighting squad headed to *Valiant*'s berth. By the time the latter arrived the fire had been extinguished, but no one remembered to cancel the original message to me, stating erroneously that the reactor compartment was on fire.

In August *Valiant* undertook an eight-day goodwill visit to Kiel in Germany. After another series of Spearfish firings at BUTEC, we headed on the surface through the Pentland Firth and down through the Skagerrak Strait to a much looked-forward visit to the German port. With a pilot embarked, I enjoyed the passage in calm conditions through the many narrows separating Denmark and Sweden. During the final stages of the passage, an East German intelligence-gathering vessel approached close abeam of *Valiant*. On her upper-deck I spotted a photographer, head under a cloth hood, handling slides behind an ancient tripod camera. Giving him a cheerful wave, I reflected that evidently the East German Navy had not caught up with camera films, never mind digital technology.

The visit to Kiel gave the Ship's Company the opportunity to relax and enjoy themselves. Warm hospitality was extended from both the German Navy and members of the local population. One of the most memorable events was a match against members of a golf club in nearby Ekelsfjord. I recall a Stoker Petty Officer, attired in scruffy submarine sweater, to my despair, taking two air-shots on the first tee before shanking his ball into the rough. There also was the need to despatch one of our team back to the clubhouse to purchase more balls as so many had been lost. Of course, we were heavily defeated. That said, our hosts were very patient and after the match we enjoyed a convivial drink in their prestigious clubhouse.

For many of the crew, a visit to the sobering U-boat Memorial, and the nearby historic Type VII submarine, was a must. The memorial's commemorative plaques recorded the deaths of over 30,000 submariners and the loss of 739 boats during WW2. Most of the crew lost in these boats were in their early twenties and in the listings there were few submarine pennant numbers missing. Towards the end of that conflict, Allied ASW capability was absolutely overwhelming and most U-boats sent on patrol never returned.

Meanwhile, a year into command, I had firmly established a sound rapport with the wardroom and Ship's Company and was extremely pleased with their high level of competence and support. I instigated the humble Mars bar as an incentive commodity within the wardroom. Should any officer make a mistake I would fine him Mars bars, the number proportional to the seriousness of the error. These I would keep in a drawer in my desk. If an officer, on the other hand, did well I would summon him to my cabin and award him with a Mars bar(s). All this was very light-hearted stuff but, particularly based on my *Sealion* experience, I avoided calling out my officers in front of the crew if an error occurred. Instead, there would be the cry – 'That will be . . . Mars bars!'.

After a Base maintenance period in September, it was a return to more mundane operations and exercises. Several series of Spearfish trials firings took place and a deep water towed array tactical evaluation exercise sponsored by STWG was conducted with the brand new SSN, *Turbulent*, as opposition. *Valiant*'s highly experienced control room and sonar teams again excelled and emphatically demonstrated her to be capable of successfully taking on much more modern platforms.

I always felt nervous and on edge when taking a submarine into a commercial port. Perhaps this nervousness harked back to the hazardous entry I experienced when taking *Otter* into Birkenhead. In November, I took *Valiant* into the port of Liverpool in stormy weather conditions with a strong flood tide running, creating an angry-looking sea. Accordingly, in this my second venture into the Mersey when in command, I was highly apprehensive. My big challenge was to safely negotiate the narrow entrance into the historic Gladstone dock system on the east side of the river. Tugs were secured at the bow and stern to swing *Valiant* sharply round to align with the line of entry. However, these vessels were used to manoeuvring slab-sided merchant ships where impact with the dock wall was not of great significance. This was not the case with the sonar and other sensitive underwater fittings of a nuclear submarine. Therefore, I was not terribly confident of the tugs' ability to get me into the dock system unscathed.

As I arrived at the dock entrance, the bow came out of the strong effects of the flood tide and swung rapidly to port heading towards the western wall of the dock. Applying urgent stern power together with the rear tug checking the swing, we avoided hitting the dock wall – just! Then, after a few more engine and rudder movements, I was safely in the dock system, the entire length of the boat out of the tidal stream, and heading towards a secure berth in the Seaforth container terminal. I was much relieved and the crew went onto enjoy the immense hospitality of Liverpool and its surrounding communities. Six months later I undertook a second visit to Liverpool in much more benign weather conditions and, on this occasion, with no near misses. Nowadays Liverpool, for reasons of the significant costs of meeting over-demanding nuclear safety criteria, is off limits to submarine visits. Indeed sadly, our few SSNs rarely make home-port visits.

This was in an era when there was ease of access to families and friends to our nuclear submarines when alongside in Faslane. Both the wardroom and senior rates mess hosted occasional parties, sometimes with a theme which involved fancy dress. The cooks often excelled on such occasions delivering magnificent buffet spreads. Additionally, on Base open days, members of the public would be able to tour the forward compartments of an SSN or the entire length of a diesel boat. Today, because of security concerns, access to our nuclear submarines when berthed in Faslane, is rather difficult and I doubt if there is the same level of socialisation between the respective crews and their families, or the local community.

Aboard *Valiant*, engineering problems were becoming all too frequent. A steam leak occurring on one of the many engine-room valves when 'flashing up' the propulsion plant in preparation for sea was a common occurrence. Sometimes this delayed departure but was never serious enough to compromise an operational commitment. The deteriorating condition of the steam pipework in the engine room was of also of serious concern. Hot, high-pressure steam inevitably causes corrosion with a consequent weakening of the piping. At worst, a major failure could have caused serious injury to the engine room watchkeepers. The occurrence of an accident was a constant worry to me. That said, the base and our own engineers, by constantly monitoring the state of the piping, and fitting replacement sections where necessary, markedly reduced the chance of this happening.

At the end of February 1986 *Valiant* headed for the Mediterranean to take part in two major NATO submarine exercises. In the event, this two-month deployment to the Mediterranean was beset by more engineering problems than usual. On passage to Gibraltar, the first port of call, a significant seawater flood occurred in the control room. This happened when the command team was closed up in the control room carrying out attack training drills in preparation for a forthcoming annual squadron inspection.

A coupling on the officers' heads flushing water pipe failed with a loud report followed by a roaring sound, as highly-pressurised water sprayed into the wardroom passageway. Immediately I ordered an increase in speed and a twenty-degree bow-up angle to reduce depth and consequently the pressure of the flooding seawater. However, the steep angle of the submarine caused a bore of water to flood out from the wardroom passage, along the deck into the control room. The nimble remained dry by leaping onto chairs and the plotting tables. The water then poured down the hatch to the compartments below, much to the alarm of the repair team trying to get up the ladder. However, the failed pipe was quickly isolated and the ingress of water halted before any serious damage was done. The only casualties were sodden trousers and socks – the attack training drills continued with hardly a pause.

Towards midnight on the same day, a second incident occurred when proceeding at depth and high speed. A high-pressure steam leak, this was much more serious than the flood. Relaxing in my cabin with a book, I heard a shrill report from aft – 'Major steam leak in the engine room!' A seal had failed on a steam-driven pump, causing a violent emission of high-temperature steam into the cramped, stygian confines of the engine room. As it could have seriously scalded anyone in its vicinity, this was a life-and-death situation. The compartment was instantly evacuated, steam shut off to the pump and the problem tackled by a repair party. Once again, the engineering staff rose to the occasion, quickly fixing the defect and soon we were underway again in full power.

Despite the efficiency with which both these incidents were dealt, I was aware of growing concerns amongst the Ship's Company regarding the safety of *Valiant*'s systems and machinery. I, therefore, spoke to the Senior and Junior Rates in their respective mess-decks a few days later, hopefully allaying their concerns. Thankfully, thereafter, there were no further serious engineering system problems, albeit a reactor instrumentation fault was to arise which caused the deployment to be curtailed.

On arriving in Gibraltar, the stalwart Andrew Miller was relieved, departing for a very well-deserved rest in a much less demanding shore appointment. There then followed a Squadron sea inspection in the local sea areas, led by Captain Roger Lane-Nott who had taken over from Mike Harris as SM3. By this time *Valiant* had excelled in a number of Flotilla-wide competitions, including such disciplines as torpedo firings, underwater photography and intelligence-gathering. I, therefore, viewed the inspection as being fairly perfunctory, rather a tick-in-the-box event. A cynic would perhaps have concluded that it did give the Squadron Staff a few days of relaxation in Gibraltar.

The first of the NATO exercises, code-named Dogfish, and inevitably re-named by the Ship's Company as 'Dogshit', took place in the Ionian Sea, the area of the Mediterranean Sea between Italy and Greece. This was a submarine versus submarine exercise and *Valiant* was cast in the 'Blue' NATO role throughout. We had, in error, received the exercise instructions setting out all the tracks and navigational way-points of the 'Red' submarines. It was thus all too easy locating and carrying out simulated attacks upon the opposing 'Red' forces which included the American SSN *Tullibee* and a number of NATO diesel submarines. From underwater telephone exchanges at the end of each attack phase, I noted a degree of despair on the part of the *Tullibee*'s crew as they grasped that they were being successfully engaged with unerring accuracy by *Valiant* in every section of the exercise.

However, to myself and the command team, these proceedings were a sideshow as we were determined to detect a 'Victor II' class

SSN which was known to be in the central Mediterranean. It had been trailed for a period by an American SSN which I was thoroughly familiar with – the *Dallas*. She was now commanded by Commander Frank le Croix who had been a near neighbour in Mystic, Connecticut. Contact had been lost with the Russian for several days but I suspected that Dogfish would act as a lure to any inquisitive Soviet submarine – the mirror-image of our shadowing of the Russian convoy in the North Atlantic the previous summer. Sure enough, with the exercise a few hours old, *Valiant* gained firm sonar contact with the 'Victor II'. However, the need to adhere to the exercise instructions meant we could not commence tracking it. The exercise was also evidently being monitored by a Russian 'research-ship' bulging with sensor equipment; she was on more than one occasion sighted by *Valiant*.

During the final phase of the exercise, after conducting a successful approach against the 'Red' Italian submarine *Guglielmo Marconi*, *Valiant* was at periscope depth about two miles to the south of her. A USN Orion aircraft had been operating with *Valiant*, dropping active sonobuoys around the *Guglielmo Marconi* to emphasise the firmly detected status of the Italian boat. Suddenly *Valiant*'s sonar team reported a fast moving submarine contact about four miles to the southward; it was tracking aft and emitting classic Russian SSN characteristics. Before going deep to start following it, there was the need to pass locating details of the Soviet submarine to the aircraft. This took some time as a cumbersome NATO numeric code had to be used to transmit the information. Meanwhile the tactical situation was confused by a high density of merchant shipping passing through the area and intense levels of biological noise from dolphins and other creatures in the vicinity.

When it appeared that the aircraft had got the message, I ordered *Valiant* deep to close with the Russian but, on leaving periscope depth, the sonar contact was lost. However, soon afterwards a number of active sonar transmissions, characteristic of Soviet SSN sonar equipment, were intercepted coming from the general direction of the Russian boat. These were followed by brief bursts of Soviet underwater telephone communications which made me think that the Soviet submarine commander was in conversation with either the so-called research ship or another submarine. What was certain, was the increasing confusion of the underwater tactical picture. *Valiant* was surrounded by a cacophony of noise: to the sound of passing shipping and noisy porpoises, there was now added the vocal Italian submarine captain of the *Guglielmo Marconi* chatting away on the underwater telephone, an Orion aircraft dropping numerous active sonobuoys and at least one Russian submarine which appeared to want to be part of the action. Looking back, I reflected that the whole incident was a rather amusing finale to my last operational engagement with a Russian submarine.

The exercise over, *Valiant* headed on the surface through the Sicilian Channel to La Maddalena in Sardinia to leave her towed sonar array with the American submarine depot-ship moored there. Before heading for a port visit to Naples, we embarked my friend, Captain Ken Cox, who now was Chief-of-Staff to the US Admiral commanding submarine forces in the Mediterranean. I can recall his surprise at the amount of defect repair work which was ongoing in the machinery spaces. To the American, the exceedingly cramped engine room, was in extreme contrast to the well laid out, easily accessible compartments of most American nuclear submarines.

Once in Naples the majority of the Ship's Company, except the engineering department, could relax. On the second day alongside, Ken C. invited me to attend the morning high-level briefings in the American Naval Headquarters. At the final and highest-level of these briefings, I noted that I was the only foreigner present as the presentations focused upon the forthcoming deployment of a three-carrier battle-group across the so-called 'Line of Death' established by Colonel Gaddafi of Libya. This ran east-west across the Gulf of Sidra but, although unrecognised by international law, Gaddafi had declared the sea to the south as Libyan territorial waters. Three days later, on Monday, 24 March 1986, the battle-group crossed the line. Libya responded with the use of anti-aircraft missiles and fighter aircraft, challenging the battle-group's right of peaceful passage in international waters and air-space. In retaliation American aircraft attacked several missile radar sites and destroyed or disabled several threatening Libyan naval vessels.

Having left Naples, a few days later *Valiant* berthed at La Spezia for an informal six-day visit and a further break for the crew over the Easter Holiday. Flag Officer Submarines, Rear Admiral Dick Heaslip, was embarked for the short passage from Naples and took the opportunity of visiting the messdecks and thanking the crew for their achievements. This was much appreciated. The Ship's Company was billeted in a hotel in the seaside resort of Viareggio some 20 miles south of La Spezia. This location proved to be a great success and the crew were particularly warmly feted by the many charming local girls who, of course, had never before encountered the Royal Navy submariner. Meanwhile I and some members of the wardroom had another opportunity to demonstrate our lack of golfing prowess. Playing on Easter Sunday at a local golf course, our attempts to get our balls across a pond caused great mirth at the clubhouse. Indeed, at the end of the round, we had generated so much amusement that the club professional warmly invited us to join his family lunch party on the terrace.

The officers were accommodated in a small local hotel. It came as a surprise to myself and fellow officers that among the other residents included a number of Libyan naval officers. They were standing by new patrol vessels under construction in the local Fincantieri shipyard. As one Italian admiral visiting *Valiant* cynically explained to me 'We build vessels for the Libyan navy, the Americans sink them and then Gaddafi asks for more to be built. It is all very good for business!'

On leaving La Spezia, in early April, we embarked a Spanish submarine commander as an observer for the second NATO submarine-versus-submarine exercise. This would be under the operational control of the Spanish navy, and was planned to culminate in a port visit to Cartagena. There, as part of the arranged visit activities, I and my fellow submarine commanding officers would be invited to partake in bull-fighting. However, I was assured that the bulls were young and matadors would be present to ensure none of the visitors came to harm. In the event, I was to miss this unique experience.

Meanwhile, the number of engineering defects occurring in *Valiant* continued to mount and I was aware that these were putting a severe strain on the engineering department. In particular, when starting up the reactor before leaving La Spezia, a problem had occurred with one of the reactor's key instruments. This meant that, should the reactor be shut down for any reason, it might prove difficult to start it up again. The inherent risk in such an event was exacerbated by a defect in the back-up emergency propulsion motor which would render *Valiant* without any form of propulsion.

Given the general state of *Valiant*'s machinery this 'worst-case scenario' was not far-fetched and was extremely worrying, particularly as the exercise would be taking place in the Strait of Gibraltar. Crowded with international shipping, this was not an area where any vessel, submarine or surface ship, would want to entirely lose the ability to manoeuvre. Two days into the exercise I therefore reluctantly withdrew *Valiant* and headed for Faslane. This was a great disappointment to me as it was the only commitment which had not been met during my time in command.

Before heading north, *Valiant* surfaced to disembark the Spanish officer by helicopter transfer. He had been curious about our engineering problems and, of course, I had to be circumspect in explaining why we were withdrawing from the exercise. Unfortunately, the bag the helicopter lowered to take up his possessions and the exercise records was not properly attached to the transfer wire. As the wire was hauled in over the sea by the helicopter, the bag detached and plunged into the depths. Observing this mishap before being lifted off, I thought the Spaniard, on bidding farewell, was remarkably relaxed about the loss of his possessions. Nevertheless, albeit trifling in nature, I realised afterwards that this marked the last of a series of mishaps.

After a week's repairs, *Valiant* was back at sea doing what her crew did best – covertly trailing another submarine for over 12 hours. On this occasion it was a British SSBN, *Resolution*, being worked-up before deploying on patrol. But it raised issues regarding the vulnerability of Britain's ageing SSBN force. Nevertheless, it was appreciated by HQ that *Resolution* was up against one of the Royal Navy's most capable and experienced SSN crews. Highly pleased for my Ship's Company, disappointments over the Mediterranean deployment began to fade as accolades followed.

On 26 April 1986 the world was shaken by the disastrous Chernobyl reactor accident. This had the outcome of vast quantities of radioactive material being released into the atmosphere which exceeded that of hundreds of nuclear bomb detonations. It is highly undesirable for radioactive matter to be trapped in the confines of a submarine. Consequently, in the days and weeks after the accident frequent radiation measurements were undertaken around the submarine. Whilst *Valiant* was docked, undergoing pre-refit tests, a radiation hot-spot was detected on the deck of the wardroom passageway. The cause was soon established to be rainwater dripping off hanging raincoats and was easily cleaned up. Nevertheless, this small incident emphasised the severity of the Chernobyl radiation release.

One of *Valiant*'s final commitments before refit was to embark a number of NATO ambassadors for a day at sea. Together with *Trafalgar*, we were tasked to take them to sea in the Clyde Estuary to observe a nuclear submarine being put through its paces. A full-blown rehearsal was staged on the preceding day. This included the cooks proving that they could deliver an absolutely splendid gourmet lunch and, indeed, they fully rose to the challenge. On the actual ambassadors' day at sea, lunch having been completed and the galley secured, I enjoyed demonstrating *Valiant*'s superb underwater manoeuvrability.

Importantly, on this significant occasion, the propulsion plant and auxiliary machinery worked perfectly. All the visitors appeared to have thoroughly enjoyed their day at sea and were highly impressed by the demonstration of the nuclear submarine's capability.

The following day there followed an even more enjoyable event when the families of *Valiant*'s crew were invited aboard for a day at sea. Ever resourceful, the cooks had sequestered sufficient of the NATO ambassadors' luncheon supplies to lay on a spectacular repast for the crew's wives and girlfriends. Rarely would lunch on a family's day have included lobster, followed by fillet steak and an array of delicious, innovative desserts.

In the closing weeks of *Valiant*'s third commission, while alongside at Faslane preparing for an impending refit and nuclear refuelling at Rosyth Naval Dockyard, the boat was visited by a group of distinguished veterans. These were former midshipmen who had served aboard the battleship *Valiant*, which was commissioned in 1915 and was a veteran of the Battle of Jutland. These WW2 inhabitants of the battleship's gunroom, thoroughly enjoyed both a tour of the submarine and afterwards drinks in the wardroom, but the one notable absentee was HRH The Prince Philip. He had sent a telegram regretting very much that he could not join the gathering owing to other commitments. Of note, he had served onboard *Valiant* as a midshipman during the period 1940–2 and had experienced some of the most intense fighting which took place in the Eastern Mediterranean, including the Battle of Cape Matapan.

Prior to arriving at Rosyth, Flag Officer Scotland Northern Ireland, Vice Admiral Sir George Vallings, embarked for the passage up the Forth. He was somewhat surprised at the good condition and cleanliness of *Valiant* at the end of a long commission. This reflected the consistently high standards delivered by XO, Huntly Gordon. Shortly after arriving at Rosyth on 19 May, I handed over command to him at a final wardroom dinner held in one of Edinburgh's finest restaurants.

During my brief few days in the dockyard, I was dismayed to observe how quickly parts of *Valiant* were being taken apart with scant regard for their reassembly. There had been intensive, detailed planning for the refit by *Valiant*'s officers and the senior dockyard managers. However, there was a serious lack of communication and control between the planners and project leaders in their cosy offices, and what was actually happening onboard the submarine. Inevitably this dysfunction was to come at a price and the refit was to over-run, extending from two to three years with a corresponding escalation in costs.

After nursing *Valiant* throughout the final phase of her third commission, I regarded the achievements of my crew as second-to-none and watching the boat being carelessly disassembled by the dockyard was saddening. However, this type of costly inefficiency has proved too often to be the case in the refitting of nuclear submarines.

My tenure of command of *Valiant* had been by far the most satisfying period of my naval career. I was sad to leave the 'Black Pig' but I was extremely lucky to have avoided a serious, even a catastrophic, breakdown or failure. Furthermore, after almost three years of continuous command, including my time in *Courageous*, I realised that almost certainly I no longer had the stamina and drive required to fully meet the demands of SSN command.

Valiant was in desperate need for a refit and during her final few months before refit, I had pushed her to the limit. I had owed much to the unsung heroes of the engineering department under Andrew Miller. Their tremendous commitment and sheer hard work, often in awful conditions, had managed to keep the submarine going against the odds. Furthermore, I had been blessed by an exceptionally competent and talented sonar team which, combined with my own experience and tactical knowledge, had enabled *Valiant* to achieve unprecedented success in hunting and tracking Russian submarines. And there was Linda, who had so patiently and understandingly, supported me through long periods of separation and the uncertainties arising from *Valiant*'s many engineering travails

I had pressed for a *Swiftsure* class command on my return from USN exchange duty. In the event, I was extremely fortunate to enjoy a highly varied operational programme in both the SSNs I commanded. As a bonus, I had undertaken six overseas and two home-port visits, where the Ship's Companies had the opportunity for foreign experiences and the enjoyment of warm local hospitality. For myself, I was highly privileged to be awarded the Order of the British Empire (OBE) in the Queen's Birthday Honours List of 1986. Very pleasingly, in the following New Year's Honours List, the outstanding leader of the engineering team, Andrew Miller received the honour of MBE.

Valiant was my last seagoing appointment but I continued to go to sea in submarines during my following appointments. In the near term, my next posting was a year at the United States Navy's War College at Newport, Rhode Island. Here I would serve as the Royal Navy's representative on a prestigious international course. It was time for Linda and myself to again pack up our possessions and head back to New England.

Chapter 23

Submarine Under-Ice Operations

The first known attempt of a submarine to operate under the ice occurred in 1931. Polar explorer Sir Hubert Wilkins, having acquired an old USN 500-ton 'O' class diesel submarine, that year led a private expedition to the Arctic, sponsored by an American businessman. Fitted with crude equipment to enable operating under the ice, including upward ice drilling mechanisms designed to allow ventilation of the boat, she was named *Nautilus*. Nevertheless, the boat was in poor mechanical condition and, having set out from North Norway, it was discovered her dive planes were missing, perhaps due to sabotage. In the event, the crew somehow managed to work around this serious deficiency, and they succeeded in making a few brief forays under the Arctic ice pack.

Since that first venture, a number of diesel submarines have made penetrations under the ice and, indeed, some have surfaced in open water. However, due to main-battery endurance limitations, and unable to use the snorkel, these conventional submarines were restricted to a range of less than 100 miles into the ice pack. Additionally, there was always the concern that, when under the ice, strong winds could cause the pack to move, possibly significantly increasing the distance to the safety of the open sea.

One of these short forays into the ice pack was undertaken by the British A-Boat, *Artemis* in April 1964. With a film crew embarked, she penetrated several miles on the surface through loose pack ice. At one point, way was taken off and the boat was secured to a large ice flow. Many members of the crew then landed onto the ice to take part in an improvised game of cricket. Cricket match over, all members of the Ship's Company, except one communicator who remained onboard, gathered for the film team to take group photographs on the ice with the boat's fin as a backdrop.

It was intended to film *Artemis* diving through the ice. To undertake this, the film crew was left on the ice flow as the boat prepared to dive. As the dive commenced, the Coxswain manning the after planes, alarmingly shouted across the control room 'What about Polar bears!' These had recently been sighted at a distance and the camera crew were totally unarmed. The Captain, Lieutenant Commander Jol Waterfield, immediately ordered the dive reversed and the boat surfaced. This sudden reversal caused a bit of bemusement on the part of the film crew who were wondering if *Artemis* had encountered a problem. However, this little episode with the crew members on the ice, with neither life jackets nor safety gear, reflected an era where there was much less consciousness of Health and Safety.

In the summer of 1958, the nuclear submarine USS *Nautilus* conducted a dived passage from the Bering Strait to the Atlantic, passing under the North Pole on route. She was the first submarine to do so. The following year a second nuclear submarine, the *Skate*, surfaced at the North Pole: again this was a first.

In August 1960, *Seadragon*, sister vessel to *Skate*, became the first submarine to achieve the remarkable feat of conducting a dived transit of the Northwest Passage which separates mainland Canada and Greenland. Proceeding along the Parry Channel, *Seadragon* undertook a series of hydrographic surveys and collected substantial oceanographic information. She also became the first vessel to navigate under an iceberg, one of many she encountered. On leaving the Parry Channel and entering the Beaufort Sea, she then headed to the North Pole where she surfaced through thin ice. Members of the crew laid out a baseball diamond with the pitcher's mound on the ice at the Pole. Uniquely, the Captain claimed he hit a ball at 4:00 pm on Wednesday and, because the ball crossed the International Date Line, it wasn't caught until 4:00 am on Thursday.

The Soviets were not far behind and, in June 1962, their first nuclear submarine, the SSN *Leninsky Komsomol*, surfaced at the Pole. All these early expeditionary cruises under the ice emphatically demonstrated the nuclear submarine's ability to safely operate under the Arctic ice pack. They also heralded the Arctic becoming of strategic importance during the Cold War. In the case of the patrolling SSBN, it offered potential sanctuary from the West's ASW forces. Indeed, in recent times, Russia has demonstrated an SSBN surfacing through the ice and proceeding to fire a ballistic missile.

The Arctic ice cap, although currently shrinking in size due to global warming, during the winter months can still only be freely navigated by submarine. The average thickness of the ice is about 8ft but ridges of ice can be as deep as 50ft or more. The protection of the ice sheet means that a submarine operating under the ice cap can only be attacked by another submarine. While sonar noise conditions in the depths of the pack ice are extremely quiet and conducive to long range detections, the MIZ is normally acoustically noisy. The movements of ice in the latter causes significant background noise which makes it a good area for submarines to hide in.

At all times of the year, there will be areas of thin ice, less than 6ft deep, allowing submarines to surface by punching their way through it. There will also exist lakes of open water, known as polynyas. In winter, polynyas having re-frozen, have features of thin ice of uniform thickness. This offers the SSN a highly suitable surfacing location.

The prime method of submarine navigation under the ice is by the SINS set to a polar configuration. Using the North Pole as a heading reference becomes impractical at very high latitudes and SINS and the submarine's gyro compasses are switched to a heading reference at a fixed point in space. As a back-up, the Loran radio navigation system allows the fixing and confirming of the submarine's SINS position from signals received via the long, floating wire aerial it trails astern. Unless the submarine is surfaced through the ice or is in a polynya, its main method of communications reception will be via this wire. To utilise satellite or conventional High Frequency (HF) communications or to undertake a Global Positioning System (GPS) navigational fix, requires at least the boat's fin to be above the ice. This enables a communications mast to be raised for GPS reception and transmission of signal traffic.

To profile the surrounding ice, a high-frequency ice detection sonar system, if fitted, warns of ice features ahead of the submarine. This allows avoiding action to be taken if there is a risk of collision. This aid is vital if passaging in shallow water, such as in the Bering Strait, where the ice sheet may reach the seabed or in sea areas where there are icebergs. Upward-looking echo sounders enable the thickness of the ice above the submarine to be measured, key information in determining whether it is practical and safe to surface through the ice. Side-scan sonars, either fitted on the hull or mounted in small Unmanned Underwater Vehicles (UUV), can provide further data of the surrounding ice features and profile.

To surface in the Arctic, the crew locates either open water or a suitable flat area of thin ice using their ice profiling sonar and upward looking echo sounders. If damage is to be avoided, it is vital to avoid ice ridges. Having selected the exact surfacing position, the Captain brings the boat to a stationary status and, when it is confirmed that the surfacing conditions are right, the main ballast tanks are blown. The boat then rises vertically passing through the layer of relatively fresh and less dense water directly under the ice. If actually under the ice sheet, the fin can punch through it.

In the case of the ice being too thick and breakthrough not being achieved, the boat is potentially in a precariously unstable condition owing to its positive buoyancy pressing up against the ice covering – like a beachball being held underwater. If the crew were to actuate the submarine's powerful emergency blow system in response to a serious flooding incident, the boat would be highly positive in buoyancy with the risk of a catastrophic roll of over 60 degrees. This would severely damage equipment, placing the vessel into an almost irrecoverable situation and imperilling the crew. In such an extremely dangerous situation, immediate steps would need to be taken to vent air out of the ballast tanks to remove the roll angle and regain neutral buoyancy.

Operating under the ice does have additional risks with, in some areas, a margin of only 25 ft between the ice cover above the submarine and the seabed below it. During early American submerged passages of the shallow Bering Strait, one boat encountered ice all the way down to the seabed and found itself in a canyon with ice closing in on all sides. Her Captain had to stop the submarine and, using the boat's ability to hover, reverse course whilst stationary. Meanwhile the crew hoped and prayed that they could then get out the way they came in.

Under the ice, any accident or technical failure, such as loss of propulsion or navigation systems failure, can have highly dangerous consequences. A serious fire onboard a submarine in this environment is a particular hazard, forcing the submarine to seek open water or thin ice to surface through to ventilate and clear out the smoke. Until this can be achieved, the crew may well need to resort to wearing emergency breathing masks.

If a submarine becomes stuck under the ice due to catastrophic loss of propulsion, even if she is able to communicate her plight and position, a swift rescue would be impossible. The assembly of assistance in such circumstances must inevitably be a race against time to reach the distressed submarine with suitable excavation equipment to dig her out from under the ice. In summary, the risks inherent in operating under the ice very much add to the normal operating stresses the Captain and his crew have to contend with.

The first British nuclear submarine to reach the North Pole was *Dreadnought*, arrived on 3 March 1971. Her charismatic Captain, Commander Alan Kennedy, very much aware of the Arctic's strategic importance, persuaded his superiors to send his boat on an Arctic patrol. Apart from some additional navigational equipment, she undertook the deployment with a standard equipment fit. It was fully recognised that, with one single main propeller shaft and an extremely limited small retractable electric outboard motor, she would be vulnerable to any serious collision with the ice.

After several attempts to surface when the Pole had been reached, *Dreadnought* broke through about a foot of ice. Prior to blowing the main ballast tanks, the Captain assessed the boat to be stationary by the rudimentary arrangement of viewing through the periscope a piece of floating cord attached to the top of the fin. When vertical, this simple device indicated that the boat was completely stopped. Eight hours were spent on the surface and many of the crew, suitably attired against the minus 38°C temperature, took the opportunity to leave the boat and walk on the ice sheet. Some even attempted playing football until their improvised ball, a plastic bucket, shattered because of the cold.

An attempt was made to contact headquarters using the radio mast, announcing that the Pole had been reached, but initially this was unsuccessful. An improvised radio transmission was then made using the floating wire aerial laid out on the ice, pointing in the general direction of the UK. In the event, the only contact made was with a taxi rank in Canada. However, eventually, the conventional method of transmission worked and Flag Officer Submarines received the good news of this Royal Navy first.

As *Dreadnought* headed out of the ice pack and started her transit south, the crew became aware that, at high speed, the stern vibrated badly. Her speed, therefore, had to be kept at moderate levels. On reaching harbour, checks of the propeller indicated that one of its blades had been bent by contact with the ice. *Dreadnought* arrived in Faslane to a rapturous welcome, having steamed over 1,300 miles under the ice.

The USN run an approximately biennial series of submarine exercises under the ice, known as ICEXs, sponsored by the Arctic Submarine Laboratory (ASL), based in San Diego. Frequently, Royal Navy SSNs participate in these exercises, operating together with American boats. Quite separately, after *Dreadnought* made that first passage of a British submarine to the North Pole, a number of our submarines have conducted exclusively national exercises or trials under the ice pack.

I assumed command of STWG in September 1987 and my immediate priority was taking the lead in the planning and execution of RN participation in ICEX-88. This took place at the USN's Applied Physics Laboratory Ice Station (APLIS) on the frozen Beaufort Sea to the north of Alaska. Two British SSNs were involved, *Turbulent*, Commander Ian Richards, and *Superb*, Commander John Tuckett. They would be joined by the USS *Lapon*, passaging from the Pacific Ocean, and conducting a dived transit through the Bering Strait. On arrival at APLIS, she would undertake a series of trials and tests for the USN. The British boats were each carrying eight Tigerfish Mod 2 practice torpedoes to test this weapon system for the first time in the under-ice environment. The Mod 2 variant incorporated a number of features and improvements which, some 12 years after Tigerfish entered service, at long last had transformed it into a reliable and effective weapon system.

In preparation for the operation, I had burned the midnight oil, carefully reviewing the plans and orders and all aspects of submarine safety. I was seriously concerned that both *Superb* and *Turbulent* were fitted with a new type of SINS which had not been fully tested in high latitudes. A submarine under the ice losing its prime positional and heading reference would be in trouble. Accordingly, I spent much time gaining assurance from its designers that this equipment would be totally reliable when the boats headed over the top of the world.

Never before had British submarines ventured so far under the ice, proceeding over 1,000 miles south from the North Pole to the Beaufort Sea. The British submarines had high definition sonars which mapped the ice on either side of them, but they were not fitted with ahead looking ice detection equipment which would be needed to navigate around deep ice ridges. Therefore, the shortest route to open sea via the Bering Strait, with its ice canyons, was not an option should they get into difficulty.

April 1988 saw me clambering out of a twin turbo-prop Casa aircraft, gingerly stepping onto the ice of the frozen Beaufort Sea to the north of Alaska. The cutting blast of Arctic air reminded me that this was an odd place for a submariner to be; it was a lot more comfortable under the ice, cocooned in in the warmth and security of the pressure hull of an SSN. I had arrived at APLIS to supervise the start of the Tigerfish torpedo firings. The camp had been set up on an area of first year ice at latitude 72 degrees north, about 200 miles north of the oil town of Prudhoe Bay.

A landing strip had been established on the flattest area of the ice as well as a number of temporary pre-fabricated wooden huts which included a command post. Accommodation at the site for the fifty-plus personnel (including several female scientists) consisted of framed PVC ridge tents fitted with up to six bunks. A diesel heater in each of these kept the temperature at an acceptable level and provided hot water for washing. Good-quality meals were served in a tented mess hall. Toilet cubicles were placed over holes cut in ice, supplemented with open air, wood-frame surrounded 'urination stations'.

The base facilities included a three-dimensional range which enabled the accurate tracking of both the submarines and the torpedoes they were to fire. This was a technical challenge, as the range equipment had to contend with the complexities of ice drift, caused by the effects of the wind, which could be up to six or seven miles a day. Additionally, there was the Coriolis effect, a phenomenon caused by the earth's rotation which creates a slow anti-clockwise rotation of the ice sheet around the Pole. The setting-up and running of the APLIS organisation had been contracted to the University of Washington State, which would also remove all equipment and debris when the tests and trials were completed by the end of April. Two helicopters were permanently on station, ready to respond at short notice to any arising contingency or emergency. The station was under the command of the Officer-in-Charge (OIC) of the Arctic Laboratory, Captain Merrill Dorman USN.

In addition to observations, measurements and other data acquisition, there were the practical problems of recovering torpedoes at the end of their run. This was to be achieved by a combination of American civilian divers and helicopters. After recovery, the weapons were shipped by light aircraft to Prudhoe airfield where a team of civilian specialists from the armament depot at Coulport near Faslane made them safe to be transported by RAF Hercules back to Anchorage airport for onward shipping. As these experimental firings were highly classified, the cover story for the Coulport team was that they were researchers from Nottingham University. For some reason they were dressed in Royal Marine camouflage jungle fatigues as the Arctic equivalent was not available. Since they all spoke with strong West of Scotland accents, few of the locals were unaware of their actual mission.

One of the greatest dangers to the people working on the ice was the presence of Polar bears. Several had been spotted near the ice station and all personnel were warned to be careful when leaving the immediate environs of the camp. In the station command hut there was an array of rifles and shotguns and it was normal routine to select a few weapons before any foray was made away from the station in case of having to deal with an aggressive bear.

A prerequisite for spending time at APLIS had been to undertake Arctic survival training in case the ice under the station unexpectedly broke up. This training largely consisted of surviving for several days in a snow hole in Maine but, as the decision that I would direct the initial phases of the firings was made late in the day, I had been unable to complete this requirement. In the event, I found life at APLIS with its accommodation in the heated framed tents very tolerable. During the time I was at the camp the temperature never dropped much below minus 25°C. However, all personnel had to be careful to protect themselves against frostbite induced by the wind chill factor in high winds and when subject to the downdraft from the blades of helicopters operating above them.

The danger of camping on first-year ice was demonstrated one night when the ice separated and a large polynya formed, taking a chunk out of the landing strip. Immediately after this event, I was awoken by a Chinese-American scientist who knew I was interested in observing any major ice movements. He invited me to join him on the back of a snowmobile and, in the Arctic twilight, soon we were heading at speed across the landing strip towards the open sea. There ahead was the unforgettable sight of recently-opened water with a shroud of sea smoke rising from it. But any exhilaration at this spectacle was suppressed by the realisation that the scientist's goggles had misted up and he could not see the edge of the ice perilously close ahead. Alarmed thumping on his back made him quickly realise the danger and we came to a halt a few yards from the open water.

However, the following morning, a second foray to the ice edge did not end so happily when three Americans and myself took two snowmobiles to reconnoitre the extent of the polynya. One of the party incautiously approached the edge in his snowmobile and whilst getting off it, stepped onto a layer of soft ice which suddenly gave way, pitching him into the sea. As I helped pull him out of the freezing water, out of the corner of my eye I spotted his snowmobile, disappearing into the depths of the Arctic Ocean. Almost immediately his wet clothing totally froze and he risked both frostbite and hypothermia.

Fortunately, a helicopter quickly arrived on the scene and flew him back to the camp where he rapidly recovered in a sauna which had been put in place for such an emergency. As the senior officer present, I had to explain to Merrill Dorman how one of the party ended up in the sea with the loss of an expensive snowmobile. The whole incident was a reminder of the hostility of the Arctic.

At the scheduled time of the arrival of the two SSNs, I was crouched in the command hut next to the underwater telephone receiver. As the minutes and hours passed with no contact from either, I became increasingly concerned that they had experienced significant problems on route. It was therefore a great relief to eventually hear faint and distant sonar transmissions, indicating the boats had successfully made their passage and would soon arrive at the APLIS site.

On arrival, the Captain of *Turbulent* reported a serious problem with his oxygen-making electrolysers. Having had to resort to burning special devices which generated oxygen – called 'oxygen candles' – she needed urgent replacements. Indeed, having penetrated the pack ice, Ian Richards had made the brave decision to press on to APLIS past the point of no return in terms of having enough oxygen candles to return south to the edge of the ice. His engineer officers did a tremendous job in calculating the number of oxygen candles needed to be burned, assessing the point of no return and determining how often there would be a need to ventilate the boat with fresh air. I swiftly made arrangements for a supply of oxygen candles, while *Turbulent* headed to a polynya located several miles distant from the ice station, in order to surface and ventilate.

The APLIS OIC and myself, having been landed by helicopter beside the polynya to await the surfacing, suddenly realised that the guns usually carried on such forays had been left in the helicopter. Preoccupied by carrying a portable underwater telephone and other equipment from the aircraft, the weapons had been forgotten. During the next few hours, I was seriously apprehensive about the danger of a Polar bear stalking us from behind the surrounding ice ridges. Even my conviction that I would be able to outrun the heavily built Merrill Dorman, did not ease my tensions.

In the event, *Turbulent*'s Captain was uncomfortable about surfacing in that location and we were picked up by helicopter soon after this plan was abandoned. In due course, at a successful later surfacing, and in what may well have been the most unconventional 'Replenishment At Sea' ever, an adequate number of oxygen candles were supplied to *Turbulent* together with electrolyser spares.

On reaching APLIS from the Pacific through the Bering Strait, the San Diego-based USS *Lapon* conducted the first of a number of under-ice surfacing tests. I witnessed this evolution in the company of a number of scientists who were collecting data. A few minutes before the event, Captain Dorman arrived at speed on a snowmobile and declared that 'two bears were on the way' and would shortly reach the surfacing site. However, observing some people starting to check out their rifles, he quickly made it clear that the bears in question were actually Soviet 'Bear' reconnaissance aircraft. Indeed, a few minutes after the *Lapon* surfaced, her fin having broken through the ice, she was overflown by the two Russian aircraft at extremely low altitude, in close company of two USAF F-15 fighters. The sight of the submarine's fin protruding through the ice being overflown by the huge Russian aircraft in an Arctic-blue sky could have come straight from the film *Ice Station Zebra*. But there were no Soviet paratroopers.

Shortly after surfacing, the *Lapon*'s Captain, Commander J. Mackin, climbed out of his submarine and joined the welcoming party on the ice. He was accompanied by his Arctic pilot, an experienced under-ice navigator who had provided guidance and advice to Mackin and his command team during the passage. After an exchange of pleasantries, the Captain revealed that he had concerns about a steam leak on his propulsion machinery. This potentially involved shutting his plant down to effect repairs. San Diego must have seemed a long way away.

In the following few days both *Turbulent* and *Superb* fired their sixteen Tigerfish Mod 2 torpedoes in a near flawless series of evaluation firings, and all the weapons were successfully recovered. Most of the firings were conducted against each other, the submarines alternating as targets; however, some weapon runs were against static acoustic targets. These were configured to represent a stationary 'Typhoon' or 'Delta IV' SSBN hiding under the ice shelf. The weapons performed extremely well in the quiet Arctic conditions, achieving long-range passive homing detections. Even in the active mode where the torpedoes' homing systems had the problem of resolving the real target from contacts generated by returns from the ice features, the weapons homed remarkably reliably. Accordingly, the Americans observing the firings were impressed by both the weapons' solid performance and their precision guidance, which enabled them to be parked under suitable flat, thin ice at the end of their run, ready for recovery.

At about 1,000ft or more, the underwater visibility was remarkable, so helping the job of weapon recovery. The routine for this consisted of creating two holes in the ice about 3ft in diameter, one for a diver and the other for the torpedo. Once the diver had attached a harness to the weapon, it was connected to and drawn upwards by a helicopter. Perhaps surprisingly, no weapon was significantly damaged, although at least one had to be recovered from underneath ice rubble about 20ft thick.

With the trials successfully progressing, my spell at the ice station was over. I soon found myself the sole passenger in the back of a Casa aircraft on the way back to Prudhoe, sharing a noisy hold with two Tigerfish. About half an hour into the flight, I awoke from a doze to the noise of a distinct change of pitch from the aircraft's engines. Alarmingly, at the same time, the pilot was wildly gesticulating downwards, pointing to the ice and circling the aircraft to lose altitude. The prospect of a crash landing on the ice seated between two torpedoes filled me with real horror but then I spotted why the pilot was becoming so excited. There, on an ice flow a few hundred feet below, were Polar bears – a magnificent mother and her two cubs.

The 1988 under-ice Tigerfish firings had firmly demonstrated the Royal Navy SSN's capability to successfully engage submarines under the Arctic ice pack, putting its hunter-killer submarines' capability on a par with the American Navy in terms of under-ice warfare. The Submarine Service hierarchy was extremely pleased with the efficient performance of both *Turbulent* and *Superb*, given the difficulties of navigating and operating for over 2,000 miles under the deep ice pack. Both Captains and their respective Ship's Companies had clearly demonstrated competence of the highest order in conducting a series of torpedo firings unique to the Royal Navy. In reflecting upon the tensions and stress the two crews endured whilst under the ice, Commander Bob Dean, *Turbulent*'s XO, recalls 'When we came out of the Marginal Ice Zone for the last time and we passed into open water, the Captain and I looked at each other across the control room. Simultaneously, we both breathed out a mutual sigh of relief that the strain was over.'

When FOSM, Rear Admiral Frank Grenier, subsequently briefed the Prime Minister, Margaret Thatcher, about the operation, she was reported to have been 'absolutely spellbound', declaring great pride in what had been achieved. Despite having impressed the Prime Minister, there were no honours awarded to individual members of the submarines' crews which struck me as a missed opportunity. Neither was there any media publicity about this unique operation.

I was not to know it at the time, but the under-ice firings almost certainly marked the zenith of the Royal Navy SSN force's history, in terms of both its number of boats and their overall capability. Extraordinary, unprecedented and unforeseen events in the following year, both at a grand-strategic and tactical level, were to have dramatic effects upon the Submarine Flotilla. Unbeknown to any of the participants – British, American and the reconnoitring Russian airmen – their activities in the high Arctic in those weeks of April 1988 marked the end of an era.

After the ending of the Cold War, heralded by the dissolution of the Soviet Union in 1991, the Royal Navy's participation in under-ice operations, unsurprisingly declined significantly. However, there remained periodic participation in ICEXs. One of these involved the SSN *Tireless* operating with USS *Alexandria* during ICEX-07, to the north of Alaska. Unfortunately, *Tireless* suffered a serious fire in an oxygen generator and, although it was quickly brought under control, sadly two of her crew lost their lives as a consequence. More recently during ICEX-18, *Trenchant* undertook joint exercises with the US submarines *Connecticut* and *Hartford*, at the 2018 APLIS base camp set up on an area of ice to the north of Alaska. During these exercises, *Trenchant* surfaced and crew members laid wreaths on the ice in commemoration of the two *Tireless* men who had died.

At the time of writing, none of the Royal Navy's latest SSNs, the *Astute* class, have demonstrated being able to successfully operate under the ice. If the UK is to continue to maintain a viable under-ice warfare capability, this deficiency will need to be addressed.

For myself, the successful Tigerfish under-ice firings, which much impressed the USN observers at APLIS, effectively marked the end of my professional journey with this weapon system. This had started in 1977 when this torpedo was notoriously unreliable and the naval hierarchy was not according it the requisite high priority in the rectification of its shortcomings. All hopes for RN future submarine torpedoes now lay with the Spearfish weapon which was under development. With a top speed of over 60 knots, it was designed to successfully take on the most capable Soviet nuclear submarines. However, in 1988, it already was late in entering service and, like Tigerfish, it was to endure a difficult gestation.

Chapter 24

New Submarine Weapons

My family and I had experienced a most pleasant and enjoyable year living in Newport, Rhode Island, while I attended the Command Course at the USN War College. Besides undertaking a comprehensive postgraduate study of the history of war at the college, visits were made to a number of states across the Continental USA. The aim of these trips was to learn about USA's society, institutions and history. The course members enjoyed a wide variety of visits such as, at one end, gaining insight to treatment of prisoners in a dismal Arizona county prison and, at the other, being welcomed to US Senate chambers at Capitol Hill. Besides being a unique opportunity to gain firsthand knowledge of many sectors of US society and industry, for me these visits were an ideal opportunity to develop strong friendships with officers from a number of allied navies. The membership of my Command Course consisted of senior officers representing the navies of thirty-six nations, several of whom, later in their career would go on to head their respective naval service. That said, in the case of the Egyptian officer, who in due course headed up his navy, if during the course of our travels I got onto a bus with him, almost certainly it would be both the wrong bus and we would be late.

In the final weeks of the course, a war game was played out over a period of several days. The game scenario was two medium-sized powers commencing hostilities against each other. The course was divided into the two opposition camps, each making force deployment and manoeuvre decisions from separate headquarters rooms. I was pleasantly surprised that the author Tom Clancy joined my group, conducting research for a sequel to his best-selling book *Red Storm Rising*. Quietly and unobtrusively sitting in a corner, he made copious notes of ongoing decisions and resultant actions, periodically interjecting with sharp, incisive 'what if?' questions. Nevertheless, I doubt witnessing the interactions of a truly international bunch of naval officers, most of whom were distinctly individualistic, would have been much help in developing his narrative.

Towards the closing months at my time at the War College, I had to submit my appointment preference for my next posting when I returned to the UK in the summer of 1987. The personal advice from my ultimate superior, the Washington RN Naval Attaché, was that I should seek an appointment in the Ministry of Defence (MoD), London. He strongly advised that this would be a natural career step towards my promotion to the rank of Captain. However, after undertaking four family moves in the preceding six years and, only four years earlier, having acquired a substantial house in Garelochead, I opted for family stability and an appointment in the Clyde Submarine Base. Besides, I was under no illusion that while it was probable that I would achieve promotion to Captain in due course, it was highly unlikely I would reach the rank of Admiral. Therefore, I viewed family considerations as high priority. A few weeks later, I was informed that I would be going back to STWG as its commander.

In the intervening nine years since my previous appointment at STWG, there had been several solid advances in the Submarine Flotilla's weapon systems. At long last the design deficiencies and unreliability of the Tigerfish torpedo had been rectified with the introduction of the new Mod 2 variant. The challenge now was for STWG to develop tactics and crew expertise to ensure the effectiveness of Tigerfish was exploited to the maximum. An early priority for me was STWG's planning and execution of the previously described under-ice Tigerfish firings.

Another of STWG's top objectives was to develop tactics for the use of the Royal Navy submarine's first underwater launched anti-ship guided missile – the 65-mile range American Sub-Harpoon system which came into RN service in 1982. At the same time, the organisation was responsible for analysing the results of ongoing firing trials of the Spearfish heavyweight torpedo which was planned to replace Tigerfish in the 1990s.

On completion of the Tigerfish under-ice firings I had to make a swift journey from Alaska to the tropics where, at the AUTEC range in the Caribbean, another evaluation of the Tigerfish Mod 2 torpedo was underway. Handing over my Arctic clothing to a MoD agent in Anchorage, I collected my tropical uniform which I had deposited with him and, after a succession of flights, arrived at Andros Island in the Bahamas to join the SSN *Sceptre*. Together with the SSNs *Courageous* and *Churchill*, *Sceptre* was conducting tactical evaluation exercises run by STWG. These boats had the additional the role of acting as target for test firings of the Royal Navy's Stingray torpedo, a weapon launched from aircraft, helicopters and surface warships.

It was one thing to evaluate Tigerfish's performance in the benign environment of AUTEC, but it was also necessary to test the weapon in the more challenging deep ocean conditions to the west of the UK. To achieve this, in the summer of 1989, a series of evaluation firings took place in sea areas in the vicinity of the remote island of St Kilda. The latter was used as a base for two helicopters, which would recover the torpedoes, and a torpedo recovery craft stationed in the sheltered waters of Village Bay. Two SSNs participated, alternatively acting as firing and target vessels. At the end of a torpedo's run it would surface, where it would be captured into a cage suspended underneath the recovery helicopter. Then it was flown to Village Bay where it would be released into the sea adjacent to the recovery vessel.

Overall, the firings were successful and much data was gained of the torpedo's performance in the deep ocean. However, on one occasion a glitch occurred when the recovery helicopter experienced strong downdraft winds coming off the cliffs surrounding Village Bay. This caused the recovery cage to start dangerously oscillating and the pilot had no option but to urgently release the torpedo out of the cage. It fell several hundred feet onto a beach area where it split into several bits on impact. Unfortunately, in the vicinity was a group of birdwatchers who did not appreciate two tons of torpedo falling out of the sky, although it was some distance away from them. In consequence, Flag Officer Submarines received a strongly-worded letter from the leader of the birdwatchers complaining about their lives being imperilled by the Submarine Service.

Besides these Tigerfish trials and exercises, there remained much work to do in evaluating the new Spearfish torpedo. This weapon was already significantly late in entering service. In 1982, recognising the performance deficiencies of Tigerfish and, in particular, its limitations against high-speed, deep-diving submarines, the MoD had invited companies to tender for a replacement heavyweight torpedo ready to enter service in 1987. In the event there were only two contenders: an advanced version of the United States Navy's Mark 48 torpedo known as the 'Adcap', and the British GEC-Marconi Spearfish torpedo. On paper the latter was the better weapon, being considerably faster and more advanced in its homing system than the Adcap. Furthermore, it would be a British weapon and its selection would ensure a heavyweight torpedo design and manufacturing capability would be maintained in the United Kingdom. It was, therefore, no surprise that the contract went to GEC-Marconi, notwithstanding it was the same company which had manufactured the troublesome Tigerfish, with its unenviable record of poor components and general unreliability. The Adcap version entered service in the USN in 1988, but it would be another six years before Spearfish was sufficiently reliable to be adopted by the British Submarine Flotilla.

Spearfish was a very ambitious project, as the torpedo incorporated a new type of turbine engine which used a highly volatile mixture of two fuels. It also had a sophisticated homing system which was able to contend with the target submarine which had laid a trail of powerful noise countermeasures aimed at deflecting an approaching torpedo. Furthermore, when used against a surface ship, its homing system was designed to place the weapon under a precisely specified part of the hull to achieve maximum damage. Combine all these novel features into one weapon and significant development challenges were bound to arise.

In studying the results of the Spearfish trials analysis, I was able to gain first-hand knowledge of the many problems the project was encountering. My main concern was the weapon's performance against surface ships, because its homing system appeared to be too easily seduced onto the target's wake. Raising these concerns with the project's managers, their response was that depth ceilings set on the weapon to prevent it actually striking the target during trials were inhibiting its successful final-phase homing. However, I was not convinced.

On submitting my concerns up the command chain, the issues I raised were to an extent undermined by the contractor's manipulation of the results which I despairingly observed first-hand when I was on location at several trial firings at AUTEC. Nor was I helped by the attitude of the Naval Captain heading up the project, who proved to be over-optimistic about the progress of the weapon's development. Worryingly, he was far from being inquisitive about evident potential problems. In sum, I was to learn that it was one thing to identify torpedo deficiencies, and quite another to persuade the hierarchy that they actually existed.

In addition to its performance vagaries, the trials firings indicated that Spearfish was unreliable. It gradually percolated through to those responsible in the MoD that they were grappling with another problem project and that, before acceptance into service, a costly programme to improve the weapon's reliability had to be put in place. This would finally be achieved in the early 1990s, but not before the introduction of the new torpedo had slipped several years beyond its projected acceptance date, leaving myself and the STWG team with the disturbing sensation of having been there before.

At the time of writing, Spearfish has been updated to both improve its performance and to enhance the safety of its fuel system. Nevertheless, in consequence of cost savings arising from the end of the Cold War, there has been a paucity of funding to progressively update the weapon. It has not received the requisite series of modifications to ensure it remained a highly viable torpedo system. Of note, in the same timeframe, the Adcap torpedo has received eight major updates.

There was, however, one conventional submarine weapon system that was proving extremely reliable for the Royal Navy. This was the Sub-Harpoon missile, the effectiveness and performance of which was absolutely outstanding. The missile was enclosed in a canister which, having been fired from a torpedo tube, rose to the surface of the sea. Here the missile's ignition system fired and it took off on its trajectory to the programmed target.

The introduction of Sub-Harpoon marked the culmination of a long search for such a weapon. Earlier initiatives to put conventional missiles into Royal Naval submarines included the Submarine Launched Airflight Missile (SLAM) which *Oberon* had been fitted for – but not with – in 1972 after her return from the Far East. A Vickers initiative, SLAM featured a retractable mast in the submarine's fin containing a pod of four Blowpipe missiles. These were intended to shoot down an anti-submarine helicopter hovering in the area dipping its sonar into the sea. However, the pod was conspicuous – particularly from the air – protruding above the sea. Furthermore, the missiles required visual guidance onto the target through one of the periscopes. This was not a practical proposition and, after a series of trials firings from the diesel submarine *Aeneas*, the project was dropped.

Another project which failed to get off the ground was Hawker Siddeley's Sub-Martel anti-ship missile. Fired from a torpedo tube, this would have been driven to the surface by a booster stage at which point a separate rocket motor took over. I had witnessed handling trials of a prototype Sub-Martel onboard *Swiftsure* in 1974 and was unimpressed by its features. Therefore, the Submarine Service was extremely pleased when the MoD cancelled the Sub-Martel project in 1976 and went for the much cheaper option of the proven, more powerful and longer range American Sub-Harpoon.

As described previously, the Royal Navy deployed the missile for the first time onboard HMS *Courageous* in June 1982, at the end of the Falklands War.

STWG was responsible for the routine proving firings of Sub-Harpoon. Normally these were carried out on the Army-run Benbecula missile range in the Outer Hebrides. Fired against remote-controlled target vessels, the missiles were fitted with telemetry equipment which enabled range control to destroy them if they deviated from their intended flight path. This equipment replaced the warhead.

However, the periodic testing of a randomly selected Sub-Harpoon war-shot was a very different matter. These were conducted well to the west of St Kilda, using a warship hulk as target, which had been towed into place by a tug which then retreated to a safe distance. As there were no range tracking facilities, a RAF Nimrod aircraft provided confirmation that there was no surface ship contact within the missile's 65-mile maximum range from the firing submarine. A Buccaneer low-level strike aircraft would also be involved, ready to take up a station behind the missile as it emerged from the sea, following it and filming its flight until its impact on target. This in itself was a coordination challenge. Responsible for the safe conduct of these tests, it was always a worry to me that there might be a small, undetected vessel within the missile's 'search and acquisition envelope'. Furthermore, an errant missile could fly in any direction with no method of destroying it in flight until it ran out of fuel at the end of its range. However, at least during my own watch, the Sub-Harpoon missiles performed flawlessly during these firings.

Meanwhile life in the Clyde Base was subject to increased security as the result of the potential threat of an IRA attack. However, in the event, there was a more significant base security threat from the establishment of the so-called 'peace camp' near the base entrance. This had the full support of the local Labour-controlled Dunbartonshire council which rather illogically had for many years declared the county a 'Nuclear Free Zone'. The only serious breaches of security at the base during the 1980s happened because of the occasional penetration of its security perimeters by peace camp activists bent on discrediting the security of the deterrent. The most spectacular of these was the boarding of the SSBN *Repulse* by two peace-campers who were lucky not to be shot by the armed Marine on duty on its casing.

The base MoD police force was responsible for physical security but, sadly, none of its seniors was held accountable for this serious security breach. Instead, it became the responsibility of the Royal

Navy duty Lieutenant Commander to personally check the several miles of perimeter fencing during the night. This angered me, as my officers were busy enough during the day undertaking their prime responsibilities, without, when off duty, incurring the additional task of spending a large part of the night checking the perimeter. Harking back to my time in *Otter*, it was clear that the Faslane MoD police continued to put more effort into making life difficult for the base personnel rather than ensuring that the base was secure from attack or illegal penetration.

Naturally security was tightened when a VIP was planned to visit the base which included an extensive search for explosive devices. When Viscount Trenchard, Minister for Defence Procurement, visited, a bag containing a friend's sports kit which had been left outside the wardroom changing rooms was towed away and blown up on the base sports field. Pieces of his shorts and sports shirt were seen flying up in the air.

Just before the arrival of the Commander-in-Chief, Admiral Sir William Staveley, undertaking a formal visit, a colleague's presentation aid caused the entire waterfront area to be urgently evacuated. This prop, which was the model of a submarine fin containing wires and a battery, had been discarded in a skip near the jetty. On being discovered during the security sweep, the Fleet Commander's car was urgently halted outside the base main gate and his guard of honour stood down. Meanwhile, my colleague, joining the hurried evacuation, suddenly realised it was his presentation aid which had caused the panic button to be pressed. A hasty explanation to the base commander allowed an order to be broadcast that permitted personnel to the return to the waterfront area and the Fleet Commander to enter the base.

There were no such problems when Rear Admiral Frank Grenier, Flag Officer Submarines, arrived for his final visit to the Base prior to retiring. Highly popular, he was given a spectacular send-off, which included being embarked in a launch and being cheered by the crews of the submarines alongside as he passed them. Then completely unexpectedly, an 'O' class submarine surfaced very close to the launch.

In 1989 the Berlin Wall came down which effectively ended the Cold War in a kind of victory for the West. The Soviet Union could not match the West's technological and economic might, and the pace of its rapid collapse in the early 1990s was remarkable. There had been many signs that the Soviet infrastructure was crumbling and while on the surface its armed forces appeared absolutely formidable, there were serious underlying organisational and material weaknesses.

A sign that all was not well in the Red Banner Fleet came in April 1989 when a fire broke out onboard the modern Russian 'Mike' class SSN *Komsomolets* in the north Norwegian Sea. The *Komsomolets* was a prototype third-generation submarine which came into service in the early 1980s and, with its pressure hull built of titanium, could dive about three times deeper than its Western equivalents. The fire spread, causing a catastrophic chain of events which resulted in her sinking and the death of over half of her seventy-strong crew.

Captain Evgeny Vanin brought the *Komsomolets* to the surface using an emergency blow system and ordered her abandoned, but the sea conditions were rough. Although the majority of the crew escaped onto the casing, the submarine was so badly damaged that she sank several hours later, leaving the survivors wallowing in the fatally cold water of the Norwegian Sea. Many perished, long before any form of rescue could arrive.

Vanin and several of his crew, still below as the *Komsomolets* began her final plunge, retreated to an escape capsule fitted under the superstructure. Wracked by extreme sea pressure and heading for the abyss carrying two nuclear-tipped torpedoes, the *Komsomolets* started to break up as Vanin and his colleagues released their capsule which succeeded in making it to the surface. Tragically, the inside of the capsule was at a high atmospheric pressure so that, when its hatch was opened, it depressurised with catastrophic force, expelling and killing all but one of its occupants. The *Komsomolets* death toll might have been much reduced if Norwegian search and rescue support had been sought promptly but, true to character, the Soviet Union was a secretive state, reluctant to seek the help of others. Considerations of humanity and the wellbeing of its citizens were not accorded priority by its leaders.

On a warm, sunny, spring morning, a few weeks after Captain Vanin and his crew had been fighting for their lives, several hundred British submariners and their families gathered on the parade square of HMS *Dolphin* for the Monarch's presentation of her colour to the Submarine Flotilla. This flag is periodically presented to branches and regiments of the armed forces, and this occasion reflected the nation's recognition of the Submarine Service's achievements and its contribution to national security since the colour's previous presentation in 1959. It was also a rare opportunity for submariners –

traditionally the more relaxed wing of the Royal Navy – to enjoy and participate in a gathering of some pomp and ceremony.

The Royal Navy's Submarine Service was reaching its zenith, with twenty nuclear and twelve diesel submarines in commission, including the brand-new *Upholder*, first of a new class of conventional submarines. Three of these were under construction in Cammell Laird Shipyard in Birkenhead and, further up the coast in Vickers Shipbuilding & Engineering (VSEL) Barrow, *Talent* and *Triumph*, the final two SSNs of the *Trafalgar* class, were being completed. Work was also progressing apace on the build of the first two Trident class submarines, *Vanguard* and *Victorious*. Added to these projects, the MoD was drawing up the specification for a new, highly capable third-generation SSN which would eventually replace the ageing *Valiant* class. The future of the Submarine Flotilla seemed very bright and this was reflected in the happy, family atmosphere of those gathered for the colour presentation, with a Royal Marine band playing and a spectacularly smart guard of honour paraded to greet the Sovereign.

I and a contingent from STWG were invited to attend the occasion with our wives and partners. I proudly presented my team members to the Queen, relating to her their individual achievements and successes in trials and evaluations from the High Arctic to the tropics. My early days in STWG, struggling with Tigerfish submarine certification in the rain swept mountains of north-west Scotland, seemed a lifetime away.

In the years of chaos in Russia in the following decade of the 1990s, its submarine force, like most of its military arms, suffered serious neglect and upheaval. Added to the difficulties of running a large submarine arm with many different classes of boat, dangerous weapon systems and conscript crews of varied ethnicity, was a chronic lack of money for pay, fuel, stores, maintenance and upkeep. 1987 had seen the last major surge of Russian submarines into the Atlantic and this was not to be repeated. Many hulls were laid up for disposal and the number of operationally available submarines decreased significantly. The Russian navy withdrew its warships from the Mediterranean and other distant theatres and, in due course, with the rise of new nations within and outside the Russian Federation, the old Soviet navy was split up. The most significant break-away was the transfer of most of the Black Sea Fleet to the Ukraine. All of this resulted in the Russian Navy and its offshoots tending to stay in harbour and the tempo of its submarine operations declined remarkably.

Any sense of triumph in the Royal Navy was muted by sobering news from Devonport Dockyard. There in November 1989, the SSN

Warspite was undergoing a routine refit when a technician inspecting part of her reactor system discovered alarming cracks in critical welds in her two steam-generating boilers. This discovery was to have a crucial impact on the Submarine Flotilla.

The defective welds joined two 14in diameter pipes – colloquially known as 'trouser legs' because that was what they diagrammatically resembled. Through these the highly pressurised reactor cooling water flowed from the reactor core into the boiler heat exchanger pipework, which generated the steam necessary to drive *Warspite*'s turbines. The welds were about 1in thick and, in *Warspite*'s case, the cracks extended across half their depth. This was extremely worrying because, if a weld failed, an uncontrollable loss of reactor coolant could cause a major accident. Furthermore, it had to be assumed that, potentially, all the Royal Navy's nuclear submarines might well be in a similar condition.

In the prevailing international uncertainty, it was necessary to limit submarine operations pending a thorough investigation but, most importantly, there was the imperative to sustain one SSBN on deterrent patrol. As the problem was considered to be age-related, the older *Valiant* class boats were immediately withdrawn from sea service whilst a testing and repair regime was developed, the newer *Swiftsure* and *Trafalgar* SSNs having priority for checking and repairing. The ageing SSBN force was equally affected by the 'trouser leg' problem but, somehow, continuous deterrence at sea was maintained by a thread. On occasion, deterrent patrol durations were significantly extended beyond the normal 60-day mark, while the SSBNs in port had their steam generator welds examined and made good. Since access to the affected welds was through a small hatch on the bottom of the generator, this required the innovative design and manufacture of robotic welding equipment. Such was the concern generated by this serious flaw that even the new Trident submarines under construction had their 'trouser leg' welds strengthened. Sadly, all this appeared to fulfil Admiral Rickover's prediction – made in the 1950s when American nuclear reactor technology was passed to the British – that the Royal Navy would be incapable of meeting the technical challenges of maintaining a nuclear submarine fleet.

As a consequence of this technical crisis, the MoD decided to rapidly decommission three older SSNs, *Warspite*, *Churchill* and *Conqueror*. The two boats of this class remaining in service, *Valiant* and *Courageous*, were to fall victims to the British Government's post-Cold War defence cuts in the early 1990s – the so-called 'Peace

Dividend'. Other savings in the defence budget were effected by decommissioning *Swiftsure*, along with the remaining diesel-powered *Oberon* class, six of which had been modernised. Finally, the decision was made to dispose of the four brand-new *Upholder* class diesel boats. The result was to reduce the Royal Navy's Submarine Flotilla to an all nuclear force of four SSBNs and twelve SSNs.

In this period of rapid retrenchment, I was selected for promotion to Captain and in August 1990, I left STWG. In my last few months in Faslane I had noticed with sadness the bored crews of the submarines tied up alongside whilst the 'trouser leg' rectification progressed. For many it was up to 18 months of inactivity, against a background of uncertainty about their boat's future. For some junior officers, this prolonged hiatus was to become a void in their career development, while the overall erosion of their core operational skills was an irreparable loss. The high standards achieved and maintained by my generation of highly competent submarine commanders, inevitably waned with only a single intelligence-gathering SSN being tasked to patrol the Barents Sea to conduct surveillance of the now largely supine Russian fleet.

Even though the full impact of the 'trouser leg' problem had still to be revealed and, as yet unaware of the extent to which Soviet submarine activity was in decline, I left a depressed Faslane. A hint of the future could be discerned from the parting remark of one frustrated submarine Captain. 'You were very lucky to see the best days in submarines,' I was told. 'The good times are over.' The words rang in my ears long afterwards.

With the Navy significantly shrinking in size, I sensed a possible threat of redundancy despite my recent promotion. There was bound to be a culling of senior officers within the ambit of a wide-ranging redundancy programme. Before taking up my new job as the deputy to Commodore Ship and Submarine Acceptance, part of the Royal Navy's procurement organisation at Foxhill in Bath, I found that I had time on my hands. Not due to start at Foxhill until April 1991, I took a six-month sabbatical at Strathclyde University Business School, undertaking a Master's Degree in Administration (MBA). I figured that such a qualification would be an advantage if I was required to leave the Service.

Chapter 25

Frustrations at the Procurement Executive

S elected for the rank of Captain at the age of 44, I was a late promotion and fully appreciated that, with the exception of being appointed to a post with the honorary rank of Commodore, this was as far as I would progress. Nevertheless, I was certain that my new job in the Procurement Executive (PE) would be highly satisfying, notwithstanding many likely frustrations ahead. As an aside, on promotion my entitlement to Submarine Pay ended which meant, initially, my increase in salary was marginal. The appointment at Bath involved a family move from Garelochead to Wiltshire, but we did not regret leaving behind the Scottish midges and 65in of annual rainfall. That said, we had had a wonderful time living in Scotland and left behind many close friends.

My studies at the University of Strathclyde were cut short by Saddam Hussein's invasion of Kuwait in August 1990. Just before the US and its allies launched Operation Desert Storm to retake Kuwait in January 1991, I was temporarily appointed to the MoD in London as a member of the Naval Advisory Group. This small section of officers had the responsibility of advising Ministers, senior Civil Servants and the military hierarchy of arising key naval logistic and force deployment issues. It was headed up by Rear Admiral Sam Salt, who had been Captain of *Sheffield* when she was hit by an Exocet missile during the Falklands War.

During the next three months I gained an insight of the workings of the MoD. In particular I was surprised by the Defence Minister's (Tom King) micro-management of the UK's contribution to the operation. For example, an urgent request for two additional Royal Marine helicopters as reserves for a squadron deployed required his personal approval. At the same time, it was evident to me that inter-service rivalry was alive and well. I had also observed that the warships operating in the north Persian Gulf, where there was a threat from both Iraqi naval forces and mines, were either American or British. Vessels of other navies were generally deployed well to the south, out of harm's way. However, the first force to land in Kuwait from the sea was a French mine-clearance contingent and, while the French tricolour was clearly evident, there was no sign of a British White Ensign as Royal Navy mine clearance was being conducted well offshore. Indeed, when hostilities ceased there was little visible presence of British 'boots on the ground' in Kuwait. Needless to say, this was not the case with our French ally, ever aware of the potential for lucrative contracts to be awarded from the reinstated Kuwait government.

The crisis organisation at the Ministry of Defence wound down at the end of March. A few weeks later I reported to the Commodore Naval Ship Acceptance (CNSA) organisation. This small division consisted of about a dozen officers and supporting staff. As its name suggested, it was headed by a Commodore who was responsible for formally accepting ships and submarines from their builders on the completion of construction and successful sea trials. The section was also responsible for advising when new weapon systems had met their MoD specification and that they were fully ready for operational service. This seemingly straightforward process was full of pitfalls which often arose from loose and imprecise specifications. Furthermore, as part of the PE organisation, I soon learned that CNSA had limited leverage or influence in rectifying serious shortfalls in equipment performance.

On joining, I found the Foxhill site depressing. It consisted of a sprawling complex of single-storey buildings which had been built in 1944 as a temporary hospital to receive the anticipated high level of casualties from the D-Day landings. In event, it was never used for this purpose and instead became home to the Royal Navy's division of the PE. I was one of only a handful of Seamen Officers in a very large organisation dominated by the Civil Service and the Royal Corps of Naval Constructers, the MoD's naval architects and ship equipment designers. Despite a cadre of Weapon and Marine Engineer Officers in senior posts, I recognised a strong vein of arrogance running through the establishment, manifested by a degree of disregard for the advice or opinion of the Royal Navy's Seamen Officers. This was not new. During WW2 the advice of accomplished submarine commanding officers, fresh from intensive campaigns, such as in the

Mediterranean, was often ignored or delayed by prevarication. The distinguished WW2 submarine Captain, Rear Admiral Ben Bryant, wrote in his autobiography 'To one who had spent two years at sea, the peaceful, unhurried atmosphere at Bath, seemed surreal'.

I thought that my extensive operational experience and knowledge of sonar – including state-of-the-art American systems – would be of value to those in the PE involved in sonar projects. Sadly, this was not the case and I soon realised that there was no interest expressed in learning about their features or characteristics. I sensed a firm belief within the organisation that Royal Navy sonars were superior to their USN equivalents and there was nothing to learn from the latter's design or characteristics. My assertion that the USN BQQ 5 sonar was superior in its capability to track and derive accurate fire-control solutions, in comparison with RN submarine sonars, was discounted.

I discovered an organisation which tended to be more focused upon process than outcome, and which was guilty of 'Group Think' as opposed to original thought. It also appeared that key decision-makers were sometimes pulling in different directions. Perversely, politicians could direct contracts to under-performing firms in areas where they had strong political support or obligations. On the other hand, civil servants might be bent upon slowing down the whole procurement process to meet annual budget targets. These problems were compounded by many senior individuals, particularly Service personnel, normally being in post for only two or three years. This was an unacceptably short period of time when compared to the extended length of modern procurement cycles. A lack of 'process ownership and responsibility' had a debilitating effect upon both continuity and accountability, exacerbated by weak project management in many areas. Rarely, if ever, was someone sacked for blatant incompetence. In sum, it was little wonder to me that, whilst it had had its highly commendable successes, the PE had an ongoing history of complex projects running into severe problems of overspend, under performance and late delivery. And this is still the case at the time of writing.

Soon after being appointed to the PE, a new Commodore arrived in post, Stephen Taylor, who despite this being his last job before retiring was full of energy and initiative. Under his leadership the CNSA organisation was much invigorated and I was to benefit from his highly professional support.

I found myself very busy when I joined CNSA. The Cold War might have been over, but there was an intense submarine building programme ongoing. The final submarine of the *Trafalgar* class,

Triumph, was almost ready to commission at Vickers Shipbuilding & Engineering Ltd (VSEL). At the same time, the first Trident SSBN, *Vanguard*, was nearing completion in the same shipyard. Additionally, the final three diesel boats of the *Upholder* class were at advanced stage of build at Cammell Laird. This Birkenhead yard had been the Barrow yard's strong rival in the UK's early years of building nuclear submarines but it had been taken over by VSEL in 1986. In addition, I had challenging responsibilities in the realms of submarine escape and rescue. These are described in the next chapter.

The submarine acceptance process involved conducting a series of material inspections. The first of these confirmed that the submarine was safe to proceed to sea on Contractor's Sea Trials. It addressed such issues as ensuring all safety critical systems were in good order. The final inspection occurred when the submarine build was totally completed, just prior to commissioning. A key element of the procedures involved identifying and listing all defects and agreeing the rectification costs with the shipbuilder. Handover of the vessel and authorisation of the final staged contract payment occurred only after the successful completion of the post-commissioning sea trials – these ensured all important defects had been rectified and the submarine demonstrated that it could perform to its full capability.

Soon after taking up my post, I and my team visited VSEL which was now an employee-owned consortium that had taken over the yard when it was de-nationalised in 1986. We were escorted on a tour of the Devonshire Dock Hall, a massive six-acre covered fabrication facility. This had been constructed in the 1980s to make a step improvement to the existing submarine build processes carried out in the open air. Within it were three Trident SSBNs in various stages of construction, *Vanguard*, *Victorious* and *Vigilant*. On boarding *Vanguard*, I was immediately disappointed by the layout of her machinery spaces. The highly significant decision had been made to reduce the hull length by wrapping the forward and after ballast tanks around the pressure-hull, thereby reducing the hull diameters at either end. This design was chosen, instead of adopting the precedent of the United States Navy's Trident SSBN in which uniform pressure hull diameter was maintained throughout its length, with the ballast tanks attached at either end, so creating much more internal space.

The resulting non-uniform hull diameter, in addition to constraining the design layout and adding complexities to the construction, produced cramped propulsion spaces with extremely difficult machinery access. Indeed, I assessed that the engine room was even more congested than *Valiant*'s which, when combined with the complexities and space constraints of the other machinery spaces, signalled a high future maintenance load and significant challenges in future refits. This has proved to be the case and difficulty of accessing equipment has resulted in the *Vanguard* class being highly challenging and costly to maintain and refit. This has been exacerbated by its designed life of 25 years being extended to well over 30 years until the *Vanguard* replacements, the *Dreadnought* class, come into service in the 2030s.

During this first visit, I called upon the Chief Executive VSEL, Noel Davies, to introduce myself and hear his views about the progress of building the *Vanguards*. On entering his office, in a corner I immediately spotted a bent aircraft propeller blade. When asking the CEO of its significance, he explained that when he was on a recent flight on the firm's twin-prop aircraft, owing to pilot error, it had run out of fuel mid-flight. The pilot had to make an emergency landing into fields, crashing through several hedgerows in the process – the badly-bent propeller blade had been kept as memento of the accident. His account of this event opened the discussion of what was to be a highly depressing meeting.

The CEO explained that VSEL had originally assumed ten *Upholder* class being completed, but it had been the MoD's decision to procure only four. An order for ten of this class would have bridged the gap at his shipyard until construction of the next generation of SSNs commenced in the mid-1990s. The latter, however, known as the SSN20 project, had recently been cancelled and now VSEL had an unprecedented small order book of only the three *Vanguards*, with the fourth yet to be contracted by the MoD. He went onto warn that large scale redundancies amongst his workforce were inevitable and there was likely to be a haemorrhaging of high-quality engineering and technical talent. As I left this gloomy meeting, I could only speculate whether the MoD hierarchy and politicians appreciated that the impending submarine construction void might seriously impair the UK's capability to build nuclear submarines in the future.

As part of the peace dividend at the end of the Cold War, all four of the *Upholder* class were planned to be sold. However, it was intended that the three boats still under construction at Cammell Laird would be completed and demonstrated as being fully operational before being put up for sale. Designed to replace the *Oberon* class, the *Upholders* had the specific wartime role of conducting a six-week patrol in the Iceland/Faroes gap. Designed by VSEL, they were the first British single-screw diesel submarines of streamlined, teardrop 'Albacore' form. With a much smaller crew than the *Oberon* class, many of the systems fitted to the *Upholder* were highly automated, but this was to cause a number of problems.

It soon became evident that the class had several serious technical deficiencies. The first of these occurred in *Upholder* during her sea trials in 1989, when she suffered a complete loss of power and propulsion. This, it was discovered, had been caused by a design defect which was only rectified after several months. Significantly, there were two serious safety concerns. The first of these was the torpedo tube operating system – described as being like a computer driven by hydraulics. The second was the snort exhaust system which, on shutting down, incurred significant seawater ingress. Other problems, which soon became evident, included a very limited range of about 5,000 miles, compared to the *Oberon*'s 15,000 miles. This was because all fuel was carried internally within the pressure hull, taking up valuable space. Past practice had been to carry fuel in external tanks wrapped round the pressure hull.

Arriving at the Cammell Laird Shipyard for the first time, I was briefed by Gordon Howell, its managing director. He was an extremely experienced and astute ship and submarine constructor who had started his career as an apprentice with Vickers at Barrow. His yard was a sprawling 150-acre site on the west bank of the Mersey, a rundown complex of old buildings and sheds which, like many British shipyards at that time, was quite unsuitable for modern and efficient shipbuilding, though it did possess a covered construction hall. When I arrived, *Unseen* lay in the fitting-out basin with her sisters, *Ursula* and *Unicorn*, yet to emerge from the hall.

Similar in theme to my meeting with the CEO of his parent company, the Managing Director briefed on the dismal outlook for the yard. He explained that, because there were no further orders in the offing, the workforce of about 1,000 faced redundancy on completion of the three *Upholder*s. Although he was trying his best to find a buyer for the yard, he was hamstrung because the yard did not qualify for either British or European Union intervention funding support for merchant ship building. In the meantime, he was downsizing the estate, selling off pieces of land and other facilities where he could. He assured me that, notwithstanding this grim situation, he and his workforce were determined to complete the three boats to first class standards. For my part I soon came to have the highest regard for Howell and, together, we formed a strong professional partnership.

Within a few weeks I and my team were off to sea aboard *Unseen* in the early phases of Contractor's Sea Trials in the Clyde Estuary. Climbing onto the bridge, I noted her slow speed as she headed on the surface to her diving areas; about 10.5 knots was her maximum on the surface although she was capable of 18 knots dived. I joined the bridge watchkeepers in an unhealthy cloud of acrid diesel exhaust fumes which was clearly reducing their ability to keep an efficient lookout. There was a following wind and the exhaust from the boat's two diesels was being sucked up to the bridge. For some reason, the designers had not built in a bulkhead under the casing to prevent the exhaust causing this serious problem. I could not understand this extraordinary deficiency – the bridge diesel exhaust problem must have been learned about years ago. However, it was the 1930s when Vickers last designed a submarine, the *Kalev* class delivered to Estonia. Prior to the *Upholder*s, British submarine design had been within the exclusive remit of the Admiralty.

Having dived in the North Channel between Scotland and Ireland, our priority was to assess the leaking snort exhaust hull valve problem. A series of trials runs indicated that, when the snorting evolution was ended and the engines crash-stopped, this important valve did not seat properly for some time. This allowed several tons of seawater to pour into the engine room. If urgently going deep after a period of snorting, with a steep angle, this had serious safety implications. However, I reluctantly accepted that there was to be no quick fix before commissioning of the boats, other than ensuring the crew had a drill and equipment in place to immediately pump out the engine room bilges after completing snorting.

The most worrying safety defect was the low probability, but plausible, risk of the torpedo tube flood valves opening to the sea when the tubes' rear doors were open. This type of problem was the cause of catastrophic flooding, resulting in the loss of the submarine *Thetis* in Liverpool Bay in 1939. Again, owing to the complexity of the torpedo tube control system, the only immediate solution was to introduce strict operating procedures to avoid serious flooding. Indeed, as the submarines were due to be disposed of and the costs for the four boats had escalated to about £1.9 billion at 2024 prices, there was no real impetus to fix the problems other than the torpedo tube defect, which had the most serious implications.

Despite these dispiriting observations, I accepted that the *Upholder* class did have some commendable features. They handled well underwater, had an extremely quiet acoustic signature, and they had an excellent fire-control and sonar suite. Indeed, in the realms of war-fighting capability they were a real improvement on the *Oberons*. Unfortunately, these advances were offset by other shortcomings, such as equipment accessibility and the crew accommodation standards, both of which left a lot to be desired. Moreover, with only two modestly-powered diesels, the *Upholders* lacked power generation capability. Overall, I considered the design to be disappointing and it compared unfavourably with the contemporary Dutch *Walrus* class. I concluded that the acceptance process would largely be confined to ensuring the Shipbuilder had built the submarines to the contract terms.

In October 1991, I was off to sea to accept into service the last of the *Trafalgar* class, *Triumph*, commanded by a fellow member of the commissioning *Spartan* wardroom, Commander David Vaughan. Conducting a deep dive and full power run in the North-west Approaches, the boat performed flawlessly. Therefore, I had no hesitation in authorising the final stage payment to VSEL. At the time of writing, more than 30 years later, she still is in service.

The following April, I was at the Cammell Laird yard having been invited to the launch of the final *Upholder*, *Unicorn*. On a sunny spring morning, she was named and the traditional bottle of champagne struck the hull. However, *Unicorn* did not move and there followed several moments of anxious pause. Then, suddenly, she was on her way down the launch slip and, to the loud cheers of the remaining few hundred shipyard workers and their families, she slid gracefully into the Mersey. The occasion marked the last launch from the yard of the long established Cammell Laird Company, ending a history stretching back 165 years. It was also the last dynamic launch down a slipway of a submarine from a British shipyard. Future submarine 'launches' would be achieved by gently lowering the vessel into the water using a huge lifting assembly known as a synchronised ship-lift. In the interim, *Unseen* and *Ursula* had been accepted into service after final trials in the Clyde. The acceptance formalities with the shipbuilder were completed onboard each of the boats in a very subdued atmosphere. I and my team were only too aware that many of the shipyard managers and workers aboard for the trials would be made redundant when they returned to Birkenhead.

In June 1993, *Unicorn* was commissioned in an eerily empty shipyard. At the commissioning lunch in the boardroom, surrounded by the paintings and the other memorabilia of what had been a great shipbuilding company, each of the guests was presented with a small crystal bowl. It was engraved with the words *Semper Commemoranda Unice Optima* – 'Always Remember they were the Best'.

The *Upholder*s were all paid off by 1994 and, in due course, were sold to the Royal Canadian Navy where, at the time of writing, they are still in service. They have since proved extremely expensive and difficult to maintain and operate. In October 2004, the *Chicoutimi* (ex-*Upholder*), when crossing the North Atlantic on the surface in rough weather, took a considerable quantity of water down the conning tower. This caused a serious fire in which one officer died. The cause of the fire was eventually discovered to be the fitting of the wrong type of watertight bulkhead electrical cable sealing arrangement. When salt water came into contact with the seals, they combusted.

Aside from the *Upholder*s, there was much more important business for CNSA to deal with. *Vanguard*, the first of the new Trident submarines, was approaching commissioning and there were many problems to address. In the event, perhaps the biggest challenge I and my team would confront would be getting the Trident Submarine Project team and the relevant MoD staff to accept the serious deficiencies or defects which we identified. The former was headed up by a senior naval constructor, who in turn reported to the Chief of the Strategic Systems Executive (CSSE), Rear Admiral Ian Pirnie. Responsible for all aspects of the Trident Project, he had a daunting remit, including the procurement of the missile systems and the construction of the requisite shore facilities.

Similar to the *Resolution* class, but about twice their displacement, the *Vanguard*s would be fitted with sixteen missile tubes capable of embarking the Trident D5 missile. This missile, with a range of over 6,000 miles and six or more independently targeted warheads, is a marked improvement on the Chevaline (Polaris A3) system. Furthermore, in terms of detonating on a specific target, it is far more accurate. Therefore, there was no need to fit it with the type of decoy package which was introduced within the Chevaline project.

There was nothing that could be done about the SSBNs' compartment layout other than press hard for improvements to the crew messdeck areas. These had been completed as dining halls, as opposed to the submarine practice of doubling as recreational spaces. There was no provision for a recreational space where individual members of the Ship's Company could relax in peace and quiet away from their crowded messdecks, particularly when meals were in progress or movies were being shown. This facility had been called for in the MoD requirement, but had been missed in the design. The project management conceded this deficiency and, in due course, agreed to adapt redundant space in the missile compartment. They also consented to the messdecks being improved. These were small triumphs, but they would make a lot of difference to crew comfort during long patrols.

It was in the area of the sonar fit where I had most contention with the Trident Project. It was evident that several key aspects of the submarine's sonar suite had been under-specified, resulting in a number of operational deficiencies which would be either costly or difficult to rectify. I had been briefed by sonar experts that, owing to design shortcomings the sonar system – which was unique to the Trident class – would be unable to provide comprehensive protection against third-generation Russian submarines. These were the stealthy and capable 'Victor III' and 'Akula' classes, which would be the SSBN's main future threat. Another important shortcoming was that, in a high-density shipping situation, the command team would find it difficult to resolve the movements of individual sonar contacts. Incomprehensibly, it was evident that no expert operator input had been sought during the design stage of the sonar system. Even worse, weak and inexperienced project management was handling this vitally important part of the submarine's defences.

These views put me on a collision course with the upper echelons of the Trident Project, who saw me as awkward, unduly demanding and – from their perspective – of questionable judgement. However, none of them had knowledge or experience of operating submarine sonar in the contemporary threat environment. Due to the arising friction, a formal complaint was made by the Project Director to Commodore Taylor, to the effect that I was being unreasonable. With little or no support from either the Naval Staff or the specialists on the staff of Flag Officer Submarines, my voice was a rather lonely one. But, harking back to my tribulations with the Tigerfish Project, it was not for the first time in my career that I was up against a stubborn hierarchy.

In March 1992, Linda and I received an invitation by VSEL to attend *Vanguard*'s naming ceremony, as part of the VIP group of guests. As *Vanguard* had been lowered into the water using hydraulic lifts, the naming replaced the traditional launch ceremony. The occasion did not go well. On our arrival at the Shipbuilder's head office, we discovered it to be blockaded by a large group of chanting anti-nuclear protesters. In picking our way through a cluster of squatting, banner-holding protesters, we and other guests eventually made it into the building. There we were urgently ushered into one of several buses to transport us to the berth where the naming ceremony would take place. Meanwhile *Vanguard*'s sponsor, Princess Diana, arrived at the yard by helicopter.

The VIP bus convoy, on setting out to the berth, entered the yard by an unfamiliar entrance and soon the lead bus got lost in the myriad of fabrication buildings. This resulted in its occupants arriving at *Vanguard* many minutes late, consequently delaying the start of the ceremony. The Princess, who had been standing on the after casing for some time, was not appropriately dressed for the Barrow March weather. Clearly, she was cold and not pleased by the delay in starting the proceedings. The VIPs in place, the short naming ceremony began and culminated in the eight harbour-facing missile tube hatches being opened in sequence with the large letters VANGUARD marked upon them. During the fine lunch which followed, the Princess was accompanied by the Procurement Minister, Mr Jonathan Aitken, but it was evident from her demeanour that she remained unhappy.

On 14 August 1993, *Vanguard* was commissioned at the VSEL yard, with Princess Diana again the guest of honour. On this occasion the event organisation was absolutely outstanding, no doubt the boat's respective crews taking a lead on the arrangements. Clearly it was a happy occasion for all levels of participant and, hopefully, it was an enjoyable one for the Princess.

In the interim, in the autumn of 1992, I embarked in *Vanguard* for Contractor's Sea Trials. Before getting underway I was briefed by *Vanguard*'s Port crew Captain, Commander David Russell, and given a tour of the boat. I was immediately struck by the awesome array of coloured displays in the control room which, as a first, was situated two decks below the conning tower. The primary means of visual surveillance was through remote periscope camera images which were then displayed on the submarine's state-of-the-art command system. There was a traditional optical periscope installed as a back-up to the two electronic ones, but this was operated from the deck above the control room. A WW2 submarine captain would have been reasonably familiar with *Valiant*'s control room with its two periscopes, mechanical torpedo course calculator and navigational plotting table. But in the case of *Vanguard*'s banks of highly sophisticated computer screens, he would have been in totally unknown territory.

The 14,000-ton SSBN was much bigger than the SSNs I was accustomed to, where most command positions, including the bridge, were a few feet away from each other. Accordingly, I judged that operating on the surface would be more complex and difficult to undertake. In short, I did not envy the challenges the *Vanguard* class Captains would confront when the boat was on the surface in dense shipping or poor visibility conditions.

Once dived, I did a walk round the various compartments. *Vanguard* was a big, spacious submarine, most notably so in the missile compartment, known as 'Sherwood Forest'. She was a far cry from the cramped, confined environs of a diesel boat, but I wondered if all members of the crew were aware that the boat was operating in a hostile external environment with high seawater pressure bearing down on the hull and its fittings. As the senior sea-rider I had the novelty of being berthed in the boat's sickbay but, at least on the first night, I had a somewhat disturbed sleep. There was a surprising number of crew and shipyard workers who entered it, requiring medical attention to minor cuts and burns.

On the day prior to *Vanguard*'s commissioning, the CNSA team, headed by my Commodore, undertook a thorough inspection of the material state of the boat. Overall, the condition of the boat was highly satisfactory with the exception of the more difficult-to-access machinery areas. The application of paint to these left a lot to be desired. Unsurprisingly, there was a substantial number of build defects, mostly minor, but it was my job to chair a two-day conference where the liability for all arising build defects was determined. I was pleased that, with few exceptions, the Shipbuilder accepted responsibility for them and agreed to a plan to fix the faults. During post-commissioning trials, I authorised the acceptance of *Vanguard* into service on behalf of the project and the final-stage payment of £80 million to VSEL was endorsed (she had cost about £850 million to build). Overall, the first-of-class trials were successful and in late 1994 *Vanguard* deployed on patrol for the first time. She had been delivered to time and cost, albeit the latter helped by a favourable US dollar/sterling exchange rate. I had to concede that it was a substantial achievement which – despite my misgivings – reflected well upon the MoD and British industry.

Predictably, however, soon after the submarine started sea trials, many of the sonar problems I had warned of made themselves evident. The Trident Project senior management at last woke up to my concerns and began to investigate these emerging deficiencies, most of which would take both time and significant resources to fix. Although totally vindicated, I deeply regretted that the lack of expert operator input at the outset of the design process and inept project management would result in the British taxpayer being confronted with a substantial bill to fix the problems. But I was also aware that few in Foxhill were commercially minded beyond meeting their own budget targets, and this too was part of the problem.

During the course of my appointment, my responsibilities were extended to taking part in the acceptance of surface ships from the shipbuilders, from the firms of Swan Hunter (Tyneside), Vosper Thornycroft (Southampton) and Yarrow (Glasgow). Sadly, in subsequent years the first two of these have ceased shipbuilding. On the submarine weapons systems side of my remit, there were many projects long overdue for final acceptance, including the Spearfish torpedo, which a small section of my officers, based in an outpost of the Procurement Executive at Portland, were addressing.

As referred to earlier, the SSN20 project had been cancelled. This class of SSN was intended to replace the *Valiant* class in the 1990s and featured a large, highly capable nuclear attack submarine with enhanced sonar and weapon systems. However, on the grounds of cost and against the background of a significantly diminished Russian submarine threat, the project was terminated. In 1993 the MoD set out a requirement for a new class of SSN to replace the five *Swiftsure* class boats still in service. It was envisaged that this new type of submarine would be a second batch of the *Trafalgars* – and the project was initially known as the Batch Two *Trafalgar* class (B2-TC). During the closing months of my time in the PE, I witnessed the beginnings of the unfortunate history of the B2-TC acquisition programme which, in due course, became known as the *Astute* class. At these early stages of the project, CNSA's role was constrained to an advisory one and that of attending progress briefings.

The initial MoD requirement stipulated that the BT-2C be fitted with the latest sonar and combat systems and the PWR2 type reactor being fitted in the *Vanguard* class. The PWR2 reactor was chosen for both its improved nuclear safety features and commonality of equipment. However, this type of reactor required a wider pressure hull for this new class of SSN. There were also demanding radiated noise targets but, significantly, there was no definition of the maximum speed required. Like the *Upholders*, this new class broke with tradition in that it would not be designed by the MoD. Furthermore, it was planned that the prime contractor awarded the contract would be required to conduct all the post-build and first-commission trials before acceptance by the Royal Navy. Cutting steel was envisaged for the first of class, *Astute* in 1997, sea trials in 2003, with commissioning and final handover in 2005.

VSEL submitted a design with an indicative cost of £1.7 billion for the first three hulls and GEC Marconi submitted a costing of £1.6 billion. The VSEL outline of design was essentially a *Trafalgar* with a bulge of its hull diameter where it had ingested the PWR2. On the other hand, the GEC offering was a much larger SSN of about 8,000 tons displacement, substantially larger than the circa 5,000 tons of the VSEL option. It also offered a greater number of torpedo tubes and a significantly increased torpedo and cruise missile load.

Clearly the MoD and FOSM were seduced by the prospect of getting the concept of the SSN20 into service at a potentially lower cost than the conservative VSEL design. In 1997 GEC were, therefore, awarded the contract, notwithstanding they had never previously built a submarine, never mind designed one. The contract cost for the first three submarines had also leapt from £1.6 billion to £2.4 billion. The overall decision-making process was to prove one of hope over experience and wishful thinking regarding British industry's ability to deliver.

In 1994, my final year at the PE, GEC bought VSEL. The share price at the point of sale was substantially more than the 1986 original offer to the employees. Therefore, many VSEL directors and senior managers who had retained their shares, pocketed their gains and left the company. About the same time the Royal Corps of Constructors was being run down and several key senior staff with submarine expertise within in the PE were accepting early retirement. Within a decade or so the United Kingdom had lost the core of its nuclear submarine design and building expertise.

In 1999, BAE Systems acquired the Barrow shipyard from GEC. For the first time Computer Aided Design (CAD) was used to design a British SSN, rather than build a full scale wooden mock-up. Unfortunately, employment of CAD ran into serious problems and US expertise was called in to sort it out. This, together with the existing void in build expertise, resulted in the project running five years late and heavily over budget. The first three boats cost over £3 billion and the British taxpayer was required to meet over half of the £650 million cost overrun.

Astute finally commissioned in 2010. The *Astute* class has proved to be stealthy, emitting minimum radiated noise, and it has an excellent sonar fit. Indeed, it has demonstrated several significant operational successes. However, though much larger than the *Trafalgar* class, it has essentially the same size of main engines and reportedly its maximum speed is unsatisfactory at less than 25 knots. This is a distinct disadvantage when opposing submarines can do over 30 knots. More importantly, much of the *Astute* equipment and systems is challenging to access and this class has proved difficult and expensive to maintain. Accordingly, *Astute* operational availability has for many years been at unacceptably low levels.

I left the Procurement Executive in the summer of 1994 to take up an appointment in the Nuclear Policy division of the MoD in London. I was not sorry to go. Although I had much enjoyed working with the shipbuilders and taking brand-new submarines through their early sea trials, there had been too many frustrations. Most notably, these included my personal inability to achieve significant change under a hierarchy which believed it always knew best. My strife with the Trident Project had achieved successes but, in pressing the case for improving the SSBN's sonar system, I felt I had ploughed a lonely furrow. Many of my colleagues in the Procurement Executive had brilliant intellects and were dedicated and committed to the Royal Navy. I could, therefore, not comprehend why the organisation was so dysfunctional.

Chapter 26

Submarine Escape and Rescue

One of the key roles during my time at the Procurement Executive was Chairmanship of the Standing Committee On Submarine Escape and Rescue (SCOSER). Essentially, I was responsible for the overall stewardship of the Royal Navy's submarine escape and rescue organisation. I was assisted by a small team of officers and could draw upon expertise across a number of specialist disciplines within the MoD, such as submarine bio-medicine research. Annually I submitted a report directly to the Admiralty Board, outlining the status of the Royal Navy's escape and rescue systems, together with a review of crew training and the exercises which had been carried out.

In view of the Royal Navy's poor record of success in crew escaping from a stricken submarine, after WW2 a comprehensive review took place of its entire submarine escape and rescue organisation. This investigation, known as the Ruck-Keene Report, amongst many key recommendations, set up the SCOSER organisation. Perhaps one of its most important findings was that escape is best conducted using the 'free-ascent' technique where the escapee uses the air in his lungs to reach the surface rather than rely upon breathing apparatus. To train in the free-ascent technique, the 100ft-deep escape training tank was built at HMS *Dolphin* in the early 1950s. Subsequent trials demonstrated that free ascent could successfully be achieved down to a depth of 600ft from an escape chamber. However, none of these deep trials involved 'compartment escape'.

'Compartment escape' involves rapidly flooding up an entire submarine compartment to balance its internal pressure with the external sea-pressure. Once this is achieved, an escape hatch is opened and rapid egress of the crew members can then take place. To escape, a crew member immerses himself in the flood water and ducks under a canvas trunk securely attached to the deck of the compartment.

He then quickly thrusts himself up to the open hatch. Once outside the hatch, he is carried rapidly to the surface by a buoyancy device. However, to avoid an air embolism, during his ascent he must continuously blow the air out of his rapidly expanding lungs. Most navies now provide Submarine Escape Immersion Suits (SEIS) instead of inflatable vests. The SEIS suits provide total containment of the escapee, making it much easier to exhale air in the ascent by simply keeping the mouth open. Most of these suits are also fitted with a one-man life raft that can be deployed at the surface.

If the distressed submarine is fitted with an escape chamber – a small pressure-tight compartment with an internal and external hatch – this provides an alternative to flooding up the entire compartment. Some escape chambers allow two crew members to escape together but it takes about 10 minutes for the full flooding-up and draining-down cycle to be completed. Therefore, even assuming two crew escaping simultaneously, it would take approximately eight hours for a crew of 100 to escape. Furthermore, the escape chamber relies upon it being operated by competent crew members. The latter is not a given, as deteriorating atmosphere conditions in the boat are likely to weaken and disorientate the crew.

Numerous risks are associated with escape, including nitrogen narcosis, barotrauma (a type of high-pressure injury to the ear drum, lungs or bowel), arterial gas embolism, decompression sickness, hypothermia and drowning. Accordingly, escape will always be a hazardous option. As previously stated, training in the *Dolphin* escape tower took place in a benign environment: the water at body temperature, the lighting excellent and instructors on hand to assist the trainee. In reality, escaping from a stricken submarine on the seabed would be an extremely frightening and risky experience.

Use of a rescue vehicle, which mates with the submarine and enables the crew to be safely brought to the surface, keeping their feet dry, is the safest method of extracting personnel from a submarine crippled on the sea bed. Furthermore, it can be conducted down to great depths, beyond those where free ascent is possible. However, this method depends upon the timely deployment of the rescue vehicle to the location of the stricken submarine. There is likely to be a race against time to get the crew out before their life support systems are exhausted.

Between the world wars, as related earlier, the Royal Navy experienced a dismal peacetime submarine accident record. Eight submarines were lost with, in most cases, their entire crews perishing. In

1927 the Davis Submarine Escape Apparatus (DSEA) was introduced together with the requisite systems to enable a compartment escape. The DSEA was a re-breather system where the escapee breathed oxygen from an attached cylinder and the exhaled CO_2 was absorbed in a separate compartment. It was not straightforward to use. Furthermore, it had a maximum operating depth of about 150ft due to the risk of oxygen narcosis which was likely to occur at deeper depths. Nevertheless, it was the primary method of escape from Royal Navy submarines during WW2 and into the 1950s.

In August 1939, whilst conducting post-build sea trials, *Thetis* foundered in Liverpool Bay as a result of major flooding through an opened torpedo tube rear door. Despite being in shallow water and the boat's stern protruding from the surface of the sea, only four personnel successfully made an escape using DSEA. Ninety-nine crew members and Cammell Laird's employees perished. One lesson learned from this tragedy was that crew members needed to undergo realistic training in the use of the DSEA.

Of a total of seventy-four British submarines lost in WW2, seven of these losses were as a result of friendly fire or accident. Two of the accidental sinkings were caused by serious flooding through breaches in the pressure hull. A third boat, *Vandal*, which disappeared when at sea to the north of the island of Arran, almost certainly foundered for the same reason.

The newly-commissioned *Umpire*, when on the surface in a convoy, sank in shallow water in the North Sea in 1941 after collision with an armed trawler. Sixteen of the crew successfully escaped using the DSEA, one of this system's few successes. Nevertheless, most of the crew who were forward at the time of the collision, perished. One of the survivors, Sub Lieutenant Edward Young, went on to successfully command *Storm*, and was the first Royal Navy Volunteer Reserve (RNVR) officer to be appointed Captain of a submarine.

In May 1943 *Untamed*, also recently commissioned, was lost with all hands whilst exercising in the Kilbrannan Sound in the Clyde Estuary. The boat was salvaged, enabling a detailed reconstruction of events which led to her sinking with the loss of the entire crew.

Due to both crew error and a build defect, the submarine flooded forward and ended up anchored to the sea bed at a depth of about 150ft. Use of main motors and blowing main ballast failed to free the boat and the crew prepared to undertake a compartment escape from the engine room. DSEA breathing sets were donned. The Ship's Company had been trained to use these but, in the rapid evacuation of the fore-ends, no sets had been brought from this compartment, leaving ten of the thirty-seven crew to go without. Rather pathetically, these latter individuals made do by lashing empty oil cans around their waists, in the vain hope these would provide them with enough buoyancy to get to the surface.

Also, counterintuitively, a valve on the DSEA set had to be switched to the 'off' position to make oxygen available to the user after inflating the buoyancy stole. This vital action might easily be forgotten in an emergency, and indeed was by several of the confused and frightened crew. The escape hatch canvas twill trunk was lowered and lashed to the deck plates. Meanwhile the engine room had been sealed up in preparation for flooding it up to equalise the pressure inside and outside the submarine. As the flooding commenced, it would be essential that it was completed quickly and that the crew had started breathing from their escape sets. As the air compressed in the compartment, the toxic gasses in it would become lethal and the unfortunates with no DSEAs were destined to succumb before getting into the escape trunk.

With the crew crouching on top of the two engines to ensure they would be above the level of water when the compartment was flooded to equalisation pressure with the sea, the Captain ordered the large escape flood valve opened. However, much to the crew's despair, no water entered the compartment. In the cramped conditions, the dark and confusion, it was not recognised that a downstream back-up valve had been incorrectly assembled during build, and, although indicating open, was in fact shut. Other slower methods were then used to flood the engine room, but these took time and those men who did not have DSEA sets, or who had their valve in the wrong position, started to suffer as they inhaled the increasingly toxic air.

With those crew who were still conscious, sitting up to their armpits in very cold water, Chief Petty Officer Challenor (one of those whose DSEA was not switched on correctly) pulled himself down under the water to the base of the escape trunk. Managing to climb up to the hatch, he valiantly succeeded in unclipping it before he passed out through lack of oxygen and drowned. His fellow crew members, who were successfully breathing from their DSEA sets were unable to help him and, with their escape route now blocked, when their oxygen ran out, they also lost consciousness and died.

On the surface, after several hours, a rescue vessel with divers arrived and immediately tried to locate the submarine but, because of strong currents and poor underwater visibility, it was 36 hours before divers finally reached the *Untamed*, which was discovered lying on an even keel on the sea bed. There was, though, no response to tapping her hull. The after escape hatch was discovered unclipped and the Chief Petty Officer's body was recovered from beneath it. The submarine was salvaged some weeks later and re-commissioned as *Vitality*.

After WW2, serious Royal Navy submarine accidents continued. As described earlier, in January 1950, *Truculent*, passaging on the surface up the Thames Estuary at night, was involved in collision with a Swedish freighter. She sank in shallow water, and while most of the crew quickly escaped to the surface, sixty-four crew and shipyard workers died. They had been swept away by strong tides and consequently drowned or died of hypothermia. The key lesson of this tragedy was that, where possible, escape should await the arrival of rescue craft to recover the crew members when they arrived at the surface.

When in 1951 *Affray* sank in deep water in the English Channel, all those onboard were killed. Four years later, when an HTP-fuelled torpedo exploded onboard *Sidon* in Portland harbour, fourteen of her crew were killed and the boat sank. Meanwhile in April 1963, the year I joined the Royal Navy, as described earlier, the nuclear attack submarine USS *Thresher* was lost with all hands while conducting trials in deep water in the Western Atlantic. Therefore, when I started submarine training in 1967, it is was not surprising that submarining was still viewed as being hazardous. Thankfully, there have been no further serious Royal Navy submarine accidents since the *Sidon* explosion.

By the time I assumed SCOSER chairmanship in 1991, there had been significant improvements in free-ascent escape techniques. All RN submarines had their escape compartments (one forward and one aft) fitted with an Emergency Breathing System (EBS). This system is essential for crew to breath from when flooding up to make a compartment escape. Each submarine had been fitted with two escape chambers and there had been successful demonstration of their use by ordinary crew members down to depths of 600ft. Additionally, indicator buoys were fitted under the casing which, when released would reach the surface and start transmitting a radio distress signal. As the buoys were tethered to the submarine, they also would precisely mark its position.

Another initiative was the formation of the Submarine Parachute Assistance Group (SPAG) to provide the capability of rapid deployment of assistance to surfacing escapees. This group, mainly drawn from escape instructors, is trained to be parachuted into the sea at the location of a distressed submarine. Making use of a static line from the rear ramp of an aircraft, equipment pods are dropped alongside the team. These contain life rafts, food, water and medical supplies, quickly providing on-the-spot medical and life support.

In July 1987, a team of British, Commonwealth and international submariners took part in escape trials in a Norwegian fjord from *Otus*. During the final phases, at a depth of 600ft, a senior rating got caught up in the chamber ladder as he attempted to start his ascent to the surface. Quickly realising the danger, he made the emergency signal by rapidly banging the side of the chamber. In response, the submarine was immediately surfaced with the escapee still in the chamber. He was lucky to only suffer a barotrauma in the stomach but, thereafter, no more of these trials were conducted.

Soon after taking up my appointment, I was surprised to learn that there was still ongoing research into submarine escape technology. In particular, a shore sited research chamber was being developed at the Haslar section of the Admiralty Research Establishment (ARE), situated not far from HMS *Dolphin*. To initially test this system, the intention had been to use goats as, in terms of the effects of decompression, their physiology closely resembles that of humans. Indeed, at ARE Haslar, a small herd of goats had already been used in a number of decompression trials and were still being looked after. Sensibly, the escape research project was soon terminated as not being required. I, therefore, was happy when passing the establishment, to see the goats in their retirement, peacefully grazing on the surrounding pastures.

In 1939 the USS *Squalus* sank off the coast of New Hampshire due to a serious flooding incident. Thirty-three of the crew were rescued using a McCann rescue bell suspended from a support vessel. Once mated onto one of the boat's escape chambers, groups of the crew were lifted to the surface. The *Squalus* incident remains the only case of successful rescue from a distressed submarine, and this type of rescue system is still in service. Nevertheless, being tethered to a support vessel, it is very much sea-state limited. Furthermore, if the distressed submarine is at a severe angle, mating might be impossible. Since the *Squalus* loss, there have been significant advances in developing submarine rescue systems and, in the 1970s, rescue mini-submarines were introduced into service. An autonomous, untethered submersible is a much better option than a bell chamber, as it has the potential to achieve success in a wide range of conditions.

In 1978 the USN brought into service two Deep Submergence Rescue Vehicles (DSRVs), the *Mystic* and *Avalon*. These were capable of operating to depths of 5,000ft and could embark up to twenty-four survivors. At about the same time, the Royal Navy commissioned the ex-North Sea oil industry mini-sub *LR5* as a rescue system. It could take up to fifteen passengers and had a maximum operating depth of 2,000ft. Both these rescue systems were air-portable but the DSRV had the advantage of being able to deploy piggy-backing on the rear of a nuclear submarine. The *LR5* required to be launched from a surface vessel with a suitable crane, incurring the drawbacks of being more weather-dependent and likely to take longer to reach the site of the stricken submarine.

Part of the *LR5* system was a small Remotely Operated Vehicle (ROV) known as *Scorpio*, which could rapidly be deployed to the accident scene before the arrival of the *LR5*. Its purpose would be to bring down to the bottomed submarine, life support stores and other equipment which could be locked into the boat through an escape chamber. This would extend the crew endurance conditions onboard the stricken boat before the arrival of *LR5* at the accident site, ready to enter the water. The operation of *Scorpio* had been contracted to a company owned by a colleague and friend – Roger Chapman. He had been navigator of *Swiftsure* during her build and contractor's sea trials, when it was discovered that his eyesight had deteriorated to the extent that it no longer met bridge watchkeeping criteria. Without recourse to appeal, this very promising officer had his service in submarines terminated. Accordingly, he chose to leave the Navy and in early 1973 joined Vickers Oceanics as a pilot for the company's mini-submarines. This company, a subsidiary of Vickers Shipbuilding, was involved in undersea support services, primarily for the oil industry.

In August 1973 Roger's submersible, *Pisces III*, was involved in an accident whilst being recovered by its mother ship in the South-west Approaches. A towline pulled the pressure-tight hatch off of one its machinery compartments which flooded and the mini-sub plunged to the bottom at a depth of 1,575ft. Upside down in darkness for over three days, eventually Roger and his co-pilot were rescued when the sister submersible, *Pisces II*, managed to successfully secure a recovery line to the stricken craft. They only had a few hours of oxygen left. David Mayo, another submarine officer retired because of eyesight deterioration, on the mother ship, led the recovery, the deepest-ever successful rescue from the seabed.

Roger went onto to be a leading international expert in submarine rescue systems. His company in due course was contracted to provide the *LR5* submersible and *Scorpio* ROV rescue systems for the Royal Navy and did so up until 2009. In August 2005 the *Scorpio* system was deployed to the Pacific where it successfully rescued the crew of the Russian mini-sub *AS28* which had become entangled in cables on the seabed. For his part in the rescue, Roger was awarded a medal by President Putin at Downing Street in October that year. He also was a leading instigator and key expert in the procurement of the NATO Submarine Rescue System which came into service in 2008. This system, jointly owned by the UK, Norway and France, replaced *LR5*.

Although during my time at SCOSER there were no further escape exercises conducted, *LR5* and the *Scorpio* system were deployed annually. These evolutions normally involved chartering a ship with a specialist 'A Frame' crane arrangement to launch *LR5* over the stern. Rather than use a real submarine to mate with, on occasions a replica escape chamber situated on the sea bed sufficed. In the spring of 1993 a major NATO submarine escape exercise was conducted in the Mediterranean off the coast of Spain, near Malaga, involving the participation of three submarines. The USA, UK and Italy respectively deployed the DSRV *Avalon*, *LR5* and a McCann Bell recue system. As I chaired a NATO Committee tasked to achieve compatibility and commonality in submarine escape and rescue systems, I was invited to attend as a key observer.

Early on the first morning of the exercises, I and fellow sea-riders arrived by boat off Malaga to embark into the Netherlands submarine *Zwaardvis*. On our arrival below, we were made very welcome by the Dutch crew and were ushered into the wardroom to enjoy a hearty breakfast. While the crew prepared the boat for diving, we were a briefed on the day's events. Once the submarine bottomed, at a depth of about 300ft, the *LR5* rescue vehicle would mate and carry out several trips around the boat to give some of the crew the experience of being in a rescue submersible.

Having dived the submarine, the bottoming procedure was flawlessly executed by the Dutch crew. This involved achieving neutral buoyancy and a perfect fore and aft trim, a few tens of feet above the sea bed. Speed was then decreased until the boat was stationary. The next step was to gently ballast the boat and let it gradually settle on the seabed and finally add additional ballast forward to, in effect, anchor it. The impact of the submarine touching the bottom was barely discernible.

Once the boat was on the sea bed, *LR5* mated and made several trips around *Zwaardvis*. I participated in one of these and, seated behind the pilot, got a close view of the submersible's controls. Besides camera systems, a pressure-tight glass dome in the bow provided excellent views of the bottomed submarine and facilitated the delicate manoeuvres required to position precisely above the escape hatch and to conduct the mating procedure.

The following day there was another early-morning embarkation, this time into the Spanish submarine *Galerna*. The bottoming on this occasion was very different from the previous day's demonstration of precision manoeuvring: *Galerna* hit the bottom with quite a thud and shudder. When confident that the boat was firmly settled on the sea bed, contact was made by underwater telephone with the US nuclear attack submarine *Batfish* which was acting as mothership for the *Avalon*. Soon the DSRV arrived to begin the mating process on the boat's forward escape chamber in the control room. As a first step it formed a pressure-tight seal on top of the escape hatch, pumping out the water in its the dome-like sealing structure attached underneath its main body.

Meanwhile I noticed underneath the chamber hatch, an oilskin-clad Petty Officer clutching a clipboard of instructions. Somewhat concerning, he appeared unfamiliar in operating the various valves on the escape tower. Having been informed that the DSRV had successfully mated, he was then directed to open the lower hatch. This completed, with a flourish he then produced and opened up a black umbrella. On opening the chamber upper hatch, he was deluged by seawater – hence the useful umbrella. The chamber should have been absolutely dry and I could only guess why there was water in it.

When instructions were received from the DSRV pilots that they were ready to receive passengers, I clambered up through the chamber and was invited by the two pilots to sit behind them. About a dozen *Galerna* crew followed and seated themselves to the rear. The submarine's escape chamber hatches having been shut and secured, the DSRV uncoupled itself from *Galerna* and did a brief tour around its hull. *Avalon* was certainly much more sophisticated than *LR5* but had been significantly more expensive to procure. I was highly impressed by the array of controls and displays in front of its pilots, rather akin to a jet airliner's cockpit. However, I did miss the ability to look directly through a pressure-tight window ahead of the craft. Instead, there was reliance upon an array of cameras and remote sensors.

Returning to *Galerna*'s escape chamber, problems arose in making a pressure-tight seal. The pilots having unsuccessfully tried several procedures, it appeared that the only option would be to return to the mother-submarine *Batfish* to disembark the passengers. This alternative was not received well by the SSN's Captain because, as previously mentioned, the USN was particularly sensitive about nuclear plant security. The prospect of a dozen Spanish submariners entering his engine room and tramping through the reactor compartment tunnel, no doubt greatly concerned the Captain.

The pilots after some discussion decided, as a last resort, to attempt the highly unusual procedure of using metal clamps to pull the DSRV down onto *Galerna*'s chamber seal. I was extremely impressed when they produced a check-off list for this emergency and, akin to airline pilots, methodically took actions strictly in accordance with the set-out instructions. The procedure worked and the seal successfully made, we all clambered down into *Galerna*. Once inside, I and the embarked USN liaison officer, were treated in the wardroom to a real feast of Andalusian leg-of-lamb accompanied by very acceptable local wine. Meanwhile, the submarine gradually de-ballasted and got off the bottom followed by surfacing and heading to Malaga for a passenger boat transfer.

In 2000 the Russian nuclear submarine *Kursk* suffered a catastrophic torpedo explosion in the Barents Sea and sank in relatively shallow water. Belatedly, the Russian authorities requested the assistance of *LR5* to rescue the members of the crew who had survived. However, those crew members in the after section of the submarine who were not killed in the initial explosion, did not survive for long. By the time *LR5* arrived on the scene, all had perished.

In 2012 the Royal Navy ended pressurised training at the *Dolphin* escape training tank but continued to use the facility for training at normal atmospheric pressure. This decision was partly made on grounds of cost but there were also small but quantifiable risks of serious injury to the trainee escaper ascending from depths down to 100ft. In 2020 this iconic building finally shut. In lieu a new escape training facility was commissioned at the Clyde Naval Base. This facility enables the trainee to thoroughly familiarise himself/herself with the operation of the escape chamber and, importantly, undertake realistic survival training in rough weather surface conditions.

There will always be financial pressures to reduce the cost and weight of installing and maintaining escape and rescue systems in submarines. Indeed, in 1994 towards the end of my time in SCOSER,

I chaired a thoroughly comprehensive review of the submarine escape and rescue organisation. A key conclusion was that, despite a good accident record since 1955, the Royal Navy needed to continue to provide effective escape systems and crew training, together with a capable global rescue system.

In 2017, the Argentinian submarine *San Juan* sank in deep water in the South Atlantic, possibly due to a battery explosion. All of the crew died. In 2021 the Indonesian boat *Nonggala* imploded in deep water off the island of Bali with, again, loss of the entire crew. Both these accidents, and that of the *Kursk*, attracted worldwide media attention and speculation over a period of many days. For those nations that operate submarines, these tragic accidents reinforced the imperatives of maintaining viable escape systems for their crews and having access to an effective submarine rescue service.

Epilogue

My appointment at Commodore Naval Ship Acceptance ended in the summer of 1994 when I was assigned to the Nuclear Policy Directorate in the MoD, London. One of my responsibilities in this new appointment was managing a team of experts who produced the strategic targeting plans for the UK's SSBNs. It was very much a desk job and consequently my career of going down to the sea in submarines was effectively over.

Looking back over that career, I count myself very fortunate to have taken part in the Submarine Flotilla's greatest ever peacetime expansion, during a period of unprecedented technical change and challenge in the years of the Cold War. I had served in various capacities at the cutting edge of the Royal Navy's undersea confrontation with the Soviet submarine force. I can think of no greater privilege than to have commanded both diesel and nuclear-powered submarines during this time.

My service in submarines from 1967 to 1994 was characterised by considerable political and military tension between the Soviet Bloc and the Western Allies which fuelled a technological arms race particularly in the design and operation of submarines. One factor, however, remained pretty constant during this period. We knew who our enemy was and were able to focus our attention almost exclusively on Soviet Russia. There were exceptions, of course, notably submarine operations in the South Atlantic in support of the Falklands campaign of 1982 and, later, submarine-launched cruise missile support to ground forces in conflicts in Iraq, Kosovo and elsewhere. However, in the main, our submarine technological and operational capabilities were primarily directed towards the Soviet submarine force, either avoiding detections in the case of the SSBNs or seeking detections in the case of the SSNs.

Today's geopolitical picture is much more complex. In the Far East, an unstable but increasingly aggressive North Korea is testing ever-more-capable missiles and China is flexing its superpower muscles, establishing unfounded territorial claims to vast tracts of the South China Sea and sabre-rattling over Taiwan. The 2021 deployment of a UK Task Force led by the carrier *Queen Elizabeth* demonstrated the necessity to confirm rights of international passage in these areas but ruffled Chinese feathers, leading to encounters with submarines of the Chinese Navy. Closer to home, Putin's Russia seeks to reassert control over the old Soviet territories and has increased defence spending on all three service arms. Although currently (2024) preoccupied with the land battle consequent upon the invasion of Ukraine, the Russian submarine force continues to be modernised and increasing numbers of highly capable submarines of the 'Borei' and 'Yasen' class are coming into service and are deployed in the Arctic and North Atlantic oceans. While their submarine activity levels are lower than during the Cold War, the Russians continue to probe the West's ASW capability and remain just as keen to detect the Western nation's SSBNs as they always have been. Worryingly, there are also many indications that Russia is developing the potential capability to attack and seriously debilitate Europe's vital undersea energy and communications infrastructure. Add to this the almost permanent conflicts in the Middle East, it is clear that there is still a key role for our Submarine Service to undertake in support of NATO and other international treaty organisations.

Against this background, Britain has unfortunately undergone a rapid downsizing of the Submarine Flotilla as a consequence of the end of the Cold War and the perceived reduction of the Russian submarine threat. This decrease in nuclear submarine numbers, has resulted in a severe contraction of the UK's specialist nuclear technical and engineering support capability. Furthermore, a hollowed-out UK industrial base has caused serious shortages of key skills within its shipbuilding and warship maintenance infrastructure and the associated supplier companies. This is exacerbated by inadequate nuclear submarine docking facilities. Only one ship-lift in Faslane and one dock in Devonport are available to conduct refits and essential repairs out of the water. This shortfall has resulted in significantly extended duration of refits and has contributed to unacceptably low nuclear submarine operational availability since 2010. Worryingly, with a planned future force level of only eleven nuclear submarines, there are many signs that this number is below that critical mass required to build and sustain a viable nuclear submarine force in the long term.

Continuous At Sea Deterrent – CASD

Since 1969 Britain has achieved credible nuclear deterrence by having at least one SSBN on patrol – Continuous At Sea Deterrence (CASD). For 25 years this was delivered by the Polaris-armed *Resolution* class. In the mid-1990s the *Vanguard* class came into service with, as previously described, the much more effective and accurate Trident D5 missile system, capable of assuring unacceptable levels of damage upon any belligerent country which has attacked the UK with nuclear weapons. In the same timeframe the RAF's tactical nuclear bomb was phased out thus leaving the Trident weapon system as the UK's only nuclear weapons capability, delivering both strategic and tactical nuclear deterrence. This system is committed to NATO and in addition to the important issue of 'burden sharing', the UK and French independent nuclear deterrents provide 'a second centre of decision making'. This deters a potential aggressor, such as Russia, from taking the risk that, in some scenarios, the US leadership might judge that a nuclear response may not be justifiable because of the potentially catastrophic consequences to its own country.

In 2016, the British government very belatedly made the decision to replace the existing *Vanguard* SSBNs with a successor class named *Dreadnought*, planned to have a design life of over 30 years. This programme, involving the build of four new submarines and updating existing shore infrastructure, will incur significant costs, £31 billion with £9 billion of contingency. However, remarkably, the Trident weapon system is likely still to be in service until the 2070s. The US and UK have jointly designed the missile compartment which will be common to both the *Dreadnought*s and US *Columbia* class SSBNs, the latter coming into service at the end of the 2020s. The *Dreadnought*s will have twelve missile tubes and have been designed to ensure that the through-life costs of upkeep and refit are kept well under control. Thankfully, the past constraints in sharing nuclear propulsion technology have been lifted and the US has very much contributed to the design of the *Dreadnought*'s propulsion system. This bodes well for ensuring ease of access to the equipment and machinery, a feature absent in the *Vanguard*s. However, there are many challenges ahead in successfully delivering the *Dreadnought*s, the first of which is not planned to enter service until the 2030s, stretching *Vanguard* hull life towards a highly challenging 40 years.

CASD has in recent years been perilously fragile because the *Vanguard* class SSBNs are now well exceeding their planned 25-year lifespan and, as a consequence, serious machinery reliability and technical problems have been experienced. This fragility will remain until the *Dreadnought*s start entering service. During the peak of the 'Trouser Leg' crisis (see Chapter 24), the Polaris SSBN *Resolution* completed a 108-day patrol, but this has subsequently been greatly exceeded on many occasions by the *Vanguard*s. Of note, in 2023 *Vigilant* undertook a six-month patrol due to the relief boat being seriously delayed by technical problems. For my part, I find it difficult to comprehend the level of the strain and demands upon the crew undertaking a patrol of that duration, without any communication to family or friends.

Owing to such patrol lengths and a number of other factors, the retention of highly-trained nuclear submariners has been a significant problem in recent years. The basing of all operational submarines in Faslane, has also had an adverse influence upon retention for several reasons, including for many crew members a long distance from families and friends.

The SSN

At the time of writing, in addition to the SSBN on patrol, there are likely to be only two or three SSNs simultaneously at sea. Long gone are the days of over twenty SSNs and SSKs being available for deployment. However, there are perhaps signs of a significant uplift in the Royal Navy's SSN capability within the recently agreed AUSUK agreement, between the governments of Australia, USA and the UK. In order to counter an increasingly assertive and potentially aggressive China, which is currently at pace building up a large, modern navy, this agreement sets out the aim of Australia developing its own SSN force from the mid-2030s onwards. Initially Australia will acquire three to five US *Virginia* class nuclear attack submarines. These will be followed by a number of SSNs of a joint Australian/UK design, which will be constructed with US assistance, and partially built in the UK.

Furthermore, as a demonstration of the AUSUK resolve to meet any future potential Chinese maritime threat, a USN or Royal Navy SSN will rotate operating out of Fremantle, Western Australia from 2027 onwards. Besides the industrial capability and skilled manpower difficulties this project brings, there will be the challenges of operating and maintaining an SSN at a great distance in Australia. Of note, there has been no commitment by the UK as yet to augment the seven planned Royal Navy *Astute*s with a number of the AUSUK designed boats.

The UK's international and military strength may no longer have the leverage or influence as in the past, but I am certain the Royal Navy still has an important global role to play in an era of significant threats from a number of sources across the globe. I firmly believe that our submarine force is still, and will be, key to the UK's national security. I am confident, too, that today's and tomorrow's Royal Navy submariners will rise to many similar challenges to those that confronted me and my peers and that they will continue to demonstrate the dedication, professionalism and innovation, so characteristic of the British submariner since the force's inception in 1903.

My last trip to sea in a submarine was in August 1995 onboard HMS *Victorious* in sea areas off Cape Canaveral, Florida, when she was conducting a full-scale rehearsal for her first Trident missile demonstration firing. My role was minder of a BBC team which was filming an episode of the documentary *Defence of the Realm*. The following day I observed the actual firing from the tracking ship, *Range Sentinel*. As the powerful missile broke surface, ignited and climbed into the sky on its way to the target area many thousands of miles away, a shiver ran down my spine at the thought of this awesome weapon ever being used in anger.

I had come a long way from that day I had at sea in the WW2 diesel boat *Totem*.

Index